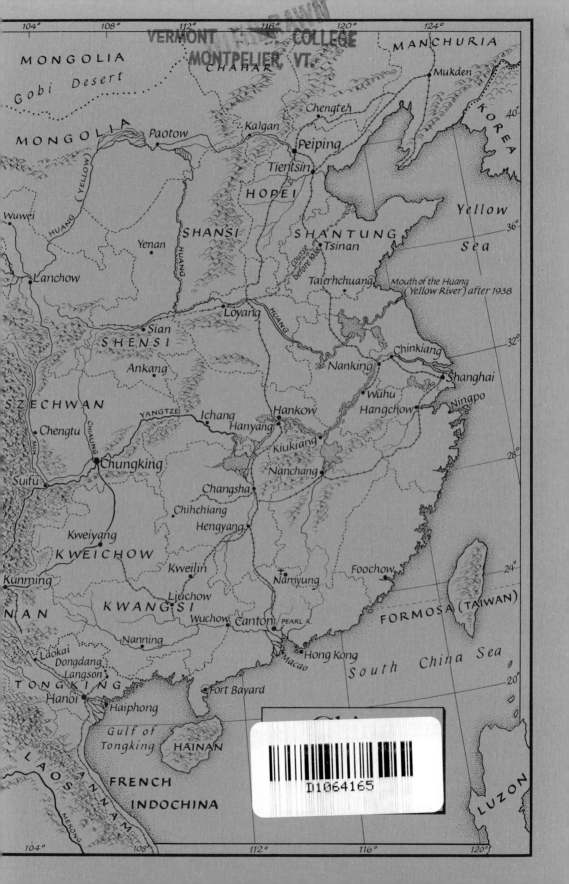

MONGOLIA

Gobi Desert

MONGOLIA

CHAHAR

MANCHURIA

Mukden

Chengteh

Paotow

Kalgan

Peiping

Tientsin

Wuwei

HOPEI

HUANG (YELLOW)

SHANSI

SHANTUNG

Yellow

Yenan

HUANG

Tsinan

Course before 1938

Sea

Lanchow

Taierhchuang

Mouth of the Huang
(Yellow River) after 1938

Loyang

HUANG

Sian

SHENSI

Chinkiang

Ankang

Nanking

Shanghai

SZECHWAN

YANGTZE

Ichang

Wuhu

Hangchow

Ningpo

Chengtu

CHIALING

Hanyang

Hankow

MIN

Kiukiang

Chungking

Nanchang

Suifu

Changsha

Chihchiang

Kweiyang

Hengyang

KWEICHOW

Kunming

Kweilin

Namyung

Foochow

NAN

KWANGSI

Liuchow

Wuchow

Canton

PEARL R.

FORMOSA (TAIWAN)

Nanning

Laokai

Dongdang

Macao

Hong Kong

South China Sea

Langson

TONGKING

Hanoi

Fort Bayard

Haiphong

Gulf of
Tongking

HAINAN

LAOS ANNAM

FRENCH

INDOCHINA

MEKONG

LUZON

CHINA
and the Helping Hand

1937–1945

CHINA
and the Helping Hand
1937-1945

Arthur N. Young
Former Financial Adviser to China

HARVARD UNIVERSITY PRESS
Cambridge, Massachusetts
1 9 6 3

Distributed in Great Britain by Oxford University Press, London

Preparation of this volume was aided by a grant from the Ford Foundation. The Foundation is, not, however, the author, owner, publisher, or proprietor of this publication and is not to be understood as approving by virtue of its grant any of the statements made or views expressed therein.

Library of Congress Catalog Card Number 63-20774

Printed in the United States of America

Foreword

A S Financial Adviser to China during the crucial years 1929 to 1947, Arthur N. Young functioned in two traditions, ancient and modern. On the one hand, he was a skilled foreigner invited, like Marco Polo or Robert Hart, to participate in the governing of China, which he thus observed from a privileged position on the inside. On the other hand, he was a pioneer in the then new field of foreign economic aid, bringing to China his special competence in government finance. In this capacity he studied from day to day how to meet the mounting crises of the war period and on behalf of China often dealt with representatives of the United States and other governments.

Mr. Young's personal records concerning the Chinese Government's financial problems and policies are in themselves of unique value; his critical analysis of foreign aid to wartime China, based on these and other records, is a unique contribution. He not only puts American aid programs in the context of foreign aid to China in general; he also views them from the receiving end.

Mr. Young was born in Los Angeles, was graduated from Occidental College, and holds a doctorate in economics from Princeton and a law degree from George Washington University. After teaching at Princeton be began in 1918 his career as a financial adviser, in Latin American countries—Mexico and Honduras. Since leaving China in 1947 he has worked on financial problems in a dozen countries in Latin America, the Middle East, and Southeast Asia. He served as the Economic Adviser of the State Department from 1922 to 1928, before going to China in the early, hopeful days of the National Government. With the perspective of his previous experience, he saw both the rise in Nanking and the wartime decline in Chungking of our ally the National Government. His sober and informed reflections on foreign aid, and lack of aid, to China and on the use and misuse of it there, provide both a factual account of a little known subject and insight into a tragic and important turning point in history.

East Asian Research Center
of Harvard University

Preface

WHEN the fighting at the Marco Polo Bridge near Peiping on July 7, 1937, led to a general conflict, it ushered in a new era for China and indeed the world. The stakes of the battle thus joined were tremendous. There were three chief possibilities: Was China with its 500 million people to fall a prey to Japan? Was it to fall to Russia and Communism? Or could China succeed in her promising yet precarious efforts toward an independent democracy?

China unaided could not expect to fight for long. Aid from abroad—its time, nature, extent, and how China might use it—was of critical importance. From the start China's leaders felt, and history has shown they were right, that China was fighting and suffering bitterly in the cause of liberty, justice, and the future of a world in which men could have security for life, liberty, and the pursuit of happiness.

In 1931, when Japan began the seizure of Manchuria, the rest of the world should have joined to stop the aggression, even at the risk of war. Then war probably could have been avoided. The United States and all Europe, including Germany and Russia, were opposed to Japan's action. Firm joint action might have forestalled the later adventures of Mussolini and even of Hitler. But by 1937 Japan had enjoyed six years of apparently successful aggression. Only overwhelming force, or the threat of it, could then have stopped Japan's China adventure. Japan might have backed down, as many Japanese opposed the militarists. Even if war had come then, it would not have been as bad as the war that finally followed. The risks of firm action were well worth taking. But in 1937 a combination to check Japan was even more difficult than in 1931. Unhappily Japan gauged the international situation only too well.

This book concerns what China did for herself and what other countries did for China during the more than eight years of war from 1937 to 1945. It also concerns what China and other countries did not do. It centers upon financial, economic, and international affairs, with which in particular I had the privilege of being connected, and deals also with internal political and military affairs. Some matters of currency, the inflation, and foreign exchange are inseparable from the story. Here I have tried to present them in nontechnical form for the general reader. Another book, more technical than this one but closely related to it, centering upon China's fiscal and monetary experience in this period, is to be published by Harvard University Press in the near future: "China's Wartime Finance, 1937–1945."

Events in this period in China foreshadow issues that have grown in importance in the postwar world. Among these are the degree of ability of the peoples of less developed countries to manage their affairs under what the Covenant of the League of Nations called "the strenuous conditions of the modern world"; the effects of strong nationalism; the roles of self-help and foreign aid; the timeliness of aid; Russian compared with Western aid; whether there should be "strings" on aid; and inflation, as it affects the economy, internal stability, foreign aid, and international relations. Finally, there is the situation of attempted Communist subversion of an unready government facing difficulties of all kinds. The experience dealt with herein teaches, at least, that success in dealing with the difficult two-sided problems of aid calls for the highest degree of understanding, cooperation, ability, and character of those responsible, and that mistakes are unavoidable.

The fall of the National Government and the Communist take-over on the mainland in 1949 have been a subject of controversy, often emotional, and will long be debated. So long as the understanding of what happened is clouded by major doubts, we shall be hampered in making policy about China. The causes of these grave events in China are to be found mainly in the war years, since before the war Communism in China was a distant and perhaps a diminishing threat. Here I have tried to shed light on what happened in those tragic years, drawing freely on the contemporary record. Also I have analyzed and interpreted—since the situation was highly complex and a bare statement of facts would not only be of less interest but of less use as a record.

As one who lived in the midst of these stirring events, I am sensible of the enormous difficulties under which China labored during the war. Trading space for time, China's resistance was almost a miracle, considering Japan's great superiority in land, air, and sea forces; the blockade; and the slowness and meagerness of outside aid in the critical period. In 1937 few thought that China could resist more than a few weeks or months. Anyone who might have said then that China would fight Japan alone for over four years and continue to resist for over eight years would have been thought a rash prophet. The marvel is, not that there were failures and sordid happenings, but that the National Government lasted through the war at all. I am reminded of what the poet Walt Whitman wrote of Lincoln in March 1863: "I think well of the President . . . I do not dwell on the supposed failures of his government; he has shown I sometimes think an almost supernatural tact in keeping the ship afloat at all."* Where I have occasion to criticize acts and omissions by China, the criticism is that of an old friend who is deeply distressed that China's outstanding people had to face, unready, the ordeal of the war years and the suffering to which they have since been continuously subjected. Since there are cycles of Cathay, let us hope for the time when China's people may emerge from their suffering with happier prospects.

A word is due about Japan, whose international conduct in these years I often have occasion to criticize strongly in this book. I do this with all respect for the many Japanese who opposed or were unsympathetic with the aggression, or who were unwittingly caught up in its results. I wish no one to take my criticism as a reflection upon these people, or upon present-day Japan, whose position as a good member of the community of nations is cause for gratification. As a postwar Japanese view, I quote the comments of Masatake Okumiya and Jiro Horikoshi, respectively a leading air commander and a plane designer, who in *Zero!* give an account of the air war:

It has been the tragedy of modern Japan that those great and humane statesmen who attempted to follow the principles of "fair play" in international conduct often met death, and that several cabinets composed of such men fell by the wayside before the pressure of the military cliques . . .

No Japanese citizen can recall the events of these years and find justification for the *national* conduct of our country. No one can deny the record, for history will relate only that Japan forced her friendly neighboring nations

* Quoted in Carl Sandburg, *Abraham Lincoln: The Prairie Years and the War Years,* one volume edition (Harcourt, Brace & Company, New York, 1954), p. 401.

into an unreasonable and unnecessary war, transformed their fields and cities into battlegrounds, and visited misery and deprivation on millions of innocent people.*

This book is both a history and a memoir. As to sources, besides my own recollection I have used the papers which I gathered and preserved without loss during nearly 19 years as Financial Adviser to China in 1929–1947. Of that period more than 14 years were spent in China, and the rest on Chinese business in the United States or on leave. The Chinese Government has consented to my use of these records, which, because of the loss of many official records during and after the war, are more complete on many topics than any collection elsewhere existing. Also, I have had access to the records of the Department of State and to pertinent data of the Department of Defense. I have consulted a considerable part of the Morgenthau Diaries, in the records of the Internal Security Subcommittee of the Senate Judiciary Committee, which made them available to me without restriction when I testified before them in 1956. What I then saw seems to cover the most important part of the record of the American Treasury's dealings with China in 1940–1945. I sought access to the rest of the Diaries covering the war period, but they are closed except to Mr. Morgenthau or his agent until after 1965.† Besides I have made use of the great volume of official and private materials published about the war period, in China, the United States, Europe, and Japan. To illuminate the subject further I have talked with many participants in these events, Chinese, Americans, and Japanese. Although a participant myself, I have tried to be objective. Whether I have been fair at all points will be for the reader to say. But if not I hope it is from unawareness of some of the facts, and not from lack of having tried.

Arthur N. Young

San Marino, California
1963

---

* Okumiya and Horikoshi, with Martin Caidin, *Zero!* (New York, 1957), pp. 9, 24.

† The diaries are to be made available to qualified scholars 25 years after the close of successive Roosevelt terms. See J. M. Blum, *From the Morgenthau Diaries: Years of Crisis, 1928–1938* (Boston, 1959), p. x.

Acknowledgments

I AM grateful to the following American and British publishers and authors' agents for permission to quote from publications: Brandt & Brandt, William D. Leahy, *I Was There;* Columbia University Press, A. S. Everest, *Morgenthau, the New Deal, and Silver;* Department of the Army, C. F. Romanus and Riley Sunderland, *Stilwell's Mission to China, Stilwell's Command Problems,* and *Time Runs Out in CBI,* Washington, 1953, 1956, 1959, in the series U.S. Army in World War II, published by the Office of the Chief of Military History, Department of the Army; E. P. Dutton & Co. Inc. and Cassell & Co., Ltd., Masatake Okumiya and Jiro Horikoshi, with Martin Caidin, *Zero!;* Harcourt, Brace & World, Inc., Milovan Djilas, *Conversations with Stalin,* and Carl Sandburg, *Abraham Lincoln: The Prairie Years and the War Years;* Harper, for the Council on Foreign Relations, W. L. Langer and S. E. Gleason, *The Undeclared War;* the Controller of her Britannic Majesty's Stationery Office, S. W. Kirby, *The War Against Japan,* volume 2; Holt, Rinehart and Winston, Inc., A. C. Wedemeyer, *Wedemeyer Reports!;* Houghton Mifflin Company, Sir Winston Churchill, *Closing the Ring,* and J. M. Blum, *From the Morgenthau Diaries: Years of Crisis, 1928–1938;* Princeton University Press, F. F. Liu, *A Military History of Modern China, 1924–1929;* G. P. Putnam's Sons, C. L. Chennault, *Way of a Fighter;* Henry Regnery Company, Don Lohbeck, *Patrick J. Hurley;* William Sloane Associates, *The Stilwell Papers,* by Joseph W. Stilwell, arranged and edited by Theodore H. White, copyright 1948 by Winifred A. Stilwell; and The University of Chicago Press, W. F. Craven and J. L. Cate, *The Army Air Forces in World War II,* volumes 1, 4, 5, and 7, copyright, 1948, 1950, 1953, and 1958, respectively, by the University of Chicago.

For critically reading all or most of the manuscript, and giving wise counsel and suggestions for improvement, I am indebted to J. B. Condliffe and Choh-ming Li of the University of California, Berkeley; to Allan Nevins of the Huntington Memorial Library; to Tsuyee Pei, formerly of the Bank of China and Governor of the

Central Bank of China; and to my former colleague Stanley K. Hornbeck, formerly Director of the Office of Far Eastern Affairs of the Department of State and Political Adviser to the Secretary of State, with whom I have discussed many points, and whose experience in the midst of these events has greatly aided me in their interpretation. Also, for critically reading parts of the manuscript and making valuable suggestions, I am indebted to W. L. Bond, formerly in charge of the operations in China of the China National Aviation Corporation; to J. Lossing Buck, formerly of the University of Nanking; to Kia-ngau Chang, formerly Minister of Communications and Governor of the Central Bank of China; to Owen L. Dawson, formerly Agricultural Attaché of the American Embassy in China; to L. K. Little, formerly Inspector General of the Chinese Customs; to Oliver C. Lockhart, formerly Financial Adviser and Associate Director of the Salt Revenue Administration of China; and to Ralph L. Powell, formerly with the American army in China.

To the East Asian Research Center of Harvard University I am grateful for sponsoring issuance of this volume, for bearing some of the costs relating thereto, and for helping to prepare the manuscript for publication. In particular, I am indebted to the Director of the Center, John K. Fairbank, for helpful advice on many matters, for more than ordinary interest and encouragement, and for facilitating the process of publication. The staff of the Harvard University Press have been most helpful in suggesting ways to improve the presentation of a complicated subject. I am grateful also to the John Simon Guggenheim Memorial Foundation for encouraging my work by honoring me with a fellowship and grant.

For access to American governmental materials, and for aid in their use, I am indebted to G. Bernard Noble, Chief of the Historical Division of the Department of State, and to E. Taylor Parks of that office; to Francis T. Murphy, Chief of the Surplus Property and Lend-Lease Division of the Department of State; to Ruth Stout of the Office of Military History of the Department of Defense; to Edwin G. Beal, Jr., Director of Orientalia of the Library of Congress; and to members of the staff of the Subcommitee to Investigate the Administration of the Internal Security Act, of the Senate Committee on the Judiciary.

For valuable help in a number of ways I am indebted to Shinji

Arai and Takenosuke Ebihara, formerly of the Yokohama Specie Bank, to Taro Sekine of the Bank of Japan, and to the Japan Defense Agency; to John Morton Blum, of Yale University; to Dorothy Borg of the Institute of Pacific Relations; to Claude A. Buss of Stanford University; to Robert J. C. Butow of Princeton University; to Jerome B. Cohen of the City College of New York; to Alexander Erlich of Columbia University; to E. Kann, veteran authority on Chinese finance; to Y. C. Koo, former Vice-Minister of Finance of China; to Douglas H. Mendel, Jr., of the University of California, Los Angeles; to A. J. Meyer of Harvard University; to Jerry Nisenson and Philip H. Trezise of the American Foreign Service; to Henry Rosovsky and Kobo Odaka of the University of California, Berkeley; to Richard L. Walker of the University of South Carolina; to Louis B. Wright, Director of the Folger Shakespeare Library; to my brother, John Parke Young of the Department of State; and to my son, Allen Young, who suggested the title. My sister, Sarah Adele Young, has carefully and laboriously prepared the manuscript. Throughout, my wife, Nellie May Young, has provided invaluable suggestions, criticisms, and encouragement.

For the work as it stands and any errors or omissions, those who have helped me are of course in no way responsible.

A. N. Y.

Contents

PART TWO
THE FOURTH POWER, 1941–1945

PART THREE
CONCLUSION

APPENDIXES

Introduction
China Before the War

A GUIDE FOR READERS

1. The Introduction, chapter I, deals with the situation in China on the eve of the hostilities.

2. The setting in which wartime aid was provided, and the earlier aid in the supply of essential materials and services, in military matters, and in communications, are discussed in chapters II, IV, in part of V, and in VII and VIII. For the period of the Pacific War, these matters are treated in chapter XIII, in part of XIV, and in XVI and XVIII.

3. Inflation and monetary and foreign exchange policy were inseparably involved with aid to China. I try to present these matters nontechnically. Chapters III and V deal with the earlier developments. The action of China, Britain, and the United States in 1939–1941 in connection with currency support is treated in chapters IX and X. For the period of the Pacific War, chapter XII describes the effort to aid China by massive financial injections. The Chinese-American controversy over money matters is treated in part of chapter XIV and in XV, and over gold in chapter XVII.

4. Sino-foreign organizations had long provided technical assistance to China in administering the customs and salt revenue services, and in strengthening security for most of China's debt. A section in chapter III describes developments early in the hostilities, and chapter VI deals with the efforts to preserve this setup, especially by British help.

5. Planning for postwar problems of rehabilitation and development, and the inadequacy of such planning, are treated in chapter XIX.

6. A summing up and appraisal of the over-all situation in 1937–1941 and during the Pacific War, respectively, are given in chapters XI and XX. Chapter XXI contains a general appraisal.

I. CHINA BEFORE THE WAR

IT is a far cry from today's Communist China of 5-year plans and communes, Mao's "contradictions," Korea, Quemoy, and Matsu to the China of 1937. Likewise it was a far cry from the China of 1937 to that of a decade earlier, before the National Government took over. In 1927 internal conditions were chaotic. There was no real central authority and China was torn by incessant civil war and banditry. Railways were disrupted and roads and airways hardly existed. The currency was a complicated mixture of weights and coins varying from place to place. Medieval fiscal practices ruled, except for the foreign-run customs and salt services. Most of the debt was in default. The older republican governments were caught in a vicious circle. They could not gain strength or make reforms because of lack of funds. But due to lack of authority they could not install an adequate revenue system. Internationally, China was a center of friction among the powers.

THE NATIONAL GOVERNMENT

During a turbulent decade, the National Government, following its take-over in 1928, wrought under Chiang Kai-shek's leadership a transformation with few parallels in history. In 1929–1934 the government put down the chief ambitious warlords. It survived the Japanese seizure of Manchuria in 1931–1932. This seizure was a bitter loss, which cut off from China 40 million people who lived in an area enormously rich in iron and coal and fertile land. Manchuria was productive both of revenues and of large exports which China needed to pay for imports and for costs of borrowing abroad. Early in 1932 China showed unexpected strength in the brief encounter with Japan at Shanghai. Determined resistance forced the withdrawal of Japanese forces, on terms that amounted to a stalemate. For China that was electrifying, since for the first time in 150 years of external pressure China had been able to oppose without immediate rout a force using modern arms. Aided by German military advisers, the Nationalists had begun to create the nucleus of a modern army. After the

Japanese attack in Manchuria, Chiang pushed this program. Also in mid-1932 China engaged American advisers to help build a modern air force. Chiang, however, as a military man and a realist knew that China could not win a war with Japan. With difficulty he held back influential elements from forcing a premature show-down.

In 1934 the government had driven the Communists from their stronghold in the Yangtze Valley to the far northwest. There they were a distant threat that seemed likely to lessen. They had joined early in 1937 in a United Front against Japan.[1] It suited Moscow to have them accept Chiang's leadership for the time being. He was implacably opposed to Japan's aggression, and Japan was a grave threat to Russia in Asia, as well as to China.

By 1937 the country internally was at peace. Chiang's prestige was high. In May, Ambassador Nelson T. Johnson reported that it was the prevailing idea in China that "Chiang's leadership is necessary to the nation's survival."[2] He was not, however, a dictator in the ordinary sense. Within the government his word carried great and often decisive weight as to policies, action, and personnel. But the delicacy and difficulty of his task as leader have not been sufficiently recognized. After he put down the major warlord and Communist opposition in 1929–1934, public opinion in China was strongly against more civil wars, especially in view of the threat from Japan. Yet political generals still controlled many troops, and were not fully amenable to Central Government directions. China was still strongly regional. Such central influence as there was over some armies depended upon subsidies or payment of troops, political favors, coaxing, or appeals. The government had full authority in the central Yangtze Valley, and while its word was gaining more and more weight in the further regions, it still fell far short of full country-wide authority. Though the strongest government in China for generations, it was still not strong enough. A main measure, for internal as well as external ends, was the progress in developing a disciplined and loyal army.

The government's over-all position left much to be desired. Like underdeveloped countries generally, China lacked the traditions of democratic government. The National Government was theoretically the creature of the Kuomintang. But in fact it was a self-perpetuating body, including many leaders and rank and file who were nonparty, and the party influence as such seemed to be waning. Government policy was too much dominated by the military. There was too much dependence on the political and military leaders who were veterans of the revolution and too often incompetent and corrupt, and there was far too little effort to enlist men of good will and patriotism from all elements and all major regions. The tutelage foreseen by Sun Yat-sen clearly had to continue for an indefinite time, especially in view of the succession of emergencies. Yet serious political thought about how to broaden the base of the government and enlist wider support was conspicuously lacking. And while definite progress was being made in administration, the government was proving a poor organizer. To its credit, however, it did not dream of trying such ruthless use of force as enabled its successors to organize China in such complete detail.

Another shortcoming was failure to apply effectively the "social welfare" principle of Sun Yat-sen. Quite conservative elements were in power or close to the centers of power. The crying need for reform of land tenure and the land tax, and for reform of local government which was so largely dominated by landlords and moneylenders, failed of serious attention. Here was a grave failure. It allowed the Communists to gain heavily, and perhaps decisively, by deceiving the people with promises of land and democracy. A partial and very real extenuation of this failure was that the government was very busy throughout the prewar decade in establishing its authority and in resisting Japan.

THE FINANCIAL TRANSFORMATION

In the years from the collapse of the imperial regime in 1911 until 1928, a lack of income blocked the growth of a real central authority. The customs revenue was mostly pledged for foreign debts, and warlords consumed most of such internal revenues as existed. The Peking governments could not finance essential services, and remained weak and ineffective. Their defaults ruined China's credit. They were unable to reform China's heterogeneous currency.

Beginning in 1928 the National Government carried through

a program of major financial reforms, without which it would have had small chance to survive for long. Due to these reforms the contrast between the financial chaos of mid-1928 and conditions in mid-1937 is impressive. In these reforms the leader in 1928–1933 was T. V. Soong, and then H. H. Kung, as Ministers of Finance. The reforms were an impressive example of self-help. The only sizable foreign governmental credits were American loans of 1931 and 1933, totaling US$26 million (utilized), to buy wheat and cotton for flood relief and other uses.

China had considerable technical aid in this period from advisers, as well as continuing administrative aid from the long-established Sino-foreign customs and salt revenue services (see chapter III). In 1928 China engaged in the United States the Commission of Financial Advisers, headed by Professor E. W. Kemmerer, who were in China during most of 1929. The fruits of the commission's efforts were chiefly realized through the work of members who remained for varying periods. Those who served in China for a considerable time were: F. A. Cleveland, who after a brief period as Adviser on Budget became Associate Chief Inspector of Salt Revenue until 1935; Oliver C. Lockhart, Financial Adviser with special reference to taxation, who succeeded Cleveland in the salt revenue service and served until 1940; Fenimore B. Lynch, Adviser to the Central Bank of China until tragically lost in an airplane accident near Kunming in 1942; and the writer as Financial Adviser with special reference to currency and credit, until 1946. Others who remained for shorter periods were Benjamin B. Wallace and William Watson, as experts respectively on tariffs and accounting. For aid in minting, China engaged Clifford Hewitt, formerly of the United States minting service, who was supplanted about the end of 1933 by Robert J. Grant, former Director of the Mint of the United States, who remained until about 1939.

China also received advice from European experts. In 1931 and 1933–1934 Sir Arthur Salter made brief visits to China to advise on economic and financial matters, and he arranged for the coming of a League of Nations mission headed by Dr. Ludwig Rajchman, which advised on agricultural and industrial development. In 1935 an international mission to help China with her finances was discussed, but the only representative to come was Sir Frederick W. Leith-Ross of Britain, who aided in the currency reform of 1935. With him was Cyril Rogers of the Bank of England, who remained to advise China.

In mid-1928 the Nationalists, after taking over from the Peking regime, began at once to develop solid revenues. The grant of tariff autonomy led to a big increase in the yield of customs. An internal revenue system taxing salt, tobacco, cotton yarn, and other goods yielded growing returns. The government gradually suppressed *likin*, the long-existing collection of taxes on internal movement of goods. There were, however, weaknesses. The government failed to make a serious effort to reform and develop the land tax, in a nation that was 80 per cent agricultural. As to direct income and profits taxes, the government accepted for several years the Kemmerer Commission's recommendation of 1929 that China was not yet ready for them. An income tax, began shortly before the war, had little success. Regionalism remained strong in finance and administration as well as in military affairs; and Nanking often had to rule with a light hand, though there was growing respect for the central authority. Despite progress in public administration, the age-old systems of official "squeeze" and multiplication of unneeded staff persisted to all too great an extent.

The succession of internal and external emergencies prevented budget balance. But dependable revenues made possible borrowing, without which the new government could not have stayed in power after 1931 and pushed its program of unification and resistance to Japan's encroachment.* To its credit, the government in the prewar decade never gave serious thought to using printing-press money. There was progress with a system of budgets and accounts. For the first time the government issued regular and fairly complete and accurate financial reports. With rapid growth of revenue, a balanced budget was becoming feasible in 1937. But a serious weakness was domination of government by the military, and failure to require from them an accounting of payments and supplies. Commanders still got the pay for their units in lump sums, inviting corruption.

* Partly offsetting the borrowing to cover deficits were heavy payments to retire older debts. These payments in the prewar period totaled well over half the amount of the deficit.

A major strengthening factor was the currency reform of November 1935 put through by H. H. Kung as Minister of Finance, which succeeded beyond anyone's expectation. In 1933–1935 the American silver-buying policy, with callous disregard for its effect in disrupting the economic life of a friendly country, and over China's repeated protests, drained away huge amounts of China's silver reserves. An argument cynically used in its favor was that raising the price of silver would help China by increasing the buying power of its huge population. But instead it raised China's silver dollar to a seriously high and overvalued level, and brought a severe deflation, credit contraction, and slump. It forced China to give up her historic silver standard. China then adopted a managed currency, not linked either to the dollar or to sterling (which was then fluctuating). After the reform China's currency, then commonly called *fapi* (herein the symbol C$ is used), was maintained by the Central Bank at about US$0.30 and 14½ pence.* There was a free market, with no controls of exchange or trade.

The hectic monetary events of 1933–1935, however, were not without eventual gain for China, after absorbing the losses. For the first time in history China's money had a value that was stable in foreign exchange. At long last the American silver-buying policy was becoming helpful to China, as Secretary Henry Morgenthau, Jr., felt his way to cooperate by converting some of the silver reserves into usable dollars and gold. American buying of Chinese government silver began shortly after the currency reform, and to mid-1937 totaled about US$67 million, for 125 million ounces.[3] Aided by this addition to dollar funds, the Central Bank made speculation against *fapi* after the reform a costly failure for the speculators. The new Shanghai mint was on a 24-hour schedule making subsidiary nickel and copper coins, which were held firmly at par value. These were in great demand to replace the old silver and copper minor coins of uncertain value and the fractional paper money, which had given China so confusing a monetary system.

Adoption of a sound and stable level of exchange rates, in place

---

* *Fapi* means legal tender notes. China's money, often called the *yuan,* has been variously designated as $, Mex. (Mexican) $, CNC$, NC$, or C$. American dollars are herein designated as US$.

of the overvaluation of currency forced by American silver-buying, brought a favorable balance of payments. Foreign trade was flourishing. China made advantageous trade agreements with leading countries, including Japan. Foreign trade in the first half of 1937 was up 40 per cent over the first half of 1936. A fifth of it was with Japan.

There was a steady growth of foreign currency assets. Total holdings of gold, silver, and foreign exchange rose to US$379 million as of June 30, 1937. These holdings equaled about 67 per cent of China's total note issue, estimated at C$1,897 million equivalent to about US$565 million. The holdings included US$45 million of gold; dollar deposits of US$74 million; deposits of pounds in London and holdings of some other sterling currencies, equivalent to US$92 million; and silver equivalent to US$168 million.* But the silver was unsold; and an attempt to realize rapidly on it would have broken the market. Moreover, the silver was mostly at Shanghai and hence vulnerable to enemy attack.

In 1928 the government created the Central Bank of China. Originally little more than a fiscal agent for the government, it was taking on more and more functions of regulating the currency. It was growing in prestige. As it first established accounts in New York and London only in 1930, it was no mean accomplishment to accumulate and hold by 1937 the major part of the US$211 million of holdings of gold and foreign currencies. In the early days of July 1937, the government approved a plan to convert the Bank into a Central Reserve Bank, but Japan's attack prevented action.†

The fillip to confidence due to the success of the monetary reform of 1935 and the favorable balance of payments made possible a move to complete the settlement of defaulted debts of the old Peking regimes. The National Government had resumed payments on some of these debts beginning in 1928. By mid-1937 the government had settled about US$250 million of

* The statistics herein cited and the quotations and statements based upon Chinese government data, are from the papers which I collected during my service for China unless otherwise stated.

† The plan was drawn by a Sino-foreign commission of which F. B. Lynch and I were members, the heaviest burden of the work having been borne by Cyril Rogers, also a member of the commission, who had been loaned to China by the Bank of England.

defaulted debts. That was about 80 per cent of the principal amount due Western creditors, and the rest probably would have been settled soon had not war supervened. Japanese claims had to stay in abeyance, but these might have been compromised had Japan stopped encroachments. In ten years to 1937 the leading issues of China's foreign debt about doubled in price. Some were selling above or near par, to yield about 5 per cent, and at better prices than comparable Japanese issues. Also, the position of the internal debt was steadily improving. The average yield on leading internal bonds traded at Shanghai in mid-1937 was under 8 per cent, prices having improved greatly in 1937. That yield, of course, was high compared with yields in more developed countries. But for China it showed a big improvement over the earlier years, when yields had been in the range of 12 to 15 per cent.

Now, however, outbreak of the fighting put in jeopardy most of China's hard-won financial progress.

ECONOMIC DEVELOPMENT

Despite great difficulties, China made notable economic gains in the prewar Nationalist decade, especially toward the end of that period. A precondition of progress was the restoration of a reasonable degree of internal order and national cohesion. The National Government accomplished this despite, and to some extent aided by, Japanese aggression. It was not until 1934 that the major revolts of the chief warlords and the Communists had been defeated. The civil wars and banditry of 1928–1934 hampered production and trade in the interior and affected the whole country. In 1931–1932 came the Japanese seizure of Manchuria and the abortive attack upon Shanghai, followed by continuing encroachment in North China. In 1931 the Yangtze Valley was afflicted by one of the worst floods in China's history. In 1931–1935 China suffered a severe deflation and depression, with the index of wholesale prices falling by 30 per cent in four years. A chief cause was the American silver buying.*

Throughout there was the hang-over from older days of condi-

---

* The world-wide depression following 1929 did little harm to China in 1929–1931, because the silver price fell and internal prices on the silver standard did not slump, while the fall in exchange rates maintained and even stimulated sale of China's exports and encouraged remittances to China.

tions and institutions unfavorable to economic progress. These included general absence of modern agricultural techniques, unjust incidence of the local land taxes, exploitation by local moneylenders and landlords, the tendency of those gaining wealth to invest in land rather than in business enterprise, too great reliance upon family rather than corporate business organization, lack of proper accounting methods, and the tendency in both family and corporate business to distribute earnings rather than reinvest a suitable proportion. There was no major governmental effort to reform faulty social and economic institutions; drastic changes were to await what the Communists so brutally imposed. But there were encouraging tendencies to deal with deeply rooted abuses, and gradual and orderly betterment seemed inevitable.

Over-all conditions of the 1930's did not favor formation of capital. Military demands for funds were insistent to promote internal order and, after 1931, to prepare eventual defense against Japan. Revenues doubled in 1929–1936, because of a strong government policy. But they could not meet the needs. A series of deficits drained away, via continuing bank investment in bonds, savings that might have stimulated greater growth. Government spending should have been better controlled, and tax-building more aggressive, especially by reform of the land tax; but governments rarely achieve perfection. Basically, heavy spending and deficits were unavoidable. The government deserves great credit for finding means to cover its outlays by taxation and borrowing, without use of inflationary credit. At stake during these years was nothing less than survival of the first promising effort, since the fall of the old regime in 1911, to build a unified, strong, and increasingly democratic China. Lack of money would have meant internal chaos and external disaster.

In spite of these handicaps, the economic progress achieved during this period was highly creditable. The government restored broken railways, built and imported new equipment, and extended the lines. It improved harbors and river navigation, strengthened flood control, developed air transport, and built over 60,000 miles of roads. Both local and foreign capital were showing vigor, especially in developing many light industries. The government was actively making plans for further development, many of which, however, were not ripe for public disclosure. These included railway extensions and improvements, roads, river and port works, irrigation, mineral development, power, industries, and regional development of such areas as the northwest and Hainan Island. These plans, as supplemented during and after the war, were the foundation of Communist planning after the take-over—though the Communists have given no credit for such plans. After the successful monetary reform of 1935, the economy was headed strongly upward.*

Thus in mid-1937 the prospects of continuing and dynamic economic growth were promising. Reports by Ambassador Johnson in the spring of 1937 confirm the above statements about China's progress and refer to the impressive way in which the government was "pushing its program of economic reconstruction on all fronts . . . accelerated to a marked degree by the fact and fear of Japanese encroachment." [4] Johnson, long a wise observer of the Chinese scene, once commented to me that the National Government never had a real chance to show what it could do, being faced during most of the prewar period by warlord and Communist subversive action and Japanese aggression in Manchuria and North China, and then by full-scale Japanese attack. The chief reservations in mid-1937 about prospects of progress were two. Would the government overstrain the currency and economy and take the easy but dangerous path of inflationary financing of development, as have so many underdeveloped countries? And would Japanese aggression defeat the growth process?

* For criticism of Nationalist policy as to public finance and economic development, see D. S. Paauw, "The Kuomintang and Economic Stagnation" (*Journal of Asian Studies,* February, 1957, pp. 213–220) and "Chinese National Expenditures during the Nanking Period" (*Far Eastern Quarterly,* November, 1952, pp. 3–26). Paauw fails to give due weight to several factors hereinbefore set out in this chapter, including: (1) the importance of the government incurring the costs needed to restore order, establish nation-wide authority, and eventually to resist Japan (see N. S. Buchanan's criticism of Paauw on this point following the second citation, pp. 45–46); (2) the disrupting effects of Japan's seizure of Manchuria and encroachments upon North China; (3) the crippling effects of the deflation of about 30 per cent in 1931–1935, largely caused by American silver buying; (4) the fact that well over half of the borrowing to cover deficits in the prewar years was not for ordinary governmental operations, but for payments to retire 'older debt; and (5) China's improving credit from 1928–1937 despite the difficulties, as shown by the great rise in prices 'of the chief external and internal bonds, selling respectively on about a 5 per cent and 7¾ per cent basis in mid-1937.

I know of no adequate analysis of China's economic progress in 1928–1937. The subject deserves further research.

APPRAISAL

All things considered, the National Government in its first decade had made a good record in many fields of activity. The over-all contrast between 1927 and 1937 was greatly to its credit. In 1937 its prestige was rising both at home and abroad. The country was prospering—internal peace always made for prosperity in China. After a turbulent decade, the outlook was bright for an era of unprecedented progress for China, if only the country could remain at peace. Grave weaknesses remained, however, which the strain of fighting brought out.

JULY 7, 1937, A TURNING POINT IN HISTORY

Japan's attack on July 7, 1937, came as a harsh surprise. Political events visible in Japan had indicated the possibility of some softening of Japan's aggressive line. The shooting near Peiping that began on the "double seventh" seems to have been the work of local commanders provoking an incident on their own, as in Manchuria in 1931. But again Tokyo supported the local action, and fighting spread to Shanghai and throughout China. China moved into a new era, of war and inflation and eventual internal strife.

At once China began to marshal her own resources: military, political, financial, and economic. There was need for the strongest possible effort of self-help. But from the start it was clear that, without external aid to supplement what she could do for herself, she could not long resist Japan's might. There was little near-term chance of finding military allies. So the practical possibility was for "aid short of war." China needed several kinds of aid. Weapons, ammunition, equipment, and materiel from abroad were needed for military operations. A variety of imported goods was essential for the working of the economy and the minimum livelihood of the people. Communication with the outside world for persons and goods was vital. Technical aid was needed in several fields of activity. Underlying all was the need for financial support to maintain China's credit and currency, lest a too rapid deterioration impair the working of government and the economy, ruin morale, and cause China's friends to feel that any kind of aid would be hopeless.

These needs indicate the roads we shall follow in moving, for the most part chronologically, through the jungle of events. Part I deals with the period from July 7, 1937, to December 7/8, 1941, when China fought alone. Part II treats the following period of the Pacific War, to August 15, 1945, when China was recognized as the Fourth Power. Part III draws some conclusions.

Part One
China Fights Alone
1937–1941

II. CHINA IN THE CRUCIBLE, 1937

I N 1937 the League of Nations was almost impotent, after its failure to check Mussolini's seizure of Ethiopia in 1935–1936. France's foreign minister, Yvon Delbos, hoped China would not appeal to the League, since it "was a cipher and the only result of a Chinese appeal would be the cipher would become the shadow of a cipher." [1] China, however, after full consideration, appealed to the League on September 12, 1937. She wanted a forum to plead her cause and hoped for some helpful action. China requested that either the Council or Assembly take action or first refer the appeal to the Advisory Committee set up in 1933 to deal with the Manchurian conflict. The Council promptly referred the matter to that Committee, with whom an American sat but without the right to vote. While the American government favored cooperation, it would not take any initiative or engage in joint action but would consider parallel action. The League Assembly on October 6 adopted a resolution proposed by the Committee, which declared "moral support" for China, and urged members to refrain from any action that might weaken China's powers of resistance and to consider extending aid individually to China. Secretary Hull at once expressed his accord. Previously the Committee had condemned bombing of open cities, a position which Hull also promptly endorsed. [2]

The day before the League's action, President Roosevelt made his famous speech suggesting "quarantine" of lawless nations. The timing suggested a connection between the League's action and the President's speech seeming to favor sanctions against Japan. But that was not the fact. While the President's idea elicited much support, it also brought bitter isolationist attack. It was to the isolationists that the administration listened. The "quarantine" idea, whatever it meant, was abandoned. [3] Washington backed away from any action of that nature.

The League's resolution also proposed a conference under the 1922 Nine-Power Treaty of Washington. The conference met at

Brussels November 3–24, with Russian delegates present by special invitation but Japanese absent. The conference labored and brought forth a mouse. It could do no more than call for a peaceful settlement. Britain and France, busy with the threat of Hitler, wanted no further risks in Asia. Russia was ready for stronger action, despite her preoccupation with Hitler and the fact that she was still digesting the effects of Stalin's purges of leading generals and others. The United States, isolationist and neutralist, would not give a lead that might have brought serious action. For the future the peril was great. But it was not seen clearly enough to move the imperiled countries in the fall of 1937.

Immediately after the failure at Brussels, China asked for a loan equivalent to US$500 million from the United States, Britain, and France, to be secured on customs and salt revenue and by oil concessions. The money was sought to buy war materials, a list of which China submitted.[4] Though the request looked big, it was eminently realistic as to the amount China could well have used. But the request received little consideration.

To China the failure of international moves was a keen disappointment. In the fighting at Shanghai in October, China had held on despite the military disadvantage, sacrificing some of her best troops in the hope of influencing favorably action by the League powers and the United States. Early in November Shanghai fell, followed by the fall of Nanking on December 13, amidst an orgy of misconduct by Japanese troops. Yet China remained determined to fight on. Although her leaders still felt that the curbing of Japan's aggression was an international responsibility, aid from several separate external sources was encouraging to China. The German military advisers, who had been in China for some time, were actively helping. Even before China appealed to the League, Russia offered credits for military items and began to send supplies, military advisers, and aviation "volunteers." On November 3, Treasury Secretary Morgenthau agreed to buy silver from China, thus helping to convert silver reserves into dollars. China could hope for growing support by her friends, acting individually.

THE GERMAN MILITARY ADVISERS

When in 1927 Generalissimo Chiang broke with Russia and dismissed the Russian military advisers, he engaged Germans in their place. F. F. Liu, a former Chinese officer, gives a good account of the part which the German advisers played in China's military development.[5] China, like Japan, copied the Imperial German system of having the military free of civilian control, as well as the German system of organization. By 1937, China had about 300,000 troops in German-trained divisions, of which 80,000 were first-class units with German-made weapons. Influential elements in Germany were planning aid to strengthen China's air force and to build a navy. Had war been delayed a year or two, the Germans might have helped China mold a far stronger force than that which faced Japan in the summer of 1937.

General Alexander von Falkenhausen led the German advisers. He had been an outstanding staff officer in World War I, and later helped to build up the Reichswehr. He knew Japan as military attache in 1910–1914, and, speaking Japanese, could talk directly with the Generalissimo (who had studied in Japan) in that language. In 1937–1938 there were about 30 German officers in the military mission, a total of 137 having served in China in the previous decade.[6]

Characterizing them, Liu said that "the German military advisers were there to contribute to their own country's interests, business and military." He, however, appraised highly the quality of their work. They faced staggering difficulties, such as lack of full cooperation, widespread illiteracy, and China's lack of developed industry. Yet, "They had been highly successful in assisting Chiang to create the powerful Central army and the small nucleus of officers which formed China's general staff." [7] My own contact with these advisers led me to feel that they were sincerely and competently serving China.

In the early weeks of fighting at Shanghai, the German advisers deprecated China's bitter and prolonged stand in a deteriorating strategic position. After the fall of Shanghai, when the Japanese columns were advancing toward Nanking, the advisers urged Chinese counterattacks on the enemy's vulnerable south flank. But the Chinese forces were demoralized, and there was no serious effort to rally them for such action.

In August Japan sought at Berlin the withdrawal or at least a reduction in number of the German military advisers. But Germany declined, feeling a moral obligation to China, and

Japan did not press the matter. German opinion on Sino-Japanese issues was divided. The Foreign Office desired neither "a decisive Japanese or Chinese victory," fearing that a victorious Japan would interfere with German trade and investment in China.[8] German industrialists were profiting from sale to China of industrial and transport equipment and armaments. A Sino-German barter agreement for 100 million marks was made in July 1936. Strong military elements, including Goering, von Blomberg, and Beck, wanted to work with China rather than Japan in the Orient and to expand German influence in China. But influential leaders headed by Joachim von Ribbentrop, then ambassador in London, favored Japan. Toward the end of 1936 Germany signed with Japan the anti-Comintern pact. Also in April 1936, and again in June 1937, Germany made trade agreements with "Manchukuo." On September 4, 1937, while heavy fighting was going on at Shanghai, Germany granted a credit of £2 million to "Manchukuo." Ninety per cent of the credit could be repaid by shipment of Manchurian products. Thus Germany was helping Japan to develop her economic bloc.[9] Ribbentrop's policy of strengthening the German-Japanese Axis was gaining the upper hand.

RUSSIA BACKS CHINA'S STRUGGLE

Though Sino-Russian relations had long been strained, Russian policy toward China was changing in 1936–1937. Russia had a growing fear of Japan's onward march in northeastern Asia, and a common interest with China in checking Japan. Russia had been feverishly building military strength in Siberia. The process, however, was far from complete; for example, the trans-Siberian railway was not yet double-tracked. In December 1936, Chiang's release after the kidnaping at Sian by Marshal Chang Hsueh-liang, according to Russian statements, was a result of Russian intercession.[10] Ambassador Johnson believed that the price paid for Chiang's release was to tolerate the Chinese Communists, stiffen policy *vis-à-vis* Japan, and conciliate Russia. The shift in policy "was due to fear of Japan rather than love of Russia," and the Chinese "preferred that course with its uncertainties to what they considered to be a certain future with the Japanese." [11]

In the following months, negotiations led to formation in China of the United Front with the Communists. In September, after fighting began, they announced dissolution of their Soviet Republic and affirmed unity with the government. Chiang announced approval. There is good reason to believe that the policy of the Chinese Communists in these matters was decided in the Kremlin.[12]

For Russia and Communism, formation of the United Front served a multiple purpose. It focused China's political and military efforts on opposing Japan, thus keeping Japan busy and diverting a possible attack upon Russia. It strengthened China vis-à-vis Japan, by avoiding for the time being internal strife. It forestalled a possible Nationalist drive to wipe out the Chinese Communist forces, which were in a weak position in the far northwest, or to drive them into Russia. And besides preserving them, it gave them a status enabling them to operate openly and later to expand within China.

Even before the Sian incident, China's policy toward Russia had begun to change. In November 1936, T. F. Tsiang (later Chinese representative at the United Nations and ambassador at Washington) was chosen as ambassador to Russia. Known as a supporter in 1936 of Sino-Russian friendship, one purpose of his mission was to obtain assurances that if war became inevitable "the Soviet Union would support China both with supplies and armed forces."[13] In April 1937, Consul General (later Ambassador) C. E. Gauss made an interesting report from Shanghai on Sino-Russian developments. Russian Ambassador Dimitri Bogomolov had told an American journalist that Russia had been impressed with China's growing unity. Bogomolov said that at recent conferences in Moscow in which he participated the view was that "the Soviet Government would do well to support the Nanking Government as the stabilizing and paramount force in this country." Even before the kidnaping of Chiang at Sian, said Bogomolov, Russia had concluded that "a strongly united China friendly to the Soviet Union" would help to maintain the balance of power in the Far East and preserve peace. Gauss felt that the Russian action and the changed attitude of the Chinese Communists, in not opposing Nanking, were "more than coincidental."[14]

Bogomolov stated, Gauss reported, that certain negotiations between Russia and China were proceeding. These, it now appears, grew out of a Russian proposal in April 1937 to conclude with China two pacts of nonaggression and mutual assistance. China inclined to agree to the former. But a mutual assistance agreement might have been viewed as a military threat against Japan, which was then showing signs of greater moderation *vis-à-vis* China. Also, it would have hurt relations with Germany. So China would not consider a pact of mutual assistance.[15] Nevertheless, in the Spring and Summer of 1937 talk of such a pact tended to lead China to believe that, if she resisted Japan, Russia would lend armed support, but without really promising such support. Ambassador Tsiang, however, consistently reported that he did not expect Russia to join in the hostilities, and that neither Stalin, Litvinov, or any other high Russian official had ever so indicated to him.[16] Russia doubtless felt that to join the fighting directly in support of China would embroil her in Europe. The German and Italian representatives in Moscow told the Chinese ambassador in the latter part of July that if Russia intervened on China's side their countries would intervene on the side of Japan.[17]

When fighting broke out in July, China became ready to discuss with Russia a mutual assistance pact. But Russia held back. The French ambassador reported from Nanking at the end of July that Chiang, who meanwhile had committed China to a firm stand, was "furious with the Russians," since they "had led him to believe that they would support him and now had told him that they would do nothing." [18] Chinese writers have speculated whether Russia, by proposing a nonaggression pact in April and by the talk about possible military support, was making a clever move to stiffen China against Japan, knowing that China then would refuse such a pact; and also whether word of the offer came to Japanese intelligence, and so influenced Japan to start hostilities promptly, before China could become stronger.[19]

Once active fighting began, the best China could get from Russia was the nonaggression pact.* That was signed at Nanking

* Mention of nonaggression came from Russia with ill grace, since in the previous decades so much of Russia's eastward expansion had been at China's expense—in Outer Mongolia, in Siberia around Vladivostok, and in Manchuria until driven out by Japan.

on August 21, eight days after large-scale fighting began at Shanghai.[20] Analyzing the pact's effects, Loy W. Henderson, the American Chargé d'Affaires at Moscow, felt them to be of much importance. For China, he pointed out, the pact stiffened the decision to keep on fighting, strengthened the case for Soviet aid in war supplies, and brought in the Chinese Communists as supporting the struggle against Japan. But he warned that "during the course of the struggle these Communists will not fail to take advantage of the situation to strengthen their influence in China." From Russia's angle, the move put pro-Soviet elements in China in a better position, made China more dependent on Moscow, and meant that Japan "will for some time to come be compelled to dissipate in China energies which the Soviet Government has feared might be turned against the Soviet Union." He quoted Chinese Ambassador Tsiang as feeling that "Moscow was more interested at the present time in stirring up opposition to Japan in China than it was in spreading communism." Henderson thought neither signatory "has any illusions with respect to the other but each feels that the other may be of use to it in the solution of immediate and urgent problems." [21]

In October the Soviet Commissar for Foreign Affairs, Litvinov, told M. Blum of France at the League of Nations in Geneva that Japan was sure to have "enormous difficulty" in China and that Russia "hoped that war between China and Japan would continue just as long as possible and would result in an attempt by the Japanese to swallow just as much of China as possible. That would leave the Soviet Union free for operations in Europe." Litvinov indicated to Blum that Russia would not join the fighting.[22]

The possibility of Russia's taking part in the war, however, raised false hopes in some circles in China and also led to trouble within Russia. There were reports that Stalin had promised that Russia would join the war at a certain date and rumors of the coming of divisions of Russianized Mongol troops as "volunteers." But nothing materialized. Despite Ambassador Tsiang's reports, certain Chinese Communists, claiming that they could best reflect Russian views, had indicated otherwise in Nanking.

In October Ambassador Bogomolov returned to Moscow. He and his military attaché and also some of the Russian military in

Siberia wanted Russia's active military participation. A month later Bogomolov and the attaché disappeared. It developed that they were under arrest. The charge, it was said, was not so much that they had made unauthorized promises in China as that they had misled Moscow about the effectiveness of China's ability to resist Japan.[23] After China's disastrous defeat early in November when the troops were outflanked and retreated from Shanghai, Russia was worried whether Japan might not emerge from the fighting more quickly and stronger than had been anticipated. Later reports were that Bogomolov had been liquidated. To me, this was distressing. I had come to know him in China and had found him friendly, intelligent, and sympathetic with China's problems.

Meanwhile, Russia began without delay to provide China with "aid short of war." At the time of signing the nonaggression pact of August 21, 1937, Russia promised a credit of C$100 million (about US$30 million). The formal agreement was not signed until 1938, and then the amount was raised to US$50 million. But Russia, not bound by the need for legal formalities, began at once to deliver military items, including planes, and to provide "volunteer" pilots and military advisers.

AID IN AVIATION: A PATTERN OF VARIETY

In 1932-1945 I had the privilege of close association with aviation developments in China, acting, in effect, part of the time as an aviation adviser. I handled the negotiations for the coming of the American mission on military aviation in 1932; participated in some of the negotiations for purchase of planes; and, in 1938, at the request of the American partners of the China National Aviation Corporation (hereinafter called CNAC) and with the agreement of the Chinese Government, accepted appointment as a director of the company for the duration of the war, stipulating to avoid conflict of interest that I would not participate in business relations of profit and loss between the government and the American partners.

In civil and military aviation, China before the war received both nongovernmental and governmental aid. That pattern continued during the war. Here were examples of what competent foreign private technicians can do, both when engaged directly by the government and when working in conjunction with moderate investments of foreign private capital. And here also were examples of good and bad governmental aid.

Maintenance of China's civil air communications during the fighting was soon seen to be of major importance. As the government was forced back from the coast, flying played more and more a vital part in holding things together. Surface transport was too slow and undependable for many communications in the emergency. Planes were depended upon for the quick movement of persons, mail, and many essential supplies, both in and out of and within China. Those who were behind the fighting lines did not feel besieged or cut off, because planes could fly in and out to friendly areas, either above the enemy lines at night or in bad weather, or by safer routes when available. In China's skies the sight of friendly planes, and not merely hostile bombers and fighters, was a clear support for morale.

In civil aviation CNAC was a major factor. Founded in 1929, it had 55 per cent Chinese Government ownership and 45 per cent foreign, the latter acquired by Pan American Airways in 1933. Administration was handled by the Chinese side and operations by the American. To operate with this divided responsibility required constant tact, but on the whole it worked out reasonably well. CNAC was fortunate to have as the chief representative of the American partners during much of the prewar period and during the war, William L. Bond, whose energy, courage, resourcefulness, and good judgment overcame almost insuperable obstacles. There was also the Eurasia Company, formed about 1930 by the Chinese Government and the German Lufthansa on a two-thirds one-third basis; its original purpose was to link China with Europe by routes through Asia. When that service proved impracticable, Eurasia operated internally in China. Its trimotored Junkers planes gave good service in the first part of the war, especially on the Hankow-Hong Kong run. CNAC in the first two years used an odd variety of planes: a DC-2, some Douglas and Sikorsky amphibians, and a trimotored Ford. In 1939–1940, CNAC acquired three DC-3's and some old Condors. With these few planes, the companies' Sino-foreign personnel worked wonders under enormous difficulties.

The lack of a military air force was brought home to China in

1932 by Japan's unimpeded control of the air during the brief fighting at Shanghai and the havoc wrought to an almost defenceless city by hostile planes. Robert M. Short, an American volunteer pilot killed during that fighting, became a hero. With the informal aid of the American government, China engaged in mid-1932 a civilian American group of flyers headed by John H. Jouett, a retired colonel. This group started a school of military aviation at Hangchow, which did effective work and was the real beginning of Chinese military aviation. China also accepted an Italian military air mission offered by Mussolini, which arrived in 1934. Unfortunately that move introduced divided counsels and confused the issue. Jouett and most of his group left in 1935, but in the meantime they gave good training to many pilots.

When fighting began, a number of Americans were in China helping to develop military aviation. Chief among these was Colonel (later Major General) Claire L. Chennault, the dramatic figure on whom centers the story of China's military aviation from 1937. A believer in pursuit aviation, he had been unable while in the American air force to sell his ideas on air tactics to his superiors. His belief in the vulnerability of unescorted bombers to attack by determined and well-trained and -equipped pursuit pilots was vindicated later in a costly way by losses of unescorted Japanese bombers in China and Burma, German bombers in the Battle of Britain, and British and American bombers over Europe.

Chennault retired from the American army in the spring of 1937 and accepted appointment to go to China to survey aviation needs. An implacable foe of Japan, he stopped there en route to gather personally some intelligence about that country, whose planes he believed China would later have to meet. That was the beginning of a study that gave him an uncanny knowledge of Japanese planes and tactics. His pilots said, "The Old Man can smell Japs!"

Arriving in China a month before the fighting began, he found a sad state of affairs in the Chinese air force. The Italian air mission had established a training school at Loyang and an assembly plant at Nanchang, besides selling many planes to China. Chennault concluded, after his survey of the situation, that in contrast to the German military mission "the Italians did all they could to sabotage China." He said,

The Italian flying school at Loyang was unique. It graduated every Chinese cadet who survived the training course as a full-fledged pilot regardless of his ability. This was in sharp contrast to the American policy of weeding out incompetents in early training and then only graduating the best students. However, the Generalissimo was pleased with the Italian method. Chinese aviation cadets were carefully selected from the top social strata, and when they were washed out at the American-style Hangchow school, protests from their influential families caused the Generalissimo acute embarrassment. The Italian method solved this social problem and all but wrecked the air force. The influence of this kind of training continued to plague the Chinese Air Force until the return to China of the first wholly American-trained Chinese airmen in 1942.

The Italian assembly plant at Nanchang was also a fraud. It turned out large quantities of a Fiat fighter that proved to be a firetrap in combat. The Savoia-Marchetti bombers were of such obsolete vintage that the Chinese could use them only as transports.

Italians were also responsible for encouraging some quaint practices by the Chinese Aero Commission. No plane was ever removed from the official roster for any cause . . . As a result, when war came the Aero Commission roster listed five hundred planes but only ninety-one were fit for combat.

Chennault also stated that some of Mussolini's air officers made air surveys of strategic areas, which they sold to the Japanese at a handsome price.*

When fighting threatened, Generalissimo Chiang asked Chennault to whip into shape China's meager air forces at Nanchang. As to what Chennault found, he said,

There were a few American-born Cantonese and some graduates of Colonel Jouett's Hangchow school who were extremely competent. The rest, most of them Italian trained, were a menace to navigation. Fighter pilots supposedly ready for combat spun in and killed themselves flying basic trainers.[24]

The first efforts of China's air force were anything but auspicious. Instructed to bomb the Japanese cruiser *Idzumo* anchored at the edge of Shanghai's International Settlement, the airmen on Bloody Saturday, August 14, 1937, found a storm over Shanghai and violated orders to avoid the Settlement. From the Central Bank I saw the first bombs fall in the river in front of the build-

* Quotations herein are reprinted by permission of G. P. Putnam's Sons from *Way of a Fighter*, by Claire Lee Chennault, pp. 37–38. Copyright 1949 by Claire Lee Chennault.

ing, blowing in windows near which I was standing. The following raids dropped bombs in two of Shanghai's busiest streets with thousands of casualties. Soon after, Chinese planes mistakenly attacked the British cruiser *Cumberland,* luckily without hitting her. They dropped a small bomb on the S.S. *President Hoover* of the American Dollar Line at sea, fortunately doing no serious damage.

But in air fighting around Nanking, China's airmen gave a better account of themselves. From Formosa the Japanese sent several daylight raids of unescorted bombers to Nanking. Chennault had taught the Chinese squadrons how to attack, and he claimed that the Japanese lost 40 or more of 54 planes within five days. That ended the daylight raids. Then came the night bombers. But the Chinese had set up a warning net and a pattern of searchlights. Chennault showed the pilots how to attack the bombers at night in the glare of searchlights. Japanese losses were so heavy that those raids ceased. Finally the Japanese sent bombers with a heavy escort of fighters in daylight. These tactics worked. In the first such raid the Chinese lost 11 of 16 fighters. Without replacements they could not stand such erosion. By the end of October less than a dozen ready fighter planes were left. The Japanese air forces had established control of the air over Nanking and Shanghai.[25]

While these things were happening, Russia was making a serious effort to bolster China's air arm. On September 29 the American embassy at Nanking reported that 300 Soviet planes were being sent to China via Lanchow. Americans reaching Hankow from Lanchow early in October reported seeing such planes there, arriving from the north. On October 4 Consul General Gauss reported that a Russian pilot was found in a plane shot down near Shanghai in the Japanese-occupied area. On October 14 Ambassador Davies reported from Moscow that he had learned that Russia had already sent to China 400 planes and at least 40 Soviet instructors. Caravans were taking other supplies on the long trek through Central Asia, and at least 200 trucks were working on this route. Also plans were being made to send heavy items by sea via Indochina. About December 1 it was reported that 42 Russian planes arrived at Nanchang bringing about 100 Soviet fliers and other personnel and that about 50 fliers were at Hankow.[26]

COMPLICATIONS OF AMERICAN NEUTRALITY

While Japanese planes were bombing and machine-gunning at large and Russia was sending war planes and pilots, the United States was at first reacting against almost any American participation in aviation activities in China. Washington intimated in August that, under Section 4090 of the Revised Statutes (34 *Stat.* 814), the United States Court for China could prohibit Americans from advising and instructing military personnel. The Consulate General at Hong Kong even provisionally asked the Hong Kong authorities not to allow American personnel of CNAC (55 per cent Chinese Government-owned) to leave Hong Kong for China. Washington, however, said that that was to be left to the Hong Kong authorities. But the Consulate was directed to call the American law to the attention of such personnel and endorse their passports as "not valid for travel to or in any foreign state in connection with entrance into or service in foreign military or naval forces." Washington also refused passports to Americans already engaged as aviation instructors before hostilities began. Several such Americans in China left the country.

In the highest Chinese circles this attitude naturally caused bitterness. Madame Chiang Kai-shek was then handling aviation matters. She told Ambassador Johnson she hoped the United States would "not place any obstacles in China's way when it is fighting for its very life." Ambassador Johnson was sympathetic with China. He told the State Department on September 10 that, unless specifically instructed, he did not propose to seek out Americans engaged in aviation and advise them unless the United States Court for China issued a writ. Washington moderated its view and indicated that its attitude was taken in view of the strong feeling in the United States against any involvement, and not from any thought of injuring China.

Finally the State Department, in a message of September 15 to Nanking, recognized that certain agencies of the American government had aided in the original arrangements to engage aviation instructors; stated that such Americans stayed in China on their own responsibility; and said that the American government disapproved their doing anything of the nature of military service with a foreign government.[27]

Washington also, pursuant to the neutrality law and policy,

blocked the shipment to China on the American vessel *Wichita* of 19 Bellanca planes which China had purchased, together with a miscellaneous lot of small arms. Cancellation of an order by Spain had made the planes available to China. The *Wichita* had sailed from an eastern port in August and called at San Pedro before starting across the Pacific. The vessel was owned by the United States but chartered to a private company. On September 14 President Roosevelt issued a statement that vessels owned by the United States could not transport to China or Japan arms, ammunition, or implements of war, and that privately owned American vessels would do so at their own risk. The planes thereupon were off-loaded from the *Wichita* at San Pedro. Naturally this made China unhappy.[28]

The course of American policy was disturbing to Ambassador Johnson. In a telegram of September 3 to Secretary Hull he said that ". . . the march of events must inevitably bring us sooner or later where we must consider whether we are to abandon all hope of saving something, even our self-respect, from the wreckage of 150 years of cultural and commercial efforts in China." He believed that a "too complaisant surrender now may precipitate a more violent effort at recovery later."[29] Events bore out Johnson's prescient view. But it was more than three years before the United States, in permitting the organization of the American Volunteer Group, Chennault's Flying Tigers, was ready to do what Russia had done to aid China in the first weeks of fighting. And even then China had to use her own meager funds to buy the American planes, which were gotten and armed only with great difficulty.

THE YEAR-END: DISCOURAGEMENT BUT WITH HOPE

In the first half-year China suffered punishing losses, both military and civilian. The response of friendly nations to her appeals for political and military support and credits was disappointing, except for the beginnings of Russian aid. The Japanese militarists showed their contempt for what the West might do by sinking the American gunboat *Panay* and attacking British warships at the time of Nanking's fall, only paying damages. Many Japanese hoped that the fall of the capital would end the "China incident." But China set up a temporary capital at Hankow and prepared for a further move to Chungking in the western mountains. The atrocities at Nanking and Japan's unwillingness to offer terms that China could consider stiffened China's will to resist, despite disasters. Also, world opinion was moving in China's favor.

Chiang set forth China's determination in a message of December 24 to Roosevelt.

> We are fighting for the liberty of the Chinese nation and against the common menace to mankind. We are not only defending ourselves, but also the principle of the sanctity of treaties especially the Nine Power Treaty, under which the sovereignty, independence and the territorial and administrative integrity of China should be respected by Japan and other signatory Powers. We will not surrender to Japan's brutal force, but will continue our resistance until the Japanese Government abandons its aggressive policy, until our national administrations are restored to us and until the principle of inviolability of the international covenants is vindicated.

He thanked the President for America's moral support and appealed for "such effective assistance to China as will enable the struggle for the cause of world peace and solidarity to be carried on to a successful conclusion at an early date." [30]

Already, as the next chapter will show, China was encouraged by seeing a genuine "silver lining," thanks to American action.

III. THE FINANCIAL EMERGENCY, 1937:
SELF-HELP AND FOREIGN AID

WHILE China was fighting and seeking the support of friendly nations, she was facing a heavy strain on her external assets. The needs were dual: to buy abroad the munitions and other items needed for the fight and to support the currency. Reserves, equivalent to US$379 million, were relatively large, and for the time being China could deal with the situation with her own resources. But from the start it was certain that China could not fight a large-scale war for long without foreign credits.

THE SILVER LINING

It is an anomaly that the American silver-buying policy, whose hurtful impact on China the American Government largely ignored until the fall of 1935, became in mid-1937 a vitally important means of aid in China's fight for survival. That policy, first adopted in 1933–1934 because of pressure of the politically strong but economically minor silver interests backed by inflation-minded allies, forced China in 1934–1935 to give up the age-old silver standard. But although China sold all the silver that the American Government could be persuaded to buy, that metal as of June 30, 1937, was 44 per cent of the total reserves. And over a third of the reserves was in China, mostly at Shanghai, comprising US$118 million of silver and US$12 million of gold.

Enemy seizure or blockade of this silver and gold would have been almost a mortal blow. So the Central Bank urgently began removal shortly after the incident of July 7. Every American and British vessel leaving for other than Japanese ports took as large a shipment as could be insured, ordinarily about US$10 million. The writer and others from the bank stood shifts day and night, to be ready to deal with any possible Japanese obstruction, which luckily did not happen. Most shipments went to Hong Kong and London. When on August 13 fighting began at Shanghai, practically all the silver and gold had been moved from that city. But about 43 million ounces then worth about US$19 million had to stay at Tientsin and Peiping, where Japanese pressure super-imposed upon regional sensibilities had immobilized it since the monetary reform of 1935. The wisdom of promptly getting the silver out of Shanghai was proved later when, in the fall of 1938, the Japanese, through their puppets, blocked the removal from Shanghai on the S.S. *President Coolidge* of 7.5 million ounces sold to the Chase Bank. This was mostly silver contributed by the public at Shanghai after August 13, 1937, in the form of jewelry and plate. Despite official American protest, the ship was forced to unload this cargo before being allowed to sail.[1] The Central Bank inquired whether an American transport calling at Shang-hai could take the silver as "ballast." Understandably, the Amer-ican government felt that such a deal would not be a purchase of silver so much as "purchase of a diplomatic incident."

While silver was 44 per cent of China's monetary reserves, it was only so much metal in the world's market, and large amounts could have been sold only at a ruinous discount. Earlier in 1937 Minister Kung, in Europe to attend George VI's coronation, had arranged with continental banks three credits totaling US$12 million secured by 35 million ounces of silver. He wanted the credits partly because sale of silver to the United States was then uncertain and partly because he felt announcement of the credits would strengthen confidence since negotiations for a large British loan had not succeeded. Later in 1937 he arranged other like credits, secured by a further 30 million ounces. But these were makeshift arrangements at best.

Clearly China should try to sell as much silver as possible to the United States. The Treasury, besides buying US$67 million worth of silver from the Chinese Government before mid-1937, had authorized a credit of US$20 million on 50 million ounces of silver held in the United States. But the credit was on a month-to-month basis, in view of American silver politics. In June, Kung visited Washington. He offered that 50 million to Morgenthau, plus 12 million held in San Francisco. On July 8 they reached agreement for sale of the 62 million at 45 cents per ounce. At that moment word had not come of the Marco Polo Bridge incident of the previous day. In describing the negotiations from an account in the Morgenthau Diaries, A. S. Everest wrote:

None of the group yet knew of the Peiping incident of the night before, so Kung's acceptance "for the sake of a strong China and for security and peace in the Far East" did not appear ironical at the time. In his effusive thanks he called Morgenthau "a far-sighted statesman," to which the latter jokingly replied, "Listen, Dr. Kung, I bought all your silver; you don't have to give me anything more."

Not to be outdone, Kung responded, "Well, I sold the silver to you cheap. I bought your surplus gold." [2]

Also the agreement of July 8 provided that the Federal Reserve Bank of New York would grant a credit of not over US$50 million against gold deposited by China. This credit was to be available to December 31, 1937, and was repeatedly extended during the war for half-yearly periods. China's prewar silver sales to the Treasury, including the sale of July 8, 1937, were 188 million ounces for a total price of US$94 million.

After the fighting began, it was clear, as a writer in the London *X-Ray* of August 30 said, that, "Giving China a good price for her silver is one of the few ways in which the Washington Administration can favour China without getting into trouble with (a) Japan, (b) Congress, and (c) the Supreme Court." That statement accurately foretold the shape of things to come. But actually Morgenthau had bought no silver beyond the deal of July 8, and the American attitude was uncertain. There was the neutrality law, with its restrictions on financial dealings with nations at "war," and strong sentiment against involvement in any hostilities. As time passed, however, and neither China nor Japan declared war, action under that law did not go much beyond warnings to Americans in the danger area and to American shipping.

Until the American attitude became clearer, it seemed wise for China not to press for sale of more silver to the United States. But in the fall of 1937, after Kung returned to China, the need became urgent. Morgenthau promptly responded to China's approach. On November 3 he undertook to buy 10 million ounces at 45 cents. On November 8 the Treasury bid for a further 10 million, in anticipation of which the bank had already arranged shipment by an American vessel from Hong Kong on that day. Further bids for lots of 10 million ounces each followed, to bring to 50 million ounces the total bought in November. Since the Japanese had captured the Chinese Municipality of Shanghai early in November, the bank, despite having its office in the International Settlement, arranged to send and receive telegrams about silver through an American bank, because Japanese censorship was feared though it did not develop.* On December 2 Ambassador C. T. Wang telegraphed that Morgenthau agreed to buy another 50 million ounces at 45 cents, in semimonthly installments of 10 million each from December 15 through February 15, 1938. As to this Everest wrote:

On the first of December, after Shanghai had fallen and Nanking was under attack, Morgenthau became extremely anxious to help the Chinese before it was too late. He wired the President for permission to purchase 50,000,000 ounces of silver and to extend the foreign exchange agreement for a year. Roosevelt gave his consent, subject only to State Department concurrence. Herbert Feis of State agreed to the purchase.[3]

These various purchases after July 8, 1937, were not made public for nine months. But the market realized, long before the announcement, that the Treasury continued currently to buy.

With the outbreak of fighting, the government redoubled its efforts to collect silver from the people. Huge amounts remained in the country as hoards of coin and bullion. The government offered a premium on handing in silver and it also gradually gained possession of stocks held by provincial authorities.

American support through silver purchase was vitally important in China's struggle and a great encouragement to China, especially in the first months of fighting. This was fully realized by Morgenthau, who had Roosevelt's backing. On several occasions Kung expressed China's great gratitude. China had reason to be thankful for Morgenthau's ready response, in face of a difficult internal political situation because of the silver controversy and problems of the neutrality law.

Some end results of the American silver policy, however, were less immediately obvious than aid to China's war chest. The historic silver standard was deeply ingrained in China's economy, and there is considerable doubt whether China would have abandoned it in the mid-thirties without pressure from the American silver policy. Had China stayed on a silver money basis, she would not have attained the momentum of progress in 1936–1937 that apparently had its part in stimulating Japan to attack before China became too strong. But, had the attack come with China

* Similarly the Central Bank arranged as a precaution that any letters of credit opened abroad by the government be handled through the Central Bank's office at Hong Kong rather than Shanghai.

on a silver basis, she could not long have found the means to fight Japan. Ability to borrow silver internally would have been slight compared with the need for money. And emergency issuance of notes payable in silver would not have commanded general confidence. Almost at once they would have been presented for redemption, largely to go into private hoards. China would have had to give up convertibility into silver. Then a premium on silver would have developed and grown rapidly, and confidence would have been quickly lost. The resulting rapid inflation would have threatened early financial collapse. Instead the 1935 reform, by nationalizing silver, gave China large reserves which she could sell to the United States at good prices to realize dollars. Had the old system continued, much less silver would have been available for sale. And that, if pressed on the sensitive world market, would have led to a ruinous drop in price.

Moreover, the managed currency system, which had started out with so much promise, made it easy to issue paper currency for war needs. Under stress of war, an inflation followed which the government found itself unable to control. Although Japan was ultimately defeated, galloping inflation became a major cause of the government's downfall. If by staying on a silver basis China had found herself unable to make prolonged resistance to Japan, the later events of World War II and its aftermath would certainly have been different. Whether for better or for worse is an interesting intellectual speculation.

Thus it is ironic and indeed frightening that an American policy promoted by special interests, and apparently when adopted of rather minor importance to the United States, changed world history in a way that could not have been foreseen.

THE EARLY MONETARY EMERGENCY

The outbreak of fighting in North China on July 7 was a rude shock to confidence. Immediate effects were felt in the most sensitive markets, for foreign exchange and securities. From July 7 until major fighting began at Shanghai on August 13, there was a constant succession of disturbing events, along with the rumors for which Shanghai was so justly famous. The outbreak of major fighting there intensified the crisis.

For the country's chief financial center to be in the very front line was an unprecedented situation. The international settlements and concessions were exempt from Japanese seizure. In occupied China these became islands, which the Japanese for the most part precariously respected until the Pacific War. That the Central Bank's office could continue in the International Settlement at Shanghai was a key element in financial events until the latter part of 1941.* The Central Bank was damaged by the first bombs that fell on August 14, and most of the bank's staff fled, leaving a few higher officials to deal with the crisis.

Immediately after July 7 there was a rush to buy foreign currencies. From then to August 13 the Central Bank sold US$42 million to support exchange. Those responsible for policy decided without hesitation to meet demand and maintain rates. The currency had been stabilized only 20 months. The reform had been highly successful, but confidence in it had not been fully established. Certainly it would have been wrong to allow the market to break at the first severe strain. Reserves were large and the currency, if anything, was undervalued. Also, previous Sino-Japanese incidents often had not proven serious, and there was no certainty that this would be the one leading to full-scale war. To let exchange slip in July would have gravely hurt China's position at home and abroad. In order to ease the strain on the market, the foreign exchange banks at the Central Bank's request undertook in July, as a "Gentlemen's Agreement," to confine exchange operations to "legitimate purposes" and to sell foreign currencies only to their normal customers.

Fears of the worst were realized when fighting began at Shanghai early on Friday, August 13. The main dangers were two-fold: the banks could not provide enough cash because of a general illiquidity and a heavy drain of foreign exchange was sure to come. The first measure was to declare a bank holiday, from 10:15 a.m. Over the week end, measures to cope with the

---

* The chief international settlements and concessions in China of significance for matters of currency and exchange were at Shanghai and Tientsin. Others existed in other leading cities. Many leading Chinese had wanted to do away with these remnants of foreign control, but with the fighting they took on unexpected importance to China. There was also the system of extraterritoriality, or "extrality," under which foreigners were not subject to Chinese jurisdiction but rather to courts of their own nationality. This system and the system of international settlements and concessions were abolished pursuant to agreements of 1943.

emergency had to be devised. This was the first of a series of heavy week ends during the war for key officials. As Finance Minister Kung was in England, the burden of financial affairs fell upon the two Vice-Ministers, Hsu Kan and Tsou Lin. T. V. Soong, throughout this period, was influential as Chairman of the Bank of China, as was also its Assistant General Manager, Pei Tsu-yee. In the Central Bank the main responsibility rested on the Manager of the Banking Department, Hsi Te-mou. For advice on these difficult problems the government and the Central Bank leaned on three foreign advisers: Cyril Rogers, who had been loaned to China by the Bank of England with special reference to creation of the contemplated Central Reserve Bank; F. B. Lynch, who had been Adviser to the Central Bank since 1929; and the writer, as Financial Adviser to the Ministry of Finance and concurrently to the Central Bank. On Saturday, August 14th, the three advisers presented a memorandum urging temporary limitation of cash withdrawals from banks, supply of currency to the banks by the Central Bank through loans "at a price," tightening the Gentlemen's Agreement, and firm support of exchange rates. The government accepted the advisers' recommendations.*

With these steps taken, the banks opened again on August 17. Business was done behind doors and windows that were heavily sandbagged. As expected, the money market was very tight. This limited the availability of funds for speculative buying of goods and flight of capital. The virtual blockade of Shanghai, which was in the midst of land fighting and naval and air operations, further added to the money stringency. Temporarily, the drain of exchange was reversed, as the tightening of the market

---

* These were embodied in Ministry of Finance Orders 34 and 37 of August 15 and 16. These Orders limited withdrawals from current bank accounts to 5 per cent per week, not to exceed C$150—later amended to exempt accounts below C$300. Deposits made on and after August 18 were to be free of the restrictions. Fixed deposits were frozen to maturity and if not renewed were subject to the same restrictions as current accounts. Currency could be withdrawn by special arrangement with the respective banks to meet payrolls or expenses related to military operations. Cashier's orders could be used for interbank settlement only. The government also authorized transfer money known as *wei wah*, that is, cash orders of commercial and native banks. These could be transferred only between Shanghai banks and could not be exchanged either for currency or to buy foreign exchange. For a time *wei wah* were discounted at up to 6 per cent but the discount soon fell to 1 per cent and for some months varied around 1 to 2 per cent.

forced some sales of exchange to raise local currency. In the second half of August the Central Bank was able to buy back in the market foreign currencies amounting to nearly US$5 million.

The market for government bonds also suffered a severe shock. From a price of 87 to 88 and a yield of about 7.75 per cent for the 6 per cent Consolidated Bonds A in the week July 5 to 10, there was a drop to a range of 75½ to 82 and yields of 8 to 9 per cent in the next week. From the latter part of July, the government for a time pegged bond prices on about a 9 per cent basis, to avoid a panic that might follow a bigger drop. Knowledge of this action checked the urge to sell or speculate. With the outbreak of fighting at Shanghai on August 13, the Stock Exchange was closed. Thereafter unofficial prices fell, to a yield-range of about 11 to 15 per cent in 1938–1941.

Advance of the enemy forces raised difficult problems for the government banks. When in November the Japanese captured the Chinese Municipality of Shanghai and surrounded the International Settlement and the French Concession, they made threats about use of these areas for Chinese Government operations including activities of the banks. To quiet the situation, a spokesman of the Central Bank stated on December 8, 1937, that under government instructions these banks "would continue functioning here for the sole purpose of maintaining the local money market for the benefit and interest of all concerned." He further stated that "with the removal of the Head Offices of these four banks, government business is no longer being conducted by them in Shanghai and that the only activities being carried on here are confined to the maintenance of currency and ordinary business of a commercial nature." Government instructions to these banks provided that in these and other similar areas they were to avoid cooperation with the enemy, to keep going as long as possible, and to close only if coerced. In regions near the occupied areas they were to maintain offices as long as they could, but take such precautions as removing valuables and settling loans. When a city was captured by the enemy, offices and depositories in China and abroad of the government banks there were instructed not to honor drawings from the captured city as from the date of capture.

Whether China should try to impose controls of exchange and

trade had careful attention in that first hectic week end. The advisers rejected the idea for several reasons, and the government agreed. China could not enforce its measures in Shanghai and in the other foreign settlements and concessions, which were the country's financial centers. Foreigners, under extraterritoriality, were not under the Chinese jurisdiction. Japan was blockading the coast and overrunning ports and other large areas. How then could China control trade and exchange? Even if there were full cooperation by friendly powers, to control part of the imports and some exchange transactions, the Japanese would oppose and evade the controls. Especially China's exports, which were mostly from or through areas vulnerable to Japan, could not be controlled. China, therefore, would not receive most of the foreign currencies realized from exports. So the drain of providing exchange at official rates for imports and other needs would deplete reserves, without replenishment by export exchange. Even if these obstacles could somehow be overcome, China lacked the needed administrative personnel to operate such controls effectively. Finally, exchange restrictions were sure to give rise to a black market. Depreciation of the newly stabilized currency in a black market would seriously hurt confidence in the critical period at the very start of war.

The decision to maintain exchange rates involved no net cost from August 13 until the latter part of October. The emergency measures had tightened the money market so that little money was available to buy exchange. But in November the Central Bank sold exchange equivalent to US$28 million, and in December to US$18 million. From July 7 to December 31 the total was US$89 million.* These sales, while costly, were holding back inflation by withdrawing in the first half-year nearly C$300 million from circulation. The Central Bank lent this money to the government, reducing the need to issue more notes. That enabled the government banks to limit to 16 per cent the increase of note-issue in that first half year, and the average price increase

---

* In the summer a study disclosed that a large demand for exchange would be met in the late fall and winter. Exchange covering exports already shipped had been sold in the market at the time of shipment. But exchange for imports had not been generally covered, imports being sold on three or four months' credit for distribution throughout the country, and remittances from outlying districts had not yet reached Shanghai. It was felt that this demand could be worked off in two or three months, and by February 1938 it had mostly dried up.

was 18 per cent. In view of the difficulties, that was a creditable showing. Moreover, currency maintenance was a defense against enemy penetration by introducing Japanese and puppet money. Externally, currency maintenance, like the military stand at Shanghai, showed strength which China hoped would influence the conference meeting at Brussels in November to provide financial and other aid to China and to press Japan. For all these reasons, currency maintenance in these early months seemed to justify sacrifices as a part of the war's cost.

But this drain of exchange was in addition to heavy payments for imported war supplies and debt service. In six months China had spent or committed over 40 per cent of her prewar external assets. Without foreign aid available in cash—and such aid was not in sight—China could not long stand such a drain. To withdraw exchange support, however, would be a severe shock. The national currency was a symbol of China's unity and of the National Government's strength. A serious break would aggravate inflation, causing a flight from money into goods and foreign currencies. Thus, as 1937 drew to a close, China faced a grave question as to how long she could or should continue to support the currency at the prewar level.

Credit from friendly nations could help China to buy abroad items needed in the war and to provide foreign currencies to support exchange. But for internal resources China was on her own.

THE OMINOUS DEFICIT

During the war, the government did not lack for money to spend, because the printing press was always at hand. In the early stages inflation is a simple and easy means of finance and can raise adequate funds as long as the rate of price rise is moderate. But as time passes it gradually tends to lose effectiveness, until at the stage of "galloping inflation" governments find the greatest difficulty in raising enough from fresh issues. In China there was grave danger of the onset of this stage as the war dragged on, especially in the later war years. Although the financial situation became very critical, fortunately there was no wartime breakdown.

The outlook in 1937 for meeting the heavy wartime costs by

noninflationary means gave no ground for optimism. The modernized part of China's economy, even if it could have produced adequately the modern-type goods needed for the war, which it could not, was vulnerable to attack because it was located on or near the seaboard and along the Yangtze River. There were located, besides the financial markets, the sources of most of China's revenue, and most of the trained workers and administrators. To avoid such vulnerability for the future, the Chinese Communists since their take-over have been setting up centers of industry in the distant interior. In the early months of the war over 600 factories, 120,000 tons of industrial equipment, and many stocks of finished goods, were moved hurriedly from the seaboard to the interior. Some went directly to Szechwan Province in the distant west, while others went to the Central Yangtze region and later inland when Japan's armies drew near. Also 10,000 skilled workers were moved westward.[4] This transplanting of enterprises and much of the key personnel, often under air attack, was an epic affair. The government encouraged it with transport facilities and credit.

In the early months of fighting, Japan seized or destroyed the sources of a good part of the National Government's revenue. Occupation of the chief ports cut off most of the customs yield. The salt revenue did not suffer so badly, but it fell drastically because much of it came from salt produced from sea water in areas that the enemy soon occupied. The consolidated excise taxes were hard hit, because they came from factory production which mostly was in the occupied regions. China had no productive direct taxes. The loss of major cities in east and central China containing the only important capital markets made it harder to borrow from the public for war costs.

Meanwhile, the government's need for money rose by leaps and bounds. The army was enlarged and there were all kinds of emergency costs. The government placed big orders abroad and spent heavily for goods and services within China. So the gap between revenue and outlay grew rapidly wider. China faced what proved an insurmountable task in building other adequate revenues. Even under the best of circumstances, the building of a new revenue system in the interior would have been a huge task and would have taken a long time. But under war conditions, with the Japanese marching through the country-side and bombing indiscriminately and China's leaders fully occupied with grave emergencies, little constructive action proved to be within the government's capacity. Later events showed how serious was Japan's destruction of China's not yet completed financial and administrative structure.

There was little possibility of covering any large part of the deficit by borrowing internally from the public. The government made a good start a few days after fighting began at Shanghai by announcing the Liberty Loan. The amount was C$500 million, equivalent to about US$150 million, of 4 per cent 30-year bonds, to be redeemed by yearly drawings. In view of the surge of patriotism, the bonds carried no security of pledged revenues, as had been customary. Subscription at par to a 4 per cent bond involved in effect a gift to the state. Nevertheless, the Liberty Bonds were sold in a burst of enthusiasm. T. V. Soong, Chairman of the Bank of China, headed the committee to promote sales. The success of China's armies at Shanghai in holding the city for three months against Japan's attack buoyed patriotic feelings. Subscriptions poured in, aided by pressure on some well-to-do individuals and enterprises. Overseas Chinese subscribed generously. Public subscriptions in China were C$146 million and abroad C$37 million, a total of C$183 million, equivalent to about US$55 million. That was a creditable showing in a weak economy. The rest of the Liberty Bonds were pledged to the four government banks for advances.

It would have been most helpful for China's wartime finance if large sales of bonds to the public could have been repeated. But an early obstacle arose when some who had been pressed to subscribe made objection in influential quarters, directed particularly against T. V. Soong who had promoted the idea and pushed the sale. Also internal bond prices fell drastically as the war news got worse. With yields in the range of 11 to 15 per cent reflecting the risks, it was obviously hard to sell bonds. There were no organized financial markets in the interior, individual savings were small, people had little knowledge of securities, and the rate of inflation grew steadily more serious.

These conditions made for a long, drawn-out financial crisis. Nothing humanly possible could have avoided severe inflation.

From July 1937 onward, there was no choice but to bridge the gap in income by loans from the government banks. Most of the business in China, especially in the interior, was done by cash rather than checks. The main recourse was to the printing press. Yet the inflation, while unavoidable, could and should have been held back by wiser and firmer measures, both by China and by China's friends, as this story will repeatedly show.

Since the government found no alternative to using inflation to mobilize national resources, it was fortunate for China's resistance that by mid-1937 the currency reform of 1935 had built up so much confidence in the currency and also in the government. That made possible reliance for a considerable time on inflationary finance. It allowed China to gain time and prolong the fighting, despite Japan's great superiority in equipment and military training, with the hope of finding strong allies. But for the future it brought grave dangers.

Appendix I contains a note on The Budget and Inflation, 1937–1945. A graph showing prices, foreign exchange rates, and note issue is on the opposite page.

THE HOSTILITIES, THE SINO-FOREIGN REVENUE SERVICES, AND CHINA'S CREDIT

The outbreak of fighting at once threatened the yield of customs and salt revenues pledged as security for debts. It threatened also the integrity and working of the Sino-foreign collecting agencies, which provided technical help to China. Their personnel was international, and they were affected with a strong international interest because of foreign trade and business investment as well as ownership of bonds.

Since 1854 China had been receiving foreign technical aid in the customs, and since 1913 in the salt revenue.* The venerable

---

* Under the 1898 Loan agreement China was obligated to maintain the customs service "as at present constituted during the currency of this loan," that is, until 1943. The Inspector General was to be British so long as British trade with China predominated. In 1936 China's total trade with the British Empire, including the large *entrepot* trade through Hong Kong, exceeded trade with the United States and other countries, though trade with Britain proper was less than with the United States, Japan, or Germany.

The agreement for the Reorganization Loan of 1913 provided for joint Sino-foreign collection of salt revenues, deposit in foreign banks, payment of collection costs and debt service, and turning over the surplus to the government. In 1913 President Wilson made his famous statement that the American Government

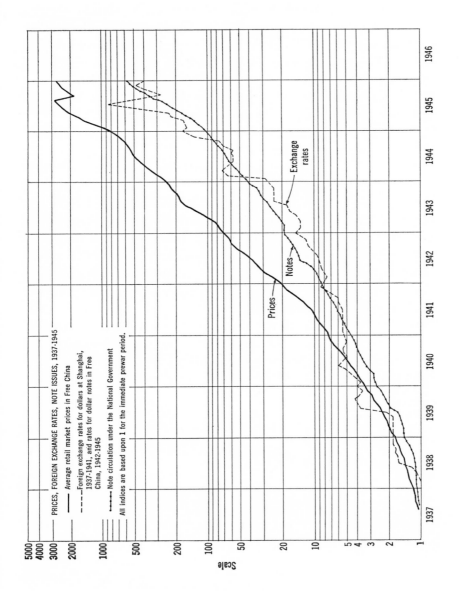

PRICES, FOREIGN EXCHANGE RATES, NOTE ISSUES, 1937-1945

——— Average retail market prices in Free China

– – – – Foreign exchange rates for dollars at Shanghai, 1937-1941, and rates for dollar notes in Free China, 1942-1945

++++ Note circulation under the National Government

All indices are based upon 1 for the immediate prewar period.

Scale

5000
4000
3000
2000

1000

500

200

100

50

20

10

5
4
3

2

1

1937   1938   1939   1940   1941   1942   1943   1944   1945   1946

Prices

Notes

Exchange rates

Maritime Customs, originally under the remarkable leadership of Sir Robert Hart, had long been the mainstay of China's credit. The British-dominated though internationally staffed service was a Chinese government organ. The Inspector General of Customs was Sir Frederick Maze, an experienced career customs officer.[5] The Salt Revenue Administration had a Chinese Chief Inspector and a foreign Associate Chief Inspector. It first had British leadership, but since 1930 the Associate Chief Inspector had been an American. The incumbent in 1937 was Dr. Oliver C. Lockhart, who was concurrently Financial Adviser with special reference to taxation.[6]

It was only natural that foreign participation in the collection of important revenues was not pleasing to many nationalistic Chinese. Yet thoughtful persons well realized that China not only was bound by agreements but that the agreements worked for China's benefit. It was not merely that the foreign personnel were generally well-qualified and efficient. They also could better resist pressures for unsound measures and for practices of favoritism and squeeze that were opposed to China's interest. On the whole the Sino-foreign customs and salt organizations worked smoothly and effectively in 1937 as an important part of China's administration. They were making more and more use of trained Chinese personnel. After the National Government came into power in 1928, the customs service had ceased recruit-

---

would not ask American bankers to participate in that loan, whose conditions "include not only the pledging of particular taxes, some of them antiquated and burdensome, to secure the loan but also the the administration of those taxes by foreign agents." China and the other national groups, however, went ahead, and the Salt Administration was duly organized under British auspices. But between 1913 and 1937 China, while keeping a system of joint Sino-foreign administration, departed from some terms of the 1913 agreement. That was of only nominal importance to holders of the 1913 loan, since in 1917 its service was transferred to the customs, a better security, pursuant to the 1913 agreement. In 1936–1937, however, China referred to the Inspectorate General of Salt Revenue in announcing settlement of certain salt-secured loans, creating a moral though not a contractual obligation to maintain the substance of the collecting system as it then existed. Shortly before the hostilities China adopted a new Organic Law for the Salt Administration. Members of that agency drafted it and took it up with the Legislative Yuan without the courtesy of consulting Lockhart. Parts of it could be interpreted as impairing the position of the foreign Associate Director General and the foreign staff. The bondholders' representatives inquired, and in reply the Finance Ministry stated in a letter of May 25, 1937 (translation), that "in our interpretation and implementation of this law the foreign associate officials continue to have joint responsibility as to essential functions and thus no material change in the established practice is being introduced."

ing foreigners, but those already in that service were retained. Both the customs and salt services were becoming more and more integrated in the over-all financial administration of the Ministry of Finance and the Central Bank. China was making rapid strides in improvement of the working of government and was moving gradually to a position in which in due time Chinese would be ready and able to operate effectively these important services. The Internal Revenue Administration, entirely operated by Chinese, worked well and already had much improved the administration of miscellaneous commodity taxes. As to foreign participation in the customs and salt services, the tendency in China in 1937 was to recognize the value to China of abiding by the agreements made and to make changes by evolution rather than by violations and seizures.

China's credit had never stood higher than when Japan attacked. Debt receiving service comprised, in principal amount, foreign debt equivalent to US$448 million and internal debt of C$2,285 million (US$675 million), a grand total equivalent to US$1,123 million. In addition, there were recognized debts in arrears of about 10 per cent of that total, some of which were under negotiation for settlement, in line with the policy which had led to completion before the war of settlements for about US$250 million of such debt. About three-fourths of the total debt was secured upon customs and salt revenues, mostly the former, and the rest was mainly railway debt. Yearly debt payments in foreign currencies called for the equivalents of about US$26 million from customs, US$4.5 million from salt revenue, and about US$15 million from railways and tele-communications, a grand total of about US$45 million. The foreign customs- and salt-secured debt was well covered by revenues at a prospective yearly rate in 1937 equivalent to about US$125 million and US$75 million, respectively.

The Japanese seizures of ports and territory raised difficult issues about the customs and salt revenue.* The most immedi-

* These seizures, in effect, were extensions of earlier Japanese acts. After the invasion of Manchuria in 1931, Japan took over the customs there. Her puppets of "Manchukuo" offered to make some provision for foreign debt payments, but no way was found to obtain payments without prejudicing China's rights in Manchuria. In the fall of 1935, Japan set up a puppet regime in East Hopei Province on the coast south of Manchuria. This created a gap in China's tariff

ate issue was the integrity of the customs as an international service that insured a uniform tariff and an open-door policy throughout China. The chief Western countries were concerned, because of their support of China's integrity and the stake of their citizens in trade and investment. Britain had a special interest in maintenance of the prestige coming from leadership in development of the customs system. In mid-September Britain, France, and the United States pressed Tokyo to safeguard the administration of the customs and salt revenues and the debt secured thereby.

Meanwhile, on August 30 the Japanese consul general at Tientsin told the local customs commissioner that Japan had no wish to interfere with the customs service if foreign loan quotas were remitted, if surplus collections were put in the Yokohama Specie Bank or other arrangements made to prevent them from being "improperly administered," and if arms shipments to the Chinese government were not admitted. That led to active negotiations, in which China sought deposit in neutral banks and quotas for internal loans. But in October the Japanese military put pressure on the Japanese negotiators, and the local customs commissioner agreed on October 22 to put collections in the Yokohama Specie Bank with withdrawals only for expenses and nothing for foreign loan quotas. The British embassy at Nanking thought that the commissioner had exceeded his authority,[8] but it later developed that his yielding was affected by the garbling of the instructions sent to him through that embassy. Maze managed to stave off the Japanese demand to extend the Tientsin arrangement to Shanghai, after that city fell early in November. But this was only by agreeing that Shanghai customs collections be put in the Hongkong and Shanghai Banking Corporation and in effect blocked there. Finance Minister Kung only learned of this six months later, and the agreement was to be the cause of later trouble, in connection with British efforts to bring about a temporary adjustment of the customs issue (see chapter VI).

The salt revenue service also was having its difficulties. Major salt-producing areas were not far from Tientsin and Shanghai and were overrun early in the fighting. Foreign and Chinese

_____

structure, depriving her of revenue and permitting smuggling of goods inward and of silver outward.[7]

officials were forced to leave. Beginning in August, the Japanese set up rival local organizations to administer salt revenues in North China and elsewhere. They made use of renegade Chinese, some of whom had formerly been in the service and had left with none too savory reputations. There were reports that the Japanese might try to set up a rival organization at Shanghai for general control. To hold back such schemes, Lockhart, with Ministry acquiescence, in the latter part of 1937 called back for service two Japanese who had been on leave, one of whom, however, did not return. The apparent alternative was military pressure to take on other Japanese who would have been less amenable. That move helped to tide things over. In August when the Japanese forces overran the Tientsin area the Japanese consular authorities gave some indication of respecting foreign loan quotas. Tentative plans for loan quotas and deposit in neutral banks were discussed among Chinese officials and representatives of creditors and of friendly foreign governments. But there were no concrete negotiations, since the pending customs issue impinged more acutely on foreign and Chinese rights and was considered the test case.

As to the foreign currency debt, maintenance of payments involved more than getting quotas from customs and salt revenue in occupied areas, which quotas were in local currency. China faced the problem of paying in foreign currency while external assets were dwindling. Soon after fighting became acute there was talk in some government quarters that China should suspend foreign debt payments. The talk was sufficiently serious to cause me to telegraph on September 3 to Minister Kung in Europe, and to say that to sustain confidence at home and abroad it was "absolutely essential in China's interest to make determined effort to maintain service in spite of grave difficulties." He replied on September 5 that the policy should be to maintain service "despite grave difficulties as long as we can, but if we should ever be compelled to suspend service, it will be due to circumstances created by Japan." About mid-November he issued a statement that, despite enemy seizures, "China will still do her utmost to meet her obligations arising from both the foreign and domestic loans." The Minister of Railways, Chang Kia-ngau, also strongly favored doing all possible to maintain debt payments. That remained the firm policy of the government. From time to time unauthorized officials made embarrassing comments about curtailing payments, but Minister Kung repudiated them.

Questions arose also about payments to Japanese creditors, which are discussed in chapter VI. From September 1937, the government took away from the Yokohama Specie Bank the handling of the "Japanese portion" of the service of the 1913 Reorganization Loan, and also withheld from Japan the monthly installments of Boxer Indemnity, about £33,000 each. These installments were accrued in a special account in the Hongkong and Shanghai Banking Corporation, pending later settlement. At one stage, the Ministry of Finance ordered the Customs not to pay the monthly installment due on the "Japanese portion." But these payments were restored, though through the neutral banks, after I pointed out that Japan's original participation was only nominal and that hardly any of the bonds were currently held by Japanese but rather by foreign nationals and to a large extent also by Chinese. To stop these payments would have damaged China's credit needlessly.

From the start of the fighting it was clear in China's inner circles that, if the war continued, China could not long maintain foreign currency debt payments without large foreign aid in cash. The matter was carefully and secretly considered. Everyone agreed that carrying this heavy burden in the face of Japan's invasion and seizures ought not to prejudice the prime object of fighting the war. But no one could know how long the war would last. It was vital for China to make every effort to honor her pledged word and to do what she could to keep up payments as long as possible. China needed to keep open the channels of commercial credit to buy war supplies. A moratorium would have severely shocked confidence by advertising a shortage of foreign funds, which China needed not only to buy war supplies but also to sustain the currency. Finally, a moratorium might prejudice getting loans which China so desperately needed from friendly governments.

IV. TRADING SPACE FOR TIME IN 1938:
COMMUNICATIONS AND MILITARY AID

CHINA had to trade space for time, both to organize nation-wide resistance and in the hope of getting and using foreign aid. A high priority was to prevent Japan's blockade from cutting off communication with the outside world. The way had to be kept open to receive war supplies, whether bought by China herself or gotten as aid from friendly nations. And, psychologically, it was important to avoid a feeling of siege.

FORESTALLING A SIEGE
The Backdoor Surface Routes

China's long seacoast was vulnerable to blockade. By early 1938 Japan had seized all the Chinese coastal ports she wanted. The only usable routes to and from friendly countries were via Hong Kong, Indochina, and Russian Central Asia.

The main route during 1938 was via Hong Kong. Fortunately before the war China completed the rail link from Canton to Hankow. Over that line a stream of war supplies now flowed into China, an average of 90,000 tons per month from May to September.[1] So urgent was the need that for a time the Chinese military would not allow cars to stay at Wuchang, opposite Hankow on the Yangtze River, long enough to load the export goods—largely wood oil, bristles, tea, silk, tungsten, antimony, and tin—whose sale abroad would augment the war chest. But in time improved organization overcame that difficulty.

Japan was well aware that there was a leak in the blockade at Hong Kong. But fear of complications with Britain held back action to stop the leak. The British authorities at Hong Kong were cooperative with China all through this period and until Japan closed the door by attacking Hong Kong on December 8, 1941. In the fall of 1938, however, Britain's weak attitude in facing Hitler apparently helped to embolden Japan. Early in October a strong mechanized Japanese force landed near Hong Kong and by October 21 had taken Canton and cut the railway.

So China was forced to use other and less effective routes to bring in war supplies and to move out the bulky exports. The loss of Canton thus was a hard blow to China, not only militarily but also to the economy and finances. By curtailing exports, it reduced China's receipts of foreign currencies.

In Indochina the French-owned railway from the port of Haiphong ran via Hanoi to Laokai at the Chinese border. Thence ran a meter-gauge line, ascending 6,500 feet on a fantastically engineered route to Kunming in Yunnan Province. This railway, built by French capital early in the century, was said to be the most costly line ever built because of its numerous bridges and tunnels in some of the most rugged mountainous country in China. Movement of supplies into China via this route began early in the fighting. The line, however, was not very efficiently run, and it was reported that monthly inward freight for a time did not exceed about 5,000 tons, though later raised to 15,000. Also after the war began, a French banking group financed building a railway from the Indochina border to Nanning, in Kwangsi Province. They advanced French francs 150 million and £144,-000, equivalent in total to about US$5 million, and the French Government Credit Insurance Department guaranteed 80 per cent of the credits.* Unfortunately this railway did not prove to be of much value, since not long after its completion the Japanese captured Nanning.

In the fall of 1937 France under heavy Japanese pressure had to order stoppage of arms shipments to China via Indochina. Japan threatened to bomb the railway. France's move distressed China, coming just after the League of Nations resolution calling on members not to do anything to lessen China's power of resistance. But France, worried about Hitler and lacking an effective common front against Japan with the United States and Britain, was in a weak position. Asia was a long way off. Japan could exploit France's weakness.

But for some time the actual situation as to transit proved not so bad. The Indochina authorities were as lenient as they dared to be. First they allowed transit of all items enroute. Then military items were allowed to pass when disguised or mixed with

---

* Interest was 7 per cent, principal repayment ran from the 4th to the 15th years, and security was the surplus of salt revenue and the Kwangsi mining taxes.

nonmilitary goods. They tried to be liberal in interpretations, for example, allowing trucks to go if not clearly of military nature. They let in anything that could be classed as commercial, even airplane engines and gasoline. French opinion was overwhelmingly for China. But action had to be governed by expediency depending upon the appraisal of Japanese threats and pressure.

Meanwhile Chinese laborers were improving the desert route to Russia, the old Silk Route which ran 1,700 miles from Lanchow through Chinese Turkistan (Sinkiang Province) to the Russian border. Hundreds of trucks and thousands of camels and other pack animals were working on this route, bringing in war supplies. These largely comprised fuel and ammunition for the Russian planes and gasoline for the trucks. The return cargo comprised the metals, wood oil, tea, silk, and other goods to repay the Russian credits. But a major part of Russia's aid to China came by sea. In the first 18 months deliveries of ammunition via Odessa were said to have been 60,000 tons.[2] Much of this entered China via Hong Kong and Indochina. Russian tanks and guns, entering by these routes, played a part in China's victory at the important battle of Taierchwang in Shantung Province in March 1938.[3]

The vulnerability of Indochina and the desire to avoid being unduly dependent upon access via the route to Russia made clear the need to develop the backdoor route via Burma, the famous Burma Road. This road followed mostly the ancient trade route from Yunnan's capital, Kunming, to Lashio in northeast Burma. Of its 715 miles, 115 were in Burma. About 265 miles of it, to the west, from Kunming to Hsiakwan, had been built before the fighting. The building of the road was an epic affair. To complete it in remote and jumbled high mountains and valleys in a matter of months, without benefit of modern machinery, was a marvel of work. Hundreds of thousands of men, women, and children toiled with simple tools, moving dirt and rock in baskets carried on poles. Blasting was done largely with black gunpowder in bamboo tubes. Labor was conscripted by the Yunnan Provincial Government, which paid in food only. In the more distant regions they had to deal with local tribal chieftains, sometimes called "kings." Thousands died from malaria and other ailments. While such labor could not be very efficient, the job was done.

On December 2, 1938, the government announced the road's completion. But it was not yet really usable. In November, C. W. Hunter, who was manager of the Central Aircraft Manufacturing Company at Loiwing near the Burma border, went over much of the road. In a memorandum of November 28, 1938, I thus summarized his findings:

The road is well located and well designed, but . . . it will not be usable effectively for some months because (a) severe land slides have carried away parts of the road in some places, especially beyond the Salween River; (b) "fills" have not settled sufficiently; (c) bridges and approaches thereto are not yet complete and temporary wooden bridges are not well maintained, while the temporary suspension bridge over the Salween River is dangerous for heavy traffic, having a capacity of only two tons; (d) the road is not yet surfaced with gravel or other material to prevent it from being too slippery for effective use in wet weather; (e) many of the sections of the road cannot be reached by telegraph and the telegraph system is often out of order for other sections and thus prevents the headquarters from knowing about the happenings in these districts until some time later; (f) there are no depots with supplies of gasoline, etc., or repair shops; and (g) the conscript labor being used is not very efficient because of not receiving cash pay. The report also states that for stretches of many miles the road is not wide enough for more than one-way traffic and therefore there would have to be some control of traffic.

Because of the difficult nature of the country, which is liable to continuing land slides and fall of boulders, the road will require a great deal of expert attention for a considerable time, even in dry weather.

Shortly afterward Ambassador Johnson traveled the road, with his naval attaché Major James McHugh, USMC. They felt that the difficulties of making the road an effective route for heavy traffic were enormous; that gasoline consumption and costs generally were bound to be very high; but that the road could become of growing value to China as time went on.[4]

The first vessel bringing to Burma war materials for China reached Rangoon November 3, 1938. In December small shipments got through to Kunming but not much moved until early in the next year.

The Air Routes

Hong Kong, up to the outbreak of the Pacific War, remained open as the main air terminal for outside contact with China. Until August 23, 1938, the unarmed civilian planes of the two

Sino-foreign lines, CNAC and Eurasia, were free from enemy interference. But on that day Japanese fighter planes shot down a DC-2 plane of CNAC. The American pilot, H. L. Woods, made a difficult landing on a river, the only level spot at hand. The enemy machine-gunned the plane even after it struck the water. It was hit by more than a hundred bullets. Those who survived and could swim dove off and made for the shore, staying under water as much as possible to dodge the bullets. Only four, including Woods, got to land.

But that attack did not stop the air service to and from Hong Kong and elsewhere in the fighting zones, as the Japanese militarists must have hoped. CNAC soon pioneered flying in and out of Hong Kong at night and in bad weather. After Canton fell in October 1938, these flights had to be made over enemy lines and past the enemy air base near Canton. The difficulties were unprecedented for a civilian air line. But CNAC developed a remarkable corps of American and Chinese pilots who had the reputation of being the best in the world for that class of flying. So good was the safety record that passengers thought almost only of risks from the enemy and rarely of the other risks of air operations under difficult conditions. A quip of CNAC personnel at Hong Kong, on occasions, was that the weather was too bad for the trans-Pacific Clipper to take off, but not bad enough for CNAC to start to Chungking (that is, with cloud cover). Planes that elsewhere would have been discarded for damage were rebuilt. Woods' lost plane was raised from the river, put on a barge, and towed to Hong Kong, where it was repaired and again put in service. A DC-3 that lost a wing by enemy bombing in China's Far West was fitted with a DC-2 wing. The spare wing was attached to the belly of another DC-3 and flown to the site from Hong Kong by Captain Harold Sweet, in a hazardous flight that could barely maintain flying speed. The damaged plane was then flown back to Hong Kong to await import of the proper wing, and meanwhile christened a DC-2½.

Just before Hankow fell in October, CNAC was able to evacuate key personnel, including Generalissimo and Madame Chiang Kai-shek, in 15 flights, mostly at night and under bad weather conditions. After loss of Hankow the Chungking-Hong Kong route took first place. Later CNAC opened routes to Indochina,

Burma, and India. The development and maintenance of these routes under an unparalleled combination of difficulties was an epic affair—in the face of enemy action, with only meager supplies of gasoline and parts, over rugged terrain without usual aids to air navigation, and in regions affected by some of the world's worst weather.

RUSSIAN PLANES, "VOLUNTEERS," AND ARMS

During 1938 Russian aid continued with the momentum it had gained in the fall of 1937. Russia assigned some of her best talent to the program. Marshall Klimenti Voroshilov took personal charge. His deputy, M. Smirnov, replaced Bogomolov as ambassador to China late in 1937. General Georgi Zhukov, who later won fame in World War II, was sent as military attaché. General Vassily Chuikov, later the defender of Stalingrad, was a military adviser. China in turn, says F. F. Liu, "gave ample evidence (if more were needed) of the military nature of the short-lived Sino-Soviet alliance" by sending to Moscow as ambassador General Yang Chieh, former deputy chief of the general staff.[5]

Delivery of Russian planes enabled the Chinese air force early in 1938 to put up renewed opposition to enemy air operations in Central China. But, beyond that, Russia provided squadrons of pilots and other personnel, with the planes. Although the pilots wore civilian clothes and were generally called "volunteers," they were actually Red Air Force personnel. Their rear base in China was in the northwest at Lanchow, a center whose defense Russia considered strategically important to her.

The biggest aerial battle in history before World War II took place near Hankow on April 29, 1938, the Japanese Emperor's birthday. The Chinese and Russian commanders with Chennault planned a trap for the Japanese, being confident that they would come for this occasion. On the previous day the Chinese and Russian squadrons ostentatiously flew away from Hankow, and moved out the ground echelons by truck. They were sure that enemy spies would report this. At dusk they slipped back to auxiliary fields at treetop level without circling. The next day the enemy planes came as expected. From the roof of the highest building in Hankow I watched part of the thrilling air fight. I recall a pilot parachuting to safety, his 'chute opening overhead, after a dive through the Japanese formation. The Chinese intelligence service reported that only three of the 39 enemy planes returned to their bases. Chinese fighters shot down part of the flight near Hankow. When the Japanese fighters were low on gas for the flight eastward to their bases at Wuhu and Nanking, the Russians ambushed the rest. The Chinese lost nine planes and four pilots, and the Russians two planes and no pilots. Yet the Japanese claimed a great victory, alleging they had shot down 52 Chinese planes.

But gradually during 1938 continuous fighting whittled away the good Chinese pilots. By the time Hankow was captured in October 1938, little remained of China's air force. In the meantime, they had landed some effective blows. Chennault had a high opinion of the ability of Chinese pilots when properly trained, equipped, and led. Beginning in 1938 and until formation of the Flying Tigers in 1941, however, he could do little but plan for the future. He helped to start a flight school at Kunming in the fall of 1938, to aid the rebuilding of an air force. Also he promoted the building of air fields at strategic points throughout the country. Besides, he planned a comprehensive warning net, which became so effective that it kept track of nearly all enemy plane movements. This net was invaluable in warning threatened bases and cities. When the Flying Tigers were ready to fight late in 1941 it helped them to face an enemy who had overwhelming superiority in numbers.

Chennault gives an interesting picture from the inside of the operations of the Russian air forces in China:

The Russian squadrons were regular Red Air Force units commanded by their own officers and complete with ground crews and Russian supplies. A General Asanov commanded this expeditionary force in China and worked with the Chinese Generals Mow and Chow and myself in planning operations. Professionally we got on very well. Socially the Russians kept to themselves in hostels, similar to those that later housed all American personnel in China. Jerry Huang's War Area Service Corps built a chain of Russian hostels all the way from Hami in Sinkiang to Nanking. Russian hostels had their own guards and were well supplied with vodka and Chinese prostitutes. Off duty the Russians behaved themselves riotously. No Chinese town that had quartered Russians ever complained in later years about the boisterousness of the American Air Forces.

On duty the Russians enforced iron discipline. In contrast to the American custom of standing alert duty lounging or playing poker in an alert shack, the Russians sat stiffly all day long in their cramped cockpits. They parked their planes in a circle around the field. When the air-raid warning sounded, they took off madly in all directions. I never saw a Russian scramble that failed to produce at least one collision. On several occasions I elected to take my chances against enemy bombs on the ground rather than participate in one of those wild scrambles. Russian pilots were tough and determined with a tremendous vitality. They could combine twelve-hour alerts, bitter air combat and all-night carousing to a degree I have never seen remotely approached by other breeds. They were considerably older and more mature than American pilots and had never heard of combat fatigue. They wore civilian clothes but retained their Red Air Force rank and got an automatic promotion on their return to Russia. Most of their pay was kept in Russia pending their return.

Their combat behavior was unpredictable. Some days they just decided not to fight and scuttled off full throttle over the treetops. When they decided to fight they did so with the teamwork and tenacity of ants, swarming over the Japs and overwhelming them with sheer determination. Like the Japanese, the Russians had an overfondness for a rigid air discipline that often backfired when something happened to their leader. The Russians took one of their worst lickings on this score when the Japs sent a wave of fighters to precede bombers attacking a Russian field. The Russians took off into the midst of the Jap fighters and were heading for a hot fight when their leader was hit in his engine and turned out of the fight to land. The entire Russian group turned and followed him down. The Japanese bombers appeared just after they landed and smashed the Russians into a bloody pulp. Generally, though, the Japanese avoided a field where they knew the Russians were based . . .

After the odd assortment of American, Italian, German, and French planes the Chinese accumulated in prewar years disappeared in combat, Chinese pilots flew Russian fighters and bombers for more than two years until United States lend-lease planes began to reach China in the summer of 1942.[6]

Russian aid, however, had its problems. In October 1938, there were reports that the Russian Mission in Hankow was not on very cordial terms with the Chinese authorities. On January 9, 1939, Chennault told the American Embassy at Chungking that "there was a considerable force of Russian aviators operating Russian planes on duty in China but this force was comparatively inactive because the Chinese failed to cooperate loyally in tactical operations."[7]

Throughout this period, and thereafter during the war, Russia gave indirect help to China by keeping strong forces in Siberia along the Manchurian border. Japan did not trust Russia, and kept countervailing forces in "Manchukuo." Several times there were border battles, involving large numbers of troops, tanks, and planes, although neither side sought an extension of the fighting.[8] Japan had 200,000 to 400,000 men in Manchuria in 1937–1940, and 460,000 to 784,000 in 1941–1945.[9] China would have found it harder to resist Japan's invasion if these forces from Manchuria, which were among Japan's best troops, had been available for use south of the Great Wall.

About the beginning of 1938, Sun Fo, head of China's Legislative Yuan, went to Moscow as head of a Chinese Mission and after some delay found a favorable response. On May 8 Sun told Ambassador William C. Bullitt at Paris that to date Russia had supplied C$150 million worth of military items. Russia, said Sun, "had not asked China for any payments on these purchases and indeed had shipped some of the munitions even before China had promised to pay for them. The road across Sinkiang had been kept open all winter by an army of snow shovelers." Sun also reported a six-hour talk with Stalin:

> He said that Stalin had assured him that he knew that China was fighting Russia's battle as well as her own; that it was the ultimate objective of the Japanese to capture the whole of Siberia as far as Lake Baikal; that China would continue to receive all possible assistance from Russia in the form of munitions, airplanes and other supplies; that the Soviet Union would not, however, intervene militarily in the war.[10]

Two agreements, each granting credits of US$50 million, were signed as of March 1 and July 1, 1938.

Chiang was determined not to accept strings on Russia's aid. Apparently there were no strings.[11] The aid was provided as loans, on which China made current payments by deliveries in kind.

Russia's aid went to the National Government, and there is no evidence of any significant aid to the Chinese Communists during the war. Likewise, there is no evidence of direct Russian participation during the war in subversive activities in China. Russia wanted China to remain able to continue to fight Japan. But apart from anything else, Russia had no need to try subversion in the interest of Communism, because Mao Tse-tung and his cohorts were far from idle. The fighting and disruption gave them the chance they wanted to expand.

In 1937–1938 the Central forces had all they could do and more to confront the Japanese forces in large-scale combat in Central China and deploy to defend Hankow and other key areas. The government could spare little for North China, where the enemy advanced rapidly, facing mainly ill-equipped provincial forces. By early 1938 Japan had occupied most of the main cities and railways north and east of the Yellow River. In the huge area of North China Japan could garrison only a limited number of posts, patrol the railways, and from time to time send out punitive and foraging expeditions. There were thousands of villages which Japan could not garrison, connected by paths, streams, and canals and rarely by roads. When the Chinese forces retreated or were dissipated, many of the provincial and local officials fled. The vacuum was often filled by organizations which the local people formed to give protection from the enemy, bandits, and looting defeated Chinese troops. The Communists whenever they could joined or took over these organizations. They organized guerrilla forces from local elements, often using scattered bands of defeated troops. That applied Mao's theory of guerrilla war, which had been used effectively before 1937 against superior government forces. Deliberately the Chinese Communists showed for the time being a deceptive front of democracy, bringing in all elements of an area. Often they carried out land reforms, but without the extreme violence used later. Whenever they could, they spread into other parts of China. It was not surprising that their strategy fooled many Chinese, as well as many foreigners in China and abroad, who regarded them as mere "agrarian reformers." In fact, however, the Communists were cunningly plotting an eventual take-over of all China. In the fall of 1937 Mao gave secret instructions that "Our fixed policy should be 70% expansion, 20% dealing with the Kuomintang, and 10% resisting Japan." He saw three stages: compromising; laying the foundations of political and military power; and finally an offensive to take control.[12]

In the late summer or early fall of 1937 Mao Tse-tung proposed the policy of "Defeat for All!" He meant defeat first for Japan, and then for the National Government by the Communists. Rightist elements led by Chang Kuo-t'ao proposed instead "Victory for All!," meaning to cooperate sincerely with the government and try to liberalize it. Chang claimed that there was a majority for his proposal, including Chou En-lai, and that Mao, realizing this, cut off discussion and closed the meeting. Chang escaped but many of his followers were caught and executed. Thus Mao's policy prevailed.[13]

HITLER PULLS OUT THE GERMAN MILITARY ADVISERS

On April 4 Japan protested in Moscow against Russian planes and pilots fighting for China. Litvinov rejected the protest. He said that volunteers of various foreign countries, including those (meaning the Germans) with whom Japan had "the closest treaty relations," were fighting for China.[14]

Until about the beginning of 1938 German Far Eastern policy was ambiguous, with pro-Chinese and pro-Japanese groups seeking ascendancy (chapter II). But early in 1938 the trend began to be more clear. In February Hitler recognized "Manchukuo," and made a treaty with it in May.[15] In the early part of 1938 Germany tried to mediate the Sino-Japanese clash on terms which China regarded as unduly favorable to Japan. Thus it was no surprise when on May 25, 1938, German Ambassador Oscar P. Trautmann announced that his government had asked China that the German military advisers be allowed to cancel their contracts and return to Germany. Also Germany announced cutting off shipment of military supplies. These actions were put on the ground of neutrality, but seemed to have been an unavoidable yielding to pressure from Japan, as Germany's associate in the anti-Comintern pact of November 1936. The timing may have been explained by reports that in the spring of 1938 these advisers had an important part in helping Chinese forces to slow the Japanese drive on Hankow.

The Generalissimo objected to the advisers leaving because they had China's military secrets. But on June 22 the German Government gave them a 24-hour ultimatum, threatening a charge of high treason punishable by deprivation of citizenship, confiscations, and other penalties, and in von Falkenhausen's case reprisals against his family. As a result the advisers left on July 5. Von Falkenhausen took precautions that none of them should return via Japan, and that they should not communicate to China's enemy their knowledge of China's military affairs. Before their departure the Chinese Government feted them and announced that they were "leaving with our assurance of high appreciation of their past service and also with our very best wishes." [16] Von Falkenhausen, while passing through Singapore en route home, issued a statement that he was convinced of China's ultimate victory. His views were based on the idea that Japanese forces would be mired down in China's vast spaces.[17]

After calling back the military mission, however, Germany's attitude was ambiguous. Shortly before the capture of Hankow in October 1938, Germany made with China a second barter agreement covering shipment of goods on liberal terms. But loss of Canton along with Hankow made it hard for China to benefit from it. The view was widely held at this stage that Germany and Italy, notwithstanding their link with Japan, did not want to see Japan succeed in China. Ambassador Johnson in a report of November 4 stated that these two countries along with the rest of Europe "are convinced that the victory of the Japanese Army would result in their partial or complete exclusion from trade with China and that they privately would prefer failure of the Japanese attempt to dominate China although their aid to China is nicely proportioned to avoid provoking war with Japan." [18]

V. BACK-STOPPING RESISTANCE IN 1938:
THE SINEWS OF WAR

IN 1938 the American Treasury continued to buy China's silver, beginning in February with a purchase of 50 million ounces in five semimonthly lots. For the last three lots bought from April 1 to May 1 the Treasury reduced the price from 45 to 43 cents. The reduction seemed related to the American controversy with Mexico, the major silver producer, about Mexican expropriation of American oil companies.[1] On April 12 a United Press despatch from Washington stated it was officially announced, "The United States has purchased in excess of US$50,-000,000 of Chinese silver since the outbreak of the Sino-Japanese hostilities." Again, at the end of April, China asked the Treasury to continue purchases, explaining that China still had 100 million ounces to sell. Morgenthau was once more responsive and agreed to a further purchase of 50 million in semimonthly lots of 10 million each. In July he agreed to a further similar deal for 50 million ounces, carrying purchases through September. On June 20 a State Department telegram to Ambassador Grew in Tokyo authorized him to explain that the Treasury was acting pursuant to its policy of "buying gold and silver the world over whenever offered, upon delivery in New York."[2]

At the time of the first American purchases of China's silver in 1935–1936, it was agreed that the proceeds were to be used exclusively for currency stabilization, to ensure that the transactions were purely financial and not for such purposes as to buy ammunition. But, for the purchases in 1938, the Treasury abandoned this point.[3] The Treasury also helped China by not insisting upon two other former requirements: that China hold 25 per cent reserves of silver against note issue, which was somewhat on the lines of what the United States was trying to do under legislation of 1934; and that China issue silver coins, the Treasury buying 3 million ounces of these that had not been shipped from the San Francisco Mint.

In the first year of fighting, through July 1938, the Treasury agreed to buy 312 million ounces, for a total price of US$138 million. In September K. P. Chen, prominent Shanghai banker, and Hsi Te-mou, Manager of the Central Bank's Banking Department, were sent to Washington to seek financial aid. High on their agenda was silver. They were instructed to sell China's remaining holdings of about 85 million ounces, all of which was in London except for 9 million in Hong Kong. But the remaining available silver which China now wanted to convert into dollars included the 65 million ounces pledged for various credits by European banks. The Treasury was unwilling to buy silver to facilitate paying debts to non-American interests. The solution found was for China to repay the credits from other funds, thus releasing the silver. In the latter part of 1938 that was done. That silver, except for 14 million ounces which the Treasury bought directly, was shipped to New York and sold in the market there, which the Treasury was supporting. It was an advantage to dispose of the silver and clear the debt, even though China got only a relatively small net amount in free dollars.

Later in 1938, about 12.5 million ounces of silver that had accumulated in the interior was shipped to Haiphong, Indochina, and thence to Manila by a small French vessel specially chartered. The handling of this lot required careful planning and secrecy in view of fear of Japanese interception. An American vessel carried it to the United States via Suez, and it was later sold to the Treasury. Shortly afterward a further lot of 6 million ounces was shipped via Rangoon. The Treasury's final purchases were another lot of 6 million ounces in 1940–1941.

Altogether the Treasury's prewar purchases of silver from the Chinese Government, including the purchase concluded July 8, 1937, were 188 million ounces, and the purchases thereafter during the war were 362 million, valued respectively at US$94 million and US$157 million.

MONETARY CRISIS: EXCHANGE RATIONING ADOPTED

By early 1938 it was clear that the drain of reserves for currency support had to be drastically reduced. China had received no foreign credits available in cash. Even if the United States bought all China's free silver, assets abroad would last but a few months if the drain continued at the rate of the first half year of fighting. China had to hold sizable funds abroad to buy war supplies and for other essential needs. The Chinese Government carefully guarded its figures but the Japanese either knew the situation or guessed it fairly accurately. The *China Mail* of Hong Kong, February 8, 1938, reported that a Japanese Foreign Office official had told a committee of the Diet that China had about C$1,200 million at the outbreak of the conflict (equivalent to about US$360 million), and that the total at the end of January was about C$600 million (equivalent to about US$180 million). He added that China should be able to continue importing war material at the then current rate for another year. These figures were not far wrong.

Of the US$379 million of reserves in mid-1937, US$85 million had gone for war supplies in the first eight months. Currency support took even more. To the US$89 million spent from July 7 to December 31 was added US$32 million paid out from January 1 until the change of policy on March 12, a total of US$121 million. While the support was costly, it brought important gains. It withdrew about C$400 million from the market, helping to hold the average price rise to 28 per cent in eight months—which compares with a rise in British prices of 37 per cent in the first nine months of World War II in 1939–1940. It strengthened confidence in the face of military defeats.

Moreover as prices rose the monetary situation was getting out of balance, with the currency's value becoming too high at the former rates. The overvaluation unduly stimulated imports and discouraged exports and, despite the "Gentlemen's Agreement," was encouraging capital flight and speculative buying of foreign currencies. The government was pushing the campaign to collect gold and silver for the war chest—Madame Chiang Kai-shek took charge of a station to collect gold in the center of Hankow, and Madame Chou En-lai did the same across the river at Hanyang. Yet the gold going out to be sold passed other gold coming in from Hong Kong for hoarding, which was about US$1 million in the first half of 1938.

On top of these difficulties came the announcement on February 15 that the Japanese intended to open a puppet bank in North China. Before then sales of exchange had been tapering off, from

US$28 million in November to a monthly rate of US$10 million in January and the first half of February. The news about the bank reversed the trend of falling sales and caused a heavy increase in capital flight and speculation.

Thus in early 1938 China faced the first of a series of agonizing decisions as to how and when to let the value of her money adjust to a level of reality. The value of money in foreign exchange is something all can see and is widely viewed as reflecting a country's strength. And China, thanks to long experience with fluctuations in the value of the old silver currency, was unusually exchange-minded. For the government to recognize the deterioration that had occurred, by dropping rates, was bound to hurt confidence and stimulate price rises. Yet action had to be taken. Frequent moves were bad, like cutting off the dog's tail by inches; but if long delayed, adjustments had to be larger and were more of a shock. The inevitable result was postponement. As to timing, it was necessary to search for as favorable a situation as possible, based on the military, international, economic, and technical conjuncture.

The question of when to act was answered early in March. The Japanese announced that the puppet regime in North China would open on March 10 the so-called Federated Reserve Bank. Clearly, the public would take this as justification for drastic action. On Friday, March 11, the government at its temporary capitol at Hankow decided to act over the week end. The question was just what to do. A series of conferences of the highest officials of the Ministry of Finance, the Central Bank, and the other government banks and their advisers began and lasted through most of the next 48 hours. There was strong advocacy of a general exchange control of the usual type, and the first plan was to try this. But the view finally prevailed that it was impracticable for reasons already stated (see chapter III).

The solution adopted was a scheme of temporary exchange rationing, for devising which the main credit belongs to Cyril Rogers and Tsuyee Pei. The plan was to supply substantial sums to the market weekly for legitimate needs at official rates, but on a declining scale. Banks would forward lists of their customers' needs weekly to the Central Bank for consideration. Each bank would receive an allotment, the Central Bank basing the proportions broadly upon the amount of its sales of exchange to the respective banks under the former system of free selling. Thus there would be neither stoppage of the supply of exchange or devaluation, either of which would have been bad psychologically. The scheme was a stopgap, giving time for the government to consider further policy.

The new measure, effective on Monday, March 14, successfully cushioned the shock. There were some disorderly markets, but on the whole rates were adjusted to a lower level without too great an undermining of confidence. In three months to mid-June rates fell by nearly 40 per cent. The weekly allotments were large enough to give some support to the market and to avoid a too abrupt drop in rates. The government cut its costs by gradually reducing allotments, which after a few months became only of nominal amount.* Shanghai naturally complained about not getting enough exchange. But at Hankow and Chungking there was always an argument whether to cut allotments faster or even to stop them. Reserves were shrinking, and many felt that support of the Shanghai market mainly helped the enemy and speculators and those sending capital abroad. Yet a realization of the importance of sustaining the national currency as far as practicable prevailed. Also the plan, announced as a means to combat enemy currency schemes, proved a strong weapon against these schemes, especially as they were developing in North China.

THE CURRENCY BATTLE IN NORTH CHINA

The master financial plan of the Japanese, said the *Oriental Economist* of Tokyo of November 1937 (page 651), was that "North China, like Manchukuo, will form a part of the gold yen bloc and a link in the chain of the currency system by which Imperial economies will be bound." When the Japanese armies moved into North China in the summer and fall of 1937, they flooded the area with notes of the Bank of Chosen (Korea). These yen notes, which had been worth about par in Chinese money,† promptly fell to C$0.82 in October and for the next few

---

* Weekly allotments in March–June 1938 were in total equivalent to US$22.5 million; in July–December to about US$4 million; and thereafter, up to the termination of allotments in June 1939, to US$0.5 million.

† In July 1937, the average exchange values were US$0.2888 for yen and US$0.2949 for C$.

months were around C$0.90. Meanwhile, Chinese currency stayed firmly at par in terms of foreign exchange. The Japanese military became impatient and demanded action.

The solution was the Federated Reserve Bank, later generally called the Federal Reserve Bank (hereinafter called FRB), which opened in Tientsin and Peiping March 10, 1938. Reportedly, the Japanese military hurried the plan into effect without consulting the Bank of Japan, which had wished to be consulted, and against the wish of local Japanese businessmen. To make the bank more acceptable to the public, eight leading Chinese banks were to be pressed to put up the capital. But the biggest two, the Bank of China and the Bank of Communications, refused under instructions from their head offices.[4]

This bank of issue was intended to provide the Japanese with currency for military uses and to promote economic exploitation, for example, to buy goods and services for operation and extension of Japanese enterprises in North China and items for export. Also, it was an offensive weapon politically in the war. It aimed to oust national currency from the regions which Japan occupied and partially controlled. There was danger that substitution of Japanese-sponsored money might threaten the allegiance to the Central Government of many of the people of North China. And the process, if it succeeded in North China, might be repeated in Central and South China. It was therefore of utmost importance to China to do all possible to sustain her currency and to defeat or at least slow down the enemy program.

When the bank opened the Japanese-controlled regime decreed that national currency could circulate in the area for only one year, that is, to March 10, 1939. But existence of the foreign-administered Concessions at Tientsin now gave China unanticipated help in hampering the Japanese plan. The Concession authorities resisted Japanese pressure, and kept receipts and payments, including public utility charges, on a national currency basis until the latter part of 1938. The Japanese sent agents to the Bank of China and the Bank of Communications, in the French Concession, to demand handing over the silver reserves of about 40 million ounces. But the French authorities courageously told the agents to leave the banks' premises. These measures strengthened confidence in the national currency. Meanwhile the FRB notes were unpopular, and for months most of them remained in Japanese banks and in the Treasury of the puppet regime.

On August 7, 1938, that regime decreed that national currency would be worth only 90 per cent of FRB notes. But this had little effect. To the embarrassment of the Japanese, national currency continued to command a premium over FRB notes in Tientsin. That did not fit with the Japanese claim that the Central Government was a mere local regime on the verge of collapse.

By the fall of 1938, six months after the bank opened, its notes had made some headway in the areas of Japanese control in North China, namely certain strong points and communication lines. But elsewhere no. The Border Government of Hopei, Shansi, and Chahar, which later came under Communist control but which had been set up in January with National Government approval, forbade use of the new notes and even executed persons found with them. So except with *fapi* neither the Japanese nor others could buy goods from the hinterland for use or export. The national currency notes gradually became a "special commodity" in the concessions. They were wanted for hoarding, to buy remittances to Shanghai and Free China, for bank reserves and clearing, to buy goods in the interior, and above all because they could be used freely to buy exchange at market rates.

The notes of the new bank labored under disadvantages. They were not acceptable for exchange transactions. It was next to impossible to buy dollars or sterling, or even yen, through the Japanese exchange control, even though the new notes were nominally tied to the yen at 14d. The foreign banks said they would take them in payment for foreign exchange when the Yokohama Specie Bank would, but that bank refused since, as *Finance and Commerce,* Shanghai, put it on September 14: "The entire resources of the YSB would be paid out for the output of the Peiping printing presses." Japanese businessmen were hard hit. They could not easily refuse to take the new notes, but they got loaded up with them and could not even use them to pay their bills in Japan. In July and August the Japanese forbade sale of certain important items for FRB. Wrote *Finance and Commerce (idem)*: "If you wish to buy Japanese machinery, cloth or other staple goods, you must pay for them in National

Government notes"! The *Oriental Economist* of Tokyo said that "the results have been unexpected currency complications throughout the Japanese-occupied areas." [5] With unusual frankness, the Economic Adviser to the Japanese Military HQ in North China was quoted as follows in a United Press report of September 7 from Peiping: "The attempt at withdrawal of the old notes within six months was a big mistake. Even Manchukuo took two and a half years. The depreciation of exchange below 1s.2d. was not envisaged in the original plan." He went on to indicate that the muddle was "due to the Japanese Special Military Mission's anger against the foreign banks' refusal to accept new notes at the [Japanese] Government's valuation." [6]

Moreover the lack of success of the monetary program in North China was delaying similar schemes for the rest of the country, which, it appeared were to be based "largely upon allegedly inexhaustible resources of goodwill." [7] In November, the Japanese press reported that their government had decided to rely on military notes (*gunpyo*) to pay for their expenditures and seizures in Central and South China.

Gradually, the Japanese tightened their measures of control. It became difficult to get fresh Chinese notes into the area. On one occasion the Bank of China ran short of notes because of loans to foreign banks. A fresh supply, camouflaged as supplies for the British garrison, had to be brought from Hong Kong to Tientsin by a British warship.[8] Also, shortage of national currency in enemy-controlled areas of North China created a vacuum into which FRB notes could flow. Being the less wanted money which people would spend first, and also backed by military and political pressure, FRB notes became in these areas the chief medium of exchange for day-to-day transactions. The foreign banks began accepting them for deposit in special accounts. The new bank won a point when, on December 1, 1938, the authorities of the British Concession in Tientsin agreed under Japanese pressure to accept FRB notes for payments due to them. The French Concession shortly followed suit. The Chinese government on December 21 urged the American, British, and French governments to do all they could to oppose the Japanese currency measures in North China. This communication said that if Japanese-controlled currency should supplant Chinese in North China,

It seems inevitable that they would introduce currency and trade control like that enforced in Japan and China's Northeastern Provinces. Under such a regime individual exchange transactions could take place only with the consent of the Japanese authorities or their agents. This would effectively close the door to freedom of economic opportunity and be contrary to the rights and interests of foreign nationals.

The British Embassy explained, in response to the Chinese representations, that the money was in general use and that in view of pressure brought on the local authorities they had no choice but to accept the notes temporarily and as a measure of expediency.*

SELF-HELP IN CURRENCY STABILIZATION WITH PRIVATE FOREIGN AID

Exchange rationing was only a temporary expedient. It had tempered what was really a devaluation and was better than stopping all currency support or formal devaluation. But it had not prevented wide fluctuations and some disorderly markets. Shortage of reserves forced the Central Bank to reduce allotments, and these soon became only a minor factor in the market.

By June, conditions were ripe for another policy. The currency had become undervalued, since its exchange value had fallen more than prices had risen.† With exchange rates abnormally low, operations to steady the market at Shanghai by selling and buying foreign currencies were feasible. Early in June, Tsuyee Pei of the Bank of China recommended such operations. Minister Kung was then ill but T. V. Soong, Chairman of the Bank of China, and I called on him and proposed the program. He was at first doubtful but agreed.

The Bank of China brought in the leading British bank, the

---

* Before the Concession authorities agreed to take the new notes, the Federal Reserve Bank had promised to grant to each concession £20,000 monthly for foreign currency needs. But the Japanese military intervened 'to prevent this, so the authorities had to sell FRB notes at a discount to buy *fapi* for foreign exchange needs.

† In June 1937, the average costs of US$1 and £1 were C$3.36 and C$16.60, respectively. At the lows of June 1938, these costs had risen to nearly C$6.00 and C$30.00, respectively, or over 75 per cent. But the average rise of general prices was about 40 per cent.

Hongkong and Shanghai Banking Corporation, to work with it and to take the main burden of actual market operations. This bank had a leading position, had long worked closely with the Bank of China, and had acted as a market regulator before the currency reform of 1935. It shared equally with the Bank of China in putting up the funds for the operation. Sometimes the Bank of China, to hide its hand, had the Chartered Bank of India, Australia and China operate for it. The operation was handled under the immediate supervision of Tsuyee Pei and Cyril Rogers. Both were unusually resourceful and intimately understood China's problems of currency and exchange.

Operations began on June 14 and were successful from the start. The first sales of foreign currency brought a prompt recovery of steadiness. The operation successfully met a severe test when Canton and Hankow both fell to the enemy, on October 21 and 25. What then happened was thus described by *Finance and Commerce* of October 26 (page 325):

Every fresh report of Chinese troops retreating sent timid people running into the market to buy sterling or U.S. dollars, but on discovering that sellers were still firm in offering 8d. or a fraction over, and that the market continued to receive the support it had been enjoying for so long, the demand for foreign currencies subsided as quickly as it came into being.

This journal in its issue of November 2 (page 345) said that "influence 'from a certain quarter' was exercised very skillfully and promptly," and that, "Throughout a week of intense outside excitement the exchange-market remained remarkably placid, to the astonishment of those who foretold a financial typhoon to follow the fall of Hankow . . . The net result of these carefully planned activities has been to maintain a remarkable degree of confidence on the market, in spite of most unfavorable influences elsewhere." Altogether, the banks then sold the equivalent of about US$15 million. As the shock wore off, they were able to buy back. By December 2, sales were entirely covered. E. Kann, the well known financial authority of Shanghai, wrote in *Finance and Commerce* of December 28, 1938 (page 513): "The management of China's currency since June was most skillfully handled, and the result of these endeavors can only be presumed a complete success."

In October, Minister Kung had been worried about whether

rates could be held without undue cost. Without cash aid from abroad, China's reserves were shrinking dangerously. His was the primary responsibility, and a heavy one, to meet China's needs for money. In a memorandum of October 23, I pointed out that exchange rates had fallen more than prices, and that, "On economic grounds, the currency is in a relatively favorable position." I urged the importance of keeping confidence: "In this critical time people must not be allowed to think that China's national structure is breaking"; and said, "To prevent this idea from gaining ground just now, the expenditure of a substantial amount of funds is fully justified." Kung asked me to seek the views of Rogers, who replied on October 25 to my telegram:

> More than ever believe that the only policy is not to let the Chinese dollar go, because of undervaluation and political importance. If we do not hold the currency we "let down" the Chinese people who have great faith in the Chinese dollar and hence in the Government. We also sell out to puppets and give Japanese control over currency, financial system, et cetera, which otherwise they would not have in spite of all military successes.
>
> Last four months proved we can hold market at little or no cost though might possibly have to adjust rate at future date.

He said that the Japanese banks did not appear to figure largely in the buying of exchange.

Certainly the stabilization policy in this period, in which a British bank aided, proved its value by helping China to keep morale in the face of two grave defeats. Maintenance of an orderly exchange market in China's chief financial center checked the price rise throughout the country by sustaining confidence in the currency and in the future outlook. Strong elements in the government, however, were irked by the idea of spending precious funds to support the market in Shanghai. They thought of the International Settlement and French Concession as a small island surrounded by the Japanese tide and filled with enemy agents and speculators. Also, the operation at Shanghai was associated with the name of T. V. Soong and led his political opponents to criticize. The policy and conduct of stabilization operations, which better could be called operations to check undue fluctuations, became little by little a bone of contention in China. From there the argument spread to the United States and Britain in connection with their later aid (see chapter X).

From the start of these operations, it was clear that they called for larger funds than China alone could supply. The Bank of China's operation was a considered risk, undertaken for large gains, in a favorable technical situation that could continue only a few months. Getting foreign aid to bolster the currency was a high priority, along with credits for essential purchases abroad.

A YEAR OF FAILURE IN THE SEARCH FOR WESTERN CREDITS

In the first year of fighting, the only major aid which China received from friendly governments was from Russian credits and "volunteers" and American buying of silver. The only credit by a Western government providing additional funds to China was the French-guaranteed Nanning Railway loan equivalent to US$5 million.* Whatever the future perils in Asia, Britain and France were busy girding to face Hitler, and the United States acted unconcerned with matters outside the Western Hemisphere. Let us review the record.

In mid-1937, substantial American and British credits to China were pending. The Export-Import Bank granted in the spring a credit of US$1.6 million for locomotives, and further credits for transport and industrial equipment were under discussion. British private interests were arranging to advance £6 million for railway construction. After the fighting started, Minister Kung, who was in Europe, sent word to President Roosevelt that he hoped the further American credits would go through. He did not want the Japanese to "become convinced that their invasion had succeeded in scaring off all the friends of China." The State Department told the Bank it would be favorably disposed to the credits if the Bank felt they were commercially sound. But on August 11 the Bank postponed a decision due to the fighting.[9] The British credits also stayed in abeyance.

Prior to the hostilities, China had replaced in Washington the veteran and much-liked Ambassador Alfred Sze with Ambassador C. T. Wang, hoping that the latter would be more aggressive in seeking aid. In the fall and winter of 1937–1938 there were rumors of big American loans, US$125 or 150 million, about to

* There was also a not very significant agreement made just before the fighting began, and repeatedly renewed for six-monthly periods, whereby the Federal Reserve Bank of New York granted dollar advances against US$50 million of gold deposited with it.

be granted to China. The State Department had to deny the reports. Early in 1938, Wang talked with New York banks about a loan of US$10 million secured on silver and securities.Then there was a scheme for a three-year loan of that sum secured by deposit of cash of the same amount, or alternatively by American government bonds possibly to be bought from the loan proceeds. This was "window-dressing" carried to the extreme. These efforts had no success, and later led to complications with private American parties. Wang was recalled and replaced by the distinguished scholar Hu Shih.[10] One Rudolph Hecht later sued the Universal Trading Corporation, China's purchasing agency in New York under the American credits, for US$1 million as a commission for allegedly helping to procure the US$25 million credit announced in December 1938. Hecht alleged that Wang had retained him to arrange a loan, and claimed without foundation to have procured that credit. The New York *Times* said Hecht had been "arrested several times on larceny charges, but was discharged each time." [11] Morgenthau wanted to find some way to help China but, understandably, had no confidence in Wang's efforts.[12]

In April 1938, Ambassador Johnson reported on Sino-British conversations concerning the conditions upon which China might get British credits. Ambassador Sir Archibald Clark Kerr, he said, intimated that Britain wanted T. V. Soong to supplant H. H. Kung as Finance Minister; this led to the Generalissimo's consideration of such a shift; but Soong's conditions were unacceptable to the Generalissimo, who "was quoted as saying that he could not possibly work with Soong and that if his failure to do so meant the forfeiture of foreign assistance he would accept this fact and continue to fight the enemy without such assistance." [13]

In June, Cyril Rogers flew to London to press for British aid. The British Foreign Office then favored a large loan to China, and there was much British public support for it. In a letter to the London *Times,* July 4, 1938, Lord Lytton, who had headed the League of Nations commission on the Manchurian affair in 1931–1932, said that Britain should help prevent the collapse of China's currency. Otherwise, he said, "not only shall we be open to the charge of placing a quarantine on the victim of aggression instead of the aggressor, but we will also be neglecting our own manifest interests." In France, Foreign Minister Henri Bonnet told American Ambassador Bullitt on July 6 that "he was certain that both Great Britain and France would be prepared to advance money to the Chinese Government at the present time if the United States should be able to take similar action," which would be "separate but simultaneous." On July 11, British Foreign Secretary Halifax told Ambassador Joseph P. Kennedy that Britain was considering a loan of up to US$100 million to support China's currency. He said that "he is in the toughest spot he has been in to advise the Cabinet on this particular question because he is convinced that unless the British do something on currency the Chinese will go bad financially and that the party will be over as far as the Japanese are concerned. If on the other hand the Chinese get some help for their currency they would go along for a year and at that time a better settlement all around could be made." [14]

On July 13, the State Department sent a telegram authorizing Kennedy to indicate the American Government's sympathy for the contemplated British action, along with its doubts about joint as compared with separate moves within the limits of each country's situation. But Washington got cold feet and canceled the message the next day before Kennedy had acted. So the United States remained silent. On July 15 the British government announced in Parliament an adverse decision. Kennedy understood that "the Cabinet had been impressed by the desirability of avoiding antagonizing Japan gravely unless Great Britain was in a position to defend its Far Eastern interests without jeopardizing those in Europe and in the Mediterranean.[15] The canceled American message might have weighted the balance in favor of the proposed loan, since the British Cabinet were divided.

In July at Hankow the Generalissimo had a second talk with Clark Kerr, in which the matter of British credits came up. In reporting later on this talk, Ambassador Johnson placed the date "about the middle of July." The report indicates that it was before the Generalissimo learned of the British announcement of July 15 turning down the loan project. Chiang said he "would be glad to receive and consider any advice which the British Ambassador might have to offer." Clark Kerr replied that if the inquiry were serious his advice would be to bring Marshal Chang Hsueh-liang out of retirement and "call all the Soong family to Hankow" to "present a solid front to Japan"; retain Kung as President of the Executive Yuan, but implying he should be relieved of financial responsibility; bring Madame Sun Yat-sen into the government; and "award posts according to merit and to include all factions rather than to give the plums to his former comrades." The Generalissimo "received these suggestions coldly, commenting that Madame Sun would be only a mouthpiece for the Communists" (whom she later joined). Johnson believed that "the British Ambassador's reply was a second hint that financial assistance would be forthcoming from British sources provided Soong assisted by Rogers (of Bank of England) might have the management thereof and that a second time the Generalissimo refused assistance with strings attached." [16]

In the Spring and early Summer of 1938, a courageous American attitude could have led the leaders of the West to take action to check China's deterioration under Japanese military pounding, and might have changed history. But American leadership was not forthcoming. Some members of the State Department and Foreign Service saw the issues clearly and favored strong action. Secretary Morgenthau had long wished the United States to take a stronger line against Japan. Besides buying China's silver, Morgenthau, after the sinking of the American gunboat *Panay* December 12, 1937, even thought of sanctions against Japan, such as freezing Japanese assets in the United States. [17] But Secretary Cordell Hull and others were timid. The most vocal American opinion was strongly pacifist and against involvement. This was reflected in Congress, which would have had to appropriate the money with which China might have been helped. Even such shocks as the sinking of the *Panay*, brutal treatment of the Chinese at the taking of Nanking, bombing of undefended cities, and disregard of American rights and treaties did not at once change the dominant isolationist views.

AN AMERICAN CREDIT AT LAST

Soon after the first year's failures came the breakthrough. Although not then known to China, in June Secretaries Morgen-

thau and Wallace tried to arrange a loan to China to buy flour
and cotton goods. But, according to Morgenthau, Hull felt that
in such case a like offer should be made to Japan. Colonel (later
General) J. W. Stilwell, American military attaché in China,
recommended a credit for military equipment as the cheapest
way to buy national defense.[18] Also, members of the State Department and Export-Import Bank continued to think about aid.
At a conference on July 15 Stanley K. Hornbeck, Director of the
Department's Far Eastern office and later Adviser on Political
Relations, told President Warren L. Pierson of that Bank that
"there had been developing an increasing feeling that, from the
point of view of the general interests of the United States, it
would be undesirable that China be defeated by Japan, and,
hence, a tendency to feel that effort should be made toward
giving China assistance when, where and as legitimate methods
may be available." Pierson said he had long had the same view.
They agreed that the United States was more free to act because
nobody had declared "war" and the neutrality law did not apply.
They agreed that a beginning might be made by the Bank helping finance sale of trucks to China.[19]

In July, Morgenthau was in Europe, and on July 26 he talked
with Ambassador Wellington Koo in Paris. Morgenthau said
that while he could make no promises it might be well for China
to send to Washington K. P. Chen, with whom he had "negotiated in the past with pleasure" about silver purchase, to look
into the possibility of a credit to buy flour and grain. Ambassador
Bullitt at Paris wrote to President Roosevelt on August 8 supporting such a credit.[20] Morgenthau had the highest admiration
for Chen. He later said, ". . . it's entirely on his personal word
that I recommended the first and second loan. . . . He's a grand
fellow. He's everything that a story-book Chinese business man
should be and most of them ain't!" [21]

On August 3, the Chinese Ambassador asked Hull to look into
the question of reviving the US$50 million Cotton and Wheat
Loan of 1933, of which US$32 million had not been used. But
nothing came of this, especially since it seemed doubtful whether
China could effectively use much of these goods.[22]

At the end of July, when word came of Morgenthau's invitation to Chen, China was facing difficult decisions. Most of

China's silver stocks had been sold. External reserves had fallen to a dangerously low level because of large costs of currency support and purchase of war materials. Though the cost of currency support was not then very heavy, with the currency undervalued, no one could tell what strains the future would bring. And the need for financing further purchases would continue indefinitely. Also, service of China's foreign private debt was a heavy burden, equivalent to about US$30 million yearly from customs and salt revenue.* With Japan grabbing customs and salt revenues, and seizing and interfering with exports and thus cutting the inflow of foreign currency, it was clear that China could not indefinitely maintain debt payments out of reserves. China had done remarkably well to maintain them for a year. The dilemma was that to suspend payments would damage China's credit at home and abroad, shock confidence, and might spoil the chance of getting the hoped for credits from the United States and Britain. It was hard to know what to do.

Rogers had just returned from his unsuccessful mission to London. I came to Hong Kong from Baguio, in the Philippines, where I had been recuperating from paratyphoid fever. There we threshed out with some of the leaders of the Central Bank and the Bank of China policy proposals to take to Chungking. What instructions should be given Chen? Could China find a way to use a credit for cereals, which Morgenthau suggested, to meet its urgent needs which were for currency support and munitions? What chance was there that Chen could get enough aid in foreign currency to continue foreign debt payments? If not, could China find a way to stop the transfer of these payments, which were rapidly eating into vital reserves, without spoiling the chance for American aid?

Chen was not well and there was a possibility of sending to Washington in his stead Sing-lo Hsu, Manager of the National Commercial Bank of Shanghai. In any case Hsu was to be a member of the delegation. Hsu, Rogers, and I were scheduled to fly to Chungking on August 23. In view of the Japanese military threat to Hankow, many offices, including the Ministry of

---

* Payments on the foreign debt of the railways were largely suspended during 1937–1938, as Japan overran most of the railways upon whose revenue payments were secured.

Finance, had begun to move there. But about August 20 Minister Kung telegraphed to Hong Kong asking Rogers and me to come at once for urgent consultation. We left on the regular commercial flight of CNAC on the morning of the 21st. Near Canton a flight of Japanese planes appeared and flew toward us. Pilot Woods at once hurried into nearby clouds, changed course, and we lost the Japanese flight. He later came back and said to me, "Did you see the Japs? I didn't think they would bother us but I ducked into the clouds." Two days later he was not so fortunate. At about the same spot he was shot down. Sing-lo Hsu, a man of high character and ability and a real patriot, was lost.

At Chungking we completed Chen's instructions and background data, which Minister Kung approved at the end of August. But how get them to Chen, who was in Hong Kong and ready and anxious to leave on September 8 by Clipper for Washington? Japanese planes were roaming the air between Hong Kong and Chungking. CNAC's service by night and in overcast weather had not yet started. Borrowing the Generalissimo's plane, I flew with the instructions to Wuchow in Kwangsi Province, 150 miles from Hong Kong. It was a flight over country rarely seen by foreigners, and in the mountain wilderness of Kweichow Province we flew over a waterfall that looked as big as Niagara. In a small Chinese river steamer we left Wuchow, reaching mid-stream just as Japanese bombs began falling on the city. As we neared Canton, we saw on a barge the wreck of Woods' lost plane, en route to Hong Kong to be salvaged and readied to fly again. Approaching Hong Kong, to avoid risk from possible enemy interception of the boat, I put my precious documents in custody of Captain James McHugh, USMC, Assistant American Naval Attaché who was traveling with me. The documents contained many of China's financial secrets. It was a relief to enter Hong Kong waters on September 4.

Chen was instructed to thank Morgenthau for his invaluable aid in buying China's silver, which made it possible for China to maintain its financial structure during the first year of desperate struggle. He was to explain fully China's financial position and seek an early credit available in cash to be used primarily for currency support. This, it was pointed out, was vital to sustain China's financial structure and to resist Japan's efforts to destroy it by substituting puppet money and by installing a system that would throttle non-Japanese interests. It was hoped that help for the currency might be available through the American Stabilization Fund. Since Morgenthau had initiated the idea of a commodity deal, Chen was to explore this. China would find trouble in making good use of cereals to any large extent. But China could make good use of a credit to buy such items as metals, oil, motor trucks, and machinery.

On September 20, Chen and his colleagues had their first talk with Morgenthau, who told the press that they had discussed "mutual financial problems." As a first friendly gesture, the Treasury at once bought China's remaining free silver, about 20 million ounces. They found a way to help China to sell the 65 million pledged to European banks for credits. Chen reported to Chungking on Setember 23 that the President, Hull, and Morgenthau all wanted to help China but the question was to find means. In the next few days the form of the eventual credit was forecast, namely, a credit by the Export-Import Bank for American purchases, secured by delivery of raw materials from China. Also an American corporation, the Universal Trading Corporation, was to be set up in New York to handle purchases by and deliveries from China.

On September 25 Chen reported that the Treasury told him the suggested credit "could not be used for exchange, as this would encourage capital flight, nor to pay loans to other countries." In reply he was instructed on September 26 to explain that capital flight had been much reduced and would be less if exchange could be kept stable; also that overseas Chinese remittances, which were vitally important in the balance of payments, came forward satisfactorily under stable exchange but were much less when exchange was falling. The limitation about use of the credit for exchange forecast the Treasury's persistent failure to recognize China's urgent need for cash abroad to support the currency and hold back the over-all deterioration, a need outweighing the admitted difficulties and drawbacks of such support. Of course it was mainly China's responsibility to try to check the ruinous inflation during and after the war, which was a major cause of the eventual collapse of the political and social structure. But the failure of friends of China, who had vital interest in her survival, to respond to the appeal for means to check the deterioration through support of the currency places part of the responsibility on them.

On October 12, the Japanese invaded South China in force and moved rapidly on Canton. Their drive on Hankow was also approaching that city. Because even China's continuance in the war might depend upon maintaining an orderly exchange market, Kung telegraphed to Chen on October 21 explaining the situation. Despite the Treasury's earlier refusal, he asked Chen again to approach Morgenthau to find out the "chance of early help that can produce cash." The message said that "naturally we intend to avoid using resources to oppose trend that cannot be checked," but that "we feel it vital to maintain orderly market"; and continued, "We beg him to do whatever he can to help us hold our national structure together. In presenting matter use your discretion as we must not create impression China is so weak as not to warrant his help." The Treasury said that no cash loan was available, for various reasons, and that anything done had to take the form of a commercial transaction. Nevertheless, to avoid a shattering shock, we took the hard decision of selling the equivalent of about US$15 million to support exchange. Fortunately this money was bought back in the market in the next few weeks.

Meanwhile differences were developing within the American Government. Secretary Hull was doubtful about a credit to China, and Secretary Morgenthau favored it. On October 17 Morgenthau sent to Roosevelt a letter saying that without prompt and substantial financial aid "Chinese resistance may soon disintegrate," and, "It is yet possible for such aid to be of decisive help." He was pleading China's cause "with special urgency because you have on numerous occasions told me to proceed with proposals for assistance to China." His efforts "have proved of no avail against the adamant foreign policy of doing nothing which could possibly be objected to by an aggressor nation." While he respected the sincerity of the advocates of inaction, he felt that "the issues at stake . . . do not permit me to remain silent." [23] Harry D. White at this time was actively supporting aid to China and made the first draft of Morgenthau's letter—a fact which is of special interest in view of White's later anti-Chinese attitude (see chapter XVII).[24]

The fall almost simultaneously of Canton and Hankow on October 21 and 25 shocked Washington. Some elements in China wanted to make peace. The plan for a purchase credit secured by shipment of Chinese tung oil had been virtually completed the day before Canton fell. On October 24, Chairman Jesse Jones of the Reconstruction Finance Corporation informed the Treasury and State Departments that he saw no reason why the Export-Import Bank should not grant to China the proposed loan of US$20 million if the President approved and referred to China's good record in repaying earlier loans. But Morgenthau suspended discussion to watch developments. He talked with Roosevelt, who said he would carry through the project if Chiang Kai-shek gave suitable assurances of continued resistance to Japan.[25]

Chen reported this situation. On November 9 the Generalissimo and Kung telegraphed to the Chinese Embassy at Washington to assure the President of China's continuing determination to resist, saying that China had "no alternative but continue struggle." They appealed for aid both to sustain the currency and for needed purchases. The message said that "it is not only in China's interest to stop cruel systematic destruction of oldest and most populous nation but development of strong independent China best guarantee of peace in Orient and failure of Japan's aggression would contribute to more stable world situation and greatly enhance American security."

On November 18 Ambassador Johnson telegraphed to Secretary Hull:

Picture of Generalissimo . . . is of a man committed to a prolonged and bitter resistance to Japanese conquest with or without assistance from the outside; one who believes that in the end resistance will be successful and that he is not only fighting for the independence of his own people but that the success of his efforts will mean much in the future of those third powers who come to his aid now . . . he desires assistance in his struggle, feels deeply that such aid is due him from the democratic nations, whose interests he identifies with China's, but will not accept aid with strings attached.[26]

President Roosevelt was now ready to go ahead subject to acquiescence of the State Department. But Secretary Hull and some of his staff, including Maxwell M. Hamilton, Chief of the Far Eastern Division, still had doubts about the wisdom of the loan, fearing in particular complications with Japan and doubting the support of Congress and the people. Hornbeck, who as Adviser on Political Relations was Hamilton's immediate superior, favored the loan, but only if the American Government, as he thought it should, decided upon "throwing the weight of this country's capacity into a general effort to halt Japan's predatory advance." Hull finally took a timid view, fearing complications with Japan. He concluded on November 14 that he could not "either advise or concur in the course proposed." He left shortly afterward for a Pan-American conference in Lima.[27] Morgenthau persisted in urging help for China. Commenting on Hull's views on the loan, he said later that the State Department "blocked it for months but I got the thing all cooked up . . . We waited until Hull got on the boat for Rio and one week out the President said, 'Yes'." [28]

It was early in December when the President decided to go ahead with the loan. After a short delay because of his absence and after discussion among the offices in Washington of the content of the agreement, Jones announced on December 15 that "the Export-Import Bank has authorized credits to the Universal Trading Corporation of New York up to $25,000,000, the proceeds to be used in financing the exportation of American agricultural and manufactured products to China, and the importation of wood oil from China." The announcement went on to say that since 1931 China had gotten US$27 million of American credits which that bank was handling and that China had repaid US$14.4 million and was paying the balance as it matured.[29] To placate congressional and other American opinion, Jones took special pains to have the loan appear as a deal with maximum security. Besides China's pledge to repay by delivering wood oil, he insisted upon guarantee by the Bank of China, an essentially commercial bank of good standing which was partly owned by the government. This guarantee reflected upon the credit of China, but China's negotiators could not get the clause removed from the American draft.

Ambassador Grew in Tokyo was informed of Jones' statement and told to say, if the subject were brought up in Japan, that the loan "is a genuine and legitimate commercial transaction" to serve American industrial enterprises and producers. The Japanese Foreign Minister in a press conference called the loan a "regrettable act" and "economic pressure." He said that "the Japanese people will undoubtedly find new grounds for strengthening the proposed new order in East Asia." [30] To the Japanese army aid from the West, not only by credits but by the friendly British and French policies permitting transit of supplies to China via Burma and Indochina, was becoming more and more irritating. Mamoru Shigemitsu, former Foreign Minister of Japan, writing after the war about Japanese army views in 1940, said that this aid was "an insult in the face of the Japanese Army," and the only thing that made possible China's continuing resistance.[31]

In China the effect of the American credit was inspiriting. Willys R. Peck, in charge of the American Embassy at Chungking, reported on December 24 that "the granting of American credits to China and reports of similar British action have been construed by the Chinese as indicating the commencement of action by those powers to prevent Japan from achieving its aims in the Far East, and it now seems clear that this conviction has immensely stimulated and stiffened the Chinese will for prolonged resistance." [32]

The US$25 million credit was formalized in an agreement of February 8, 1939, between the Export-Import Bank and the Universal Trading Corporation. The bank was to provide "commercial credits" to Universal up to US$25 million, to buy American agricultural and manufactured goods. Payment was to be by shipment of 220,000 tons of tung oil (wood oil), beginning with 25,000 tons the first year and rising to 60,000 the fifth and final year. China agreed to use half the proceeds from the tung oil to repay the credit and the other half to purchase American goods. Interest was 4½ per cent and repayment was unconditionally guaranteed by the Bank of China. The credit could not be used for arms, ammunition, or airplanes. In practice, however, the American side took a liberal view of items that could readily be converted into military use.*

---

* For a summary of the terms of this and other credits, see appendix II, Foreign credits and Lend-Lease to China, 1937–1945.

BRITAIN FOLLOWS SUIT

By November the progress of the American negotiations led Chiang to press Clark Kerr again for aid. In a strong communication of November 4 Chiang said he appreciated having been able to get munitions through Hong Kong, and that Britain might have held off aid for fear of Japanese action in South China that would jeopardize Hong Kong. But now that the Japanese had recently seized Canton, he wanted to know whether Britain would give aid:

For the past 16 months [we have been?] hearing a lot of eloquence about loans and in addition have been put off from time to time with excuses that loans were impossible because of Parliamentary complexities. But the whole world witnessed the granting almost overnight to Czechoslovakia of a loan similar in nature to that asked for by China.

Now the moment has come when we must have definite knowledge of Great Britain's intentions.

If Great Britain [should go back?] alike upon us and her principles, then I shall never bring up this question again.

Clark Kerr reported that the Generalissimo was not making a threat, and was firmly determined to carry on the fight. He thought the Generalissimo wanted a definite statement to present in December to the Kuomintang plenary session at Chungking. As the first move, the Generalissimo wanted a loan to support China's currency.[33]

The British reply was noncommittal but left open the way for further negotiations. London had long thought, and rightly I believe, that the most effective financial aid to China was for currency support, for which a credit as large as US$100 million had been mentioned in July. Only a few days before announcement of the American purchase credit, the British embassy approached the State and Treasury Departments to express the hope that, if Britain arranged a currency credit for China equivalent to US$15 million, the United States would take "parallel and simultaneous action."[34] But the approach was unsuccessful, as Washington had other ideas and on December 15 announced the US$25 million purchase credit.

The American action encouraged the British to go ahead, but for the time being only with a purchase credit. On December 20, London announced a £500,000 credit, mainly to buy motor lorries for the Burma Road, and forecast further purchase credits.[35]

Under the agreement signed on March 15, 1939, China used
£223,000 to buy motor trucks and parts. China paid one-fourth
in cash and the remainder (£167,000) in serial notes of the
government with Bank of China guarantee, maturing during four
years bearing 5½ per cent interest. The British Board of Trade
guaranteed the other three-fourths. China did not use the rest of
the credit, since Lend-Lease and credit arrangements became
available under which no cash payments were needed.

INFLATION: TIME WORKS AGAINST CHINA

In the 18 months to the end of 1938, China made a relatively
good financial showing, thanks to the strength of the finances
when Japan attacked and in particular to possession and use of
large external assets. But time was working against China. After
mid-1938 the pace of inflation began to quicken, with the threat
of grave social, economic, and political consequences. In the face
of heavy and inescapable military costs, the government had lost
by the end of 1938 most of the customs revenue and half that
from salt. The government had not proven able to develop tax
revenues that were anywhere nearly adequate. Less than half
of the outlay in the first 18 months was covered by nonborrowed
income plus borrowing from the public and the proceeds of sale
of foreign currencies. The government had to turn to the government banks for loans, and to the end of 1938, their total note issue
grew by nearly two-thirds over the total of mid-1937. From June
1938, the stabilization operations of the Bank of China checked
the fall in the exchange value of money. But by the year end,
because of the rise of prices, the currency no longer was undervalued. And the resources that China could use to support the
currency were meager. This situation presaged difficulties in
1939.* China's assets abroad by the end of 1938 were dangerously
close to the minimum needed as working balances. Thus the
American and British purchase credits came in the nick of time.

Also, strong pressures were working against the checking of
avoidable or postponable spending. There was pressure for credits
by business enterprises unable to get normal bank accommodation
and by banks wanting funds to loan. Besides, in the Spring of 1938

---

* See appendix I and the graph on page 43 for further data about these
matters.

the government adopted the policy of "Resistance and Reconstruction." The idea was that China should modernize on a broad scale while fighting. The urge to modernize is understandable, but there was a general failure to distinguish between what was essential and what was not essential for the war effort.

Serious inflation and financial deterioration during the war could not have been avoided by any means humanly possible. But they could and should have been slowed much more than they were, both by China's action and by larger and prompter foreign aid, in the first 18 months and also thereafter.

VI. THE SINO-FOREIGN REVENUE SERVICES AND CHINA'S CREDIT, 1938–1941

BRITAIN TRIES TO SAVE THE CUSTOMS

WHILE China was struggling with currency problems and seeking foreign credits, another and related struggle was taking place with regard to the revenues pledged for China's debt and the Sino-foreign revenue services. At the beginning of 1938 the customs service in the occupied ports remained more or less intact. Maze, however, was in a difficult position as inspector general. He faced the task of trying to safeguard the integrity of the customs and the debt service, which both China and the friendly powers desired, in difficult negotiations which his subordinates had to carry on with the militant Japanese as they strengthened their grip on China's ports. He was subject to Chinese Government instruction. But he hoped the powers would dissuade China from issuing to him instructions that "might possibly conflict with the policy which the interested powers may deem it desirable to adopt in the best interest of China herself." [1] He early had to face in North China a Japanese-sponsored regime claiming authority, and he felt if he were not amenable to some extent to Japanese demands he might be replaced by a Japanese. Being an adroit politician, he decided to compromise when he felt confronted with *force majeure.* Thus he assigned Japanese already in the service to more important posts, and employed additional Japanese in lesser "outdoor" duties. He reported to Minister Kung about most, but not all, his actions. Kung was in a difficult position *vis-à-vis* his colleagues and, for the record, sent Maze instructions tending to restrain him, but in practical effect allowed him considerable latitude. For holding things together Maze deserves credit. In this, however, he was aided by Japan's willingness to have the service of an effective revenue-collecting organ.

In early 1938 there were two main sore points. Japan was blocking remittances from occupied ports for China's debt service. And Japan was flagrantly violating the open-door agreements. At

Shanghai Japanese importers were bringing in goods without paying any duties, on the fiction that the goods were military items. Ordinary Japanese vessels were designated as "transports." Japanese armed forces detained and on some occasions attacked customs craft, thus interfering with the antismuggling work.* In January Japan announced through the Peiping puppet regime a new tariff for North China, with lower rates for items in which Japan was interested.

The British Government took a growing interest in the negotiations under way to protect the integrity of the customs service and to procure loan quotas out of the seized revenues. This interest derived from Britain's long connection with the customs service; extensive trade; and investments equivalent to a billion dollars or more, specifically British holdings of Chinese bonds equivalent to perhaps US$200 to 250 million. London instructed the chargé d'affaires in China to request Maze to keep him fully informed and follow the chargé's advice, and to give Maze such support as possible. In contrast, the American Government, while pressing Tokyo to respect customs integrity and provide loan service, wanted to stay out of arranging any specific solution.[2]

China's firm attitude in the negotiations, which made it hard to reach agreement with Japan, reflected the patriotic surge caused by the fight for existence and the unexpected success in resisting a far stronger enemy. To China's leaders it was crystal clear that Japan was making an all-out effort to dominate China and to destroy both her independence and the position and influence of foreign countries, other than Japan, and their nationals. These leaders strongly felt, and I concurred in my advice to them, that China ought not to go beyond a certain point in conceding on the customs issue. What would China gain by handing over the Sino-foreign organization more or less intact to collect revenue for the enemy and to grant favors to Japanese trade, while preserving little of benefit to others? It would be better that Japan be forced to make an outright seizure. To many foreigners in China and even to some persons in their governments, the fighting seemed an episode that could sooner or later be compromised, with things going on somewhat as before. But to the Chinese Government it

* They also detained for about a year dredging equipment needed to keep the port of Shanghai safely operative.

was a showdown, forced on China after years of great forbearance and effort to stave off a fight for which she was so ill-prepared. From the time of Japan's attack in the summer of 1937 the Chinese Government and many foreigners involved with it felt that there was no promise for the future in giving way in matters of principle; that the only possible solution was in firm resistance which had to have strong backing by other powers to succeed; and that such backing could better be gained by firmness than by appeasement. Some British officials criticized China's stiff position on the customs and also my advice against "appeasement"—though one highly placed official admitted privately that he did not personally disagree with me.

By early 1938 negotiations about remitting debt quotas from occupied ports had gotten nowhere. Civilian Japanese officials wanted a settlement. But the military were getting harder to deal with. General Matsui, commander-in-chief for Central China, stated at Shanghai in an interview quoted by Reuters News Service, February 1, 1938, that he might have to take over the customs, since "the new Chinese regime whatever it may be called . . . must draw its financial resources from the customs." Payments for foreign loans could be negotiated, "but it must be understood that the sum to be allowed for such services will be much lower than before." To get away from Japanese military pressure, Britain proposed in December that negotiations be shifted to Tokyo. Washington raised the obvious question of "who or what agency is to represent the Chinese in these negotiations." The British reply on December 31 was that China of course would not be present, but that "an endeavor would later be made to persuade the Chinese to accept any understanding which might be reached." [3]

In February Britain and Japan began negotiations at Tokyo. The British embassy at Hankow kept Minister Kung informed of the general subject matter under discussion but not of the specific proposals. Kung, in written communications in March and April, reserved China's position and stated that he assumed China would be consulted in advance of any agreement to find whether it would be acceptable. But toward the end of April press reports from Tokyo indicated that an agreement between the Japanese Foreign Office and British Ambassador Sir Robert Craigie was imminent.

On May 2 Chinese leaders learned that an agreement had been concluded. On that day Ambassador Clark Kerr telegraphed from Shanghai to Generalissimo Chiang and Minister Kung that the matter suddenly had become urgent and that the agreement had to be concluded at once to prevent Japanese take-over of the customs. What had happened was that the Japanese military had told the Japanese civilian negotiators that they would not accept the terms of the agreement unless it were concluded by that date.[4] To avoid that, said Clark Kerr, and because clearly Japan would not meet China's minimum terms about the customs, Britain had deliberately refrained from consulting China during the negotiations. China, of course, could disavow responsibility but he hoped China would not do anything to make the measures unworkable. He believed that the arrangement was much preferable to unconditional Japanese seizure of the customs. A summary of the agreement was made public the same day at London.

The announcement referred to "unofficial conversations" at Tokyo, which led to Japan's notifying Britain of "the temporary measures proposed to be taken during the period of hostilities" concerning foreign debt payments and other customs matters. The revenue to be collected in occupied areas was to be paid to the Yokohama Specie Bank. Quotas for payment of foreign debt service would be remitted to the Inspector General's account at that bank in Shanghai, and the Inspector General would arrange to convert them into foreign exchange. The customs revenue accumulated in the Hongkong and Shanghai Banking Corporation in occupied ports, about C$27 million, was to be transferred to the Yokohama Specie Bank for future foreign debt quotas. The arrears of the Japanese portion of the Boxer Indemnity accumulated in sterling in that bank since September, then equivalent to well over US$1 million, and further sums as due were to be paid to Japan. Japan expressed in the agreement the intention of resuming duty payments by Japanese importers and of returning seized customs craft, "except those specially required for military purposes," and allowing them to resume preventive work. The entire arrangement might be reconsidered "in the event of a radical change in the economic conditions under which the above measures are proposed."[5]

The London announcement of May 2 said that Britain would

offer no objection to these arrangements, and also that the United States and France do not propose to offer objection. That was true in the case of France. But it was misleading in the case of the United States. Ambassador Joseph C. Grew had been instructed on April 26 that the State Department did not wish to comment, nor to have an American official participate in fixing quotas. On the 30th he was told that the State Department "reacts unfavorably" to the proposal of informing Japan that it offers no objection. On May 1 he so told Craigie, and also reminded him that Washington already was on record as wishing to make no comment. Furthermore an instruction of the 29th by the State Department had pointed to a basic weakness of the proposal, that the plan would throw on China the entire burden of providing the foreign currencies for quotas of areas in which Japan was trying to drive out national currency with puppet notes, and in which Japan was appropriating the foreign exchange derived from exports. On May 2 the State Department repeated to Grew that it wished to withhold comment "until the Chinese Government had made known its attitude toward the whole arrangement." Craigie had hoped till the last moment that the United States would let it be known that it had no objection, thinking that otherwise the plan might fail. He thought he would have time to have London eliminate from the draft announcement he had forwarded, if necessary, the statement that the United States had no objection. He apologized to Grew, saying that London issued the announcement sooner than he had expected.[6]

Craigie's mishandling created difficulties all around. Internationally it put the United States in a false light. But for the United States to make a flat denial would seem a slap at Britain, and might kill the agreement. To China in particular it was disturbing that the United States had appeared to be associated in support of the agreement. Ambassador Johnson reported on May 3 that Kung was much disturbed by the agreement, and particularly by the statement that the American Government would not object to it. Johnson told the British Counsellor, who asked his view, that the agreement would be taken as evidence of "willingness on the part of the British Government to legalize Japanese capture of customs." In reply to the Counsellor's inquiry whether he would join in urging China to accept or at least not oppose the agreement, Johnson said that he could not do so, and that if Washington asked his views he would recommend against doing so. The State Department approved his action and authorized him to explain to Kung that the American Government wished to make no comment on the agreement until the Chinese Government had made known its attitude.[7]

To China the whole affair was embarrassing. The press expressed surprise and regret. China promptly told Britain she regretted that a Chinese administration had been "the subject matter of an agreement between two foreign states." The note called attention to the obligation in the Nine Power Treaty of 1922 "not to enter into any treaty or arrangement with any power or powers which would infringe or impair the sovereignty and administrative integrity of China." It pointed out that the agreement did not bind China, whose rights and freedom of action about the customs were fully reserved.[8] But China, on the other hand, was anxious not to alienate British sympathy, being so dependent on British and other foreign aid. So the government refrained from positive steps to oppose the agreement, such as sending specific instructions to Maze.

Such steps, however, were not necessary. The agreement could not become effective, it quickly appeared, without positive action by China to make payments to Japan. But no Chinese official could put himself in the position of ordering Maze to hand over to its enemy the accumulated and blocked Boxer Indemnity payments (£260,000) plus future installments (£33,000 monthly), or the customs funds that were held in the Hongkong and Shanghai Bank (C$27 million)* even though promised to be used for future debt service.† Maze gave some indication that he might feel called upon to pay over the funds as a matter of *force majeure*, but Kung made it plain that he could not do so unless specifically instructed. The Commissioner of Customs at Shanghai, however, began early in May to deposit the daily collections in the Yokohama Specie Bank, considering it a matter of *force majeure*.

---

* The pound was then fluctuating, and worth about US$4.95. China's money was equivalent to between US$0.21 and US$0.26 in May 1938, but then slumped and in the rest of 1938 the rate was about US$0.16.

† Japan's argument was that, if she gave up part of customs receipts in occupied areas as quotas to benefit other foreign interests, she should get her contractual share in the debt payments which the quotas covered.

As soon as the Anglo-Japanese agreement was received, the Chinese Government studied very carefully the practical pro's and con's, as well as the issues of principle. In its favor was the preservation of formal customs integrity. Japan would exercise most of the control of the customs, but that was bound to happen anyway in the occupied ports. At least Japan undertook not to take over the customs and install supervisors and officials at every key spot, in place of the international personnel. On the other hand, the agreement made no provision for local currency debt, which the Japanese refused to consider. Also there was risk that Japan would try to use the agreement, if it came into effect, to maneuver the customs into the hands of the "reformed government," whose "concurrence" they had obtained. Early in May the Japanese installed a certain Li Chien-nan as "Superintendent of Customs" at Shanghai. They might claim that Britain had recognized the regime. A Japanese spokesman at Shanghai, quoted by *Transocean News*, October 27, 1938, said that the agreement "amounted in practice to a *de facto* recognition by Britain of the 'Reformed Government.'"

The financial angle also was important. China was to hand over at once to Japan the blocked Boxer Indemnity funds equivalent to about C$8 million, and about C$27 million of customs funds deposited in the Hongkong and Shanghai Banking Corporation, a total equivalent to about C$35 million (about US$8 million). Minister Kung learned of this latter deposit only in May and was much put out. Maze had agreed in November, as an alternative to accepting the Japanese demand to put Shanghai collections in the Yokohama Specie Bank, to put the money in the British bank and not to use it without Japanese sanction. Maze hoped that a negotiated deal would regularize everything. Meanwhile the British bank had used the money for local loans, including one to the Yokohama Specie Bank.[9] China, on the other hand, was to receive only about C$19 million of debt quotas as of July 1, plus about C$4 million monthly thereafter. Hence until about November the deal would be financially disadvantageous to China. Not trusting Japan, China feared that after Japan got the immediate benefits she would find some way to get out of the agreement under the clause allowing her to reconsider in case of "radical change in the economic conditions." Furthermore, China feared that if she handed over the C$27 million Japan would use it to buy foreign currencies in the Shanghai market. Japan was short of exchange and in July mobilized the foreign currency and security holdings of her nationals.

The Chinese Government had the burden of providing both the foreign and local currency for debt payments due from the entire country. On May 2, I noted on the copy of the agreement handed to me by the British representative: "Overlooks real difficulty, exchange." Reserves were shrinking and it was clear in May that regardless of what happened to the customs China could keep up debt service only for a matter of months without large aid available in foreign currency. No such aid was in sight. Thus while superficially the agreement appeared as a support of China's credit, actually it promised little help in that regard for long. Meanwhile, because of failure to get the quotas from customs collections at occupied ports, the Inspector General had to borrow local currency from the government banks.

In November, when China might have begun to get financial benefits from the agreement, we carefully considered possible indirect implementation by some informal setoff.* But by then suspension of foreign currency debt payments seemed imminent, because of shrinkage of China's foreign currency reserves. Any plan for Japan to hand over foreign loan quotas in local currency would have implied that continuance of these debt payments was assured. Moreover, any plan for setoff that China could consider would have required further British negotiations with Japan, and meanwhile China could not risk having her hands tied in the matter of suspension. Furthermore, if the agreement had gone into effect by a setoff and China thereafter suspended payments in foreign currencies, would Japan have continued to pay over debt quotas in Chinese currency? For the reasons indicated, China left in abeyance the agreement that had caused so much controversy.

A backward look indicates that the British were right in feeling that no deal was possible to which both China and Japan could assent in any formal way. The alternative was to go for an ar-

---

* A further reason for considering implementation of the agreement was the deterioration in the monetary situation. Payment of loan quotas by Japan would have reduced the supply of money in the Shanghai market and thus tended to check the inflation.

rangement that could slide into effect if China merely did not oppose. What proved to be the main obstacle at this point was inclusion of clauses calling upon China to turn over funds to her enemy. It was expecting too much to think that any Chinese official could do this, especially when the financial benefits were so one-sidedly for Japan for the first half-year. But, on the other hand, Japan would not have agreed to terms substantially less favorable to herself than those of the 1938 agreement. Hence it is questionable whether there was a real basis for a customs agreement in the spring of 1938. With benefit of hindsight, perhaps the best that could have been done about debt quotas was to acquiesce in some deal that probably could have been arranged in September 1937, based upon the proposal by the Japanese consul general at Tientsin (chapter III) to allow remittances in Chinese currency of foreign debt quotas from occupied ports, and to keep remittances going as long as possible. But then China tried to get better terms; the Japanese military intervened when there was delay; and the chance was lost.

The Anglo-Japanese customs agreement, while it failed to safeguard holders of China's foreign debt, brought limited accomplishments in two other fields. First, the making of the agreement, even though China did not implement it, satisfied the Japanese military long enough to divert their attention from threats to take over the customs. Thus it preserved a measure of "integrity" of this Sino-foreign organ, which was well worth doing because it could still be useful to China in case of a stalemate or Japan's eventual defeat. But to believe that a victorious and militant Japan would have allowed this internationally staffed agency to continue as formerly constituted, and to preserve the "open door," was wishful thinking. The *Oriental Economist* of Tokyo May 14, 1938 (page 23) called the agreement "an elegy telling of the decline of British influence in the Orient." From China's viewpoint, customs integrity in any meaningful sense was already badly impaired at the time of the agreement, since in occupied China the organization had become mostly a collecting agency for the enemy and the puppet regimes. The second accomplishment was to temper somewhat, for the benefit of non-Japanese trade with China, the Japanese interference with the "open door." Thus a prompt result was an end to the import at Shanghai of Japanese goods *sans* duty and the application of a uniform tariff, even though tailored to benefit Japanese trade.

In China the agreement was strongly resented. It was an element in Sino-British friction, which grew steadily during the war.

THE HOSTILITIES, NATIONALISM, AND THE SALT REVENUE SERVICE

While the arguments over the customs situation were going on, the problems of the salt revenue service were multiplying. By early 1938 the fighting had spread to areas that produced over half the salt revenue. Fortunately this did not seriously impair the supply of salt to the people. Salt merchants and the salt administration worked hard to remove stocks from exposed places. Also there was much smuggling out of occupied areas. Loan quotas from these areas no longer came forward. Also loan quotas from Free China fell into arrears. The local authorities needed money for war costs and kept most of the revenue under one guise or another. The Central Government tended to acquiesce, though it would have been better to have maintained revenue rights and granted subsidies.

Continuance of the fighting created conditions that gradually led to weakening the system of joint Sino-foreign authority and responsibility (see chapter III). The central administrative offices were divided between Shanghai, Hankow, and Chungking, and later further divided in other places in Szechwan Province. Lockhart felt he should stay mostly at Shanghai, to keep in touch with the coastal salt-producing areas, part of which were enemy-occupied, and with representatives of the holders of salt-secured loans; and also to avoid giving the Japanese an excuse for setting up a rival puppet organization, on the pretext that the lawful authorities had abandoned the field. Meanwhile Director General T. C. Chu stayed in the interior to look after problems of the revenue and supply of salt. In the prevailing atmosphere of strong nationalism, Chu's tendency to disregard his colleague grew. He and some associates worked to undermine the system by intrigue and indirection, rather than frankly trying to change it by agreement or openly casting it aside.

Having in mind this background, and preparatory to possible negotiations with Japan, Ambassador Clark Kerr wrote to Minister Kung on March 22, 1938, through the British Diplomatic Mission at Hankow, urging "the necessity of maintaining the authority of the foreign staff." In his reply of March 24, Kung said,

> . . . in principle I consider that as to essential functions the joint responsibility of the Directors-General and of the subordinate foreign and Chinese officers should be maintained substantially as it existed during the years prior to the outbreak of hostilities. I am issuing instructions to the Salt Administration to the effect that there should be no derogations from this principle except to such extent as is unavoidable during the emergency, and that any such derogations are only temporary in character.

The system of joint authority and responsibility remained the announced policy of the Ministry of Finance. Both Lockhart and I repeatedly argued against unilateral change, whether directly or by indirection. But the attitude of numerous persons in the salt administration and elsewhere made it hard to give effect to the policy.

After China's adverse reaction to the Anglo-Japanese customs agreement of May 1938, the British were unwilling to try for a deal about salt without a definite request by China. They sounded out the Chinese Government, but China was not ready to make such a request while the customs question remained unsettled. Sad experience with the customs made clear that cooperation with Japan to maintain "integrity" of these Sino-foreign agencies meant in practice turning over to Japan the services, in occupied areas, of experienced revenue-collecting organs.

As the war dragged on, the salt revenue service faced continuing difficulties. Under stress of growing nationalism, Chinese members of the service led by Director General Chu pushed to reduce or eliminate foreign expert participation. This went on despite the afore-quoted assurances to Clark Kerr, which Minister Kung renewed at London in the summer of 1939 in relation to negotiations for partial resumption of debt payments. Much of the pressure was not for modification by agreement. Rather it took the forms of resistance to the practical operation of a system of joint authority and responsibility, encroachment with a view to gradual complete taking over, and efforts to hold the foreign officers responsible for results even though in fact they had not been accorded the corresponding authority and power to act. The situation was further complicated by the illness, and resulting absence in Shanghai and the United States, of Associate Director General Lockhart.

In the summer of 1939 the State Department asked Ambassador Johnson's view on talking informally with the Chinese Government about the position of the foreign staff in the salt administration. His report of August 21 stated his impression was that the Chinese felt "the presence of foreigners was useless and a reflection on their capacity as Chinese"; that it seemed "regrettably probable that . . . more sinister reasons of financial irregularity have crept in"; and that it would be hard to persuade the Chinese "to restore genuine authority" to the foreign officials. He felt that insistence on this point would be "misplacing of emphasis," since "unless China succeeds in regaining its territorial and administrative integrity it seems to me safe to predict that at least the larger part of its funded indebtedness will become a total loss." It was "the Japanese invasion and not the lack of effective foreign authority that really menaces the interests of American bondholders." Washington finally authorized him to use his good offices informally "to the end that the service conditions of the foreign personnel in the salt administration may be improved." [10]

In 1937–1941, under influence of war conditions and intensified nationalism, the position of the foreign staff steadily worsened. They were gradually losing the struggle to uphold China's international commitments by maintaining joint authority and responsibility. Their pay and allowances, though partly put on a foreign currency basis, were generally below those of foreign employees of China in the customs and postal service and fell far short of keeping abreast of inflation. Granting of home leave during the war was frowned upon. The health of many became impaired and their nerves strained by lack of rest, bombing, evacuations, separation from families, bad living conditions, and infringements upon their prerogatives. Many resigned and left China, and their places were not filled. In the fall of 1941 appointment of four new foreigners was authorized, but they were caught in Shanghai and Hong Kong when the Pacific War broke out. By then the number of foreign officers had fallen to

16, from about twice that number before the war and four times that number a dozen years earlier. Lockhart left China about the end of 1940 because of illness, and resigned late in 1941.

The salt revenue made a sorry showing during the first four years of hostilities, due to the government's policies. There was a feeling in influential circles that rates of tax should not be increased, thus adding to the people's burdens in a time of stress. Rates were set in money per unit of salt, rather than on an *ad valorem* basis. As a result, when general prices rose the real value of salt revenue fell. By 1941 the salt operation had become a source of cost rather than revenue. The proposed solution, drafted by the salt administration by direction of the Minister of Finance, was clearly a blunder: to create a salt monopoly. Besides violating agreements, a monopoly would involve huge capital outlay at a time of inflation, create a large bureaucracy with infinite possibilities for corruption and mismanagement, and disrupt the salt trade. Better measures were available, that is, drastic increase of rates; measuring rates according to the value of specific quantities of salt, to keep abreast of inflation; consolidation of items of tax, which ranged from 6 to 16 in individual districts; and strengthening the existing organization. Lockhart and I pointed out the objections and urged the better solutions. The monopoly scheme fortunately met such opposition that the government, instead of adopting it as proposed, raised rates materially as from September 1, 1941. The monopoly nominally took effect January 1, 1942, but was not a monopoly in the usual sense of the word. The government collected the difference between officially set prices paid to producers and paid by distributors. Retail prices of salt were not controlled. The system gave rise to difficulties, and before the war's end the government reverted to the system of taxation.[11]

THE DILEMMA: TO PAY OR NOT TO PAY

China faced during 1938 a painful dilemma about debt payments. In the summer of 1938 China could have made a case for suspension. Japan was detaining or had destroyed about three-fourths of the customs revenue and half that from salt. China had to furnish all the foreign currencies. These could not be currently acquired but had to come out of reserves needed to support the currency and to meet other vital war needs. On the other hand, schemes for aid to China were pending which would have increased foreign currency resources and made it possible to continue payments at least for a time without radical change. The best near chance of aid then seemed to be in Britain, and drastic action on debts would have appeared as a slap at Britain, where the largest amount of Chinese foreign currency bonds was held. For several months beginning in the spring of 1938, the negotiations for aid in London went through alternate phases of hope and despair. When in July London's reply finally was adverse, Washington invited China to negotiate for aid. Although in the friendly nations some persons favored aiding China on grounds of broad policy, it was obvious that loans would have to be set up as financially justifiable.

Before K. P. Chen left for Washington early in September 1938, I orally explained the situation to him on behalf of Minister Kung. Chen was asked to discuss the dilemma most confidentially with Morgenthau and seek his informal guidance. Heavy debt payments were coming up at the end of September, and we thought seriously of a moratorium before the end of the month. A further factor in timing was the fear that Hankow would fall in a matter of weeks. Because of the effect on general confidence and morale, a moratorium ought not to come too close to a serious military defeat, before or after. So on September 21 Kung telegraphed to Chen asking for his preliminary views by the 26th. Chen replied on the 25th that cash aid looked impossible, but that an export credit was being considered. He said that a "high Treasury personage" had indicated that such a credit, however, should not be used "to pay loans to other countries"; and that "so long as U.S. loans paid, what is done as to European loans will not affect the negotiations." The reply was of little help, since clearly China could not discriminate between creditors. So China had to miss that chance for a general suspension.

Again on October 9 Kung telegraphed to Chen at length, hoping for guidance as to how China might be relieved of the impossible burden of debt payments without prejudicing the chances of American aid. But Chen feared the effect of broaching the subject in any form. Three times more, in October and

November, Kung went back at Chen, hoping to draw forth some indication of the American view, based on broad consideration of China's problem, but to no avail.

Thus China's hands were tied. American help was by no means certain, and a moratorium might prejudice getting that help. Also, the public might take such action to mean that the government had despaired of American help. A moratorium, coupled with the fall of Hankow and Canton in late October, would have been a disastrous shock to confidence in the currency and to morale in general. In that case a moratorium might not have saved as much as it would have cost in added outlay for currency support.

SUSPENSION OF PAYMENTS

The American purchase credit of US$25 million was announced December 15, 1938. A week later Minister Kung told me that the problem of foreign debt payments had been discussed in the highest Chinese quarters, that the feeling was that payments had to stop, and that if anything they had been carried on too long. December 31 was named as the deadline. I at once pointed out that in view of the American credit Washington ought to be consulted, and drafted a telegram sent on December 23 to Ambassador Hu and K. P. Chen. They were instructed to explain to Morgenthau that China no longer had the foreign currency funds needed to keep up debt payments, and would of course bear full responsibility for action; and to reiterate that China would continue payments on the prewar commodity loans granted by the American Government. China "would like to know that American Government understands and has no alternative advice to offer and will not object and will continue its friendly interest."

Ambassador Hu was ill, and Chen replied on December 29 that ". . . we have repeatedly presented all facts . . . to Secretary and important Treasury officials who expressed their personal views that our war conditions justify suspension but stressed that payments on all American debts be continued." Kung replied on December 31, pointing out that China could not continue to pay service of private loan issues to Americans, while suspending payments to others, without unjustifiable discrimination. That message drew no specific reply and, pending word, China had to make a sizable debt payment on January 5. While Kung was wondering how he could act without giving offense to Washington, after the American credit so recently granted, he was under pressure from his Chinese associates to do something.

Finally, on January 9 and 10 came messages indicating that the United States would make no official comment, and also that Secretary Morgenthau was away on holiday until January 15. China could wait no longer with no cash aid in sight, and Kung decided to act at mid-month. The policy decision and form of announcement involved most delicate problems. Happily during the discussions there was no leak. Besides the obvious dangers of speculation and damage to credit, a leak might have led to a raid on exchange, because the public might feel that reserves were exhausted. Hence China had to act suddenly and unilaterally, without talking first to the various creditor representatives and their governments—the exchanges with Washington had taken place only because of the pending American credit. China could not take the risks of leakage; and such talks would have taken time while the heavy burden of payments continued. Moreover the announcement had to stress enemy seizures and interference with the currency, instead of difficulties of "transfer."

The statement issued January 15, 1939, applied only to customs-secured debt—payments on salt-secured foreign loans were suspended a few weeks later. The statement recounted enemy seizure of pledged revenues, which forced China to advance about C$175 million for debt service. China also had provided all the foreign exchange required, although Japan was interfering with the currency. The situation had become too anomalous to continue. The government therefore had declined to make a further advance to the Inspector General of Customs. The announcement called the suspension "a temporary arrangement in view of present abnormal conditions."

The suspension of payments was a most serious step, which caused the highest officials of China much worry. I recall that just after the papers approved at the final conference had been sent forward for action Madame Chiang Kai-shek asked me whether I felt sure that the action was wise. I replied that there was no better alternative.

As a preliminary step to minimize shock to the currency, I prepared an informal "spokesman's" statement which was put out, one day before the announcement, through the foreign press agencies and especially designed for Shanghai and Hong Kong. It said that for some months China had been successfully conducting stabilization operations, for which substantial funds were earmarked, and that these operations had been conducted without loss in foreign exchange. The suspension fortunately did not cause any serious difficulty in the exchange market.

The suspension, however, was followed by a drop of about six points in Chinese bonds at London. Financial opinion there and in British circles at Shanghai and Hong Kong was critical. That was not surprising in view of large British holdings of Chinese bonds. The general comment, not taking into account the foreign exchange shortage which the government could not discuss, was that China ought to forget its objections and implement the customs agreement. Britain again urged this upon China in a note of January 25, and also urged the French to support it. The French ambassador at Washington asked whether the United States would also join in pressing China. Hamilton, Chief of the Division of Far Eastern Affairs, told him that China's suspension of payments "appeared to be not unreasonable"; that the United States had declined to urge on China any particular plan for servicing the debt; and that the basic difficulty seemed to be, "would the Japanese-controlled areas furnish their share of the foreign exchange or would the Chinese Government be expected to furnish all foreign exchange?" [12]

Unfortunately the suspension came at a time when, as we learned immediately afterward, the elements in the British Government that favored aid to China were gaining the upper hand. The misunderstanding in London was so serious that we felt it could be dispelled only by sending Rogers there. He had been ill and away for several weeks to recuperate from illness and overwork, and he returned only just before the announcement of suspension. But he willingly undertook to go and did a good job of explaining the necessity of China's action.

China maintained payments on the prewar American commodity loans, which was of course necessary in view of the 1938 credit of US$25 million. China also continued to make the payments due on the French credit of 1938 for the Nanning Railway. This was a special situation, since the loan was made after start of hostilities and with partial guarantee by the French Government (see chapter IV). The agreement for the British purchase credit announced in December 1938, was not concluded until after the January announcement; and China made the payments under this agreement, as in the case of the American and French obligations.

Railway debts were treated separately. The principle was to suspend payments when a line securing them had been fully occupied by the enemy. As Japan overran more and more of China, payment of railway debt gradually ground to a halt. In October 1938, Britain protested the proposed destruction by the Chinese army of rolling stock and bridges on part of the Shanghai-Hangchow-Ningpo Railway, on the ground that they were mortgaged to British creditors. Minister Kung replied that the authorities concerned had been instructed "to use due judgment," but said he was "sure that the foreign interests concerned will appreciate that in a major war, involving the existence of the Chinese nation, actions of such nature have to be governed by military necessity, even though sacrifices of property are entailed."

When announcing on March 26, 1939, suspension of salt revenue payments on the foreign currency debt, Kung said that China had initiated negotiations for an arrangement concerning service of customs- and salt-secured loans. The background was as follows: When Rogers reached London about February 1, he found strong feeling about China's unilaterally stopping payments. There was a bright prospect for a British currency credit; but people would feel that China, with a cash credit, ought to do something about resuming debt payments. The British Government asked no formal *quid pro quo,* but Ambassador Quo, under instructions from Chungking, addressed to the British Government on March 2 a note saying that China had suspended payments only with the greatest reluctance, wanted to do everything possible despite the difficulties to arrive at a reasonable arrangement about debt service, and would shortly transmit a proposal.

London debated whether to condition the credit upon China implementing the Anglo-Japanese customs agreement. But Ambassador Clark Kerr telegraphed in February that for China the difficulties were matters of principle, and that these views were "held in all quarters." [13] So no such string was attached.

China made a proposal on March 21 to bondholders' representatives in Britain, France, Germany, and the United States, offering partial payment of interest but nothing for principal. That led to active negotiations. While these were moving toward a conclusion, the currency situation in China was worsening rapidly. Because of this, Rogers telegraphed from Hong Kong on June 2, advising me to go slowly about concluding negotiations. By July the currency difficulties became the controlling factor. Exchange was weak, the Anglo-Chinese stabilization fund was nearing exhaustion, and the Central Bank's external assets were only equivalent to about US$30 million. On July 17 came a telegram saying that the bondholders' representatives wanted China to make her offer. The next day operations to support the exchange market had to be suspended. China then had no real option but to inform the bondholders' representatives on July 27, through their governments, that it had delayed its intended offer due to the unexpected difficulties in the exchange market and the Japanese threat to the foreign concessions (see chapter IX), and that "most reluctantly" China was unable to proceed with the negotiations. On July 19 I wrote to Rogers:

> I am far from happy about the prospect of dropping the debt negotiations when they are at the point of finality. To do so will be misunderstood and will evoke criticism and probably a feeling that there never was good faith on the Chinese side. This latter charge, if it comes to that, will be quite unjustified as Dr. Kung sincerely wishes to make a settlement. The delay is largely due to responsibility taken by you and me because we could see more clearly than others the trend of events; though even if we had tried to push the negotiation through the result might have been the same.

Clearly it would have helped neither China nor the creditors to announce a settlement that could not be carried out.

This proved to be the end of payments on China's prewar foreign currency issues. Toward the end of the war, in July 1945, I made detailed recommendations to the Chinese Government as to resumption of payments, including a plan to simplify and consolidate the railway debts. I hoped for early resumption. But to avoid a risk of breakdown of new arrangements, I recommended that "negotiations for final arrangements . . . wait until China is definitely on the path to economic and financial recovery, and until China's internal situation and the international situation affecting China show a fair prospect of stability." Unfortunately those conditions never developed. Today the creditors' prospects of being paid do not seem bright.

VII. STALEMATE, 1939–1941:
COMMUNICATIONS

THE fall of Hankow and Canton late in 1938 did not end the "China Incident" any more than had the fall of Nanking a year earlier. Japan occupied the main ports and waterways, most of the railways, and the centers of most of the modern development. But the government moved to Chungking and resistance continued in the vast area which Japan could not occupy and hold. There is a story that, at a Japanese reception, a Japanese officer asked a German diplomat whether he had ever been a soldier. The diplomat replied, "Yes, in 1914–18 I fought in the World Incident"! Japan worried about how to end the fighting. A Tokyo paper complained that China was a nation "of the lower strata of life," with no vital spot whose capture would end the will or capacity to resist.[1]

While the enemy forces were driving on Hankow, their government was debating what to do after that city's fall. One view was to push on and try for the "actual physical destruction" of China's government. The other was to consider it "crushed" and use political means, seeking to organize the conquests through puppet regimes.[2] The second view prevailed. Had the Japanese forces pushed ahead vigorously after taking Hankow, instead of stopping after limited advances, they would have had a chance to knock out serious large-scale resistance. But they halted, as after taking Nanking, and again gave China time to catch her breath to continue the struggle.

The period of three years preceding the Pacific War was, in effect, a stalemate. But there was no lack of activity on all fronts: military, international, internal, and financial. While Japan's forces made no really major military advances, they staged campaigns for limited objectives, sometimes for foraging and troop training. They were mostly victorious, but met a number of defeats, as in several attempts to take Changsha. They devised regional puppet regimes, but despite talk never joined them in a federation. Their puppets never gained real standing in the regions—not even Wang Ching-wei, the well-known leader who defected at the end of 1938 and later headed the Central China regime.

Friction between Japan and the Western nations grew, as Japan encroached on their rights and interests in China, and moved into Indochina, thus forecasting the attacks that were to usher in the Pacific War. The nations concerned, especially the United States, responded with increased aid to China, as preferable to retaliation against Japan, although that also came gradually. The start of World War II in September 1939 and developments in the war had important repercussions in China and on her international relations. Meanwhile, her internal situation deteriorated, as the Communists used the confusion to expand and as the pace of inflation became faster.

We shall discuss the events of this period of stalemate in this and the following three chapters, which deal, respectively, with (1) communications, (2) material and military aid, and (3) the finances.

THE INDOCHINA ROUTE

Early in 1939, Japanese forces seized Hainan Island, not far from the Indochina Coast. There seems to have been an informal understanding, dating from about the start of 1938, that Japan would not seize Hainan if the French checked entry of munitions via Indochina. The French countered Japan's action by liberalizing transit. In February 1939, it was reported that all kinds of goods, even artillery, were going through.

The French position in Indochina, however, remained under constant threat from Japan. On July 31, 1939, a month before the outbreak of World War II, a member of the French Foreign Office told Ambassador Bullitt, "Both the French and British Governments had decided to withdraw from every position and possession that they had in the Far East if necessary to avoid war with Japan. In view of the situation in Europe they could not take any other attitude unless they could count on the active support of the United States in the Far East." Nevertheless, the French Government did much to facilitate transit to China via

Indochina. Thus, that government, in the later part of 1939, authorized expenditure of 80 million francs to improve the railway to Kunming and 16 million francs for a new motor road northwest from Haiphong to the Chinese border, as an alternate to the road to the northeast toward Nanning, which Japan had captured.[3]

Many of the goods bought under the US$25 million American credit of 1938 were routed via Indochina. These and other goods piled up at Haiphong, and 120,000 tons of goods destined to China were there in the latter part of 1939. The railway to Kunming was then carrying only about 12,000 tons per month, and some additional freight was entering China via the road that ran northeast to Nanning. Neither route was very efficient, and efforts to clear the congestion met only moderate success. In December 1939, the Japanese capture of Nanning blocked that route. The French authorities believed that this drive toward the Indochina border was intended to intimidate them and cause them to check the movement of goods to China. Also Japanese planes bombed the railway.[4]

The Japanese continued to be unhappy about the French attitude on transit to China. Ambassador Bullitt reported to Secretary Hull from Paris on September 14 that shipments via Indochina would go through "provided they are labelled on the principle that a rose by any other name would smell as sweet." But with France enmeshed in the war after September 1, Japan was able to increase her pressure. France soon had to stop transit of munitions, motor vehicles, and gasoline.[5]

The Japanese coveted control of strategic Indochina. In September 1940, after the fall of France, they acted drastically. In response to an ultimatum, France had to agree on September 22 to let Japan garrison and use three air bases and place a few troops at the chief entry port of Haiphong. Despite this yielding, another Japanese unit, the Canton Army, invaded Indochina at Dongdang and Langson, overwhelming the small French garrisons. That was in spite of all that the Japanese negotiator at Hanoi, General Nishihara, could do to try to stop the invasion. And they bombed Haiphong. A few days later Japan joined the German-Italian Axis.

From then Indochina ceased to be a significant route to China. There remained only the Burma Road, the precarious air links, and the tenuous land route through Central Asia to Russia.

THE BURMA ROAD

Early in 1939 traffic began to roll over the Burma Road. The work of maintaining and improving it went ahead, under great difficulties. By May the official Southwest Transportation Company, directed by T. L. Soong, was operating 600 trucks. Also many private trucks found it lucrative to bring in goods to meet the many shortages in Free China. By July 22 China had received at Rangoon 1,768 American and 120 British trucks, and more were expected.[6] Assembly was slow at the start, but soon Chinese mechanics and carpenters arrived and work proceeded effectively. Bodies were made locally. The flow to China of American trucks was invaluable to China.

In June and July, Julean Arnold, American Commercial Attaché, made an investigation. He forwarded his personal comments to Minister Kung by letter of August 7. He praised Chinese morale but found serious difficulties. Chinese official organs were not coordinated, leading to indecision and waste. Congestion of goods at Rangoon and other points was alarming, leading to huge losses from depreciation, pilferage, and delay. Drivers were poorly trained and trucks badly maintained, causing heavy loss and wastage of equipment. Service stations were lacking. Trucks returned empty from Kunming despite China's urgent need to export. Responsible staff were underpaid. He ventured some penetrating views:

> The comments and suggestions offered are not new to most Chinese . . . The problem is one of organization and action. While in America, it was not unusual to be told by our educators that the Chinese students averaged higher in scholarship than any others. The mistake that the Chinese Government made was not to stipulate that every Chinese student who went to America should make a thorough study of American football . . . The son of the janitor has as good prospects as the son of the college president or the football coach. In a word, men are selected because of their ability and willingness to play the positions allocated to them . . . The big objective is to develop a winning team. . . . Face and favoritism have no place in football. And the student body is behind the team.

The Chinese Government early recognized the need for expert foreign aid in improving road traffic. It engaged as adviser D. F.

Myers, an experienced American automotive expert. Myers reported in July that the road in its then state could not serve as an all-weather road because of bad drainage, poor surfacing, and constant slides. He said there was not an adequate repair shop on the entire road, and that it was often blocked by double parking and the jamming of narrow streets in towns by long stops.

In July 1939, the Chinese Government invited to China for a survey of road problems a mission of three Americans, arranged by K. P. Chen and headed by M. E. Sheahan, an experienced truck operator from Chicago. They reached China in September. After investigation they urged various reforms: better grading, drainage, and surfacing of roads; establishment of proper inspections and properly equipped shops for maintenance; centralized purchase and handling of stores; an improved organization for road maintenance, regulation of traffic, and truck operation; and better training and pay for drivers and a plan for relay driving. Their urging brought about some physical improvement of the road, but on other matters had little immediate result.

Under the agreement covering the American purchase credit, announced in December 1938, wood oil was to be shipped in payment. Some wood oil was sent from Hong Kong and via Indochina. But exports via the Burma Road were slow to start. The first such shipment of 53 tons left August 12, 1939. By February 22, 1940, shipments to Rangoon were 1,100 tons. It was hard to get export goods moving, even though most trucks were leaving Kunming empty. There was a lack of internal transport to get the goods to Kunming, since there were but a few thousand usable trucks in Free China.

Private export trade was almost nonexistent. Exporters, besides facing transport problems, had to sell to the government banks, at semiofficial rates, the foreign currencies gotten from sale of exports. The rates first set were in line with the market. But price rises and a slump in exchange soon made the rates unrealistic. It was a year before new rates were set, and these too soon got out of line.* Exports therefore had to be handled by official agencies, because only they could pay the prices necessary to

* The first rates as from July 1, 1939, were 7d. and equivalents in other currencies. Exchange soon fell to nearly half that figure. As from August 1, 1940, the rates were changed to 4½d. and equivalents, since exchange then ruled around 4d. But these rates soon got out of line.

buy the goods and get transport to move them. Through these agencies China met her promises to ship out goods to pay Russia, the United States, and Britain.

Detailed figures of traffic over the road in 1939 and 1940 are not available. By April 1939, about 30,000 tons of war materials had reached Rangoon, but only 3,600 tons had been sent on to Lashio, the railhead where the road into China began. Only 900 to 1,200 tons monthly of war supplies were reaching Kunming. That was but a small fraction of the freight moving by rail from Indochina. Also there was much private trade over the road by Chinese and Indian merchants. The profit of this trade was so attractive that it proved hard to get the transport allocated for war needs. Nevertheless more and more essential goods were being sent to Rangoon under both the American and Russian credits. Gradually they began to reach China.

Hitler's drive on France and Britain in May–June 1940 gave the Japanese opportunity to demand on June 24 that Britain close the Burma route to transit of munitions and other essential supplies. About this time I reached Washington, accompanying T. V. Soong. On June 28, while I was talking with the Financial Attaché at the British Embassy, the Ambassador, Lord Lothian asked to see me. My memorandum of the conversation was as follows:

Lord Lothian almost immediately brought up the question of the Burma Road. He wished to know how important it was to China; whether it would be subject to serious interruption or rendered useless by Japanese bombing; and in particular, whether the Generalissimo would continue to fight if the Burma Road were closed by the British under Japanese pressure.

I stated that the capacity was several thousand tons monthly, which was susceptible of increase; that the Indo-China Railway had been considerably more important, having a capacity of about 20,000 tons monthly of late; and the interruption of this railway, as the result of the French yielding to Japanese pressure, was very unfortunate and would considerably handicap China. I pointed out Burma was the remaining link between China and the western countries and, if this were cut, there would remain only the contact with Russia. In my opinion, the maintenance of contact through Burma was of the greatest importance in preparing the way for an eventual counter attack upon Japan by China with aid from the western countries.

As to the possibility of the Japanese interrupting the Burma Road by bombing, I stated that in my opinion, traffic could not be seriously curtailed thereby. The Chinese had kept the Canton-Hankow railway going under constant bombing attack from nearby bases. The nearest point from Hanoi to the Burma Road (Kunming) was approximately five hundred miles, or over two hours for a bomber. The distance increased as the road ran westward for five hundred to six hundred miles. Certainly China would feel that the possibility of bombing was not a serious threat to this life-line.

As to China's attitude were the road closed, I said that I naturally could not speak for the Generalissimo. However, it is clear that the Sino-Japanese conflict is not ripe for settlement because with the Japanese in their present temper any settlement would amount to surrender by China. In my judgment the Chinese would feel that in any case they are obliged to continue fighting, just as the British are continuing to fight the Germans. I pointed out that the British and the Chinese were the two countries now resisting aggression, and that the closing of the Burma Road would be regarded as a serious blow to China by a country that should befriend China, and would doubtless be regarded in China and in the United States as analogous to the failure of France to support Great Britain. Certainly, the closing of the road would have a serious effect in the United States on the British cause. I felt that in recent years much had been lost from giving in to aggressor countries on matters of principle, and that the best course to follow is not to yield to improper demands of this nature, because a stand against them has to be made somewhere and it might as well be made now in order to rally the forces that should resist the aggressor countries; in particular, it would be a great wrong to China which has been fighting the cause of the democratic countries for three years, and would only encourage Japan to fresh adventure in other directions. In other words, any promise that Japan might give were the British to agree to close the Burma Road would not be worth the paper on which it is written.

Lord Lothian said that he agreed with much of what I had said, but that in the present world force was all that counted. The biggest question at present was whether Great Britain could survive, and Great Britain had to avoid bringing Japan in as an enemy at present. The British Isles were about to be subjected to a bombing attack compared to which the bombing in China was "child's play," and Great Britain had to reserve all of its strength to fight Germany. If Germany should overcome England, Germany would acquire in Europe an industrial and ship-building capacity so great that the United States, Japan, and Russia would be only second-rate powers. He stated that the British would try to resist Japan's demands and temporize, but intimated that he doubted whether the demand to close the Burma Road could long be resisted. He asked whether the United States would be prepared to join in resisting Japan by force if Great Britain refused the Burma Road demand. I stated that apparently the United States is not now prepared to resist with force; but that the tendency was in that direction and that a strong stand by the British Government and possible Japanese forcible expansion in the form of an attack on British, French, and Dutch possessions certainly would tend to bring the United States to take more active measures.

Commenting on reports that closure of the road was imminent, Secretary Hull issued a statement on July 16 that "this Government has a legitimate interest in the keeping open of arteries of commerce all over the world," and that such action and the French closing of the Indochina railway "would constitute unwarranted interpositions of obstacles to world trade."

On July 18 Prime Minister Churchill told the House of Commons that in response to Japanese demands the road would be closed to transit of munitions, trucks, gasoline, and railway supplies for three months. A like prohibition would apply at Hong Kong, though these items were not in fact moving there. Churchill said that Britain was not unmindful of its obligations to China, but was "engaged in a life or death struggle." He said in the debate that "all that happens to us in the Far East is probably likely to be very much influenced by what happens over here." The agreement he said was temporary because he hoped that time would lead to a solution.[7]

Closing the road to traffic in vital goods was a hard blow to China. Analyzing the situation for my own guidance in a memorandum of July 15, I concluded that it was hard then for the United States to do anything effective because isolationism was still strong and the political campaign was under way. Radical nationalism was gaining in Japan and should the United States take some strong action, for example, an embargo on oil for Japan, the Japanese might make it a pretext to move against the Dutch East Indies, or British or French possessions. American opinion might then blame their government for interference; whereas if American action followed fresh Japanese measures, it might be "much easier to take." I concluded that "the situation in China is critical as to morale, since China seems almost alone for the moment, and American action of some sort must not be delayed beyond the point where China's morale would crack. It appears that the latter will not take place, in any event, during a reasonable time in which negotiations are proceeding in Washington with the prospect of success."

When the three months' period of closure of the road expired, the British refused to close it any longer. They had meanwhile won the Battle of Britain. Also, after a discouraging interlude, Washington granted to China a credit of US$25 million in September just after the Japanese moved into Indochina. The American action encouraged London to take a firmer position. But China was not soon to forget that Britain had closed the road. A year later the Generalissimo was quoted as saying that this act had "permanently destroyed British prestige" in China.[8]

By the end of 1940 the road's capacity had been built up to only about 5,000 tons per month. This could gradually be raised to 15/20,000 and more by better organization, improvement of drainage, better surfacing, and reduction of curves and grades. But even so it would be far from adequate to supply China's military and civil needs from abroad for defensive warfare, not to speak of an eventual offensive. So it was desirable to push plans for a railway. In 1939 China started to build a railway from Kunming to connect with the Burma railway a hundred miles within Burma. By the end of 1940 China had done a third of the earth work on the China section, plus perhaps a sixth of the work on bridges and tunnels. Rails torn up from the then useless Indochina line had been used to start the line westward from Kunming. The cost in foreign currency was figured at US$15/20 million, and the time of completion about the end of 1942 if actively pushed forward.

China had negotiated with the French and British for aid for the railway, but without definite result. In the fall of 1940 Chinese representatives began further discussions in Washington and London. The State Department and Export-Import Bank were both sympathetic, as were the British authorities. The representatives pointed out that, if the United States should later be at war with Japan, it would need all possible transport capacity for an eventual offensive, especially to supply air bases in China. Export-Import Bank aid for the railway did not materialize. But on May 6, 1941, China became eligible for Lend-Lease aid. Under Lend-Lease China was allotted US$15 million for the railway during 1941. But the Japanese invasion of Burma early in 1942 put an end to the project.[9]

The Japanese move into Northern Indochina in September 1940 put them in position for air attack on the road. On January 23, 1941, they bombed the two Mekong River bridges, putting both temporarily out of service. But trucks were ferried across, using the pontoon ferry made from empty oil drums that was hauled back and forth by cables powered by donkey engines. There was no serious interruption to traffic. There were further bombings but they did not seriously check operations. Chinese engineers and workmen were efficient in repairing damage, just as they had kept the Canton-Hankow railway open in 1938 despite constant bombing. One engineer remarked that each bomb cost the enemy a thousand dollars gold to make a hole in the ground, but he could fill it up for a few dollars "Mex." Also the monsoon season from Spring to Fall, with its poor visibility, brought some protection.

There was grave risk that Japan would physically cut the Burma route, especially after encroaching on northern Indochina in 1940. What they could do to France they could also do to Britain. In April 1941, because no one else seemed to be doing it, I made with Chennault's collaboration a study of possible invasion routes to Burma. This I embodied in a memorandum of April 30 with maps, which I gave informally to the Chinese and American authorities and discussed with British representatives at Washington. I pointed out the grave consequences if China were cut off from aid, and also the danger to India. It had been generally thought a land attack on Burma would be impossible, but I pointed out possible routes by which the Japanese could use partly built roads together with paths from Thailand and cut the railway north of Rangoon.

I urged shipping promptly to Burma equipment that troops would need and especially aircraft; dispersal of supplies in the interior; and consideration of letting Chinese volunteers go to Burma as "tourists" or "laborers," borrowing a device used by the Axis in Europe, since the British were harassed by the Germans and could spare little from Europe and the Middle East. The Chinese and some American contacts were impressed with the need for doing something. But the British representatives, after consulting London, reported the view that the jungles were too hard for the Japanese to penetrate. Yet that was just what the Japanese did eight or nine months later.[10]

There are no complete figures of traffic over the Burma road, but the available data of goods arriving at Kunming are as follows:

1940–1941	Number of trucks	Tonnage
October 19 to November 17	1,740	4,788
November 18 to December 17	1,720	4,730
December 18 to January 17	2,448	6,732
January 18 to February 17	2,914	8,012
February 18 to March 17	2,855	7,851
March 1 to 31	3,127	8,600
April	4,004	11,100
May	4,727	13,000
June	4,573	12,850
July	5,128	14,100
August	3,345	9,200
September	5,349	14,712

By the end of 1941 about 15,000 tons monthly was reaching Kunming. Commercial truckers brought perhaps a fourth of this, mostly cotton yarn and gasoline. Outbound cargo was much less than inbound, and so far as I could learn never exceeded about 3,500 tons monthly. More than half of this was wood oil.

Gasoline was a problem. About 30 per cent of incoming cargo had to be gasoline needed for the round trip to Kunming. To Chungking a round trip from Burma would need by weight about 50 per cent gasoline. In November 1941 a scheme for a gasoline pipeline was proposed—such a line was built before the end of the Pacific War to supplement the air route over the Hump and the road from India (see chapter XVIII).

Congestion of stores in Burma and along the road in China proved serious from the start. In June 1941 I returned from the United States to China via Rangoon, with a mission from Soong to do what I could enroute to get cargo moving better. The Burmese Government was charging a transit tax of 1 per cent on goods for China. T. K. Tseng, representative in Burma of China's Foreign Ministry, and I felt that this ought not to apply on Lend-Lease goods. We got the Chinese Government to raise the question. Burma countered with a proposal to double the charge, on the ground that the traffic caused them extra expense and trouble. In the United States there was critical comment on Burma's taxing Lend-Lease goods. The solution was for Burma to make only a nominal charge per ton, this to be paid Burma as a subsidy by the British Government.

About 46,000 tons of China cargo had accumulated at Rangoon by June 1941. This included 20,000 tons of "old cargo," which had been transshipped from Indochina and Hong Kong. I urged creating a single authority to deal with all the cargo, moving it inland in Burma and into China as promptly as possible according to priorities, selling any of the "old cargo" that was not to be moved to China, and seeing that cargo was properly dispersed to reduce the risk from bombing and sabotage.

At the railhead at Lashio I found about 30,000 tons accumulated. This included a striking sight from the air—long rows of white and gray-white drums of gasoline closely packed together and inviting sabotage or bombing. They were stored on the ground and subject to tropical wetness. I urged dispersing them in the woods, raising them above the ground, and camouflaging them, which was promptly done.

Within China along the road to Kunming I found an accumulation of about 55,000 tons of general cargo and 12,500 tons of gasoline. Some months before, a dump of thousands of tons of precious munitions had exploded at Chefang, almost wiping out the town. Apparently it was sabotage. As a result of this terribly expensive lesson, cargo within China was better dispersed and protected. But I often found scores of trucks parked end to end on the road or in towns, inviting destruction by sabotage or bombing, not to speak of blocking traffic.

The trip over the road was an impressive experience. In my report of July 21, I wrote:

The road is a tremendous accomplishment, and one travelling it for the first time cannot but be impressed with the way in which it was put through so quickly under such great difficulties of terrain, labor, health and climate. Also one is greatly impressed by the energy, resourcefulness and devotion of the numerous loyal men engaged in current maintenance and operations.

I shared the feeling of one American who remarked, "Why, they dug this out with their fingernails!"

But I found many things that neded to be done to improve conditions. Near the frontier is an area subject to malignant malaria. This became a bottleneck, due to inability to get labor to maintain the road. I urged the Chinese Government to arrange for an American mission to combat the disease, and this was done. Dr. Victor H. Haas and the first members of a 16-man mission reached China about November first.

Over a dozen Chinese Government agencies were operating on the road, plus commercial trucks. Traffic control was almost nonexistent. There was no effective policing. There were many stations of national, provincial, and local authorities for collection of taxes and tolls, where convenience of the collector took precedence over urgency of cargo. The road badly needed surfacing and improved drainage. In one stretch in the malaria district, from 7:00 a.m. to 1:30 a.m. we covered just 10 miles. We spent the rest of the night in cots under mosquito netting on top of a mountain. Space at stations for parking and dispersing trucks was inadequate. There were few facilities for maintenance and repair. Tools and machinery, parts, and trained workmen were lacking.

Drivers were a problem. Chinese drivers feuded with those from Burma and India and with each other. They would add to their income by many devices. They would carry passengers, known as "yellow fish," and collect the fare, as well as carry their private cargo. They would smuggle gold and other goods into China. They would squeeze gasoline by coasting downhill out of gear at risk to them and others, and sell what they saved. They even would sell parts off the trucks. They knew little about loading, care, and maintenance.[11]

Financial procedure was bad. The agencies concerned with the road frequently needed emergency funds. Finance Minister Kung usually authorized these promptly, but it took so long to get them through because of red tape that the funds when received were not enough. The constant inflation ate into the buying power of salaries of officials, tempting them to irregular practices. As usual in China the offices were overstaffed with office personnel, many of whom would not soil their hands by going out to see what was happening on the road.

I made a full report in July on the findings of my trip, with detailed recommendations, explaining that many of these were not new and were already receiving attention. Generalissimo Chiang ordered these recommendations put into effect. He asked me to advise on communications as well as finance.

To improve conditions, Generalissimo Chiang had appointed John Earl Baker as Inspector General of the road, as from May 1. Baker had had a long experience in China, having rendered important services as adviser to the Ministry of Railways and also as an able administrator of disaster relief in floods and famine. He was appointed on China's initiative, though the American Government through Laughlin Currie, of Roosevelt's staff, backed his appointment.[12] Baker made some improvements on the road, but in practice could not quickly cope with the many difficult problems. He was given neither the power nor the Chinese backing needed, and he was handicapped by red tape. Moreover, he could not hire suitable staff because limited to salaries with a top equal to about US$30 per month. He wrote to me August 13:

> We cannot build intermediate terminals because it takes six months to get the budget approved and money in hand. I cannot put up a telephone necessary for rapid adaptations of truck movements to road conditions for not only is money absent but telephones come under the Ministry of Communications and the men around me are afraid of interdepartmental complications. This eternal fear or hurting some one's feelings paralyzes action at every turn.

Ambassador Gauss reported on August 15, 1941, that he felt that no director of the road could function effectively "unless in addition to full powers he is given efficient and adequate police or military assistance unquestionably at his command to enforce, where necessary, his directions . . ., enforce discipline and suppress all interference from whatever sources with the efficient operation of the road. He should also have virtual financial autonomy." And again on August 24 he said, "Centralization of authority over the road, in hands that are willing and able to establish needed police controls and to subordinate provincial and private vested interests to the national welfare, is imperative if American technical assistance is to be effective and if aid to China under Lend-Lease is to materialize as anticipated." [13]

In the Summer of 1941 a mission of American traffic experts headed by Daniel G. Arnstein came to China at the Generalissimo's request. After investigation they recommended centralizing managerial authority in a single Managing Director, with six sectional directors each having authority over a section comprising one day's run for a truck. They urged various improvements in operating methods. They concluded that only experienced American personnel could effect proper maintenance. They backed recruiting in the United States a maintenance supervisor with six assistants, for whom Baker had already asked, and also 15 American mechanics. These were to train Chinese personnel. The Mission urged a preventive maintenance plan, with regular inspections. Before departure from Washington, anticipating the needs, they left with Soong a full list of the equipment needed for this plan. The equipment and personnel were to be provided under Lend-Lease. They urged pressing on with paving at least the westernmost section, which had already started, because this had the worst surface and the hardest weather conditions. They made various proposals to improve traffic control, loading of trucks, handling of gasoline, and other phases of operation.

Baker had made very similar recommendations early in 1941, as had others before him. But, frustrated by the lack of authority and funds and hence of results, he resigned in September. Washington's delay in recruiting and sending the technical staff for which he had asked—they did not leave the United States until late October—denied him means to work effectively. Also China's asking for an American traffic mission in June, the month after Baker began work, and the prestige derived from its selection by Harry Hopkins, tended to undermine Baker's position and to delay reforms pending another investigation.

In September 1941, Generalissimo Chiang ordered the amalgamation of all transport agencies on the road. Its effective working was becoming more and more vital, since by October about 80,000 tons of materials for China had accumulated at Rangoon, including thousands of tons of blankets which had long been stored and were deteriorating. Also there were large supplies at the Lashio terminal in Burma and at points along the road. How far the growing American part in operating the road could have helped matters never had a chance to be known. Doubtless, with the firmer attitude of the Chinese Government, it could have helped greatly. But the Pacific War broke out before much could be done, and soon afterward Japan overran Burma.

THE AIR ROUTES

The development and improvement of civil air routes for passengers and goods continued in 1939–1941, despite hazards and difficulties. Two CNAC passenger planes were attacked during the war with loss of life. The first was near Canton in August 1938 (see chapter V). The second was two years later, when enemy fighter planes shot up a plane rolling to a stop after landing near Kunming. The landing made was to avoid an air raid; however, the American pilot, W. C. "Foxy" Kent, the stewardess, and 11 passengers were killed. There were repeated close calls, in which CNAC planes took evasive action—in four of which I was a passenger. As it became clear that enemy planes would shoot down any non-Japanese plane in China skies, there was no reason not to camouflage the planes and to carry any item needed in the war. CNAC developed a sizable freight capacity, flying about two million ton-kilometers in 1937–1941, mostly in 1941. They brought in medicines, gasoline, banknotes, and other supplies, and flew out tungsten and other essential exports for delivery to the United States in payment of wartime credits.

Always aviation gasoline was a problem, since planes could not make the round trip from Hong Kong to Chungking without taking on fuel in China. Stocks of aviation gasoline were precious and were mostly kept in caves for protection from bombing. Another serious problem was finance. Receipts in 1937–1941 were mainly in Chinese currency, and as the inflation went on it was always a battle when the time came to persuade the government to allow higher rates. Expenses for planes, parts, fuel, and pilots' pay were mainly in dollars. Minister Kung, despite his grave problems, usually found enough dollars for CNAC's basic needs. American credits to China could not be used even to buy commercial planes or for civil air operations until the spring of 1940.

Existence under war conditions of two civil air lines, CNAC and Eurasia, was uneconomic and anomalous. The Chinese Government had majority control, both lines were under the Ministry of Communications, and Eurasia's foreign partners were in Germany, the ally of Japan. With Germany's involvement in war from September 1939, Eurasia could not get parts and replacements, and its service gradually petered out. But Eurasia survived by adroit politicking and became a vested interest, with a full complement of personnel. It even came close to getting Chinese Government support for receiving planes later provided by American aid and wartime priorities. Also, China came close to setting up a third enterprise to run an air freight line, due to plausible salesmanship, instead of concentrating on development of CNAC which had performed well under trying conditions and had the advantage of invaluable experience. That episode reflected China's eclecticism, a desire to try everything, and a softness for plausible and sometimes unscrupulous salesmen. Repeatedly this weakness caused waste, confusion, and harm in the history of Nationalist China, in military as well as civil aviation and in financial and business matters. Some of us tried several times during the war to bring about a consolidation of the two civil air organizations, but with no effect.

Though in 1937–1941 CNAC never had more than six first-class planes at one time available for operations, it was able to maintain the minimum needed air routes. In March 1939, CNAC opened a route to Hanoi, after negotiations with the French authorities. In October, after negotiations with the British, it opened its Rangoon line, as Burma and the Burma Road replaced Indochina and its railway and roads as the main supply route. Also in the latter part of 1939 both CNAC and Eurasia began occasional flights to Central Asia, along the Russian supply route. But in 1938–1941 the most vital line for movement of persons and air-borne supplies was between Chungking and Hong Kong. When in July 1940 the Japanese forced Britain temporarily to close the Burma Road to gasoline and munitions, the ban included Hong Kong though few such supplies were then moving there. There were rumors that Japan would force Hong Kong to exclude CNAC. As a precaution CNAC hurried some vital supplies inland and to Manila. But nothing happened. Bond wrote June 27 from Hong Kong that he was "very much concerned," but that "there is nothing we can do about any of it. We have never had but one policy and that is to outlast this war if possible. It is still our policy."

China could not ignore the chance of needing a route further north and less exposed than between Kunming and Rangoon. In November 1940, CNAC explored a route from Myitkyina in northern Burma over the rugged mountains to Suifu, beyond Chungking at the head of steam navigation on the Yangtze. But a more feasible route for freight seemed to be to Kunming and other places in Yunnan Province, from northern Burma or Assam, in India, the eventual "Hump" route. In the latter part of 1940, negotiations began for an air route between China and India. As the world situation worsened during 1941, the chance increased that Rangoon would not be a usable port of entry. It took time to negotiate because of discussion of possible routes, reciprocal rights for British and Indian airlines, cabotage, landing fields, and technical matters. The British-Indian authorities hesitated to allow use of the big new military airfield being built in northeast Assam. Much of the country over which the new air route would pass was virtually unknown, and some of it inhabited only by wild tribesmen or not at all. The situation in the Summer of 1941 was shown in the following extract from a letter of August 28 which I wrote from Chungking to Harold M. Bixby, Vice-President of Pan American Airways, who was helping T. V. Soong in negotiations for planes for CNAC:

> . . . as to planes for freight service we have just heard from a telegram from Bondie to P. Y. Wong that we may expect five DC3's in February and five more in March and probably more soon thereafter. We know how difficult it is going to be to get them sooner with the urgent demand of the British and no doubt the Russians for transports. But I do hope that more can be done earlier, and much earlier. Before I left in June Currie told me we could have two very soon . . . could we not pry loose two say in September? Rather than have the ten in February–March, it would be better if we could get say two monthly from October. It will greatly help our preparations, and also help us in pressing the Burma authorities, if we can have a fairly definite schedule beginning soon. Since Burma may be involved in hostilities without prior announcement, a few more good transport planes would be invaluable for China. Confidentially we are pressing the British hard for the right to operate from the region of Sadiya in India. But we want something to operate with, when we encounter more trouble on the Burma route.

Finally India gave permission for the survey flight from northeast Assam, over what came to be known as the "Hump." This flight was made on November 24, 1941, just two weeks before Pearl Harbor. We flew well to the north of the direct route to Kunming, to see what sort of country was there. It was impressive to see this wild and rugged region of towering snow-capped mountains, much of which was uninhabited and which white men had never before seen. The difficulties were great, but the route could be flown. China could still have a life line. The first flight to Calcutta was made two weeks after Pearl Harbor.

VIII. STALEMATE, 1939–1941:
MATERIAL AND MILITARY AID

B Y early 1939 China had about exhausted the two Russian credits of US$50 million each granted in 1937–1938. Sun Fo again went to Moscow for help. After some delay Stalin received him cordially and another credit agreement, for US$150 million, was signed as of June 13. Russia thus provided three credits totaling US$250 million.* These bore 3 per cent interest and were repayable respectively during 5½, 7, and 13 years. China was to pay by delivering materials which Russia needed. It is a striking fact that the terms of most of Russia's postwar aid to the Chinese Communists are similar to those of the aid to the National Government in 1937–1939, that is, by medium-term low-interest loans repayable in goods, rather than as gifts.

During 1939 substantial Russian material aid and military advice continued. War supplies came overland and via Rangoon. Russian arms were sufficient to equip about 10 reorganized Chinese divisions in 1938–1940. By the fall of 1939 Russia had supplied about 1,000 planes. About 2,000 Russian "volunteer" pilots in rotation played the dual role of helping China by service in China's air force and receiving combat practice.[1] The use of "volunteers" was an extension of the policy of qualified intervention developed in Spain's civil war. Russia also had about 500 military advisers in China. They did not serve with the front line forces, but rather at training centers for aviation, artillery, and tanks. They advised the National Military Council and the higher field headquarters. Their functions, however, were mainly technical rather than concerned with war strategy. Their role was more limited than that of the former German advisers. Their presence was useful for Russia, for ". . . studying the capabilities of the Chinese and Japanese forces and of testing German concepts, training systems, and

---

* Unofficial sources mentioned by MacLane, *Soviet Policy*, pp. 129–130, suggest that there were other credits to China by Russia in this period. The official Chinese data available to me indicate that there were no credits other than those herein mentioned.

equipment on the Chinese battlefront." [2] Also they could observe how China hurriedly transplanted factories and personnel to the interior; and this apparently influenced Russia to transplant some of her war industries behind the Urals, to gain greater security *vis-à-vis* Germany.

Outbreak of World War II in September 1939 brought a new situation for China. Russian aid slackened. The Russo-German pact of August 23 worried China because it showed Russia's pre-occupation with Europe and was followed by the Russian move into Eastern Poland and the attack on Finland. China wondered whether Russia was going to make a like pact with Japan at China's expense. The pact also worried Japan, because it was inconsistent with the German-Japanese anti-Comintern treaty of 1936.

But more events were to come that suggested a lessening of Russia's interest in help to China. When the Axis pact of Germany, Italy, and Japan was signed, September 27, 1940, Japan at once sent an emissary to Moscow to discuss a possible deal for direct or indirect Russian adherence to the pact. Russia was ready to consider a deal, if Japan paid enough, and seems to have demanded cession of Southern Sakhalin Island, some of the Kuriles, and territory in Manchuria—which Japan refused. On November 15 Russia indicated the breakdown of negotiations by denying that it had agreed to end its aid to China, and soon after announced that its policy to China "remains unchanged." [3] Japanese aims in signing the Axis pact had failed. Japan got nothing from Germany. Russia refused to stop helping China. Britain's reply was to reopen the Burma Road. And the United States was not intimidated—rather the contrary—and increased its aid to China.

Russia, however, did not at once make good on assurances of aid. There was delay in responding to China's request for better types of planes. But in February 1941 China was reported to have gotten 50 new Russian pursuit planes and 50 bombers. The American and British credits announced late in 1940 may have temporarily stimulated Russian aid. [4] The newly received planes raised China's hopes. China's military aviation was at a low ebb, with less than 70 planes at the beginning of 1941, and all of them obsolete in view of Japan's newer types. But the new Russian planes proved no match for the new Japanese Zero planes. The

Chinese air force suffered a severe defeat on April 2 near Chengtu. Besides planes, other supplies from Russia continued to come overland. On April 30, 1941, a member of Ambassador Johnson's staff, who lately had been in the northwest, reported that nearly 2,000 tons monthly of artillery and munitions were entering there. Also camel caravans were bringing in gasoline at the rate of nearly a million gallons yearly.[5]

In March–April 1941, Japanese Foreign Minister Yosuke Matsuoka visited Europe. His main object was to bring Russia to associate with the Berlin-Rome-Tokyo Axis, despite the rebuff a few months earlier. Japan was plotting a southward move against the British-Dutch possessions in Asia, and wanted to protect her rear. Matsuoka's first approach in Moscow was not too promising, so he went on to Berlin. Hitler wanted Japan to make that southward move. He felt that it would attract American attention to Asia and divert the United States from sending war supplies to Britain and from helping to police the Atlantic. Hitler did not want Japan to attack the United States. But he carefully kept from Japan the plans then being made for a German attack upon Russia after seizing the Balkans. On April 4, 1941, he made an unasked promise. Casually he told Matsuoka that, if there were a conflict between Japan and America, Germany would promptly take part.[6]

Matsuoka then returned to Moscow, where on April 13 he signed a five-year "neutrality" treaty with Russia. Each party was to respect the other's territorial integrity. By a declaration attached to this treaty, Russia and Japan both struck blows at China's integrity: Russia by agreeing to respect the territorial integrity of "Manchukuo," and Japan to do likewise as to the "Mongolian People's Republic," which China still claimed to be Chinese territory. Each party of course realized that the other's promises were potentially worthless. But for the time being it suited both to abide by the pact.

From Russia's standpoint Japan's assurance of neutrality proved to be good throughout the war, and thus a good bargain. Russia, fearful of German attack, viewed a deal with Germany's Axis partner, Japan, as necessary appeasement. Stalin seemed to show his true feelings at the send-off for Matsuoka at the Moscow railway station, when press correspondents heard him say, in substance, "Now that the Soviet Union and Japan have arranged their affairs, Japan will straighten out the East, the Soviet Union and Germany will take of Europe and later on between them they will take care of the Americans." Members of the German Embassy confirmed the substance of this.[7] But Hitler had no thought of acceding to Russia's worried moves of rapprochement with Germany. His reply came on June 22 when he attacked Russia. In April, however, even though German planners were busily preparing the attack on Russia, Hitler favored the Russo-Japanese neutrality pact. His idea was that Japan should be free to attack British possessions in Asia, and thus help to finish off Britain. But a few days after the attack on Russia, Hitler pressed Japan despite the neutrality treaty to move against Siberia. Japan coyly temporized.

Japan, on the surface of things, won major diplomatic gains. First, Russia agreed by treaty to remain neutral *vis-à-vis* Japan. To Japan, that assurance proved good until Russia violated it four years later by her attack a few days before the war ended. Russia's prolonged respect for that treaty was due to her need to put every effort into a struggle for survival in the face of Hitler's drive. Also Hitler verbally promised, with no specific *quid pro quo,* that Germany would join the conflict if Japan became embroiled with the United States. Hitler honored this promise in due course, even though Japan carefully concealed from Germany the plan to bomb Pearl Harbor, just as Germany kept from Japan her designs on Russia. The news of Pearl Harbor surprised Germany, as it did the United States.[8]

Thus the way was cleared for Japan to decide on July 2, ten days after Hitler's move against Russia, to go ahead with the southward advance. That fateful decision was to prove Japan's undoing, because Japan decided to act regardless of anything the United States might do.

China naturally was unhappy with the Russo-Japanese deal of April 1941. She feared stronger Japanese attacks on China, not knowing that Japan's policy was moving toward a southward advance. The Chinese Ambassador in Moscow took up the treaty with Molotov. To the protest against implied recognition of "Manchukuo," Molotov replied that the term was used for lack of a better word. He declared that the new treaty had nothing to do with China, that aid would continue, and that Russia's policy to China would remain unchanged so long as China continued fighting Japan. The Generalissimo's first reaction, however, that the Russo-Japanese pact presaged the virtual end of Russian aid to China, proved correct. The trickle of aid that continued was mainly to facilitate China's delivery of strategic goods to Russia, and shipments of military goods practically ceased. After Hitler attacked Russia in June 1941, Russia was understandably fearful of doing anything that might provoke Japan into attacking Siberia.

What about the Chinese Communists? Russia's quick change in appeasing Japan did not shock them at all. They dutifully declared on April 23 that "by this treaty the U.S.S.R. has not disappointed and will never disappoint China." [9] Long before, in the second half of 1938, the United Front began to break. The friction soon led to outright fighting, and to the government blockade of the Communists in the northwest.[10]

Yet even while the United Front was breaking down, Russian aid continued to flow to the National Government. On August 13, 1939, Ambassador Johnson reported that Russian supplies and aid went to them and not to the Chinese Communists. On January 30, 1941, the Generalissimo told him that "Soviet Russia has not been giving the Communist armies any assistance whatsoever in the way of personnel, equipment or finances." But, said the Generalissimo, the Third International at Moscow had directed the Communists to expand in China and to prolong the Sino-Japanese hostilities—that information having been obtained from a captured Communist general.[11] C. B. McLane, in a detailed study of evidence, concludes that in the war period the link between Moscow and Yenan was nominal; that while from time to time various persons, mostly Chinese, traveled between these centers, there is little indication that Russia kept an agent in Yenan or vice versa; that, however, communication was maintained; and that the Chinese Communist Party dutifully adapted to the Russian line.[12]

For Russia the Sino-Japanese struggle was a vicarious war. Russia aided China because her main objective in Asia in this period was to divert Japan from moving against Siberia. That took precedence over immediately pushing Communism in China. Hence Russian writers talked of the "fundamental improvements" which the National Government had made before the war, which made it possible to resist Japan, and did not mention past civil wars with the Communists. They praised Chiang and gave prominence to his statements. That attitude continued even after the bloody suppression of the Communist Fourth Army by government troops early in 1941, and changed only gradually thereafter.[13] This episode showed Russia's single-minded pursuit of national interest with daring, flexibility, deep calculation, and accurate appraisal of the international scene in the Far East.

To China, Russia's aid was important in the critical first two years of fighting. It gave both weapons and moral support. China's leaders, however, were not under illusions about Russian aid. A Chinese representative in Moscow told the American Embassy in September 1939 that China was building up appreciable reserves from Russian supplies, despite Russian pressure for immediate utilization. China was doing this so as not to become too dependent upon Russia and thus become vulnerable to possible future Russian threats to shut off supplies.[14] China's leaders were convinced that Russia would provide no more aid than was necessary for China to continue resistance against Japan. They realized that Russian imperialism was only in abeyance. A Chinese representative in Moscow told the American Embassy in July 1939, that "perhaps in the not too distant future the Soviet Union would replace Japan as 'enemy No. 1' in the Far East" because of its growing military and economic strength.[15]

MORE "LIFE-SAVING INJECTIONS" BY THE UNITED STATES

The American credit announced in December 1938 opened the way for more aid. But American opinion was divided, with isolationism still strong. It was far from easy for China to get the further credits she so badly needed.

By the Fall of 1939 most of the earlier credit was committed for purchases. Ambassador Hu Shih told Morgenthau on September 26 that China was much disturbed because, under enemy pressure, the Indochina authorities had to stop the transit of munitions, motor vehicles, and gasoline. Hu asked "another life-saving injection, in the form of a loan, to sustain morale." K. P. Chen was still in the United States, helping with operation of the 1938 credit and ready to negotiate for more aid. Roosevelt, when Morgenthau reported the Chinese request, told him to "do everything for him that we can get away with." [16]

The project of aid to China was again backed by Harry D. White. Long before the 1938 credit was fully committed, he urged more aid to China, along with aid to Latin America and Russia. In a memorandum of March 31, 1939, to Morgenthau he said, "The time is ripe to propose to Congress the extension of a $100 million ten year credit to be used by China for the purchase of whatever American products she wishes . . . A loan at this time would mean much to China's stiffened resistance and would offset the effects of the Administration's neutrality legislation." * Now, in a memorandum of November 22 to Morgenthau, he again favored a loan to China, saying that a credit of US$35 million based on tin exports, patterned after the wood oil credit, might be feasible. Such a loan to China, he said, "would materially strengthen her staying power against Japan, and decrease her dependence upon Russian assistance." [17] He mentioned, however, the risk of the Japanese blockade and also that extension of the area of Communist control in China might interfere with Chungking meeting its commitments. In another memorandum at about the same time White proposed using part of the American gold reserves, of which he felt there was a large surplus, *inter alia* for a loan to China.† White's views and efforts in 1938–1939 in support of China and his statement quoted above that American aid would decrease China's "dependence upon Russian assistance," are specially interesting in view of his later anti-Chinese attitude, for ex-

---

* The memorandum, which is among the papers of Harry D. White at the Princeton University Library, also favored trying to make a deal with Russia for a credit of US$250 million at 8 per cent interest, the excess of interest over the cost of borrowing to be applied on Russian debts to the American government and private American creditors. He said, "Such action will be notice to Germany that we intend to provide substantial economic support to the enemies of aggression. Japan will be more hesitant to join Germany and Italy in their plans of aggression." Also he thought such action would stiffen Britain.

† He proposed a law creating a "Gold Investment Committee." He argued that with American gold reserves approaching US$20 billion, and likely to stay around that figure, there was a big surplus over the US$8 billion he estimated to be needed for monetary reserves. Part of the surplus gold might then be used "to carry out our Latin American program, to make a loan to China, and to participate in reconstruction loans elsewhere after hostilities cease—all without additional appropriation of funds by Congress." The text of the plan is given in the Hearings before the Subcommittee to Investigate the Administration of the Internal Security Act and Other Internal Security Laws, of the Committee of the Judiciary, United States Senate, June 15, 1955, part 29, pp. 2339–2341.

ample, in blocking gold shipments to China in 1944–1945, and the fact that he later was charged with being a Communist or at least following the party line (see chapter XVII).*

Under Kung's instructions Chen asked in October for a credit of US$75 million to be based on tin exports. But negotiations moved slowly in the winter of 1939–1940. The total that the Export-Import Bank could lend to any one country was limited by law to US$30 million. China had repaid about US$3 million of the 1938 credit, and with over US$22 million outstanding, the maximum of new money China could get was thus about US$8 million in January 1940. But on February 7, the Senate Foreign Relations Committee approved a limit of US$20 million for any one country for loans "hereafter" and also an increase of the Bank's lending capacity by US$100 million. Chairman Key Pittman proposed this, saying, "There is a great desire on the part of the Administration to make a further loan to China." Chairman Jesse Jones of the Reconstruction Finance Corporation told the Committee he would consider a further loan to China "if an arrangement could be worked out where it looked as if the loan would be repaid." [18]

A month later Jones announced the US$20 million credit, and the agreement was signed April 20. The terms were a little more liberal than those for the previous loan of US$25 million. The Export-Import Bank dropped the requirement in the previous credit that China agree to spend in the United States, over and above the credit, a sum of equal amount. Interest was 4 per cent instead of 4½ per cent, and the money could be spent for commercial but not military planes. Chen reported that it was necessary to give the loan a strictly commercial character, in view of American politics and the neutrality law which forbade credits to countries at "war." The primary security was export of tin.† There had been some question of insisting also on security of

---

* In 1938–1939 Russia was aiding Nationalist China, but Russia's line changed to strong criticism in 1943. The views and efforts of White and some of his associates also shifted in this later period.

† Chen, acting under instructions, was unable to get Washington not to insist again upon a Bank of China guarantee. This reflected on China's credit; and clearly that bank, which was mainly a commercial bank although in part state-owned, should not have been expected indefinitely to guarantee governmental debts. But Washington wanted to be able to claim that the debt had all possible security, and Chen was unwilling to press the point.

tungsten (wolfram). Chen, however, persuaded Morgenthau to have this waived, pointing out that China needed its other exports to pay for munitions and also to make deliveries to Russia. Morgenthau said in April 1940, ". . . if we tie them up, we simply tie them up in a nice pink ribbon and turn them over to Russia."[19]

In China the loan was welcomed with expressions of gratitude. In Japan the Foreign Office spokesman characterized it, translations varying, as an "unfriendly act," or "not to be regarded as friendly action towards Japan." The puppet regime was slated soon to be set up at Nanking. The spokesman said, "At a moment when a Chinese Central Government aspiring to sway the new destiny of China is about to come into existence, it is a very undesirable thing to see the United States Government decide on another of its old measures in aid of the Chiang Kai-shek regime."[20]

In June 1940, T. V. Soong came to Washington with a broad mission to seek aid. Soong asked, *inter alia,* for a credit of US$50 million secured on exports of tungsten, to buy nonmilitary goods and to improve transit to China. The credit was needed because the funds available under the two earlier credits were about exhausted. Roosevelt was anxious to aid China. But he had to move cautiously, because of the terrible uncertainty about the outcome of Hitler's drive on France and Britain and also because of the election campaign. On August 15, Soong conferred with Morgenthau and Hornbeck. The Secretary said that he had found difficult the problem of responding to China's desires and indicated that he had not so far been able to find a way to help. Soong told Hornbeck after the meeting that he was "disappointed and greatly worried." He said that unhappily China "is nearing the breaking point on the material side and is desperately in need of assistance." Hornbeck said he should not regard the negative results so far as conclusive. Morgenthau had referred Soong to Jesse Jones, head of the Federal Loan Agency. Jones talked of $5 million, a figure so small that it would have done more harm than good if announced. At this point China's prospects for aid were at low ebb. On September 12 Morgenthau remarked to Stimson, "Well, poor old T. V. Soong is here and we can't do a damn thing for him."[21]

When negotiations dragged during the summer of 1940, there was talk of a triangular deal with Russia. The United States would buy manganese, chromite, mercury, mica, and other strategic materials from Russia, making certain advance payments. Russia in turn would use the funds to provide war materials to China, which the United States could not do under the neutrality law. Some passages in the Morgenthau diaries suggest that President Roosevelt had suggested the idea to Soong, who relayed it to Morgenthau.[22] But the seed of the idea may have been planted by K. P. Chen, since his original instructions when seeking American aid in 1938 had suggested this possibility.

This episode showed how far the United States Treasury was getting into foreign affairs. It made plenty of trouble within the Administration. Secretary Hull and Under-Secretary Sumner Welles opposed the scheme. American relations with Russia, restored in 1933, had deteriorated. Russia's nonaggression pact with Hitler had helped to bring on World War II. Welles asked Morgenthau to wait. But after some delaying, Morgenthau and Jesse Jones got the President's permission to call in Ambassador Oumansky for a discussion. The State Department again objected. Welles told Morgenthau that he had gotten nowhere in trying to get Russia to allow transit of DC-3 commercial planes to China via Siberia, to save dismantling them and shipping them by sea. Russia feared to give Japan any excuse to attack in Siberia while Hitler was a menace in Europe. Welles also told him that in talks with Oumansky about treatment of American interests in Russia "the Russians have taken the most completely uncooperative attitude after the first two conversations and we haven't gotten anywhere." Also he said that what was told to the Russian Embassy went at once to Germany and Italy and probably also through Germany to Japan.

But Morgenthau went ahead. He said he had reached a point "where people like Mr. Welles and the rest of them, I am going to fight him tooth and nail up to the point that this place gets too hot for one of us . . . Now if Mr. Welles wants to go up against Jesse Jones and me and the President, okay, let's see what happens."

When Ambassador Oumansky called on September 20 he told Morgenthau that aid to China was limited by availability of materials and not by finance; also that Russia had offered to sell 800,000 tons of manganese to the United States in the previous year but had been turned down. Relations of the United States with China, he said, were good, as were Russia's relations with China. But as to Russia's relations with the United States, that side of the triangle was a "blank." On September 25, under instructions from Moscow, he offered to sell the materials to the United States, but made it clear that this had no connection with Soviet-China transactions. So the matter was dropped.[23]

But meanwhile the prospect of a direct American credit to China brightened. On September 13 Assistant Secretary of State Adolph Berle told Morgenthau that the President had approved a purchase credit of say US$20 million. A few days later the matter came to a head, thanks to the Japanese military encroachment on Indochina. The State Department wanted to announce a loan at once, as a counter-measure against Japan's move. Morgenthau thought that the time to press Japan had been before she acted in Indochina, when she might have "stopped, looked and listened." Jesse Jones proposed a credit of US$20 million, but both Hull and Morgenthau wanted US$25 million. On September 25 the loan of US$25 million was announced, and Jones left with Soong the implication that when that was gone there would be more.[24] The terms were similar to those of the former credits, with a more liberal schedule of repayment. This time the credit was extended to the Central Bank and secured by exports of tungsten. Once again, the money could not be spent for munitions.*

On October 18, Generalissimo Chiang again asked help. The purchase credit lately announced, he told Ambassador Johnson, was helpful. But he wanted planes and if possible American volunteers. He feared, more than the Japanese army, "the defiant Communists." Johnson commented eloquently in his telegram to Washington. China had been fighting desperately against enormous odds. "All along," he said, "both Japanese and Communists have stated that our aid would not go beyond sympathy and moral help." The Chinese people find it hard to believe that the United States will not prevent the closing of the Burma Road (whose reopening the British almost simultaneously announced), "thus shutting them completely off from outside assistance and force

---

* The Central Bank instead of the Bank of China was to guarantee the repayment. This clause was not proper since certainly it was not the function of a central bank to guarantee governmental obligations, though in some cases the Central Bank had done so before the hostilities but over my protest.

them to choose between the Japanese and Communism." The Russians, they believe, "would be more likely to give positive aid to a Communist China if our help is not forthcoming." Johnson felt that, "Our prestige in the Far East is directly challenged," and asked, "Are we going to abandon everything that we have stood for?" Five days later he underlined his views:

> . . . the slogan, "All aid short of war," which has come so frequently from the United States has a discouraging effect upon a people who for three years have been fighting desperately against invasion in a struggle which they identify with our interests. This is especially true when such aid is offered only at a high cost which is draining the country of the money and resources which might otherwise back the currency and prevent soaring prices. We give nothing, neither life nor treasure, to help those who are fighting against those who, if they succeed, must inevitably unite to fall upon us backed by the accumulated might of their conquests. We cannot expect this praiseworthy activity to continue in China nor in England where the people are being drained of their economic life to reimburse us for the means which they need to maintain themselves against conquest. Either we are asleep or we show a callous and dangerous disregard for the effects of this kind of a smug attitude if we really believe that "aid short of war" is enough. We should quickly awaken from this diffidence lest we find a completely unsympathetic world looking on unable to give us even the flimsy aid that we have been willing to give when we ourselves are attacked.[25]

In a further telegram of October 24 Johnson said that ". . . failure of the United States and Great Britain to afford timely aid to China may in the end result in Communist ascendancy in China." Both factions, he believed, were committed to continue the fight against Japan. But he warned, ". . . such a policy probably will benefit the Communists more than the existing government because the former is afforded the opportunity of consolidating its position in a country whose economic and social systems continue to deteriorate under the relentless impact of the Japanese military machine."[26]

Chiang's appeal and Johnson's support of it led to two concrete results. But only after delays. The first result was the announcement on November 30 of credits of US$100 million, half for purchases and half for currency support. Again the United States moved to counter Japan's aggression—this time, Japanese recognition of the puppet regime in Central China. The terms of the purchase credit, which again was granted to the Central Bank, were similar to those of the other credits. A further and very important result was to promote action before the end of the year which led to organizing the American Volunteer Group (AVG), Chennault's Flying Tigers.

MORE BRITISH AND FRENCH PURCHASE CREDITS

American support of China by granting the US$25 million credit encouraged Britain to grant in March 1939 the currency credit decribed in chapter IX.

Four months later the situation in China was especially critical. Aggressive Japanese measures against the Tientsin British Concession were damaging confidence. The exchange market had slumped badly and was almost in panic. Japan was insisting publicly that Britain stop aid to China. A joint Anglo-Japanese statement of July 24 was widely taken as British appeasement (see chapter IX). Nevertheless, on July 20 Ambassador Quo Tai-chi was told in London that Britain would grant a further purchase credit. On July 31 British Ambassador Clark Kerr telegraphed London from Chungking that Britain must not fail to grant the credit, to offset the bad impression of the July 24 statement. The next day Foreign Secretary Lord Halifax told Quo that ". . . it would be easier for this country to adhere to the policy of assistance to China if the Chinese Government for their part exercised discretion and refrained from giving undue publicity. We had to make the best of an ugly set of facts, in which simultaneous difficulties faced us in the Far East and Europe." [27]

The credit agreement, for £2,859,000 to buy British goods, was signed August 18, on the eve of World War II. The Board of Trade guaranteed payment to the exporters. Interest was 5 per cent, and payments were spread over 10 years. There was no specific security of Chinese goods, but it was understood China would earmark enough exports to cover the payments due. Because the Americans had insisted on a Bank of China guarantee, the British also required this, but stated that otherwise they would not have asked for it.

Again in December 1940 Britain announced a credit, for £5 million, to buy goods in the sterling area. This time the interest was only 3½ per cent with payments again on a 10-year basis.

China agreed to ship bristles, tea, silk, antimony, or other agreed goods to provide for payments. There was no Bank of China guarantee.

Altogether British purchase credits to China in 1938–1941 were £8,359,000. These credits, like the American grants, helped China to get a variety of useful goods and relieved some of the strain on foreign currency resources. The whole of these credits was used, excepting £277,000 of the £500,000 credit announced in December 1938. About £6.7 million or three-fourths was used by the end of 1945 and the remainder by June 1948, but only a small part has been repaid.[28]

France was the first Western nation to arrange wartime credits to China, by the guarantee early in 1938 of 80 per cent of advances for railway construction (see chapter IV). A French group and the China Development Finance Corporation, by an agreement of December 11, 1939, undertook to provide a further railway credit up to 480 million French francs (about US$10 million). This was to finance a railway from the Kunming terminus of the Indochina Railway to Suifu on the upper Yangtze River above Chungking. There was to be an 80 per cent guarantee by the French Government's Credit Insurance Department. Despatches of the Domei News Service from Nanking and Tokyo, May 29 and 31, 1940, reported that the puppet regime at Nanking repudiated the loan. During the first part of 1940 the French group placed orders in France for a considerable part of the materials required. But these remained there in storage when in May–June Hitler overran France. Soon afterward Japan's encroachments blocked that route for shipments to China. So it was not possible to proceed with the project as contemplated. Apparently a substantial amount was advanced under the agreement, but definite figures are not available.[29]

THE TRY TO BUY AMERICAN MILITARY PLANES

Part of the enemy plan to break China's will to resist was heavy indiscriminate bombing of all sizable cities of Free China. Foreseeing the need for air defense, Chennault and others wanted China to buy more planes. In 1938–1939, before the European war, deliveries were obtainable.

China's reserves of foreign currency were low, as was current foreign currency income. An air force is an expensive affair under any conditions—for planes in the line, replacements, fuel, ammunition, parts, and ground equipment. Nevertheless, China could have afforded some planes. But the government wasted its chance. When week after week went by with nothing accomplished, it was highly frustrating to Chennault in particular, and also to others of us who were pushing for planes, including W. H. Donald, Australian adviser to Chiang Kai-shek. There was inertia and ignorance on the part of members of the Aviation Commission and other high officials. Also a factor was rivalry of American sellers of planes, whose partisans within the Chinese Government showed unaccustomed zeal in forwarding the cause of one or opposing that of another. The outcome was failure to buy planes that could have checked the bombing. Instead, an airplane assembly plant and factory was set up at Loiwing in China's extreme west, which could not deliver anything soon and in any case could not provide the late model planes needed to fight the enemy successfully.

When heavy bombing of Chungking began on May 3, 1939, China could offer no effective defense. That city, with a reported 268 raids in 1939–1941, became the most bombed city in the world until the record at London and Malta. Raids were concentrated in the Summer, as almost constant haze from September to April led to the saying that there the dogs barked at the sun. The first two raids caused heavy loss of life and property, resulting mostly from fire in the congested city. Thereafter losses were less, because of the remarkable system of shelters and the effective net of warning stations. When the government moved to the wartime capital in the Fall of 1938, the characteristic sound heard everywhere was the chipping of rock by masons' hammers, interspersed with black powder explosions, as dugouts were built in solid rock on which the city stood. The city was honeycombed with caves that could accommodate the larger part of the population. The warning system was excellent—probably the best in the world at the time. Spies with radios near enemy bases spotted the take-off and movements of enemy planes, telling the number and the direction of flight. This, along with advice on the progress of the flights, was relayed to air defense headquarters in the threatened cities. Warnings there were given in the early stages by signals raised and lowered in high places, and then by sirens. People who could not take shelter had time to disperse to the countryside. The morale in Chungking was high, despite losses, at this stage of air bombardment. It had a way of stirring up the people to angry determination to resist. The clean-up, fire-control, and repair services were admirable. Yet there was a limit to the punishment that human nature could take, and there was danger that the country might come to view the future as hopeless unless China could find some means to check these largely unopposed bombings.

The building of air defense remained a high priority for China in mid-1940, when T. V. Soong reached Washington in search of aid.* He asked for US$40 million for military planes and US$30 million for munitions. But at that time Europe's crisis held first attention. France had surrendered and Britain's fate hung in the balance. The United States was characteristically unready. Earlier, China could have bought for prompt delivery all the American planes she could afford, even though output was pathetically small judged by the needs that developed with World War II. But now deliveries were booked far ahead for Britain and for the American army. Even if China had ample money, which she did not, she could not get a priority. For months, despite sympathy for China, every plea for planes and money to buy them seemed to us to fall on deaf ears. But we persisted, feeling that American opinion was changing. In September came the destroyers-bases deal with Britain, and this was heartening to China.

In October Generalissimo Chiang sent Chennault to Washington accompanied by Major General P. T. Mow of the Chinese air force. They brought with them full details of the aviation situation in China—about planes, equipment, airfields, pilots, ground personnel, et cetera. Also they brought late data as to Japanese aviation. Chennault told me at the time that the American army authorities whom he could contact were not very interested in learning what they could from him about Japan's capabilities, nor did they take seriously his warning about a greatly improved Japanese plane, the famous Zero. Two Japa-

---

* The reason for his coming then was found primarily in financial developments described in the next chapter. But his mission was to seek military as well as financial aid. I was assisting him for a year in Washington.

nese intimately connected with wartime aviation wrote in 1956
that after outbreak of the Pacific War they learned that the
Allies were astonished and caught unaware by the Zero's performance, although it had been in combat in China for over
a year.[30] The brilliant success of Chennault's Flying Tigers
against Japanese planes in Burma and West China after Pearl
Harbor was based on his careful study of enemy planes and
tactics. It contrasted with tragic failures of American and British
plane operations in the early part of the war in the Philippines,
Malaya, and the South Seas. Some at least of these failures could
have been avoided had Chennault been listened to in 1940 and
early 1941.

In November we began a series of discussions in Washington,
to prepare a program of aid in aviation for Soong to urge upon
the American Government.* Chennault and Mow reported that
China had only 37 fighter planes, and none that could cope with
Japan's Zeros. The only bombers available were 31 of slow Russian types with difficult flying characteristics, that could not
be used at night and could be used in daytime only with fighter
escort. Anti-aircraft equipment was inadequate and badly worn.
As to pilots the situation was better. China had 480 pilots ready
or nearly ready for action, and a like number who could be made
ready within a few months. In contrast they stated that Japan
had 968 planes in China exclusive of Manchuria, and 120 in
Indochina. These included late type fighters and bombers, fast
and well-armed. Japan had well-trained pilots and an effective
ground organization. But Japanese bases were vulnerable to air
attack because in a hostile countryside they had no adequate
warning net.

On November 25 Soong proposed to the American authorities
an aviation program aimed at protection of Chungking and of
the Burma Road as the first priority. It called for 250 fighters
and 100 interceptors with 25 per cent monthly replacements;
150 two-engined bombers with 15 per cent monthly replacements; 10 transport planes; 190 training planes; and such items
as spare parts, antiaircraft guns and equipment, gasoline, and

---

* Mrs. Young recalls that these discussions were largely held in our apartment,
and that although she was consigned to another room because of the secrecy, she
heard most of what took place because Chennault's deafness made it necessary
to talk with a loud voice.

ammunition. To carry out the program effectively, China would need 200 additional flying instructors and about 150 American personnel for maintenance, et cetera. On December 4 the State Department told Soong and Ambassador Hu that steps were being taken to provide 50 planes "within the comparatively near future." It was clear, however, that any large supply of planes was not easy because of the intense demand to aid Britain and build up American strength.[31]

On December 17 Roosevelt revealed the idea of what came to be Lend-Lease aid. Isolationism was weakening and public opinion approved. At first the idea of giving China planes, especially those that might bomb Japan, met with enthusiastic response in the highest quarters. On December 19 the President asked Secretaries Hull, Stimson, Knox, and Morgenthau to work out a plan. But General Marshall and the air force staff argued that planes given to China would be at Britain's expense, and that Britain needed them more. That view finally prevailed.[32]

Finally China got 100 P-40B fighters early in 1941. Britain released them from her first quarter deliveries, against promise of 200 of a later model in May–July.[33] China paid for these herself, as Lend-Lease was not then available. The planes were not of the latest model and still had to be equipped with armament and radio, but they would do. They were shipped from the United States in the spring and reached Rangoon beginning in June 1941. They proved of vital importance, because they gave a basis for organizing the Flying Tigers.

LEND-LEASE AT LAST

The Lend-Lease act became law on March 11, 1941. Four days later the President made an address in which he said, "China . . . expresses the magnificent will of millions of plain people to resist the dismemberment of their Nation. China, through the Generalissimo, Chiang Kai-shek, asks our help. America has said that China shall have our help." [34]

Lend-Lease solved China's problems of paying for needed armaments. Earlier, that would have been an inestimable boon. But now a shortage of goods replaced the former shortage of finance. On March 31, Soong presented a comprehensive request for aid of three main kinds: equipment of an air force of 1,000

planes, 700 pursuits, and 300 bombers; modern armaments to
equip 30 divisions; and improvement of communications with
China via the Burma Road and the projected Burma Railway.
Also there were such items as those for arsenal materials, medical
supplies, and cloth.

The War Department promptly studied this request and on
April 22 made a preliminary report to Currie, who had been
charged with expediting Lend-Lease aid to China. This report,
reflecting high policy, listed items "which if available could be
supplied to China without interfering to any appreciable extent
with U.S. Army and British programs." The War Department
felt that details and specifications needed for procurement were
lacking as to many items, creating a "general air of vagueness
and unreality," except as to aviation where Chennault and Mow
had stated exactly what was wanted. But planes and many items
of artillery and ammunition would be in very short supply for
a year or more. Certain items, however, mainly trucks, railway
supplies, and arsenal materials, could be spared.[35]

Meanwhile events added to the urgency of China's need. On
April 13 Russia and Japan signed their "neutrality pact," which
caused anger and disappointment in China, and fear that Japan
would now be freed for further drives. In Shanghai there was
an outbreak of enemy-sponsored terrorism, kidnaping of members of the Bank of China staff from their dormitory in the
International Settlement, and weakness in the foreign exchange
market.

On April 17 Ambassador Johnson telegraphed that the Generalissimo was being embarrassed by the lack of concrete American aid despite the promises made. The Russians in China were
spreading the word that these promises were meaningless. And
Morgenthau was insisting on the right to dole out the American
contribution to China's Stabilization Fund at not over US$5 mil-
lion monthly (see chapter X). Clearly the Generalissimo's pride
was hurt, said Johnson, and there was "a deep Chinese feeling
that China has won a right to be treated as an equal among the
nations fighting for their rights." The Generalissimo, Johnson
reported, wanted a definite statement with a schedule of war
materials to be provided, and in particular he was anxious for
planes.[36]

Commenting on this situation, Hornbeck in a memorandum of April 24, pointed out that China had gotten American loans and credits of US$175 million in about four years. Compared with the vast program of aid to Britain on which the United States had embarked, he said, ". . . the amount and the types of aid which we have given to China . . . appear insignificant in proportions . . . Suppose the United States had in 1937 or 1938 embarked upon a program of 'all-out' aid to China, how different might be the situation with regard to China (and Japan and our problems in the Pacific and in the world) now." An appraisal of the situation would show that "we have helped China somewhat and that we have hindered Japan somewhat," but, "Japan's present ability to continue her efforts in China and to give thought now to possible 'bigger and better aggressions' and even to 'war with the United States' is a consequence in no small part of the practically unrestricted access which Japan enjoyed for more than three long years to the rich and most helpful markets of the United States . . ." [37] The United States was heavily buying Japan's silk without restriction, and was supplying the major part of Japan's imports of oil, scrap iron, and automobile parts, and about 40 per cent of her needs for metals, cotton, and wood pulp.

On April 26 the President sent word to the Generalissimo that he had approved a list of items valued at about US$45 million, comprising railway and communications equipment, trucks, gasoline and oil, arsenal supplies, and textiles. Supply of airplanes and other articles was under study. A follow-up message indicated the tight situation as to aircraft.[38] On May 6 the President formally made China eligible for Lend-Lease, declaring in accordance with the law that the defense of China was "vital to the defense of the United States."

The War Department at once got busy on items immediately available. A first shipment of 300 2½-ton trucks left New York for Rangoon in the first part of May. Further items totaling US$49 million were approved in May, though largely for shipment by mid-1942. As negotiations proceeded the War Department complained, however, that China wanted "the biggest and newest equipment regardless of availability or practicability." There was friction over the kinds of equipment to be supplied.

These happenings helped to stimulate sending to China in the Fall of 1941 the American military mission headed by Brigadier General John Magruder, a former military attaché in China, an important part of whose work would relate to Lend-Lease.[39]

A letter of May 8 from the Office of Production Management to the Director of Procurement of the Treasury Department showed an attitude unfriendly to aid to China. It gave wrong data as to the asserted inadequacy of the Burma Road, alleged that China had failed to repay loans, said Lend-Lease goods might be diverted to Japan, and concluded that the United States should carefully weigh the situation before disturbing in China's behalf its normal economy or military program. The letter circulated widely in the Lend-Lease organization. Currie sent it from the White House to the State Department. That Department prepared a careful comment which it sent to the other offices concerned. It cited the series of statements by the President and other high officials declaring the policy of giving fullest aid to China and other nations resisting aggression. The President had assured the Generalissimo that a wide variety of goods had already been allocated to China and shipment of available goods would be expedited. China was taking steps to improve the Burma Road, and already the movement was exceeding the limits mentioned in the letter. As to debt, China's record "will be found to compare favorably with that of other countries including those of more advanced economic development," and China, as Jesse Jones had publicly stated, was meeting all its obligations to the United States. As to diversion to Japan, there was nothing to indicate that China had violated or was likely to violate its undertaking pursuant to the Lend-Lease Act. The State Department concluded that the United States should live up to its pledges to China, which already had resisted Japan for four years. The letter of the Office of Production Management, said the Department, was contrary to the policy of the American Government.[40]

On July 7 Undersecretary of State Welles wrote to Hopkins to urge speeding up the sending of munitions and supplies to China. He recognized the needs of other areas, but pointed out that Germany's attack on Russia two weeks earlier might lead Japan to embark on more aggressive action, and that this made it specially important to render "effective aid to China in the shortest possible time." Such aid also would help China's morale. Welles sent to General Marshall and Admiral Stark copies of his letter.[41]

Urging both China's need and the American interest, I wrote to Hornbeck on August 11 after returning to Chungking. "On a time basis," I said, "China stands where the countries of Europe were in September 1918. Morale under bombing and ruthless enemy action is truly remarkable. While in that regard I see no material deterioration after a year's absence, it is clear that the economic and financial situation has become much worse . . . The risk of asking China to wait too long . . . is very real." As to the American interest, I said that "it seems certain that very considerable American aviation forces . . . will be needed in this part of the world—either for defence of the Philippines," which I thought was not being sufficiently strengthened, or to strengthen Chennault's volunteer group. So far China's getting planes was largely a result of concessions by the British, and I hoped that the American army "might take a more liberal attitude."

On August 26 Washington announced the military mission to China. At first the thought was to have General Magruder consult with the Chinese military authorities about what to do if both countries were engaged with a common enemy. But that failed of approval. The mission was to aid China in procurement of Lend-Lease goods, to train Chinese personnel in their use and maintenance, to aid in obtaining their orderly flow to the Chinese forces, and to aid in creating an adequate line of communications. Magruder reached Chungking on the Double Tenth, October 10, 1941, the 30th anniversary of the Chinese Republic, and was warmly welcomed.[42]

On October 22 an important cargo went forward on the S.S. *Tulsa:* 48 75-mm guns, 11,000 Thompson submachine guns, 500 Bren guns, 100 .50-caliber machine guns, ammunition for the guns, and 35 scout cars. This shipment was regarded in Washington as a real sacrifice, considering American needs in the Philippines and elsewhere. By September 90 per cent of the materials for the Burma-China railway had been ordered, and the War Department had bought 125 miles of abandoned narrow-gauge railway in Colorado and begun to dismantle it for shipment to Rangoon.[43]

As Japan became more and more aggressive in the second half of 1941, Washington went ahead with further plans for China's air force. On July 23 the President approved equipping, manning, and maintaining for China a 500-plane force. The plan looked toward bombing Japan before the end of 1941, but shortage of planes and trained personnel put plans forward to the Spring of 1942. Chinese pilots began reaching Thunderbird Field in Arizona for training in October. Also there was to be a second AVG, but the first of its personnel were stranded in Australia when war broke out December 7/8.[44]

In 1941 total Lend-Lease aid "furnished to China," according to American Treasury data, was US$25,821,000 or 1.7 per cent of the total to all countries. Lend-Lease was so slow to start that China bought supplies of many kinds, especially for needs of the air force, from the proceeds of the Export-Import Bank credits. These supplies were shipped to China and proved invaluable later after the Japanese cut the Burma route early in 1942. Lend-Lease comprised both goods and services. Shipments to China began with 7,552 tons in May and totaled 66,675 tons through December.[45] Many trucks and other goods reached China before the Burma Road was closed in the Spring of 1942. Spares and supplies for Chennault were ordered. But little arrived for him until well after outbreak of the Pacific War, though what did get through was highly important. Planes were ordered for CNAC and began arriving early in 1942. Discussions about re-equipping 30 Chinese divisions under Lend-Lease began in the Summer of 1941, but nothing effective was done until much later. The services provided to China included the antimalaria mission of the Public Health Service; the Arnstein road mission in the Summer of 1941; the sending of road experts who got caught in Manila when the Pacific War broke out; and the training of Chinese fliers in Arizona.

Had China gotten more American planes, they could have been flown from Burma to China. A way could have been found to move in the more urgently needed armaments. But there was a bottleneck in Burma for heavy items that had to enter by the railway to Lashio and thence by road. That bottleneck became more and more serious as Lend-Lease shipments reached Rangoon. Magruder urged in the latter part of 1941 tighter control on shipments until the stockpile there could be cut to more manageable size. Next he suggested suspending purchase and shipment until items in Burma could be inventoried. Soon after this came the Japanese occupation of Burma.

The smallness of aid to China in 1941, US$26 million compared with US$1.5 billion to other countries, mainly Britain and Russia, reflected the "Europe first" policy. Hitler's containment and defeat was the prior strategic aim. Also American leaders and opinion were oriented mainly toward Europe, and at the start Lend-Lease was mostly thought of as "aid to Britain." They favored helping China, but China was remote and almost unreal, and some elements in official circles were unfriendly. The men with the say, especially in the War Department, thought scarce items would do more good in Europe or in arming the United States. Many felt Britain had a greater stake than the United States in keeping China a belligerent. Significantly the first planes for the Flying Tigers were released by Britain from its allocation, against delivery of a later model, rather than directly from American production lines. Yet in 1941 a beginning was made, valuable to China and promising for the future. Of special importance was the cooperation of the War and Navy Departments in helping to arm and munition the first 100 planes for Chennault, and in allowing skilled pilots and other personnel to leave the American services to join him in China.

THE FLYING TIGERS

By the latter part of 1940 Chennault had concluded that use of American pilots and ground crews in China was a key part of any successful aviation program for China. China's leaders agreed. But there were serious obstacles, apart from getting the planes. American laws were strict. While the language was not always clear, there was risk that an American serving in the forces of a foreign belligerent would be subject to fine or prison or loss of citizenship. As the fighting in China progressed, however, the State Department came to take a more liberal view than in mid-1937, and in January 1940, held that acceptance of service in China as aviation instructors by Americans not connected with the armed services was a private matter between them and China, so long as they did not join the combat forces.[46]

The War Department, however, in July 1940, notified retired officers that the Constitution forbids their serving as civilian instructors of foreign military personnel.* This raised a question whether Chennault could continue serving China. Fortunately the matter was handled so as to avoid discontinuance of his work.

It was an index of the changing attitude of Americans toward China's struggle, and toward international matters in general, that by the end of 1940 leaders in Washington were ready to cooperate in formation of the American Volunteer Group (AVG). A leader in pushing China's cause was Frank Knox, Secretary of the Navy, and Secretary of War Henry L. Stimson was favorable. Roosevelt and Morgenthau gave the idea their blessing.

On January 2, 1941, Chennault proposed a detailed plan for organization of a group of American airmen for China. This comprised both air and ground personnel, a total of about 250 men. His memorandum concluded, ". . . it is desired to emphasize the point that a group of American pilots cannot operate efficiently and successfully in China unless supported by American technical and clerical personnel and supplied with adequate operating equipment and facilities."

The plan devised was that the Americans were to be engaged by the Central Aircraft Manufacturing Company (CAMCO), an American corporation organized under the China Trade Act which operated the airplane factory near the Burma border. Active in putting the plan into effect were William D. Pawley, later Ambassador to Peru and to Brazil under the Truman Administration, and Bruce Leighton, a former Commander in the American Navy. The company's counsel first raised with us some questions about the applicability of the American laws on engaging Americans who would engage in combat duty. He wanted to try to get the law amended. But the company finally decided to go ahead. In a memorandum of January 29 I wrote that "in practice the American authorities are prepared to close their eyes if it is possible to avoid raising issues with which they will be forced to deal."

* The Constitution (Article I, section 9, clause 8) provides that persons holding "any office of profit or trust" under the United States shall not, without the consent of Congress, "accept of any present, emolument, office or title of any kind whatever, from any king, prince, or foreign state."

For weeks we discussed the problems and worked on drafting the contract, and on April 15 it finally was signed. It set forth China's intention to establish "three advanced instruction and training units," that is, three squadrons, under an "American supervisor" (Chennault). CAMCO was to engage the necessary personnel and pay all necessary expenses. being covered from a revolving fund set up in a New York bank. CAMCO also agreed to help assemble and service the planes in the field, subject however to this not interfering with present or future production programs of the factory. CAMCO was not to be obligated to do anything in violation of American law.

Recruitment was a problem. The job to be done by the group was no matter for flying adventurers, but rather for men trained in the air forces of the army and navy. Both services were rapidly expanding and did not wish to release personnel. As to this and the next developments, Chennault wrote:

The military were violently opposed to the whole idea of American volunteers in China. I tried to convince them of the large return in tactics, intelligence, and equipment evaluation they would get from a small investment in personnel. Many countries had tested their air strength in combat through the device of volunteers under a foreign flag—the Russians in China and Spain; the Germans and Italians in Spain—but nobody in the Navy and Munitions buildings would buy it . . .

It took direct personal intervention from President Roosevelt to pry the pilots and ground crews from the Army and Navy. On April 15, 1941, an unpublicized executive order went out under his signature, authorizing reserve officers and enlisted men to resign from the Army Air Corps, Naval and Marine Air Services for the purpose of joining the American Volunteer Group in China . . .

Orders went out to all military airfields, signed by Secretary Knox and General Arnold, authorizing bearers of certain letters freedom of the post, including permission to talk with all personnel. Field commanders were astonished when our mufti-clad recruiters appeared and enraged when they discovered the purpose of the visit was to lure men out of the services. Several sputtering commanders called Washington long distance for confirmation of their orders . . .

Their offer was a one-year contract with CAMCO to "manufacture, repair, and operate aircraft" at salaries ranging from $250 to $750 a month. Traveling expenses, thirty days leave with pay, quarters, and $30 additional for rations were specified. They would be subject to summary dismissal by written notice for insubordination, habitual use of drugs or alcohol, illness not incurred in line of duty, malingering, and revealing confidential information. Before the end of the A.V.G., I had to dismiss at least one man for every cause except revealing confidential information. A system of minor fines was initiated for minor offenses.

There was no mention in the contract of a five-hundred-dollar bonus for every Japanese plane destroyed. Volunteers were told simply that there was a rumor that the Chinese government would pay $500 for each confirmed Jap plane. They could take the rumor for what it was worth. It turned out to be worth exactly $500 per plane . . .

I had originally planned to give each pilot a final personal check, but in the hectic rush to get the group under way, I had to abandon the idea. We made one last desperate attempt to get six trained staff officers from the Air Corps, but Arnold was adamant. I pleaded for three and finally for a single officer as group executive, but Arnold stuck to his theme that the loss of even one staff officer would cripple the Air Corps expansion program. Later Air Corps headquarters bitterly criticized the A.V.G. and its successors in China for their lack of staff work. Not until the middle of 1943 did the Army send me any staff officers. In the meantime I had to use whatever American adventurers I could find knocking about loose in the Orient . . .

I flew to San Francisco on United Air Lines and met the first contingent of the A.V.G. in the Mark Hopkins Hotel on July 7, the fourth anniversary of the Double Seventh, the night the Sino-Japanese war began. Nobody who saw that odd assortment of young men, looking slightly ill at ease and uncertain in their new civilian clothes, could have possibly imagined that in a few months they would be making history. The first group left on July 10 aboard the Dutch ship *Jaegersfontaine*. Japanese intelligence was not fooled by passports claiming occupations of musician, student, clerk, banker, etc., with a leader who was a farmer. The Japanese radio announced that the first group of American volunteer pilots planning to fight in China had left San Francisco by ship.

"That ship will never reach China," the Japanese radio chortled. "It will be sunk."

West of Hawaii passengers on the *Jaegersfontaine* spotted two warships, steaming in loose escort formation. Navy pilots identified them as the U.S. cruisers *Salt Lake City* and *Northampton*. The cruisers stuck with the Dutch boat as it swung far south of the regular shipping lanes to avoid the Japanese bases in the Carolines. In the Torres Straits off Australia a Dutch cruiser picked up the job and convoyed the liner to Singapore.

I left San Francisco on July 8 . . . As the big flying boat roared into the air over San Francisco Bay, I settled comfortably in my seat, confident for the first time in my battle against the Japanese that I had everything I needed to defeat them.[47]

With the conclusion on April 15 of the arrangements for AVG, and the signature on April 25 of the Sino-American-British stabilization loan agreements, I left Washington for China in May. Reaching Rangoon on June 18, I found that most of the first precious shipment of planes was lying crated on the docks, in piles vulnerable to sabotage by the numerous enemy agents who infested the place. At once I had the planes dispersed to safe places until they could be assembled. A British dock official at Rangoon was irked by all the fuss. He did not see any cause for worry, because it was "only a lot of Chinese and Japanese fighting each other way off in China" and there was no danger at Rangoon. I remember warning him that as I saw it he was likely to be bombed within six months. It happened that six months proved right almost to the day, as Rangoon was first raided December 23.

When Chennault returned to China in July he faced a huge task of establishing bases and training his polyglot group for combat. He was able to arrange with the RAF for use of a paved airfield near Toungoo, north of Rangoon. The British authorities were helpful in allowing the assembly and testing of planes, and after some delay they allowed combat training provided that Burma was not used as a base to attack the Japanese. Training was a problem for pilots with varying experience drawn from the army, navy, and marines, many of whom had never flown pursuits but only bombers.

The Chinese authorities were helpful in readying hostels and air fields within China, and in furnishing many needed technicians and other ground personnel and labor.

A serious problem arose about machine guns, which were not supplied for the first 36 planes, and about current provision of ammunition. These items were gravely short. A presidential order, gotten with Stimson's backing, was necessary to cause the War Department to release these items, without which the whole effort would have failed.[48]

Chennault now had his chance to use the lore he had been storing up in the years of discouragement and little action. He drilled his men carefully in knowledge of enemy planes and tactics and how best to combat them, fighting in pairs and using the advantages of P-40 planes, in sturdiness and armament, to offset the enemy advantage in maneuverability, rate of climb, and altitude. He was careful not to let his men fight until checked out for combat. These were the reasons for the unsurpassed record of the AVG in fighting. Chennault said that "Japanese pilots were able to kill only four A.V.G. pilots in six months of air combat."[49]

The AVG suffered from lack of spares. Apart from some tires gotten from American forces in the Philippines, few spares arrived until March 1942. Planes had to be cannibalized. By early November only 44 of Chennault's original 100 planes were operative. Some spare parts were rushed by plane and boat from the United States and Manila, and enough arrived in time to get 66 planes operative by December 1, 1941.[50] Another problem was lack of an adequate warning net in Burma, which had no counterpart for China's excellent system, and where according to Chennault the local commander did not consider it important.

By the time of the Pearl Harbor attack, December 8 in the Orient, the AVG were ready to fight.

IX. STALEMATE, 1939–1940:
CAN THE FINANCES HOLD OUT?

CHINA by the beginning of 1939 had received large help in military supplies and personnel from Russia, and at last substantial purchase credits from her Western friends. American silver-buying was converting the silver reserves into usable foreign currencies. But for maintaining an orderly exchange market, and thus helping to sustain confidence and contain the growing inflation, no help had come other than the aid lent by the Hong-kong and Shanghai Banking Corporation, on the credit of the Bank of China, in the so far successful stabilization operation. The government could spare little for currency support, because its funds abroad were approaching the minimum needed for working balances.

As 1939 began, China urgently needed aid from abroad for monetary support and management. And there was need for all practicable foreign assistance to counter enemy moves to bring about the collapse of China's currency.

THE CURRENCY WAR

Japan, taking advantage of China's pronounced regionalism and wishing to strengthen it as a divisive force, planned a group of more or less separate regimes in occupied China. Each was to have its own currency displacing the national currency and, to facilitate exploitation, linked to the yen. In addition, the Japanese military, not trusting the civilian side, wanted their own currency. They issued military yen (*gunpyo*). Besides all of these currencies, the Communists issued their own money. The complex variety of monies in China, which except for the national currency were beyond China's control, was described by Harry D. White of the American Treasury late in 1940 as giving rise to "the really most difficult monetary job there is in the world." [1]

The Japanese program of currency moves in China dates back to the issuance of "Manchukuo" yen, after the seizure of Manchuria in 1931. Following the invasion of China proper in mid-1937, the first such move was to set up the puppet Mengcheng Bank in the fall of 1937, to issue currency in the Chinese provinces of Inner Mongolia. The next step early in 1938 was formation of the Federal Reserve Bank in North China. But the plan there hit a snag when China, with the cooperation of the authorities of the British and French Concessions at Tientsin, was able to maintain the position of the national currency in North China to a substantial extent (see chapter V). Japan's financial troubles in North China, with FRB notes at a humiliating discount compared with Chinese money, delayed plans to set up similar puppet banks of issue at Shanghai and in South China. Hence, for Japan there was immediate need to try to win the currency battle in North China.

On February 20, 1939, the puppet regime at Peiping decreed that national currency in North China would be worth 60 per cent instead of 90 per cent in FRB notes. But to the embarrassment of the Japanese the premium in favor of national money, which theretofore had not exceeded about 10 per cent, rose to 20 to 30 per cent in the Spring of 1939. As from March 10, the regime forbade the circulation of national currency in North China. But this had little effect beyond the range of Japanese gunshot. Where the Japanese had military control, they forced the people to sell goods and give services for payment in puppet notes. But Japanese hopes to exploit North China by drawing from it for export large amounts of food and raw materials were fading. The fighting had disrupted trade and communications. And the farmers made a rather remarkable shift from planting export crops such as cotton to wheat and other subsistence crops. The shift, to avoid helping the enemy, was urged by the Border Government and willingly accepted by those suffering the abuses of a ruthless invasion.

The existence of the British and French Concessions at Tientsin continued to be a key factor in so largely frustrating the Japanese drive for full economic control in North China. The authorities of the Concessions, though at times beleaguered, gave such support at they could.

On June 13 the Japanese suddenly blockaded the Tientsin Concessions. The basic reason was to bring pressure on Britain because of her aid to China and her resistance to Japanese encroachments in North China. The excuse, however, was British refusal to hand over four Chinese accused in a political murder case. On the pretext of searching for currency, the Japanese police held up traffic into the Concessions, causing long delays and expense, and forcing the unloading of cargoes, even coal, in the streets. Searches extended to stripping persons at barriers, including at least one British woman. The blockade was a severe blow to confidence. It heavily shocked Shanghai because of fear of like action there. When the British Ambassador protested these measures, the Japanese Foreign Minister told him that there was need for "reconsideration by the British of their attitude of assisting Chiang Kai-shek," which the Japanese felt was strengthening China's resistance and prolonging the war.[2]

To deal with the Tientsin situation, Anglo-Japanese conversations started at Tokyo. These led to a joint statement issued July 24, which leaked July 23, as follows:

His Majesty's Government in the United Kingdom fully recognize the actual situation in China where hostilities on a large scale are in progress and note that, as long as that state of affairs continues to exist, the Japanese forces in China have special requirements for the purpose of safe-guarding their own security and maintaining public order in the regions under their control and that they have to suppress or remove any such acts or causes as will obstruct them or benefit their enemy. His Majesty's Government have no intention of countenancing any acts or measures prejudicial to the attainment of the above-mentioned objects by the Japanese forces and they will take this opportunity to confirm their policy in this respect by making it plain to the British authorities and British nationals in China that they should refrain from such acts and measures.[3]

This was interpreted as showing a weak British attitude, and led to a near panic in the exchange market at Tientsin. From Shanghai Ambassador Clark Kerr telegraphed to London on July 25: "Formula has had bad reception here. Amongst British it has created something like consternation and amongst Americans bewilderment."[4]

But while Britain felt she had to make some political concessions to Japan, in view of Japanese force on the spot, the British view on the financial issues remained firm. Foreign Secretary Viscount Halifax had instructed Ambassador Craigie at Tokyo on July 4 that ". . . we regard the avoidance of a collapse of the Chinese currency as a cardinal point in the economic stability of the Far East." [5] Reflecting that viewpoint, and to correct some of the bad impression of the joint statement, Premier Chamberlain stated in the House of Commons on July 25 that "nothing would be agreed to in the negotiations calculated to impair the Chinese currency or Britain's right to grant credits to the Chinese Government for any purpose whatsoever." [6] A further boost to confidence came when the United States, on July 26, gave Japan notice of its intention to terminate the American-Japanese commercial treaty of 1911.

The Japanese press reported that Japan was demanding that Britain abandon support of stabilization of the Chinese currency and "contribute to the collapse of China's legal tender, (1) by cooperating in prohibition against the circulation of the legal tender in North China, (2) by transfer of Chinese silver stocks in the British Concession at Tientsin, (3) by British cooperation in the activities of the Federal Reserve Bank, and (4) by effective control of the business of Chinese banks and private bankers in the British Concession at Tientsin." [7] The British refused to yield to such demands.

In a telegram of June 24, 1939, British Ambassador Craigie reported from Tokyo on the failure of the puppet bank up to then, which he felt was due to "inept management on the spot, inconvertibility, insistence on link with the yen and trade control," and "refusal of Chinese population living in areas under guerrilla control to deal with new currency." [8] But from mid-1939 the Japanese program began to make some headway. The total circulation of FRB notes began to approach that of national currency in North China. In July for the first time, due to a slump in the Shanghai exchange market and the pressure on the foreign concessions at Tientsin, national currency went to a discount below FRB notes, though recovering a premium soon afterward.

Meanwhile the Japanese pressed to get the more than 40 million ounces of silver. Most of this was in the French Concession at Tientsin, but it was on the British that the Japanese brought pressure. In a telegram of August 17, 1939, Lord Halifax told Ambassador Craigie at Tokyo that he could offer no compromise on silver. China's "claim to ownership is strong," Britain could not recognize the puppet regime's authority, other powers were interested, and yielding would depress the national currency and strengthen the FRB notes, and "deal a damaging blow to the confidence of the Chinese Government (and other friendly Powers) in ourselves." A Foreign Office memorandum of August 21 for the Cabinet at London said there would be no yielding on silver and proposed that if necessary Britain should be ready to denounce its commercial treaty, following the American lead; withdraw women and children, and then others, from occupied China; impose a clearing agreement on Japan; and give further financial aid to China. It was felt that "the danger of surrender on vital principles is greater than that of a breakdown of the conversations," and that "it is better to face the situation now." [9]

When World War II broke out on September 1, the British and Japanese had not settled their Tientsin difficulties. Besides the silver issue, Japan sought to eliminate national currency in the concessions. Britain looked for a formula to satisfy Japan. As to silver, the outcome was a compromise, to which China did not offer objection, and a moral victory for the British stand. In June 1940, the silver was placed under Anglo-Japanese seal pending future agreement, except for silver worth £100,000 to be used for flood and drought relief in North China under international control. As to currency, Britain undertook merely not to hinder circulation of FRB notes in the British Concession. On the strength of this agreement, Japan lifted the blockade of the concessions, though threatening to renew it "if there is imperative need."

From the fall of 1939 until mid-1940, FRB notes and national currency had roughly similar value in North China. But then national currency gradually went to a discount, which grew during 1941. The basic reason was that the Japanese inflated the currency of North China less rapidly than did Chungking in Free China. During 1941 FRB notes became the chief currency of occupied North China.

In Central China the creation of the puppet regime of Wang Ching-wei at Nanking on March 30, 1940, opened the way for Japanese moves at Shanghai to attack the national currency. The Japanese and their puppets were in dispute about what to do. Nationalist agents kept Chungking well informed on such matters during the war. The upshot was the opening of the Central Reserve Bank in Shanghai in January 1941. Its office on the Bund, the former premises of the Central Bank of China which the Japanese had occupied in the latter part of 1940, was guarded by troops with drawn guns and nets to check throwing of bombs. It was a striking admission that it based its notes upon national currency at par. In this scheme it was assumed that the latter would continue to circulate for the time being. The new bank proceeded cautiously, and when the Pacific War broke out in December its issue was less than 2 per cent of the total issue of national currency. The puppet notes, besides being viewed as an alien currency, were unpopular for other reasons:

The Chinese quickly discovered certain ominous signs and warnings on the notes themselves. It developed, for instance, that on the red $5 CRB bills the pattern of intricate etched lines surrounding the middle part of the large figure "5" on both sides of the note formed two small, white-rimmed circles which together definitely resembled the eyes and even the head of a fox. Now, the fox, according to ancient Chinese beliefs, is a supernatural creature; a goblin which brings misfortune to innocent and honest persons. According to numerous mythological tales the fox can turn into a beautiful woman, and in an uncanny and predatory fashion lead unsuspecting men to their perdition. Hence these notes were considered unlucky.

It was further found that the blue $10 notes were equally "fishy." Along the edge of the etched frame on the reverse side of the bills could be perceived distinctly the ominous silhouettes of turtles—winged turtles at that, which is even worse. These animals symbolize in Chinese eyes a person without legal parents, an imbecile capable of the dirtiest acts of disloyalty and treachery, a bastard, a crook. So the $10 notes were hardly more popular than the "fivers."

While nothing special was discovered on the one dollar notes, there was strong suspicion that some highly unbecoming and unspeakable objects were concealed in the outer rim of the reverse side of the $100 notes.

But the most striking and sensational discovery was made on the 50 cent notes (also allegedly on 50 dollar notes) of the CRB. Some patient soul while examining the front side with a magnifying glass noticed something odd about the picture of Dr. Sun Yat-sen's mausoleum engraved in rather pretty bright orange and violet tints. Among the bushes and shrubbery on both sides of the great stone stairway leading to the tomb were six distinct and neatly drawn Chinese characters, skilfully hidden. At first no particular significance was attached to this because the characters were placed in deliberate disorder, but after a little experimenting the following sentence was formed: "Chung Yang ma hsanglai chia," meaning, "Central (Government) will soon be here!"

This discovery, of course, created a merry furore among the citizenry. The

Japs were furious and the puppet officials apprehensive. Fifty cent notes became scarce and soon disappeared from circulation. It was rumored that the mischievous Chinese engraver fled to Free China. Fifty dollar notes were never put into circulation although it had been announced in local newspapers that several hundred million dollars worth of them had been printed. Apparently, their printed value to puppets was not great enough to offset their propaganda value to Chungking.[10]

China's success in the currency battle, with foreign help, was substantial. Persistence of national currency in the concessions and much of the occupied areas was a unifying and morale-building factor, and strengthened the loyalty of the people there. It was evidence for all to see that the government was a going concern, especially since for about half the time in 1938–1941 Chinese money was at or above par with the rival notes. China's success held back enemy exploitation. And, by allowing national currency to circulate over an area broader than Free China, it tended to hold back the inflation.

The key monetary policy, which made possible operations under the noses of the invaders, was to maintain free markets for the national currency at Shanghai and Tientsin. There the currency was freely convertible, even though at irregularly falling rates. Such markets, of course, could exist only because of the shelter of the foreign concessions, where the Chinese and foreign banks could keep operating. And the Colony of Hong Kong was a vital link in communications. But many Chinese, including many of the leaders, did not appreciate the advantages being gained for the time being from these concessions and the colony, whose existence nationalism denounced. Some leaders thought Shanghai and Tientsin to be expendable and viewed the cost of supporting the currency as largely for the benefit of speculators and of foreign interests, including the Japanese.*

The advantages China gained from this battle of currencies were not without cost. At times North China was the main cause of the drain on currency reserves. The net cost of the Tientsin operations may be estimated at about US$12 million up to the latter part of 1939, and perhaps US$18 million up to the end of market operations in the summer of 1941. As an offset to the cost, besides the intangible but vital advantages, the proceeds

---

* The conflict of ideas on monetary policy is discussed in chapter X.

in Chinese currency from sales of exchange reduced the need to issue new notes, and this checked the inflation.

On balance clearly the results justified the effort and cost.

Although in the summer of 1938 Britain turned down the idea of supporting China's currency the subject was not dropped. In December Washington would not go long with the British proposal of joint measures of currency support. But early in 1939 London was ready to go ahead independently, the decision having been influenced by the success of China's stabilization operation. The example of the American purchase credit helped, along with the fact that the United States had acted without serious trouble with Japan. Ambassador Craigie in Tokyo favored going ahead, and was confident that a currency credit would not lead to war. Before public announcement, he was instructed to tell the Japanese Government of the scheme, saying that it was being done to protect British trading and financial interests, that the money would be used only for currency support, that "our intervention in support of it has been rendered necessary by Japanese action," and that if it "has indirect effect of helping Japan's opponents, Japan has only herself to blame for putting us in the position of having to take this action." [11] Britain also was influenced by world political conditions, especially Hitler's growing aggression in Europe. When the credit of £5 million was announced, the *Financial Times* of London, March 9, 1939, said, "There is a general welcome for the idea of preventing further penetration of Japanese influence in China by granting financial assistance to the Chinese Government." The *Financial News* of the same date said, "Not merely our own interests, but common decency demand that we should support China against the wanton and brutal aggression of Japan."

The agreements of March 10, 1939, set up a stabilization fund of £10 million. At the last moment Rogers was able to get the British part raised from £3 to £5 million. This was to be put up by the Hongkong and Shanghai Banking Corporation and the Chartered Bank of India, Australia and China, with British Government guarantee, at the favorable interest rate of 2¾ per cent. The Bank of China and the Bank of Communications were to provide the Chinese part of £5 million. A committee of five, "The Hongkong Committee," were to manage the Fund. Each British and Chinese bank was to name a member, and the chairman was to be appointed by China. Rogers was named to this post.* Britain, after consideration, did not attach strings, that is, that China implement the customs agreement and resume loan payments.[12]

Britain still hoped for parallel American action to support China's currency. The State Department told the British Embassy it would study the possibilities of some new and parallel step, and Hornbeck favored it.[13] But Washington was not ready to think about it seriously. There was even a question about continuing to buy China's silver, because of opposition in Congress to continued buying of foreign silver.

In April conditions were much less favorable for success of stabilization operations than when they had begun ten months earlier. During this period foreign exchange rates changed but little. But average prices rose steadily as the printing presses poured out more and more money to meet the deficit. Thus China's money became considerably overvalued in foreign exchange.

The new Fund had to sell foreign currencies heavily almost from the start. Its managers realized the need to correct the overvaluation by lowering the support level of national currency. They had to find the right opportunity; and there was delay, partly because of the opening of a new Japanese bank of issue at Shanghai about May 1. When finally the Fund dropped the support level by about 20 per cent early in June, the adjustment seemed to be a success. But, as luck would have it, the Japanese moved within a few days against the Tientsin Concessions. People wondered whether their funds in banks in Shanghai

---

* The Chinese Government gave several assurances through their Ambassador at London. During the life of these agreements "the financial, economic and monetary policy of the Chinese Government will be designed to maintain the stability of the Chinese dollar in terms of sterling." To that end the Chinese Government was to restrict its foreign exchange commitments to the greatest possible extent and not buy exchange in excess of immediate needs. All exchange was to be bought through one or more of the banks represented on the committee. The Chinese Government banks were to cooperate in every way with the committee, and foreign exchange which they acquired in any manner and not required for immediate commitments was to be sold to the fund at cost, so long as the fund was not in excess of £10 million.

were safe. Heavy withdrawals began, much of which went into buying foreign currencies. Measures to restrict withdrawal of money from banks had only a temporary effect in slowing the drain of reserves.

At the end of June the drain resumed. By July 12 the Fund was nearly exhausted. The government could spare nothing to replenish it, since the Central Bank's balances abroad were down to about US$25 million (equivalent). Britain would not put up further funds, negotiations for French aid had stalled, and there was no sign of cash aid from the United States. So on July 18 the Fund was out of the market.

Rates fell sharply, in three weeks to almost half the former level, while prices rose rapidly. The collapse was a severe defeat for China on the financial front. Failure to maintain an orderly market raised doubts at home and abroad about how long China could hold out. London was in doubt about what to do. The *Times*, reflecting official views, stated that the Chinese currency problem was very difficult, and that larger-scale aid was needed together with American cooperation in the program.[14] Likewise the breakdown encouraged the Japanese, who had been floundering in a morass of problems, despite their military victories, and wondering how they ever could bring an end to the "China incident." *

China was "practically at the end of its domestic financial resources," reported Ambassador Johnson on August 13, on the eve of World War II. Exhaustion of the small Sino-British fund and the failure to get American and French backing for the currency, he said, meant that China had, "to all intents and purposes, abandoned the Chinese dollar in the occupied areas." That, he felt, was discouraging and dangerous for China. Yet, he reported, the American notice on July 26 of intention to end the treaty of 1911 buoyed up the Chinese, who realized that this treaty had blocked possible American sanctions and felt that this action portended further steps to defend American Far

---

* Nevertheless, confidence in Japan was at a low ebb both in China and abroad. In China the slump of rates hit the Japanese currencies along with the national currency. Military yen dropped almost as much as did the latter. In Tientsin on August 10 national currency was at a surprising premium of 1 per cent over FRB notes. In London Japanese bonds fell about 15 per cent, as much as did Chinese bonds, and were at about the same level, even though Japan was paying on her bonds while China was not.

Eastern interests. In a further telegram of August 21 Johnson said that "economic assistance particularly in the support of Chinese currency would affect powerfully the outcome of the struggle." [15]

Appraising with the benefit of hindsight the Sino-British stabilization operation of April–July 1939, it is clear that the Fund should have promptly adjusted rates to a lower level. At lower rates, sale of a given sum of foreign currency would have withdrawn more national currency, for example, a third more at 6d. than at 8d. A readjustment, if not done at the start, in April, should have been done early in May, when the Fund sought and received from the government authority to do it, since by the end of May nearly two-thirds of the Fund's resources had been sold. Of course there were strong objections to either date, and British opinion would have been surprised and critical of a change of rates so early in the game. But the result of postponement proved worse than what would have then happened. At lower levels the eventual cost of support would have been less, and lower rates would have checked imports and brought a better equilibrium in the balance of payments. The American Commercial Attaché at Shanghai reported on August 11 that importers and distributors were uncertain what to do about marking up prices due to the drop of about 50 per cent in exchange, since "a proportionate increase would virtually kill business in most imported commodities." [16] At a level where technical factors were on China's side, the Fund might have retained an effective balance for an extended time and not run out of money after a little over three months. That would have blunted later criticism of the stabilization policy in Chungking. The Fund thus might have kept going until—what could not then have been foreseen—the onset of war in Europe permitted the Fund to recoup much of what it had spent.

But so much for afterthought.

OUTBREAK OF WORLD WAR II: THE FUND REPLENISHED

A startling reversal in China's currency situation followed Hitler's march into Poland on September 1, 1939. The slump of China's money in preceding weeks was extreme, and due to be corrected. Even before fighting started in Europe, people began to repatriate money to China. They felt not only that European currencies would fall in value, but that restrictions would tie up their funds abroad. Speculators, short of Chinese currency, hurried to cover their positions. In about two months the value of China's money rose in the exchange market by about 80 per cent in sterling and 55 per cent in dollars—sterling rates falling from US$4.68 in July to about US$4.00 in September. The Fund had a golden opportunity to restore its resources. By stepping into the market it recouped £4.2 million, about 40 per cent of all it had sold, and in the process prevented a disorderly rise of rates. Once more the Fund was a market factor.

Although China had a breathing spell, the fundamental situation had not changed. Prices were rising faster than ever. Japanese actions, including acts of terrorism, added to nervousness. In March 1940, Japanese agents kidnaped the chairman of the Ningpo Commercial Bank at Shanghai, holding his family as hostages. For ransom he had to hand over to the Yokohama Specie Bank C$2 million in cash and C$3.6 million in securities. Other banks got threats of like treatment if they did not sign declarations of "voluntary cooperation."

These events led to pressure on the Fund, and by April its resources again were low. On May 2 it withdrew support and rates dropped about a fourth. But on May 6 the Fund was able to announce that its resources had been strengthened. The Hongkong and Shanghai Banking Corporation came to China's aid, and joined the Bank of China and the Bank of Communications in putting up the equivalent of about US$10 million additional, known as Fund B.* The agreement for Fund B, though settled in principle in early May, was not actually signed until July 8. As to conditions in Chungking then, Rogers wrote to me on July 6 the following account of getting final approval (I was then in Washington):

> I took the draft to Chungking last Saturday but after walking around among the ruins of the Western district for several hours trying to find the whereabouts of the Ministry of Finance and Dr. Kung's Secretarys etc., I almost came to the point of leaving the documents with some trustworthy person to give to Dr. Kung. All the places which you and I normally think

* The Bank of China guaranteed the Hongkong Bank against loss, together with interest at 2¾ per cent per annum on sums it might provide in cash. The new Fund was not to operate until the old Fund was exhausted.

of when we want to find Dr. Kung were either deserted or destroyed. Dr. Kung's big house on the top of the hill had been completely razed to the ground the day before. It was impossible to find any telephone which was working so you can imagine how frustrated I felt among the piles of bricks and coils of telephone wires which lay all over the roads. By good fortune I was able to find a dugout when the expected raid came along. Even now I am still wondering how it was that I heard in the darkness that Dr. Kung "had arrived at the Central Bank." Following an instinct I crept up to the daylight and did indeed find him. We jumped into a car and tore out along the Chengtu road in a cloud of dust and sat down at some spot along the roadside to talk about the draft agreement. When 50 'planes came our way at 15,000 feet there was a certain disquiet and scrambling about among the bushes. However the chop had been placed on my pieces of paper so I was able to give myself up to an open air view of the bombing.

My main feelings that day were fatigue, hunger and discomfort from the heat and dust. Chungking most unkindly registered the highest temperature for years, viz. 98 degrees in the shade. However, I was eventually able to leave at 5:30 and arrived in Hongkong at midnight more or less safe and sound.

The new Fund, as it turned out, never had to be used. Once more events in Europe, though tragic enough there, came to China's aid. Hitler's great drive into the Low Countries and France in May–June brought fresh sales of foreign currencies to bring money back to China. By July rates of exchange recovered to around the level of April. And the Fund bought back about £2 million.

THE SEARCH FOR MORE AID FOR CURRENCY SUPPORT

In August 1939, taking advantage of a lull in government activity in the exchange market, I returned to the United States for rest and for personal reasons. In October–November I visited New York and Washington regarding certain Chinese legal business.* Though I had no negotiating mission, I thought it useful informally and personally to explain China's needs to the State and Treasury Departments. On November 12 I wrote to Cyril Rogers in China: "Events in Europe and/or Asia are likely to modify opinion toward support of a more active policy." High officials of the American Government favored support of China's cause.

* This concerned China's attempt, eventually unsuccessful, to recover on a claim against assets in the United States of the former Russo-Asiatic Bank, which failed in the 1920's while holding Chinese loan funds.

About the middle of November, I had an extended talk with Secretary Hull, in a personal capacity. I explained that China's most vulnerable spot was probably finance; that time was not all on China's side because of the risk that the "inflationary spiral" would develop at some future time; and stated that China in the fairly near future would need support for the finances. Hull was keenly interested and sympathetic but could promise nothing. Also I made a similar statement to Secretary Morgenthau, emphasizing the need for cash funds to maintain an orderly free foreign exchange market for China's currency. He stated his great sympathy for China, but said definitely that since I was about to return to China he did not wish me to carry back the idea that he was in position to give any cash aid. In the Treasury I also discussed with Harry D. White procedure and policy in the event of later American aid.

The State Department pursued with me the subject of what might be involved in support of China's currency, should this later become practicable, and especially the cost and what means China might have to guarantee payment. Also they were interested in possible future Japanese attacks upon the currency, and how such action might be countered. In a memorandum of December 22, I explained the success of the Bank of China operation in 1938–1939, and the reasons for the difficulties which the Anglo-Chinese Fund encountered in 1939. This Fund could have held the situation, I said, had it been a little larger. As to the money needed to hold the currency at a reasonable level, I thought a fund of US$75 million would be enough for a year or two, with a further US$25 million on call. China's debt, I said, was relatively small, and repayment should not be a serious problem if China "can be reconstructed." I thought that the Japanese needed most of the revenues they collected for military and civil costs, and would not have relatively large funds to buy foreign currencies in China. I stressed the need to support the currency, both to strengthen China's resistance and to check Japanese moves against the open-door policy.

Secretary Hull, on the basis of recommendations on December 29 by Hornbeck and his colleagues in Far Eastern Affairs, decided to approach Secretary Morgenthau about currency support.[17] After several discussions, Hornbeck communicated to Morgenthau on April 11 views I had forwarded through the embassy at Chung-king, that the Anglo-Chinese Fund "does not possess reserves adequate to protect the currency against such adverse develop-ments as further attacks upon the currency by the Japanese, the creation of a new central 'government,' serious military reverses, or further repressive action by the Japanese military forces against foreign settlements and concessions in China." [18]

On April 30 Morgenthau advised the State Department that he thought it would be inadvisable to undertake at that time stabili-zation activities *vis-à-vis* China.[19] He stated that he would have to obtain permission of Congress to use the Stabilization Fund for that purpose and that he did not think it would be an appropriate time to seek such permission. His reference was to assurances made public October 25, 1939, namely, a letter to Senator Vanden-berg which repeated the following statement made some months earlier to the Senate Banking and Currency Committee: "Senators, if there is a war in any foreign country, before we would use the stabilization fund or any money in the Treasury to assist any country in prosecuting that war, I would come up before the proper committee and ask for guidance." [20] Morgenthau was sympathetic to aid to China. But he wished to provide it by credits for specific purchases, and not for direct currency support, as to which he was skeptical. Also he trusted K. P. Chen, with whom he had negotiated, but did not have similar faith in the other Chinese leaders.

The Treasury's decision coincided with a serious break in Chinese exchange, of which they had not yet had word. A memo-randum of May 10 to Morgenthau from White's Division of Mone-tary Research referred to the break in exchange, and said it indi-cated that the Japanese and their puppet regime "have probably won an important victory in the currency war." White and his Division at this time were more sympathetic than the Secretary to the State Department's interest in possible cash aid to China.[21]

The currency difficulties in the Spring of 1940 were very dis-couraging to China. The Fund was about gone; Central Bank balances abroad had been for months around US$25 million, the minimum needed for working funds; and the American credits, while helpful, could not be used to buy munitions. The time had come for a fresh effort to strengthen China's resources.

On May 11, Generalissimo Chiang called me in for a discussion of the situation. I stressed the increasing rate at which prices were rising and stated that both internal and external measures were needed. I confirmed and amplified my recommendations to him in a memorandum of May 16 which urged "all practicable reduction in public expenditure," curtailment of credit "not essential to the war effort," renewed efforts to raise money by taxation and borrowing from the public, measures against hoarding of necessities, and if feasible temporary suspension of conscription during the current harvest. Also I proposed fresh efforts to add to the funds for currency support.

The Generalissimo asked me to draft for him a message to President Roosevelt. The message, as presented on May 31, stated that China was taking steps internally to curtail expenditures and credit, but urged the need "to broaden the scope of financial assistance to China by taking into consideration the possibility of supporting the Chinese currency by a cash loan or by other effective means which your financial experts may suggest." [22] Chiang was ready to send a representative to Washington to negotiate detailed arrangements. In a separate message through the American embassy, the Generalissimo proposed that part of the US$20 million credit granted on April 20 be made available in cash instead of only for purchases.

Ambassador Johnson strongly supported China's proposals, after talks which the Generalissimo, Minister Kung, and I had with him. Johnson felt that the United States had "to a large extent benefited by the efforts of others," and that if the currency collapsed the results would be serious. He said that "it seems to me that it should be found possible in some way to make a contribution to this existing fund for the purpose of aiding American commerce and objectives in China." [23]

Despite Morgenthau's doubts, the State Department was favorable to China's proposal. Hornbeck and his colleagues told Hull on June 3 that they felt that the temper of American opinion had changed so that it might be feasible for Morgenthau to gain release from his commitments to Congress; that a currency credit to China "would seem to have more to commend it than any other move of this character which we might make"; and they suggested that Hull try to get the President to talk to Morgenthau.[24]

On June 4 Ambassador Hu telegraphed that he had learned that the President told Hull that the United States should plan more aid to China. Encouraged by the ray of hope, T. V. Soong and I left for Washington on June 15, even though no reply had come to China's proposal to send a representative to Washington. On July 12 Soong proposed to Morgenthau a currency credit of US$50 million, together with credits for military and other purchases. On July 27 he gave the Treasury at their request a memorandum in support of the currency proposal.* The memorandum dismissed exchange control as impracticable. It argued strongly for a new Stabilization Fund since the total of only about US$20 million, available in the old Fund plus Fund B, was clearly inadequate. Operation of the proposed new Fund, it was suggested, should be coordinated closely with that of the existing Funds through an American-British-Chinese committee. The memorandum admitted that the Chinese Government had not been united on the merits of undertaking stabilization, but stated that the government now accepted the principle. Assistance to China was vitally important, Soong declared, and support of the Chinese currency was the most effective way in which the United States could concretely aid China.

In this memorandum was a frank account of China's financial position, including secret data. It is specially interesting, therefore, that a draft of this paper was read by Frederick V. Field. At that time he was a writer for Communist and Communist-front periodicals. He has since been described as a Communist in sworn testimony by various witnesses before Congressional committees, and has invoked the fifth amendment in refusing to answer questions about Communist affiliations.[25] Thus valuable inside information may have gone to the Chinese Communists.

The circumstances were as follows. Soong and I were working on the document at Hotel Ambassador in New York. Dr. Ludwig

---

* The memorandum described stabilization operations to date, the need to continue them, and dealt with the objections raised against the program. The first objection was that the Japanese could acquire foreign exchange in the market. But, it was explained, the indications were that they had not been able to get very much and that whatever they got was a small price to pay for the integrity of the Chinese currency. As to the objection that capital flight was promoted, the memorandum explained that maintenance of stability of rates tended to check such flight. As to the argument that maintenance of exchange encouraged import of nonessentials, the memorandum stated that on the contrary the problem was that essential imports were so heavy owing to the distressed condition of the occupied areas.

Rajchman,* who was then advising Soong on general and political matters, suggested to him that Field was a writer who might make helpful suggestions about presentation. At that time Soong had never heard of Field, and I knew his name but not his leftist affiliation. Rajchman brought in Field, to read the draft, and Field proposed some changes which were helpful but minor. Rajchman is understood to have been connected with the Communist regime in Poland after 1945, and with UNICEF.

The Morgenthau Diaries now show what was going on behind the scenes in Washington. After Soong's arrival there Morgenthau prepared for Roosevelt a memorandum of July 1, drafted in White's office. This memorandum suggested doubt about Soong's sympathy with "continued resistance to Japan"—in my view a surprising and wholly unjustified slur. It referred to his and my previous efforts to obtain support for currency stabilization, and stated that Soong was probably now going to ask for a loan from the American Stabilization Fund. The Treasury, said the memorandum, wished to help China, but felt that a stabilization loan to China was beyond that Fund's scope. The Treasury, moreover, felt that the proposed operation by China would be costly, in an area not under China's control, and that the risks would outweigh the advantages. Exchange rates could be held at a cost of US$25 to 100 million in the course of a year or so, said the memorandum; but "if the United States is willing to extend that much aid, it can be extended for more effective purposes than an attempted stabilization of the currency." [26]

For many weeks negotiations for aid to China moved slowly. Morgenthau favored aid, but remained cool to the idea of currency support. He felt that "a loan from the stabilization fund . . . was impossible because it too nearly aproximated a 'gift.' " [27] There was no encouragement for China to expect American aid in currency support, despite its vital importance.

In October–November China's situation was critical. Japan had indicated she expected shortly to recognize the puppet regime of Wang Ching-wei at Nanking. Germany was pressing China to

* Rajchman is a Polish physician, formerly head of the League of Nations public health office, and had advised Soong during the Manchurian affair in 1931–1932. Also, he represented the League in China in 1934. During his stay in Washington a writer in McCall's, September 1941 (p. 109), described him as, "A Pole with a long clever face . . . who loves intrigue as a drunkard his brew . . . The State Department does not like Raichman [sic] . . . The Government even tried to get him deported."

negotiate with Japan to end the war. Ribbentrop told the Chinese Ambassador at Berlin that Germany's relations with Russia were better; that England would be knocked out of the war in a few months; and that then no one could help China. He said Germany and Italy would also recognize the Wang Ching-wei regime if China did not make peace. This he said was China's last chance to come to terms with Japan. Japan, discouraged by not being able to knock out China, and as her interest was shifting from China to an intensified southward move, was putting out feelers indicating that China could get better terms than ever before. All this, coupled with lack of Western funds to support the currency and for airplanes and other munitions, and along with the growing Communist danger internally, added up to the gravest threat yet to China's morale and continued resistance.[28]

On October 18 and again on November 9, the Generalissimo put forward urgent pleas for help by the United States and Britain on a broad front, by planes, volunteers, munitions, and credits. He wanted "a joint loan or separate loans" of US$200 to 300 million, "with a view to maintaining China's foreign exchange and national currency." He also urged a "Sino-Anglo-American plan of cooperation," for political, military, and financial support. Reporting on this, Ambassador Johnson said, "He believes and has all along said that the fight that China is waging is intimately linked with the United States and Great Britain. He feels isolated and finds it hard to understand why China's part is not given more concrete recognition." On November 21, the Generalissimo told Johnson that if, at the time of Japanese recognition of Wang Ching-wei, "America does not show a positive attitude and give positive assistance, our war of resistance will be gravely imperilled. Only America can turn the tide and keep up the morale of the Chinese people." Johnson strongly urged maximum and prompt American action.[29] Chiang's proposal of a really big loan foreshadowed the requests a year later, at the time of the outbreak of the Pacific War.

FOR CHINA'S RELIEF: AMERICAN AND BRITISH CURRENCY CREDITS

With dramatic suddenness the situation came to a head at the end of November. On November 22 Roosevelt wrote to Under-Secretary of State Welles: "I have a hunch that we ought to do something in regard to the Chinese loan quickly or not at all—

because I have real fear that the domestic situation in Free China will deteriorate unless we do something fast. Will you work on this?" [30] On November 29, Roosevelt told Morgenthau that he wanted to announce within 24 hours a loan of US$100 million to China. Half would be for currency support and half for purchases.[31] On November 30, the President made the following announcement:

> The discussions between the American and the Chinese authorities in the field of financial cooperation have progressed. There is contemplated a credit to the Chinese Government of $100,000,000. Of this, a credit for general purposes to the amount of $50,000,000 has been decided upon by this Government. Arrangements for early allocation of the balance, namely, $50,000,000, for purposes of monetary protection and management as between American and Chinese currencies are now in process in consultation with the appropriate committees of the Congress.
>
> The Secretary of the Treasury will appear Monday forenoon [December 3] before a joint session of the Senate Committee on Banking and Currency and the House Committee on Coinage, Weights and Measures. At this time, he will bring to their attention the proposed extension of a $50,000,000 stabilization arrangement with the Central Bank of China.

This announcement coincided with formal Japanese recognition of the puppet regime Japan had created eight months earlier. On December 3, Morgenthau and Hull appeared before a joint session of the Senate Banking and Currency Committee and the House Committee on Coinage, Weights and Measures. After hearing their proposals, the two committees gave them a unanimous vote of confidence. In his report on the session, Chairman Andrew L. Somers of the House committee said that he believed "the American people are not only willing but are now anxious to help China in every practical way." *

The British Government, which for some time had been thinking of further financial aid to China, took parallel action. On December 10, they announced credits of £10 million for China, half for stabilization and half for purchases. The announcement met with whole-hearted approval in Parliament and the country at large.[32] The Generalissimo had hoped for a larger figure. But the British felt they could do no more at a time when they had far-reaching financial commitments for the war, and were seeking financial aid from the United States.

---

* I breakfasted with Chairman Somers before the session to brief him fully.

X. THE NEW DEAL IN AID FOR THE CURRENCY, 1941

WHEN Roosevelt announced on November 30, 1940, a credit of US$50 million to China for "monetary protection and management," he could not have foreseen the weighty consequences of the decision as to how China's currency should be supported. The eventual plan involved the freezing of Japanese as well as Chinese assets in the United States, Britain, and The Netherlands. For Japan that amounted to an economic blockade. Because the freezing proved to be a crucial step in the events leading to Pearl Harbor, it is important to examine how this decision came about.

HOW SHOULD THE CURRENCY BE SUPPORTED?

The American and British announcements on November 30 and December 10, 1940, assured China of large resources for currency support. But there was much to be done before China could use the money. Roosevelt's announcement was an urgent gesture, timed to uphold China's morale at a critical moment; and Britain's move had a like purpose. Washington had decided nothing definite about use of the US$50 million "for purposes of monetary protection and management as between American and Chinese currencies." London's ideas about use of their £5 million to add to stabilization funds were more concrete, but there was still much to be decided. And the arrangements and policy had to worked out with China, where there were differences of view.

The basic choice was between two main alternatives. The first was to continue the policy followed since June 1938, that is, the policy of stabilization, better described as the effort to check undue fluctuations of exchange rates in the free market. That involved selling foreign currencies in the free market at Shanghai to sustain the exchange value of China's currency, and at times buying back foreign currencies when conditions were favorable. Under that policy there was a single broad market, open freely to all. The second alternative was to undertake some form of exchange control, whereby foreign currencies would be sold only for approved "legitimate" purposes, mainly to buy goods abroad and for personal needs. Since part of the applications to buy foreign currencies would be rejected, a black market for Chinese currency at a lower level would result.

China rejected exchange control as impracticable in mid-1937 when the fighting began (chapter III). But the idea did not drop from view. Disagreements were smoldering, and the argument continued. The differences largely reflected the long-standing division within China's leading family, mainly between T. V. Soong and his brother-in-law and sister, H. H. Kung and Madame Kung. Like a continuous thread, these divisions ran through the financial problems of wartime China. Kung as Minister of Finance was of course mostly at Chungking, and Soong, who during much of this time was head of the Bank of China, was mostly in Hong Kong, where he aided in stabilization operations, which he favored and to which Kung had agreed.

As Financial Adviser, it became my task in 1938-1941 to handle stabilization matters at Chungking. I tried constantly to moderate the differences, which grew in 1939 as pressure on the Fund mounted. Regarding the Chinese Government and people as my client, I did my best to avoid embroilment in any internal political or personal differences. I tried to work with both sides and keep their confidence, in which I feel on the whole I succeeded despite repeated arguments with one or the other or both.* In the stabilization issue in 1938-1941, however, my economic experience and judgment led me to lean definitely to the side of efforts to maintain an orderly and free exchange market at Shanghai. Repeatedly I explained that exchange control would be a failure under existing conditions. Cyril Rogers, as chairman of the Sino-British Committee, had a major responsibility in developing and operating the stabilization policy, and of course backed it strongly. He and I agreed about exchange control. He had a hard job, and worked loyally and effectively in China's interest. Often after strenuous days of market operations he had to spend week ends flying under hazardous conditions from Hong Kong to Chungking, to report and discuss the always grave problems.

* Soong once remarked to me that he knew I kept his secrets; and that Kung also knew that I kept Kung's.

Cyril Rogers died in London early in 1962. The strain of his self-sacrificing exertions for China in 1938–1941 may have shortened his life.

Chungking never supported whole-heartedly the stabilization policy, and became more and more critical as the pressure grew. Minister Kung from the beginning leaned toward exchange control. He faced the almost superhuman task of financing the foreign currency costs of a full-scale war with China's scanty resources. It was but natural that he should worry when precious reserves were paid out rapidly and without restriction for currency support. In the first two years of fighting, reserves dwindled from US$379 million to under a tenth of that sum. About US$50 million had gone for debt payments, and the rest was about equally divided between war purchases and currency support.

On May 3, 1939, a month after the Sino-British Fund began operations, the issue came up when Rogers sent a message despatched at 3:00 a.m. from Hong Kong, saying that on May 2 the control had spent £1.1 million to support rates in a weak market. He urgently asked authority to suspend support and let rates adjust to a lower level. Due to heavy air raids, the message did not reach Chungking until the evening of May 3. It was not decoded and ready to take up with Kung until 1:00 a.m. of May 4. Reluctantly I got His Excellency out of bed to discuss and prepare a reply, which I encoded and took personally to the telegraph office at 4:00 a.m., to be sent urgently to Hong Kong so that instructions could reach Shanghai before the market opened.

Chungking's work was conducted with great difficulty in this period, due to protracted air raids by day and on moonlight nights. With Mrs. Young's help I personally coded and decoded messages exchanged with Rogers, in codes we jointly devised and from which we were satisfied there was no leakage. No assistant was available whom I thought should be asked to risk the charge of having received information that could win a fortune by speculation in the market. Picture the financial adviser sitting on a hillside near a dugout, or inside by candlelight, working on a code message when delay might be very costly!

Kung's reply authorized suspension of the Fund's sales, but queried whether it would be better to reduce the drain by making some sales according to merit of the applications and reject doubtful applications. Sales based on merits would have resembled the rationing scheme of 1938. While nominally keeping a fixed rate such sales would have been small, and the main market would have fallen away drastically due to lack of support. The Fund's managers therefore could do nothing about Kung's suggestion without abandoning the basic policy. Actually they waited a month to lower rates, because the drain slackened.*

After breakdown of the Fund on July 18, Generalissimo Chiang in a speech of July 24 endorsed Kung's views. He said that he had "never been in favour of indiscriminate supply of foreign exchange" in the foreign Concessions, because it "exposes our wartime currency to the injurious manoeuvres of enemy-actuated and unprincipled speculators." [1] I found no evidence, then or since, to support the charge that enemy operations in foreign exchange were an important factor in the exchange market in this period.

On July 27, 1939, the Chinese Government sent telegrams, which I helped to prepare, to the American, British, and French Governments, explaining the situation after breakdown of the Sino-British Fund, and appealing for "aid in maintaining the value of the Chinese dollar." Following these messages, however, others were sent from Chungking of which I learned only through postwar publication of the British records. These messages suggested to Britain that in fresh operations either the Fund should operate with more control of transactions or that China supply exchange for needed imports at the rate of 7d.—the market then being in the range of half to two-thirds of that figure. These messages probably tended to discourage British aid, since London thought the proposals showed "lack of understanding of the currency principles." On August 29, on the eve of World War II, Lord Halifax told Ambassador Quo that there was little prospect of further British contribution to the Fund.[2]

When Ambassador Hu appealed to President Roosevelt on May 31, 1940, for aid in currency support, he reported that the President talked freely about the German method of absolute

---

* Kung's views were responsible for measures of trade and exchange control introduced in Free China about July 1, 1939. These measures had little direct effect on the total situation.

control of the currency. Kung telegraphed to inquire what the President had in mind. The Ambassador replied that the President had said he realized such control was not possible in China. It was shortly after this episode that Soong came to Washington and urged American backing for currency support. When asking American funds, he said in his memorandum of July 27, "Hard experience has finally convinced the Government of the necessity of stabilizing the currency, and has demonstrated the impossibility of establishing exchange control in the areas where the Government cannot regulate import and export trade." It did seem then that the policy of support in a free market had won out in China. But after Washington and London agreed to provide funds for currency support, the argument broke out anew and involved all three countries.

It was clear that inflation and a falling exchange value of China's currency were unavoidable. The issue was how best to control them and lessen the bad effects. The problem was complicated by the fact that the chief market was in the International Settlement at Shanghai. There China had no jurisdiction, nor did the enemy have control until December 8, 1941.

Let us look at the case for the policy followed from June 1938, to August 1941. Maintenance of the value of the national currency in an orderly free market helped China to continue to rely upon issuing notes, as the chief and vitally important means to finance the wartime deficit. Disorderly fluctuations, on the other hand, created fear and lack of confidence in China and her prospects; were followed by a faster rise of prices and by increased speculation and capital flight; and led people to spend money faster rather than hold it, thus speeding the rate of turnover of money and magnifying the effects of growing note-issue. Orderly rates encouraged remittances of money to China by overseas Chinese—equal to about US$100 million in 1938. The stabilization operators could step in to hold rates in the face of temporary strains, such as severe military defeats, enemy action against the currency, or events abroad, thus sustaining confidence and morale. Also support of the value of China's money and its convertibility into foreign currencies in a free market sustained the inclination of the people in the occupied areas to prefer the national currency to Japanese-sponsored currencies. It thus checked enemy currency schemes, which were bound up with Japanese controls of exchange and trade and held back Japan's exploitation of her conquests. Also, an orderly market enhanced the possibilities of aid by friendly powers, for demoralized markets might suggest that China was beyond help. Finally, support of the currency, in the free and occupied areas alike, maintained it as a symbol of unity, bolstered the will to resist, and showed to all at home and abroad that despite Japan's pressure China remained a going concern.

There were disadvantages as well. Inflation proceeded inexorably, and market support had to be a holding operation—a sort of rearguard action. It was not an easy art to find the right conjuncture when rates had to be lowered. There had to be a series of devaluations and mistakes were unavoidable. Operations to support exchange were costly, China's resources that could be spared were meager, and the only foreign credit was the £5 million which Britain provided early in 1939. Fortunately the Fund could supplement its assets on several occasions by skillfully buying back foreign currencies when the market was strong, without disturbing rates.

Granting the disadvantages of the stabilization policy, there was the crucial question whether anything better could be put in its place, that is, could an attempt to operate an exchange control succeed? China had no jurisdiction in the International Settlement at Shanghai, where the main exchange market was located. China could neither regulate imports there and into the enemy-controlled areas, nor require exporters (outside of Free China) to hand over, in exchange for Chinese currency, the foreign currencies which they received from selling their goods abroad. Hence, exchange control looked like an expensive experiment, with much foreign currency handed out but little coming in.

It was not surprising that the Finance Minister, with multiple calls upon his shrinking reserves, should worry whether support of exchange was pouring money down a rat hole. The chief objection was that market support benefited mainly the enemy and speculators. *Prima facie* it was not unreasonable to query the wisdom of freely selling exchange and using precious reserves in an enemy-surrounded and notoriously speculative market, Shanghai.

What of the charge that Japan was using the free market to raid China's reserves? At the time we made every effort to learn the facts. The best evidence we could get, including the views of the banks operating the Fund, was that while Japanese banks at times were buyers of exchange they also at times were sellers; and that Japanese buying of exchange was not a persisting important factor. Postwar inquiry of Japanese bankers confirms that statement. The Japanese military and civil authorities and their puppets were spending large sums in China. Besides spending the new currencies they sponsored, whose circulation China's monetary policy tended to hold down, they needed for use in China most of the national currency they were able to get. Whatever risk there was of the enemy obtaining benefits from the policy had to be suffered in behalf of much greater gains by China.

Speculation and capital flight were bound to occur in a free market with inflation rampant, where controls could not be used. But these evils were less in an orderly market, in which the Fund from time to time could squeeze speculators, than when rates flutuated wildly. Moreover, the evil of capital flight was partly offset by two factors. First, sales of foreign currencies withdrew money from the market, thus checking the rate of growth of note-issue and helping to hold back the rise of prices. Second, a chief alternative to flight abroad, for those seeking to protect the value of their assets, was buying local goods for hoarding, often scarce goods, thus bidding up local prices. Nevertheless the situation was made no better by the fact that the speculators, flighters, and hoarders were so largely Chinese, including civil and military officials. Japanese bankers formerly in China, with whom I talked in 1958 in Tokyo, thought that in 1938–1941 the chief flight of capital came from Chinese, including insiders.

The drawbacks of the stabilization policy had to be set off against the advantages. I believed then and still believe that the plus factors far outweighed the minus. *Without this policy, there is grave doubt whether China could have avoided financial collapse during over eight years of war, perhaps even before Pearl*

Harbor. The justification of the policy, however, was sophisticated. It was politically vulnerable and never fully understood even in some high Chinese and American circles.

NEGOTIATING THE AGREEMENTS

The Treasury gave Soong the American proposal on December 26, having been delayed by urgent negotiations on British financial needs. The draft proposed a Stabilization Board, with a Chinese chairman and two other Chinese, plus an American and a British member appointed by China on nomination by the respective governments. The Board's assets, including the existing Sino-British funds and a Chinese contribution, would be nearly US$100 million.* The funds were to be used "exclusively for the purpose of stabilizing the value of the Chinese yuan with respect to the United States dollar and other foreign currencies." China would undertake to repay on 30 days' notice any dollars used.† The American draft did not predetermine any basic policy of operations and was subsequently signed with no important change except removal of a restriction which Secretary Morgenthau proposed.

Morgenthau had never liked the idea of supporting the currency in a free market. In order to assure that the US$50 million would last at least 10 months, he proposed that China limit drawing to US$5 million cumulatively per month, unless he gave prior consent. Soong at once objected. He pointed out that the Board should have unfettered control of drawings to meet possible emergencies, and that if the limitation became known it would spur demand on the Fund. Generalissimo Chiang was very unhappy about this clause, and instructed Soong not to accept it. Laughlin Currie, Assistant to the President, who was in China in February for political, economic, and military investigations,

---

* That comprised the American contribution of US$50 million, the British contribution equivalent to US$20 million, the Chinese contribution eventually set at US$20 million, and the 1939 Sino-British Fund equivalent to about US$5 million.

† A draft letter to accompany the agreement proposed that China set up an agency with power and authority to manage and control all the foreign exchange assets of China, other than those held in the stabilization fund. Such agency would have authority to set up a system of exchange control, and to require citizens of China to turn over for fair compensation their foreign exchange assets including gold and silver. China was to undertake that its financial and economic policies would be designed to achieve exchange stabilization.

reported to the President on March 15 that he hoped the clause would be waived as the Generalissimo desired. Currie thought "we would gain by making this gesture of full trust and confidence in him." Ambassador Johnson reported on April 17 that the idea of doling out the money hurt the Generalissimo's pride.[3]

On April 21, Morgenthau yielded after consulting the President, with whom Soong had discussed the matter. But he asked that Soong and Ambassador Hu give their personal word that China would not draw beyond US$5 million monthly of American funds without first consulting him. Soong said he would have to ask for instructions on this. Signature of agreements, however, did not wait for reply. In Shanghai a grave situation had arisen from terrorism. As reprisal for murder of a staff member of the puppet Central Reserve Bank, a large number of Bank of China staff were kidnaped from their dormitory in the International Settlement. Bank staffs were demoralized and the four government banks had to close for several days. The clearing system was not working. The foreign exchange market was nervous and the Sino-British Fund had to give support. The fears in the market made it urgent to finish negotiations and announce signing of the agreements. So on April 25, 1941, the agreements were signed. The Sino-British agreement was parallel to the Sino-American.

The negotiations were far from satisfactory, especially as to Anglo-American cooperation. In the latter part of 1940 the State Department worked closely with the British, and favored a joint effort to devise a plan. But the Treasury was not so cooperatively inclined. For example—after Rogers returned from England he gave the Treasury for consideration the draft of the Sino-British stabilization agreement. But a few days later on March 27 the Treasury turned up with a revision of the American draft without giving him opportunity for informal discussion to harmonize the language and policy before ideas had crystallized.

On the Chinese side, some of the reactions portended future trouble and partly involved the old difficulties within China's leading family. In a note made for my own guidance on April 1, I set down the importance of close coordination of handling the prospective problems, "Because of the personalities involved on the Chinese side which, in the absence of most skillful handling of the situation, may result in continuation if not aggravation of the serious friction that has caused so much harm to China." Also I noted that "Occasion should be taken to have a showdown about exchange policy, and to do all possible (a) to eliminate the confusion and inconsistency which have made it so hard for China to confront the grave problems of the period of hostilities and (b) to prepare China for meeting the terribly difficult period of inflation and intensified conflict that lies ahead."

As to Soong's handling of the negotiations, A. Manuel Fox, who became the American member of the Stabilization Board, telegraphed to the Treasury on August 18, that "Dr. Kung disclosed Saturday during discussion that he never liked terms of April 1 agreement." [4] And a despatch of October 14, from the American Embassy at Chungking reported that Kung had stated to the Embassy's informant (not this writer) that the text of the American stabilization agreement was not submitted to Chungking before signature and was received only a month later; that the "severity of the language employed" and some of the terms suggested that it had been drawn by "some expert mortgage attorney in Washington" and "smacked of a contract such as a money-lender might draw up"; and that he and the Generalissimo were "astounded to learn that Mr. T. V. Soong would sign such an agreement." They found the British agreement more liberal in language and terms. They hesitated to send the agreements to the Legislative Yuan for ratification because they feared it would reject them. Fox reported to Morgenthau early in 1942, "Both the Generalissimo and the Kungs have expressed dissatisfaction with the agreement, claiming that the terms were too one-sided and smacked of a colonial agreement," for example, that the United States could cancel on a month's notice but China could not.[5] These thoughts were to bear fruit in termination of the agreements at China's instance early in 1944 (see chapter XIX).

ARGUMENTS AND THEIR REPERCUSSIONS

The agreements, as we have seen, did not specify the policy of operations. But during the negotiations, the argument on policy went on. Within each of the three governments there were differences. Inclined to support of the Chinese currency in a free market were: the American State Department; most but not all of the British Government; and on the Chinese side most financial interests in China both Chinese and foreign, China's negotiator Soong, and advisers Young and Rogers. Inclined toward controls were the American Treasury; in England J. M. Keynes and others, though they later abandoned the idea; and in China Generalissimo Chiang Kai-shek and Finance Minister Kung. With both China and Britain engaged in life or death struggles and so dependent financially on the United States, American views were bound to be weighty. And since the issues were mainly financial, and the American Treasury was going far into international affairs, it was they who had the greatest say.

All recognized that controls would be unavoidable in case of a Pacific war, which looked more and more probable, or if the Japanese seized Shanghai or otherwise closed its market and that of Hong Kong. But pending such possible events the proponents of control, who shied away from supporting the currency in the free market, sought to get around China's lack of jurisdiction in the internationally controlled and enemy-occupied areas by "external exchange control." The idea was to control the transfer for China account of dollars and sterling in the United States and England. Such a plan would call for "freezing," that is, controlling China funds in these countries. This was the plan eventually adopted in July 1941.

Britain, *vis-à-vis* China, faced difficult technical problems growing out of British wartime monetary controls.* To help to deal with these problems, Rogers came to Washington at Soong's request, and shortly flew on to London. Some in London, including Lord Keynes, had been looking for a formula of external exchange control for China. But after talking with Rogers, they decided it was not feasible. This idea was discussed at length in London and in exchanges of messages between Soong and Rogers. Soong felt, and Rogers and I concurred, that adoption of such a plan would involve serious risks. The upshot of these talks was British agreement with Soong's thesis that the wisest policy was to keep the *status quo* unless China were forced to abandon Shanghai, or unless and until a change seemed in China's interest.

* Sterling was mostly inconvertible into dollars, but was traded freely in China, Hong Kong, and Japan. London was anxious to prevent leakage of sterling via the uncontrolled area.

The State Department also thought well of Soong's approach, and in January considered telegraphing to Chungking that the United States felt that China's current exchange policy was generally right and that exchange control by China was not feasible. This action would parallel a proposed British message. But the Treasury did not want such a message sent. They said that before reaching policy decisions they wanted to await the return of Currie, who was in China in February. As to China's currency problem, White commented that "this is the really most difficult monetary job there is in the world, because it is the only country which has so many currencies operating in areas over which it doesn't have complete control." [6] Yet the Treasury people were never ready to sit down and talk informally with Rogers and me, who for three and one-half years had been dealing with the problem, about the situation and what should be done.

Meanwhile there were developments in China. On December 9, Kung telegraphed to Soong that he favored protecting the stabilization fund by measures to prevent enemy and speculators from buying exchange, apportioning exchange for "legitimate" purposes, and adopting long-term stabilization.* Chungking was getting the idea that the American and British Governments favored exchange control. On January 27 the Generalissimo told British Ambassador Clark Kerr that he opposed supporting the currency at Shanghai, and two days later Kung amplified the views in a memorandum.†

When the British Ambassador at Chungking reported this to London, the British Government was busy threshing out policy for use of the £5 million credit. On February 19 they informed the State and Treasury Departments that the Ambassador had been instructed to inform the Generalissimo that, "We should

---

* This last foreshadowed the policy later adopted—setting fixed rates that got steadily out of line with the economic situation as inflation moved ahead.

† This memorandum said that holding behind the currency "adequate reserves . . . which will not be wasted" would sustain confidence. The new American and British funds should be used "entirely to strengthen the reserve of the national currency." The government was taking steps to develop the exchange market at Chungking, "which will be a free one provided purchasers have legitimate needs . . . It continues to be the Government's firm intention to maintain the value of the Chinese Dollar both in terms of foreign exchange and in prices for domestic goods and services, but this policy is in respect to the value of the National Currency as a whole and not with reference to the black market in Shanghai or elsewhere."

consider it a fatal mistake to reverse the policy of supporting FA-PI unless and until some other constructive policy can be adopted in its place. We doubt if such constructive policy can comprise exchange control in China, which would not be effectively administered under existing conditions in China." [7] The memorandum transmitted by the Ambassador at Chungking stressed the importance of convertibility into foreign currencies in the free market, that is, Shanghai. This, said the memorandum, was a main factor leading the people to prefer the national currency to Japanese-sponsored currencies, and to maintain resistance to enemy domination; if China abandoned Shanghai, the Japanese would have an excuse to push their currencies and gain full economic control of the occupied areas; any advantages which Japan gained from the free market were insignificant compared with the advantages to China; the Japanese were short of Chinese national currency and for some months had been selling dollars at Shanghai; and even in the rackets of the Nanking regime (opium, gambling, etc.) payment was demanded in *fapi*.

The Chinese reply of February 26 said, "There has never been any thought on the part of the Chinese Government to abandon the Shanghai market nor to impair the convertibility of the Chinese Dollar." But it was intended to "develop a free exchange market in Chungking, and the Chinese Government feels strongly that all requirements for exchange for legitimate demand should be fully met regardless of location of applicant." Also, the reply continued, because of the Japanese threat to Shanghai another market ought to be available. On March 1 the Ministry of Finance announced the opening of an exchange market at Chungking, in which the Central Bank would meet legitimate needs. But in two months that Bank sold less than US$200,000. Thus Chungking's action made little change.

Despite the inexorable march of inflation, Chinese exchange rates stayed surprisingly steady during most of the year up to the summer of 1941. The negotiations in Washington and news of several large credits buoyed the market. Also, people feared more and more that funds abroad might be blocked, and this not only dampened flight of capital but caused some repatriation of funds. But toward the end of December the market weakened. The rumor spread, by China's unexcelled rumor system, that the new stabilization credits would be used only in Free China. On December 23 rates broke sharply and the Sino-British Fund had to sell heavily to restore steadiness.

The Fund, nevertheless, did not have to incur large total net cost in 1940. Currency support cost only the equivalent of US$8 million, and the Fund's balance on December 31 was equivalent to about US$10 million. The supplementary Fund B had not been needed. In January 1941, there was another flurry in the market. But in 1941, as in 1940, the Fund incurred relatively little net cost for currency support, and in the Summer was able to hand over to the new Stabilization Board the equivalent of about US$5 million.

When Currie returned to Washington from Chungking early in March 1941, he reported his view that the chief advantage of continuing exchange support at Shanghai was the need to avoid a huge flow of currency from the occupied areas to Free China. He felt that support of the Shanghai market "should not be discontinued for the present." But because of that city's vulnerability he concurred with Minister Kung's view that "an open market in exchange should be gradually developed at Chungking." But Currie's most important new recommendation was that the United States and Britain should freeze Chinese assets abroad.[8] The possibility of freezing loomed large in the background, while the policy and organization for operation of the new American and British credits were being devised.

A NEW ORGANIZATION TAKES OVER

Morgenthau pressed at an early stage for K. P. Chen to be head of the Stabilization Board. The Generalissimo and Kung agreed, but apart from any question about Chen personally, who had represented China well at Washington, they were unhappy about what they regarded as interference in China's internal affairs. The other two Chinese members were Tsuyee Pei of the Bank of China; and T. M. Hsi of the Central Bank. All were well qualified for the work. The Secretary-General of the Board was Chao-ting Chi. It is not clear how he came to be chosen. He had been said to be a Communist while studying at Columbia University, but had returned to China about the end of 1938 and joined the National Government. It was then said he no longer was a Communist. Chi became a secretary to Minister Kung, before being named Secretary-General of the Board. After the Communist take-over in 1949, Chi received an important post in the Communist-seized Bank of China. During my association with him in 1941–1946 I saw no evidence of disloyalty. In 1944 Chi accompanied Kung to the Bretton Woods financial conference. In view of later charges that Harry D. White was connected with the Communist apparatus, it is of interest that White, who was in charge of planning the arrangements for that conference on behalf of the American Government, telegraphed in June, 1944, to Solomon Adler, then American Treasury Attaché in China and with whom Chi shared a house at that time in Chungking, suggesting that the Chinese Government send Chi to the conference.[9]

On May 1, 1941, Morgenthau was ready with his nomination for what White called "the really most difficult monetary job there is in the world." He announced he was recommending to China as the American member A. Manuel Fox, a member of the Tariff Commission. William H. Taylor of the Treasury was to be alternate. China agreed to these recommendations. Before Fox's nomination the Treasury considered others. Morgenthau approached Currie, who had visited China early in the year, but Currie did not want to go even for three months. The following report after the Secretary's talk with Currie is given in the Diaries of April 10:

H.M.Jr.: And he suggested one White, and I turned that down because I can't spare him, and he suggested Coe, and I can't spare him. So then he suggested Commissioner Fox of the Tariff Commission. He says it will be entirely acceptable to the President.

Bell: I don't know him at all. Harry [White] knows him. He suggested him the other day.[10]

Fox, however, was in no way a part of the White ring. Trained in engineering, he had some economic but not much financial experience. The Treasury had shown in the negotiations their intent to have a prominent say in China's monetary policy. Now, by choosing as their representative a man without previous connection with China, and who was by no means an expert in currency and foreign exchange, they showed their wish for a new deal in policy and practice. Where I am critical in what follows, it relates to the policies Fox was charged with carrying out, rather than to him personally. He and I had good personal relations. He gave himself loyally and sincerely to his hard task, the strain of which doubtless was partly responsible for his death in the summer of 1942 from a sudden heart attack. He was a true soldier of his country.* At the time of the evacuation of Chinese personnel from Hong Kong by air at outbreak of the Pacific War, W. L. Bond, who was in charge for CNAC, wrote in his report of December 17: "I would like to express my real appreciation for Mr. Fox. He organized his party exactly as requested. Also he did not include himself until he had made every effort to get all his staff out first." After the death of Fox, his alternate, Taylor, could not succeed him because he did not leave Hong Kong when the Japanese attacked. The successor was Solomon Adler of the Treasury.

Britain proposed as the British member Cyril Rogers, which was logical in view of his work as chairman of the committee operating the Sino-British fund. But on June 23 Fox reported to Morgenthau that the Generalissimo was "unalterably opposed to appointment of Rogers." [11] His rejection was unfortunate, as he had loyally and efficiently served China, even at sacrifice of health. But the Generalissimo and Kung felt that Rogers stood for the policy of stabilization operations in the free market of Shanghai, as to which they had developed increasing doubts. They felt he had been more closely associated with Soong than with them. Besides they were somewhat suspicious of British policy. As early as the spring of 1938, Ambassador Johnson reported to the State Department the British feeling, which Ambassador Clark Kerr had intimated to the Generalissimo, that China ought to rely upon Soong rather than Kung in financial matters, and that Rogers should assist Soong. The Generalissimo "received these suggestions coldly" (see chapter V).[12] So rejecting Rogers in 1941 was in part another manifestation of the long-standing differences within China's leading family. About August 1 China agreed to the British nomination of Edmund (later Sir Edmund) Hall-Patch, who had been financial adviser to the British embassies in China and Japan.

When the stabilization agreements were announced on April

* He was buried in the foreign cemetery at Chungking, which commands a splendid view of the Chialing River. Because no one of the Jewish faith was available to perform the ceremony, it was conducted in Old Testament terms by the Reverend C. B. Rappe of the Methodist Mission.

25, the exchange market in China was rather indifferent. There was known to be opposition in Chungking, and also by the Communists, to support of the Shanghai market. Nevertheless the market reaction was that "it would be exceedingly stupid to bring a huge stabilization fund into being in order to see the dollar grow weaker and weaker." [13] Discussing rumors from Chungking of exchange control, *Finance and Commerce* strikingly forecast the course of events when it said on May 21 (page 509):

> If the stabilization fund is to be used on the basis of providing official allotments of exchange under permit, it will merely have the effect of establishing a one-way traffic. Merchants, and others with legitimate claims, will apply for exchange at the official rates, but all exchange which has to be sold will naturally be sold on the "black" market, which will continue as before. The stabilization fund will feed and to a certain extent encourage the import trade, but it will do so (if it is active) at the cost of a gradual depletion of its resources.

The need, they said, is for a scheme allowing buying as well as selling that would "at the same time prevent exchange from going into undesirable channels," but they saw no indication how this problem could be tackled.

While the new organization was preparing to take over, its members did not face up to the need for a smooth transition from the old arrangements. Nor did they give due weight to the fact that the new setup could not function for some time, lacking such items as new appointees, staff, offices, codes, and above all lacking intimate familiarity with the problems at first hand. This situation reflected the friction over policies and personalities.

On June 20 Fox, shortly after his arrival in China, addressed the Third National Financial Conference at Chungking. He properly stressed the internal aspect of the currency problem and strongly urged a program of reforms. He thought the Stabilization Board should give attention to a broad range of fiscal and economic problems. He stressed the need for "new taxes, based mainly on the ability to pay" and collected "without fear or favor" by a nonpolitical civil service; and "a well organized and unified system of budgetary control." His remarks on the currency problem were necessarily very general, but he hoped the Board's work would have "favorable repercussions on the internal financial situation." He praised, however, China's program of industrial reconstruction paralleling the war effort.[14] Fox visited Shanghai about July 1 for first-hand information. *Finance and Commerce* reported that in his interviews there he always asked about the effect of withdrawing support of the national currency in the foreign exchange market. They commented that this doubtless was a necessary question, but caused some weakness in the market even though it was "unthinkable" that the Stabilization Board with its great resources would do that. The Chinese press of Shanghai as quoted by *Finance and Commerce* reported that Fox "has found adequate methods of improving the 'black' foreign exchange market here"; and that journal said that if so he "is an extremely fast worker, and will be able to report to the Government authorities that 'I came, I saw and I solved, within a week, a problem which has been worrying Shanghai banking circles for years past.' " Fox appears to have had in mind the ace in the hole—the belief that freezing was just around the corner. The market had some suspicion of this. On July 10 and 11 the Yokohama Specie Bank was reported to have sold US$1.5 million or more, and other banks sold apparently because of this belief.[15]

In mid-1941 the London *Economist* commented on China's currency problem. It was hard to prop a basically weak currency, because Japan controlled the main outlets for exports and pushed competing currencies. If Japan had *yuan* to spare they could use them to buy foreign exchange. Effective exchange control could prevent this, but it was hard enough to run it in the United Kingdom and it "would create a nightmare of difficulties in a country such as China." Hence, the *Economist* reasoned, China must remain a free market, with risk of diverting funds to "channels which neither Great Britain nor the United States wishes to feed." This risk "must be accepted in the cause of upholding Chinese confidence in the yuan," so that Japanese efforts to oust it or get much of it will fail. "The resistance of the yuan," they said, "to the heavy odds against which it has had to contend has been unexpectedly tenacious and successful." Despite its fall, "its hold on the loyalty and confidence of the Chinese population —even in the occupied parts of China—has not been shaken by this." [16]

But Fox had other ideas on policy. On July 21 he telegraphed to Morgenthau from Hong Kong his report of his visit to Shanghai. After reviewing the economic and financial conditions, he said that opinions differed on who got the foreign exchange sold by the Sino-British fund. Some thought the Japanese got much, and others thought they got little; some thought the larger part went to speculators including insiders. Fox came out definitely for exchange control and freezing. He concluded:

> It is my firm conviction after careful examination of the evidence that it would be foolhardy to subjugate (?subject) the new stabilization fund to the manipulations of Shanghai speculators and the Japanese and not provide reasonable safeguards to protect against unnecessary wastage. Before visiting Shanghai some doubts about the advisability of freezing Chinese funds might have been entertained. After visiting Shanghai I have not an iota of doubt. All (?legitimate buyers) should be provided with foreign exchange but a system should be introduced before or simultaneously with the start of functioning of the new stabilization fund to provide necessary scrutiny of all foreign exchange applications.[17]

THE FREEZING OF CHINESE AND JAPANESE ASSETS

For some time Washington had thought about freezing Chinese assets in the United States, to help China get control of private Chinese funds for the war effort. That was discussed at a Treasury conference as early as May 16, 1940, soon after Morgenthau had turned down the State Department's idea of aiding China by currency support. The two Departments then discussed freezing, but the State Department felt that the disadvantages would outweigh the advantages.[18] On December 28, 1940, the Treasury proposed that the United States freeze *all* foreign funds in the country, under a plan whose operation would rest mainly with the Treasury. But Secretary Hull blocked the move, seeing that it would have injected the Treasury very far into handling vital matters of foreign affairs.[19]

The issue whether to freeze Chinese assets became active early in 1941. The American and British Governments were thinking of freezing as a possible way to help China to work an "external" exchange control. The British then concluded, as we have seen, that such a scheme would not work satisfactorily, and so informed the Chinese and American Governments. Soong agreed with that view. In a memorandum of March 31, I concluded that a scheme based on freezing would have serious loopholes and be hard to work well, that it should not be tried unless the situation became "quite untenable," and that "the question arises whether the hurt done to Japan by restrictions imposed by the United States under a general control would offset the certain injury to China." The State Department apparently shared that view. George Luthringer of the Economic Adviser's Office stated in a memorandum of April 12 that the "disadvantage of freezing Chinese funds at this time would probably exceed the gains," especially if Japanese assets were not frozen at the same time.[20]

But meanwhile, unknown to the State Department or to me, Currie brought back from Chungking what he described as "a strongly written appeal" from the Generalissimo which urged freezing. He reported to Roosevelt, "I earnestly hope that you can comply with his wishes in this matter." [21] Roosevelt sent to the Treasury the Generalissimo's proposal. The Treasury decided to delay consideration until after the stabilization agreements were signed, the date of signing being April 25, 1941.[22]

On March 10 Ambassador Grew recommended consideration of freezing Japanese funds, as a means to reimburse owners of American business interests in Japan which, he reported, Japan was about to seize and control. The State Department's experts were divided about such freezing, and Secretary Hull opposed it.[23] In general that Department preferred aid to China to sanctions against Japan. American public opinion was hardening more and more against sending so much oil and other vital supplies to Japan, but isolationism was still strong. Also the Administration wanted to build greater military and naval strength before taking greater risks. There was real danger that to deprive Japan of oil, in particular, might bring attack upon British and Dutch possessions in Southeast Asia. With the issue against Hitler still in grave doubt, Britain did not want to see Japan in the war.

The Treasury, however, remained quite ready to make proposals on the international issues. On June 6 White submitted a memorandum to Secretary Morgenthau proposing a deal of tremendous proportions. He would try to end the fighting in China and wean Japan away from the Axis, letting Japan have Manchuria on condition of withdrawing from the rest of China and Indochina. He would give Japan financial aid and, after bringing her to friendly terms, would move the American fleet to the Atlantic. He would give Russia credits and economic aid, on condition of her stopping help to Hitler.[24]

On June 14 the United States froze German and Italian assets. The step brought nearer like action about Japan. Meanwhile in Japan fierce conflicts of policy were taking place. A strong group wanted a peaceful settlement, and sponsored negotiations with the United States through much of that troubled year. But events favored the expansionists. On June 22 Hitler attacked Russia. Not only did this remove for some time the threat to Japan from Russia, but early German victories promoted a belief that Hitler would triumph. So on July 2 Japan decided to embark upon the southward advance, regardless of the possibility of war with the United States and Britain. The background was a feeling in Japan's ruling circle that her aims could not be harmonized with the firmly stated American principles of respect for China's integrity and settlement of Pacific and Far Eastern issues by peaceful means. And there was strong resentment of the growing American support of China through credits and Lend-Lease, organization of the "Flying Tigers," staff talks with the British and Dutch coupled with supply of arms in Southeast Asia, plus tightening American restrictions on trade with Japan. Most of the July 2 decision was known in Washington by July 8, thanks to reports by Ambassador Grew and the breaking of the Japanese diplomatic code.[25]

On July 14 Japan demanded of the Vichy Government, with a deadline of July 20, permission to send land, sea, and air forces to southern Indochina, occupation of air and naval bases there, and removal of French garrisons from the places to be occupied by Japan. France had no means to resist and had to agree. On July 24 Acting Secretary of State Welles issued a statement that Japan was "giving clear indication that it is determined to pursue an objective of expansion by force or threat of force"; that the United States could only conclude that Japan was preparing further conquest; and that Japan's action tended to jeopardize American procurement of needed raw materials such as tin and rubber and endangered the safety of other Pacific areas including the Philippines.[26]

These grave events brought to a head the freezing issue. On July

18 Hornbeck recommended economic pressures against Japan as one means to show American disapproval. On July 19 Acting Secretary Welles, following Cabinet approval, asked him to have the necessary papers drawn by Monday, July 21, to effect simultaneous freezing of Japanese and Chinese assets, prohibition or restriction of imports of silk from Japan, and restriction of export of petroleum products to Japan. On July 21, also, Fox telegraphed to Morgenthau from Hong Kong, just after his visit to Shanghai, "unhesitatingly" recommending "that all Chinese funds in the United States be frozen, that simultaneous action be taken by both the American and British Governments and that a satisfactory organization be established for unfreezing Chinese funds." [27]

On July 26 Roosevelt announced the freezing of both Japanese and Chinese assets in the United States. The President's Executive Order #8389 (as amended) brought under control, as to Japan, all financial and trade transactions with the United States involving Japanese interests. It was designed, he said, to prevent use of American financial facilities and trade in ways harmful to American defense and interests, and prevent liquidating in the United States assets gotten by duress or conquest. As to China, the announcement said:

At the specific request of Generalissimo Chiang Kai-shek and for the purpose of helping the Chinese Government, the President has, at the same time, extended freezing control to Chinese assets in the United States. The administration of the licensing system with respect to Chinese assets will be conducted with a view to strengthening the foreign trade and exchange position of the Chinese Government. The inclusion of China in the Executive Order, in accordance with the wishes of the Chinese Government, is a continuation of this Government's policy of assisting China.

Great Britain took parallel freezing action, as did The Netherlands soon thereafter. Japan countered with her own freezing measures.

As from August 1 the United States also restricted oil exports to Japan, subjecting them to licensing control.[28] Freezing policy, however, started as flexible, without a policy declaration, and based on the idea of allowing limited trade but cutting oil products to about the 1935–1936 level except for stopping high octane gas. If Japan had shown any idea of desisting from expansion, the orders might have been relaxed. But Japan was preparing further moves. In practical effect, freezing amounted to an economic blockade of Japan.[29]

The amounts which the United States froze are indicated by a census of foreign-owned assets which the Treasury took a few weeks before, as of June 14, 1941. The totals were US$356 million for China; US$161 million for Japan; and US$84 million for Hong Kong, much of which was Chinese. Then and later a great deal of thought was given both in China and in the United States to China's getting possession of private Chinese assets abroad. Part of these represented flight of capital. I then opposed trying to take them over, largely because payment in China would have made available large purchasing power which would have sought refuge in buying goods for hoarding, and so would have added to the inflation. Eventually no feasible means of taking over these assets was found.

To operate the controls, the Treasury announced that it was licensing 14 well known Chinese and foreign banks as "appointed banks," and shortly increased the number to 26. These banks were to apply to the Stabilization Board for exchange to cover "legitimate imports" by their clients, and the Board would notify them whether it approved. No exchange was to be used for imports prohibited by China. Merchants receiving exchange from these banks were required to sell to them at official rates the proceeds of their exports, or set them off.[30]

The record makes clear that the freezing of Japanese assets followed Japan's fateful commitment of July 2 to expand southward, regardless of what the United States might do. Hence freezing as such could not be blamed for provoking the Pacific War. But Japan's reaction was strong. Foreign Minister Toyoda gravely warned Ambassador Grew that "the peace of the Pacific" might be involved. Grew wrote in his diary that it would be hard to stop "the momentum of this downgrade movement in our relations," of which "The obvious conclusion is eventual war." [31] Langer and Gleason reached the following conclusions based on their study of the contemporary and postwar record:

The freezing order was probably the crucial step in the entire course of Japanese-American relations before Pearl Harbor. It was not initially intended to end all American trade with Japan, but rather to serve as a means of exerting pressure as the circumstances warranted. But in practice no exports of any consequence reached Japan after August, nor was Japanese silk or any other commodity imported into the United States. Thanks to the cooperation of the nations of the British Commonwealth and of the Netherland Indies, the ensuing economic blockade of Japan was all but complete. If one thing was more certain than another, it was that Japan could not continue under such pressure for more than a few months. American officials were well aware that Japan had been given a choice between climbing down or fighting it out. Many believed that Japan was in no condition to fight and would have to climb down. Others, including a majority of the Cabinet, expected that Japan would fight, but one and all felt that Japan's chances of success in war were slim. It was therefore largely a matter of postponing the evil day as long as possible so as to gain time for further American preparations.

. . . The truth of the matter was that the policies of the two powers were no longer reconcilable.[32]

As a matter of fact, at no time in the ten years following Japan's Manchurian adventure begun September 18, 1931, had American and Japanese policies been reconcilable.

GIVING EFFECT TO THE NEW PLAN

In China opinion welcomed the freezing as a blow against Japan. Predominant official and press opinion in Chungking hoped that the resulting financial measures would provide China with needed goods and check the inflation, and wipe out the "black" market at Shanghai which many blamed for the price rises. But news of the freezing upset the Shanghai market. In two weeks rates slumped by over 10 per cent from the levels of July 25, which were 3¼d. and US$0.05 11/32. Reuter's News Service reported from Shanghai on July 28 that "repercussions are already felt in essential foodstuffs and commodities whose prices have already gone up 10 to 15 per cent." Dealings in exchange were nominal and the market was nervous, not knowing what to expect.

The striking steadiness of China's currency in the exchange market in the year prior to July 26, 1941, was due largely to talk of freezing, and even of general war with Japan. Formerly talk of war had brought buying of foreign currencies. But, said *Finance and Commerce*, April 16, 1941 (page 387): "Those days are gone. Any indication of further and more serious trouble in the Far East now brings with it a disposition to call money home from its far distant resting places, while the going is good." But the very steadiness was building up an unstable situation, and problems for the future, because prices within China were rising with no real letup, while the value of her money in terms of other currencies refused to go down. In July 1941, the buying power of China's money was 11 to 12 per cent of its value four years earlier, as measured by two indices of wholesale prices at Shanghai; and in Free China 8.7 per cent, as measured by average retail prices. But in the exchange market for American dollars, whose buying power changed little in that period, China's money was worth about 17 per cent of the prewar figure.* In a memorandum of August 9 I called Minister Kung's attention to the disadvantages of an overvalued currency.† I urged that the Board's rates be realistic and flexible, and that the free exchange market continue "at least for the present."

Effective August 18, 1941, the Stabilization Board announced its official rates, 3 5/32d. and US$.05 5/16. These official rates were 10 per cent above the free market,** which already involved a big overvaluation. The rates chosen were the average rates for July, a basis said to have been chosen at White's suggestion. With announcement of official rates, the free market came under a ban. It was commonly called the "black market"; but the government had no way to stop it in the areas outside its control and in Free China made no serious effort to stop it or to penalize those using it. Reuters News Service reported from Shanghai on August 18, "The official rate applies only to merchants able to obtain permits under the freezing regulations," and, "Bankers said that the black market dealings would continue, however, on account of the fact that many would be unable to obtain permits." On September 6, publication of black market rates ended at the Board's request.

---

* See appendix I and the graph on page 43.

† "A. Sales of exchange for currency stabilization or to support China's public finances . . . will not withdraw as large a sum from circulation as if the rate of exchange were lower. B. Discouragement of overseas remittances . . . C. Discouragement of exports. D. Increased difficulties to philanthropic and missionary institutions whose income is in foreign currency . . . E. Overvalued exchange tends to cause over-importing and an adverse balance of payments. F. Building up a false and artificial situation, which later will have to be corrected in order to effect a proper economic adjustment between China's economy and the economies of other countries."

** On August 16 (Saturday) the market closed at 2 27/32d. and US$.04 3/4.

The Board began to receive applications for exchange for "legitimate" imports. It set up its main office at Hong Kong and hurriedly got together a staff to handle applications. It began to prepare monthly programs of permitted trade. Fox reported to the Treasury in November that Shanghai had a big output of goods reaching the interior, including 65 per cent of the textiles, 45 per cent of the knitted goods, and 35 per cent of machines and machine tools. He was favorable to the encouragement of essential imports into Shanghai, believing that it cared for the needs of Chinese in that area and led to inflow of needed goods to Free China. Cochran of the Treasury, who visited China in October, took a like view after his visit to Shanghai. But there was much criticism in Chungking of sustaining that hotbed of speculators and Japanese and puppets. At the November meeting of the People's Political Council the Board was criticized for support of Shanghai and also for staying at Hong Kong rather than being at Chungking.[33]

The Board in its first six weeks to the end of September sold about US$10 million of exchange, of which about two-thirds was dollars and the rest sterling. Most of this was sold in the first ten days. It rejected applications for about half as much. These heavy sales brought in nearly C$200 million. Consul General A. E. Southard reported from Hong Kong on August 23, "The American banks in Hongkong state that their Shanghai branches did not have room enough in their vaults for the large quantity of Chinese currency obtained from the sale of American dollars at the advantageous rate."[34] These sales withdrew so much currency that they had a sustaining effect on the exchange market, but the market remained nervous though at fairly steady rates until October.

Meanwhile, with uncertainty about the future of the exchange market, speculators and those wishing to protect their funds turned to commodities and real estate. Activity in commodities became feverish. In August–September cotton yarn prices rose about 40 per cent at Shanghai, and this was important for Free China since textiles from Shanghai were shipped there in large amounts. In November the price of sugar rose by 140 per cent.

In October the market had a really bad time. Freezing checked the sale of foreign currencies that otherwise might have been repatriated. And importers hastened to buy foreign currencies, because they had reports that the Board was going to tighten up on allotments.* Also the advent of General Tojo's government in Japan hurt confidence. In five weeks to early November rates in the black market fell by 45 per cent, to about half the Board's official rates. The panic amounted to a flight from the currency. American dollar notes were in special demand. Some of us wanted the Board to sell both exchange and notes at Shanghai to restore an orderly market, and the cost probably would not have been great. But the Board would not hear of this. The disorder in the market got worse when a United Press telegram from Washington, October 14, stated that "informed sources" doubted that the Board would intervene to bolster the national currency at Shanghai. Finally the Board acquiesced in operations by the Bank of China to support Chinese currency in the note market at Hong Kong.

In the Summer and Fall, prices in China rose much faster than before. Average prices rose by over 80 per cent in the second half of 1941, compared with 43 per cent, 51 per cent, 49 per cent, and 45 per cent in the preceding four half-yearly periods.† The faster rise was not due to any material change in the proportion of expenditure covered by inflationary credit. Undoubtedly in the second half of 1941 impaired confidence in the currency caused the public to spend money sooner after it was received, and this faster turnover accelerated the rise of prices. We cannot isolate the various factors then affecting prices, for example, the growing chance of a Pacific war. But it is clear from what I have recounted that the change in currency policy was a major factor in the faster deterioration.

The Board tried to require those who bought exchange at such a bargain to pass the benefits to the consumer. There was some success in this at Shanghai. There the Municipal Council

*Importers who could not get exchange from the Board, or feared they could not, went to the black market. Linking of export-import deals began through unlicensed banks, thus reducing the supply of exchange sold in the market. From a level of about 2 3/4d. and US$.04 3/4 at the end of September, rates broke to about 1 7/8d. and US$.03 1/16 by mid-October. After some recovery they slumped again, with the dollar at US$.02 5/8 on November 5.

† The figures of average prices show a rise of 88 per cent in the second half of 1941, but I have adjusted this figure to 81 per cent to allow for dropping from the compilation in the last two months of 1941 of Shanghai, where prices were lower than the average in Free China. Data for that city for those two months were not available because of outbreak of the Pacific War.

arranged with the Board in November to provide US$4 million monthly for regular programs of imports of rice, flour, vegetable oils, and coal, to be sold at prices based on the official rates of exchange. That forced hoarders to unload stocks at a loss, and consumers gained. But there were no such controls in Free China, where they could not be administered properly, nor in enemy-controlled areas. So the benefits of cheap exchange went largely to various dealers and middlemen rather than to the ultimate consumer.

The new program was costly. In about three and one-half months to December 1, the Board spent about US$13.5 million and £1.8 million, a total equivalent to about US$21 million, an average of nearly US$6 million monthly. The sales of dollars were from the Chinese contribution, hence it was not necessary to use the American contribution of US$50 million. The sterling was from the British contribution. The Board could not recoup from the market much of their sales. The rates that gave importers a bargain had the opposite effect for exporters, who could get more national currency if they sold foreign currencies in the black market than by selling to the Board. Furthermore, the Board's receipts from remittances by overseas Chinese slowed down, for a similar reason. In about five months to January 12, 1942, the Board's total receipts in foreign currencies from exports were only US$106,500.[35] Fox estimated that for the future the net drain on the Fund would be perhaps US$5 million monthly. But that assumed receipts of several million monthly from exports and overseas Chinese remittances.[36] This expectation of receipts could have been approached only if the Board's official rates of exchange were kept in reasonable harmony with internal prices. Chungking, judging by later policy, would not have allowed this.

Chungking praised the denial of exchange to speculators and the enemy. But Shanghai was critical despite the Board's generous allotments. Comments were that the Board's work was a "virtual failure . . . due to the yuan not being stabilized," and that "Shanghai is becoming heartily sick at the mere mention of the name of the Stabilization Board."[37] In Washington the Treasury was not happy about how the program was working. A memorandum of November 18 from White to Morgenthau said, "Repeated instances of Japanese interests in China being the ultimate beneficiaries of exports to Shanghai have been received and there is reason to believe that a large percentage of the approximately $10 million worth of goods shipped from the United States to Occupied China since freezing orders were issued, found their way to Japan proper." [38] This came with strange grace from an agency that had persistently argued that the previous policy benefited the enemy.

The Treasury prepared a plan for better control of trade, and H. Merle Cochran of the Treasury took it to China in November. The plan provided that all Sino-American trade be cleared with the Board.* This plan was put in operation November 12. Britain and the Netherlands took similar action. Because Pearl Harbor supervened within a month, there was little time to see the effect of these measures. They would have checked import of less essential goods and tended to shrink the black market, but also they would have tended to divert part of China's trade to Japan and to intensify Japanese action to control trade and to push puppet currencies.

The approximate cost of the previous stabilization operations in three years and two months to August 1941, had been:

	US$ millions (equivalent)
Bank of China net sales, June 14, 1938 to April 10, 1939, taken over by Anglo-Chinese Fund	6
Ministry of Finance allotments of exchange to the market, June 14, 1938, until termination of allotments June 30, 1939	6
Anglo-Chinese Fund, net sales, April 10, 1939 to August 18, 1941, less Bank of China net sales taken over	34
Total	46

That averaged about US$1.2 million monthly for the whole period. Thus the US$21 million which the Board had spent in about three and one-half months was nearly half what the former operations had cost in three years and two months. The Board's average monthly cost was nearly five times the figure for the former operation. The prospect was for a heavy continuing cost. And these high costs were over and above the intangible, yet significant, damage which the new policy and procedure did by stimulating inflation.

* Two months previously Carl Neprud of the Chinese Customs and I recommended a similar plan.

The outbreak of the Pacific War diverted attention from this situation and saved those responsible for the plan from criticism which otherwise they would have had to face.

APPRAISAL

The freezing and resulting controls of trade and foreign exchange had far-reaching effects upon China, Japan, and the Western world. In China the measures were financially upsetting. Withdrawal of support of free market rates hurt confidence in the currency and led to a faster price rise. The measures indeed curtailed speculation in exchange, but diverted speculation to the buying and hoarding of goods—which was more damaging to China. Sales of exchange at the fixed bargain rates gave inordinate profits to importers, who sold the imports mostly at inflated prices. The exchange control proved a far more costly way to aid China than had the policy of supporting the free market from mid-1938 to mid-1941. And it was ironic that the creation with American backing of a system of overvalued exchange rates, whose operation was bound to be inflexible, set the scene for the costly financing of American military outlay in China after 1941. China's insistence upon payment in dollars, at the fixed rate of 20 to 1, for steadily depreciating Chinese currency led to serious Sino-American friction during the Pacific War (see chapters XIV and XV).

The main advantage of the measures was to give the American Treasury, and also China's leaders, a superficially plausible defense against the charge that aid to China was being "poured down a rat hole" or going to the enemy (though the working of the new policy probably helped the enemy more than had the former policy). With dollars allocated to pay for specific imports, the "end-use" could be accounted for and sales of exchange could be shown to be "legitimate." * In view of the financial detriment,

---

* Analogous to the Treasury policy of 1941 is a practice which has been used generally in providing American postwar aid. The United States commonly requires the aided countries to submit for approval import programs, listing the imports from the United States and elsewhere that are to be paid for by aid dollars and sold to raise local currency for the aid programs. To authorize and control this trade, which sometimes is a large part of the aided country's imports, the United States maintains an elaborate and costly organization. These imports are not the goods used for specific aid projects, yet the organization checks their "end-use." The justification put forward for this costly and obstructive procedure, which is

an argument in behalf of the new stabilization policy must rest on grounds of American political expediency, as judged by the Treasury. By indicating that it favored exchange control, the Treasury at once gained the support of those leaders in China who already were so inclined. The Treasury thus overrode the views of those operating and supporting the former policy in China and of its backers in the State Department, and the considered financial opinion of the British Government.

The freezing of China's assets had no necessary connection with the freezing of Japanese assets. Rather, it was done at China's request, and because it was needed for operation of the plan to control China's exchange. To have frozen Chinese assets alone would have seemed anomalous, coming a few weeks after the freezing of German and Italian assets. Thus the Chinese request and the plan of exchange control for China were intangible elements in the situation that led to freezing of Japanese assets.

As to the effect of the freezing and trade controls on Japan, the die had been cast by Japan's fateful decision of July 2, 1941, after Hitler's attack on Russia, to embark upon a southward expansion regardless of opposition. The freezing on July 26, Hornbeck has pointed out, "was only one of many indications that we did not intend to withdraw or be ousted." [39] Freezing, however, was done at about the same time by the United States, Britain, and The Netherlands. It thus may well have worked to cause Japan to attack all three of her chief Western opponents at once on December 7/8, 1941. Had Japan proceeded piecemeal against Thailand, the Dutch Indies, and the British colonies, such aggression probably would soon have brought the United States into the war. But not with the promptness and unity and fervor caused by the surprise attack at Pearl Harbor.

On the very eve of Pearl Harbor I summed up my views on the new monetary policy in a letter to Mrs. Young. I said: "If a Pacific war comes, the harm that has been done will be lost sight of; but if there is no war for a few months the effects of the policy are likely to become more clear. The Board have a bear

---

inconsistent with American advocacy of free enterprise and the ending of foreign trade and exchange controls, is that some members of Congress and others want that information—which actually has little real importance. See my letter to the *New York Times*, February 5, 1961.

by the tail. They will have to keep on putting out millions of U.S. dollars month after month unless they abandon Shanghai . . . which would be the effect of stopping. We were blamed for the cost of our former policy; but it will be nothing compared with the cost of the new one if there is no war or if Shanghai is not abandoned." [40] The day after writing this letter I recalled that I finished it at 1:05 a.m. December 8, Chungking time. A few minutes later, and five thousand miles away, the bombs began to fall at Pearl Harbor.

XI. A SUMMING UP, 1937–1941

THE AID THAT WAS NOT ENOUGH

FOR four years and five months, a period longer than World War I, China fought alone against great odds. Friendly nations helped but, over-all, their help in these years was too often too little, late, and not the kind best suited to strengthen China's resistance and add to her chance of survival as a free nation.

The American Treasury's buying of China's silver in the first two years, thanks to Secretary Morgenthau, was invaluable. Although there was no granting of credit, this buying converted unusable silver reserves into usable dollars at firm prices. Total purchases after July 10, 1937, were about 362 million ounces, for US$157 million. Adding prewar purchases, the grand total was about 550 million ounces, for US$252 million. American silver policy changed history. After this policy forced China in 1935 to give up the age-old silver standard, the adoption of a managed currency enabled China to finance the war largely by inflation. On a silver basis, China could not have found a flexible method to finance a prolonged struggle, and organized resistance would probably have been a matter of months rather than years. The very length of the war was to prove a major factor in fixing China's fate.

It was Russia that provided to China the only prompt credits and military aid. In the early months of fighting, China got from Russia large amounts of munitions and planes, and also "volunteer" pilots. Russia did not wait for the signing of formal agreements, which did not come before March 1938. The United States, Britain, and France—except for protests to Japan and American silver-buying—did little to aid China for nearly 18 months. By December 1938, when the first modest American and British credits were announced, Russia had provided US$100 million of credits, much of which had been used. Prior to 1940, Russian credits authorized were more than three times those of the West. Moreover, Russian credits, in striking contrast to those

from the West, could be used for implements of war and munitions. And Russia, although her homeland was far more exposed
to possible Japanese vengeance than that of any Western power,
promptly supplied even military advisers and "volunteer" aviation personnel who actually fought for China. This action in
China was a genuine "first" for the Russians, as they anticipated
Chennault's Flying Tigers by over three years. For Russia the
war was vicarious, to keep Japan off her own neck. Hence Russia
was "correct" in providing aid only to the National Government
and not to the Chinese Communists, even after the internal conflict was clearly growing. Russia's terms, with 3 per cent interest,
were more liberal than the terms of the American and British
purchase credits to China in 1938–1941. Russian aid had no
political strings. And the National Government was canny
enough to use the aid without becoming too dependent upon
Russia.

Total foreign credits to China authorized before the Pacific
War were equivalent to US$513.5 million. Most of this was for
purchases; US$93 million was for currency support. Details are
shown in appendix II. Russia granted US$250 million to pay for
supplies and services. Of the US$263.5 million from the Western
nations, the United States provided US$170 million, of which
US$120 million was for purchases and US$50 million for currency
support. Britain provided US$78.5 million, of which US$35.5
million was for purchases and US$43 million for currency sup-
port; and France provided US$15 million for railway construc-
tion. Also, besides credits, the United States provided US$26
million of Lend-Lease in 1941. The grand total of aid from all
countries authorized in 1937–1941, including Lend-Lease, was
US$539.5 million.

In this period, however, the amount actually utilized of the
various credits plus Lend-Lease was only about US$350 million,
or less than two-thirds of what was authorized. Using dollar figures, which give the only available comparison, Russian and
Western aid utilized before the Pacific War were about equal
in amount.* In the first two and a half years, that is, before 1940,

* Russian aid utilized in 1937–1941 is estimated at US$170 million (the total
was US$173 million and practically all was used before 1942). Western aid is
estimated thus: American purchase credits US$95 million (US$104 million had
been used as of early 1945); American lend-lease US$26 million; British purchase

the amount of Russian credits utilized was nearly thrice as great as in the case of Western credits. By 1940, however, Russian aid began to taper off; and Western aid gathered momentum, with grants for purchases and for currency support and the start of American Lend-Lease in 1941.

The Western purchase credits, US$120 million from the United States and the equivalent of US$35.5 million from Britain, helped China to get a great volume of needed goods and services which otherwise she could not have afforded. The purchasing procedure for the American credits worked efficiently, through the Universal Trading Company, a Sino-American corporation in New York. Federal procurement officers helped China to get good prices. The deals were clean, without "squeeze." The credits could not be used for munitions or currency support. But they freed other funds, even though quite limited, for these major needs. Washington allowed purchase of some partly fabricated items that could readily be converted to military use. Yet the objection to use for munitions handicapped China, and contrasted with Russia's liberality. In May 1941, China became eligible for Lend-Lease. This eased the need for use of the credits. China used about US$95 million of the American credits before Pearl Harbor, and US$104.5 million by the war's end. China delivered the promised strategic exports, despite great difficulties; and these proved valuable to the United States both before and after becoming involved in the war. China had almost entirely repaid the American credits by June 30, 1949. Of the British advances, part of the credit of £2,859,000 was repaid and about £900,000 of the credit of £5 million. Of the Russian advances totaling an estimated US$173 million used, China owed about US$55 million as of mid-1946.[1]

The various purchase credits from the West, once they started at the end of 1938, pretty well took care of the supplies China needed, other than strictly military items. Not all that China bought could be gotten into the country, because of transport difficulties. Unfortunately China lost many of the goods in transit when Japan overran Indochina and later Burma.

These purchase credits, however, involved a serious offsetting

credits US$20 million and stabilization credits US$27 million; French credits US$12 million; total US$180 million. The American stabilization credit was kept intact.

detriment. China had to provide local currency to pay her producers for the wood oil, tin, and other items exported to repay the credits. Available data indicate that in 1938–1941 payments for interest and principal, by shipments of exports, were of the order of US$85 to 90 million, of which US$60 to 65 million was for Russia. The money for such outlay, over and above other expenditures, could come only from the printing press. It thus further aggravated inflation. Ambassador Johnson saw this. In a telegram of October 23, 1940, he pointed out that American aid was "offered only at a high cost which is draining the country of the money and resources which might otherwise back the currency and prevent soaring prices." [2] Outright grants, or credits with principal payments deferred during the war, would have been far better. But, prior to Lend-Lease, grants were not politically possible, and the credits had to appear in the Western countries as commercially justifiable.

China's chief needs which aid failed to meet in 1937–1941 were for currency support and for military purchases, especially airplanes. How much could China have used reasonably well in this period?

A beginning of currency support was made early in 1939 by Britain's credit of £5 million, equivalent to about US$23 million. This was granted after Britain failed to induce the United States to take joint or parallel action. The credit was timely. But it was too small, and even 50 to 100 per cent more would have enabled China to avoid the damaging breakdown of the Fund in July 1939.

China, I believe, should have had in 1938–1941 US$100 to 125 million over and above the British credit of 1939, for currency support in the free market prior to the Pacific War. It was specially unfortunate that, in the critical years from 1938 to the latter part of 1940, the United States would not go along with Britain in a joint or parallel effort for currency support, in which for a time France was ready to join. The State Department gradually came to favor this action, but the Treasury would not agree. China's handling would have fallen much short of perfection. But I believe that the funds would have been fairly well used, judging by the experience in 1938–1941 when China had only limited funds for this purpose. With tactful negotiation, desirable "strings" could have been put on the aid, for example, management by a competent Sino-foreign committee. That would have been in the interest both of China and of the aiding countries.

Such aid would have put a brake on inflation and strengthened China's over-all position. Even the imperfect action, with inadequate resources, that China was able to take to support the foreign exchange value of the currency and to maintain an orderly market at Shanghai helped to keep confidence in the currency and in the government. It showed the people in both the free and occupied parts of China that the government was still a going concern. This was specially important at times of defeats, enemy action against the currency, or other adverse events, whose effects panicky markets would have magnified, perhaps disastrously. Currency support helped to convince friendly nations that China was not beyond help. It retarded exploitation of enemy conquests, making it harder to push the circulation of puppet currencies. China could not escape the need to issue paper money to cover much of the war's cost. While the printing presses were pouring out a huge volume of notes, support of the currency was helping to give it a value throughout the country and thus allowing the process to continue. Furthermore, when foreign currencies were sold for market support, national currency was taken out of circulation. Thus the support operations tended to hold back the inflation.

China had no spot more vulnerable than her currency. Without the stabilization operations which China conducted in 1938–1941 "on a shoestring," with relatively small British aid, there is grave doubt whether China could have avoided financial collapse during the war, perhaps even before Pearl Harbor. China did not appreciate the value of the British aid, but she should have.

American aid for currency support, although promised late in 1940, was not actually available until August 18, 1941, about three and a half months before Pearl Harbor. Then the American-British-Chinese program provided the equivalent of nearly US$100 million, an adequate amount. But the American Treasury insisted upon an experiment with exchange control despite warnings that it could not work well. The result was to aggravate China's inflation; to bring costs that were far higher than under the policy of supporting the currency in the free market; and to create a system of inflexible and overvalued exchange rates. That system greatly increased what the American army had to pay to get Chinese currency during the Pacific War, and led to serious Chinese-American friction.

Moreover, the working of the system of exchange control depended upon freezing Chinese assets abroad. That, in practice, could not have been done without at the same time freezing Japanese assets. When Chinese and Japanese assets were frozen almost simultaneously by the United States, Britain, and The Netherlands, about the end of July 1941, the nature of the action was not lost upon Japan. The Japanese militarists had already decided upon the southward advance, come what may. But the joint freezing may well have promoted the decision to attack the three nations all at once on December 7/8, instead of a piecemeal southward advance. A piecemeal attack upon Dutch and British territory probably would have brought the United States into the war, but not with the unity and zeal aroused by the attack at Pearl Harbor.

The second half of 1938 was when the friendly nations should have begun to help China to support her currency in the free market. A lead by the United States could have made this possible. Even American encouragement to Britain in July 1938 might have tipped the scales in favor of such aid (see chapter V). Then China was successfully supporting the currency with her own meager resources. Adequate help by joint or parallel action of the friendly nations beginning then could have had an important impact. It might have mitigated later frictions both within China and between China and her Western friends. It might even have provided machinery to help with China's postwar rehabilitation. It would have helped to check the deterioration that was later to have such grave internal and international consequences.

As to military purchases, it is not easy to estimate how much China could have used well in 1937–1941. Not only is military "hardware" expensive, but even with prompt and massive Western aid, to apply it effectively would have raised hard problems: how to get sizable amounts of munitions and other goods to places where China needed them, due to Japan's blockade; and how to use the items effectively once delivered. It is far from easy, as the United States has been finding out, to give large aid quickly and with good effect to underdeveloped countries. The war laid bare China's shortage of physical facilities and trained people, and the basic need for reforms in military and civil affairs.

In aviation, China could have used fairly well many Western planes, beginning early in the war, but only if providing them had been accompanied by "strings," for example, training of pilots and use of planes under Chennault or other competent officers. It would have been largely futile merely to provide planes to the Chinese Aviation Commission as it existed in this period* Moreover, provision of planes would have given an important stimulus to the output of planes in the West and could have alerted the West to Japan's capabilities and progress in aviation, for example, the development of her Zero planes by 1940. The advantages would have been greater had the West earlier matched Russia by also providing "volunteer" aviation personnel. Russia's experience indicates that this could probably have been done without war in 1938–1941; and it might have discouraged later Japanese adventures. But it was not within the realm of practicable American politics until the latter part of 1940.

In November 1937, China at the Brussels Conference asked a credit of US$500 million for war purposes, from the United States, Britain, and France. In retrospect, that proposal was eminently realistic as to amount. Had these powers found themselves able to grant such aid, the course of events might have been greatly changed for the better. A half billion spent in 1937 might have saved huge later costs, the end of which is not yet. When, a year later, there still was no western credit to China, the Shanghai British periodical, *Finance and Commerce*, made a prescient comment:

The grim fact is that, unless substantial help is very quickly forthcoming, Chinese democrats will be compelled to turn toward Communism in sheer desperation—and the democratic Powers will be left to wail exceedingly at the disaster overtaking a nation which, had it received the support that should have been swiftly forthcoming at the very beginning, would have

* That was shown later in the war, when American-trained Chinese fliers failed to do much when put under commanders without American training. When later these fliers were brigaded with Chennault's men, they did well.

developed into a most powerful ally in the cause of peaceful political progress.[3]

The four and one half years in which China fought alone were critical. The United States and the entire free world are now paying heavily for American isolationism which prevented this country from taking the lead in granting promptly to China the aid for which she pled. Even after Lend-Lease was authorized in the spring of 1941, American eyes were focused mainly upon Europe. The importance of aid to China was too often ignored, and aid was opposed in some official quarters. Then, and during the rest of the war, China felt a lack of recognition and a sense of inequality.

AID AND EQUALITY

Failure to get larger and prompter aid was disheartening enough to China. But besides this was the feeling that it reflected on China's standing and ignored her great contribution and sacrifices in fighting alone against Japan for over four years. In a telegram of August 27, 1941, Ambassador Gauss reported, "The Chinese want, as much as they want material assistance, to be recognized as equal partners in the fight against aggression." [4] They felt that China had been ignored in the Roosevelt-Churchill conversations in the summer of 1941, and that China should have participated in the Moscow conference in the fall along with the United States and Britain. In a radio address of October 10, 1941, Madame Chiang Kai-shek said:

> We feel that we have earned equality of status with the other democracies, but we do not want it granted to us in charity . . . We have an indispensable right to be consulted and to make our voice heard when others deliberate about Asia and the Pacific. We are the senior nation in the stand against aggression, therefore we ought not to be treated as a junior in the common councils of the anti-aggression nations . . . We cannot rest secure until you unreservedly recognize our right to take our full share of responsibility in planning a world order that will prevent future aggression.[5]

The long American-Japanese conversations of 1941 gave rise to great nervousness in China, and fear of appeasement at China's expense. In China it could be seen very clearly that there was no real chance of ending the Japanese occupation short of military defeat. The State Department also recognized that difficulty. An analysis of Japanese penetration of China, made a few weeks before Pearl Harbor, stated that the Japanese administered "down to small detail" the transport, communications, utilities, mails, finances, and major markets of occupied China. Hundreds of thousands of Japanese civilians were busy in these activities. The army "has a vested interest . . . in business and 'rackets' in China on an all-out scale"; ". . . is enjoying power, wealth, authority, and good living undreamed of before"; and ". . . we may be certain that the army is not going to give up China lightly." [6]

Generalissimo Chiang told Washington in a message of November 25 that enemy propaganda was spreading the idea that Japan and the United States would make a deal. He said that any relaxation of the freezing or embargoes against Japan would cause the Chinese people to feel that "China has been completely sacrificed by the United States"; that China would collapse and "every Asiatic nation will lose faith"; and that the situation would be hopeless, even if the United States later came to China's rescue.[7] Churchill also was worried by the China angle of the negotiations. In a telegram to Roosevelt on November 26 he said:

Of course, it is for you to handle this business and we certainly do not want an additional war. There is only one point that disquiets us. What about Chiang Kai-shek? Is he not having a very thin diet? Our anxiety is about China. If they collapse, our joint dangers would enormously increase.[8]

For the record, the final American proposal of November 26 to Japan was not one of appeasement. Nor was it in any sense an ultimatum. One of the vital points in the draft proposed to Japan—for discussion of a possible agreement—was that Japan "withdraw all military, naval, air and police forces from China and from Indo-China." [9]

Nevertheless China felt hurt, especially after her staunchness against Japan and almost unbelievable sacrifices, by not having a part in major negotiations that might vitally affect her future. The sense of inequality, rooted in over a century of being pushed around, rankled during the rest of the war and made it harder after the war to deal with Nationalist and later Communist China.

Part Two
The Fourth Power
1941–1945

XII. MASSIVE FINANCIAL INJECTIONS

CHINA'S leaders had been telling their people since 1937 that China eventually would defeat Japan. But thoughtful people well knew that this could come about only if stronger nations joined the war. Japan's attack of December 7/8, 1941, which simultaneously brought into the war the United States, the British Empire, and The Netherlands, gave China new hope. But that hope was quickly clouded by Allied defeats—at Pearl Harbor and in Hong Kong, the Philippines, Malaya, and the East Indies. To us in Chungking in the early months of the Pacific War, it seemed that the only saving of Western prestige was the brilliant performance of Chennault's Flying Tigers and the American stand at Bataan. By the spring of 1942 most of Burma was lost. China's only link with the Western allies was the tenuous air route to Calcutta, explored two weeks before Pearl Harbor and maintained only by four two-motored planes. China's allies could not even hold their own areas against Japan, let alone lend to China prompt and effective military aid.

After what Hornbeck called "a miracle of war-making," China was worn and weary and needed aid more than ever. But planes and other strategic items were in short supply and far away. There was no question, however, about the United States being able to deliver dollar credits to China on short notice and in whatever amounts China could use. And financially China's difficulties were as grave as they were militarily. By the end of 1941 prices had risen about 20-fold from prewar. How to cope with acute and ever-faster inflation in an overstrained economy stood out as a major issue. So it was natural to turn to financial aid. Moreover, there were questions of China's morale. China could still win some of the battles; this was shown at the turn of the year in the defeat of Japan's attempt to capture Changsha. But if Japan quickly seized all of Southeast Asia, including Burma, would China be able to continue fighting? A Sino-Japanese peace would be a terrible blow to the Allied cause.

CHINA SEEKS BIG LOANS

More than a year earlier China had begun to talk about a really big credit, of US$200 to 300 million (chapter IX). In November 1941, on the eve of the Pacific War, Minister Kung broached the idea at Chungking to H. Merle Cochran of the American Treasury. Kung thought that such a credit, used as reserve, would strengthen confidence even if the fund were not touched. In the latter part of November, I returned to Chungking, after absence in Burma, and found the idea of a large loan engaging the active attention of the highest Chinese leaders. They decided to send a proposal to Secretary Morgenthau by the hand of Owen Lattimore, who on President Roosevelt's recommendation had been serving as political adviser to Generalissimo Chiang,* and who was about to leave for the United States. I helped prepare a statement dated December 3 for the Secretary, expressing gratitude for American help by Lend-Lease and previous credits and pointing out the seriousness of the inflation. A loan of US$500 million, said the statement, would strengthen public confidence in the currency and check the price rise. While helping to prepare this presentation for Washington, I felt bound to point out in a memorandum of December 3 that although such a loan "would doubtless have some temporary psychological value" and would be "invaluable for a future currency reform," it could only be really effective if some means were found to use it to check the growth of note issue, such as to facilitate issuance of bonds subscribed in local currency.

The communication to Morgenthau was never delivered. Lattimore was to leave with it December 8. I began a letter of December 7 to Mrs. Young as follows: "I have a chance to send a letter by Owen Lattimore who is due to leave on the next Clipper—if there is one." Early on December 8, when I telephoned to learn about the time of the CNAC plane's departure for Hong Kong from Chungking, I was told of Pearl Harbor, which was attacked at 1:25 a.m. December 8, Chungking time.

Meanwhile Cochran had reached Washington and reported Kung's proposal of a month before. On December 16 Morgenthau

---

* As to the circumstances of this recommendation, see Hornbeck's testimony, Hearings, Institute of Pacific Relations, part 9, pp. 3209–3210. Hornbeck testified that Currie told him that he, Currie, had recommended Lattimore to Roosevelt, and that the State Department was not consulted.

sent word to Kung that he had not yet been able to focus on the proposal but that it would have "the attention and respect due to a nation which has so courageously and successfully resisted Japanese militarism." [1]

On December 30 Generalissimo Chiang told Ambassador Gauss that he wanted about a billion dollars—US$500 million and £100 million. Gauss was favorable to a political loan in principle, but he believed China's chance to get it would be aided by proposing how it would be used. On January 9 Kung sent to Morgenthau through Fox a message further urging such a loan. Fox supported the idea in view of "the extreme gravity of the economic situation" and "to counteract pessimism and defeatist tendency in some Government circles." He hoped it could be granted promptly to show confidence in China. He also said the Chinese attitude in recent days had changed "from one of despair to one of firm insistence on financial aid." [2] One factor in this change was the defeat of the Japanese drive on Changsha at the turn of the year. This came in the midst of heavy reverses to China's allies at Japan's hands in Hong Kong, the Philippines, and Malaya. The Changsha victory understandably boosted China's estimation of her value to her allies.

A HALF BILLION "TO TIE CHINA INTO OUR WAR"

On January 9 Roosevelt gave his blessing to the idea of a loan:

Memo for the Secretary of the Treasury: In regard to the Chinese loan, I realize there is little security which China can give at the present time, yet I am anxious to help Chiang-Kai-Shek and his currency. I hope you can invent some way of doing this. Possibly we could buy a certain amount of this currency, even if it means a partial loss later on. FDR.[3]

On January 10 Hornbeck told Hull that he felt that there was clear need to make a loan to China of "not less than $300 million —and preferably $500 million"; that commencement of action need not await talking to Britain; and that it was important to act before it was necessary to admit defeat in the Philippines and perhaps Malaya, and to assure the Generalissimo accordingly. Hull at once proposed to Morgenthau a loan of US$300 million.[4]

The Morgenthau Diaries tell of discussion of the subject at the White House and Treasury, including possible use of American currency to pay Chinese troops. Morgenthau thus reported on January 13 the ideas of the President:

> He wasn't interested in details, but he says, "If I want a million shock troops, as Commander in Chief of the United States Government, I can get them and pay for them, whether they are Chinese or whatever they are" . . .
>
> He says, "I will pay them five dollars for maintenance, to the Government to maintain them, per month, and five dollars to the troops themselves."

The President talked of doing this with a new currency that might be called the "demo"—for democracy.[5] The President's idea of using American money in one way or another to pay the Chinese army or to buy up Chinese currency was very persistent.

Early in January Soong under the Generalissimo's instructions asked Morgenthau for a $500 million credit. In talking with him Morgenthau wondered how it could be used, saying that China had had US$630 million allocated in Lend-Lease and had at Rangoon already more goods than could be moved, in view of Japan's attack; and that the US$50 million of stabilization funds was still untouched. Morgenthau was thinking in terms far smaller than hundreds of millions. He wondered whether "they would be willing to let us buy them off for five or ten million dollars a month for the next three months." Reporting to his staff a talk with Soong, Morgenthau said,

> He said, "I have got to put it in the language of the Generalissimo. He is a general. How can he say where [he] is going to use five hundred thousand troops? He has got to have them in reserve and then use them." I said, "Now, you have told your story," and he kind of laughed. But when I got on this basis of paying the soldiers in U.S. currency, he liked it. Now the difference was, there are two important things. After all, the soldier idea was yours in the first instance, and the U.S. currency is mine. If we could get out of this thing for the next two or three months at five to ten million dollars a month, and I drove it home very hard that this was a month to month basis, then we get by the point, are they going to fight or aren't they going to fight. It doesn't give them the excuse to say, 'Well, you refused us a billion dollar loan, and therefore we are going to make peace.' So I am just saying this. I am not trying to lay down the law either. But if T. V. Soong would—and the Generalissimo would fall for this, and they would be willing to let us buy them off for five or ten million dollars a month for the next three months, Gresham's law or no Gresham's law, if I could see three months ahead I would recommend it."[6]

The Treasury staff were not enthusiastic about the President's suggestion of circulation of American money in China. Jacob

Viner suggested using say US$10 million monthly to "do a little mopping up of their own money." But Morgenthau's distrust of such direct support of China's currency was as strong as ever. He said, ". . . this is a bottomless well. They will print the damn thing faster." He proposed introducing dollar notes. Viner said it was tried in Poland, and that, "It went very well, as far as the gold certificates were concerned, but it just worked hell with their own currency." Hornbeck also did not think much of the idea of using American money or trying to pay directly for Chinese troops. The Chinese likewise did not like the idea. They felt that the loan should be free of conditions. Also they thought that the idea of relating it to troops disregarded the grave economic and financial problems. *

Meanwhile the State Department was stressing the vital political reasons for a big loan. Hornbeck feared the effect in China of further enemy successes in southern Asia which seemed imminent, such as overrunning the Philippines, Malaya, the Dutch Indies, and Burma. He said on January 23, "Now is the time for us to tie China into our war (which is still her war) as tight as possible." The funds China sought were "small relative to our cheerful outlays for military equipment," and failure to provide such funds risked losing China as a valuable ally. He was distressed by "the apparent lack, of which I have evidence every day, of adequate understanding on the part of high officials of this Government of the miracle of warmaking which the Chinese have performed during the past four and one-half years, not excluding the period since we entered the war." He believed that although the war "cannot be won in the Far Eastern theater . . . it could be lost there." [8]

On January 26 State and Treasury officials conferred, and concluded that a large loan was desirable. The State Department viewed the proposal as a demonstration of confidence in China and readiness to accept China as a partner in a common cause.[9] Morgenthau, however, was far from pleased with the idea of the big loan. He said, "The whole purpose of this thing is to make

---

* With Roosevelt the idea died hard. In a memorandum of January 26 to Morgenthau he said: "If they don't want dollar notes, why don't we buy Chinese yuans and use them for paying for the equipment of Chinese troops in China itself. I would be wholly willing to go up to twenty or twenty-five million dollars a month on some such basis." [7]

General Chiang Kai-shek happy." He told Secretary Stimson on January 28 that the President had asked him to do "some very difficult negotiations with the Chinese," and as to their attitude, Morgenthau said, "really it's a hold-up." He wanted to talk to Stimson and Marshall and "go to school as to just how much are we or should we be worried that Chiang Kai-shek might stop fighting if certain things happen." Ambassador Gauss, however, had reported January 17 that the Generalissimo is "completely committed to the policy of resistance." Gauss favored the loan but also wanted certain conditions, such as better arrangements to run the Burma Road.[10]

Morgenthau also called in the Russian Ambassador to discuss the matter, as reported in the Diaries of January 29:

H.M.JR.: Ambassador Litvinoff called at my request and I said that we had been approached by the Chinese for a loan and I felt that what the Chinese did in the future was as much of interest to them as it was to us. He said it is of more interest to them than it is to us.

I told him that they had asked for a billion dollar loan, half from the English and half from us, and the English said they would go up to fifty million dollars but couldn't go any further. I told him what I had offered to do about the soldiers and he said, "Have they a million troops under arms?" I said, "Well, I believe so."

He said he didn't know anything himself but he would get off a wire right away. He said, "I question whether the Japanese would make any peace with the Chinese now because they are drunk with victory," and he said, "If Singapore falls we are firmly convinced . . ." He said, "We believe that the Japanese will synchronize with the Germans and will attack us in about two months' time. That is what we expect." He said, "Once we begin to fight the Japanese, that ought to greatly encourage the Chinese."

He gave me the distinct feeling that he questioned that the Chinese would stop fighting at this time. I said that I personally wasn't so worried because after all, the Chinese had gone through this for four years and now that they saw that we were in this thing I just didn't see how they could quit at this time.

He kept repeating over and over again, "Well, this is nothing but black-mail," and I said, "Yes, and at a time when we have our back to the wall in the Pacific, and I don't like it." That is that. But it is interesting, what?

MR. WHITE: He agreed with the opposition.

H.M.JR.: Yes, but it is interesting that he is convinced that they will be attacked in two months and are ready for it.

"Oh, yes," he said, "Can't you drag these negotiations out as long as possible?" I said, "Well, that is what we are trying to do by making payments on a monthly basis." He said, "Yes, that is the way to do it."

He said, "Well what can they use it for? What can they use it for? They can't get any more material up the Burma Road." I said, "I have been all over that with T. V. Soong and I pointed out to them several weeks ago that we had committed five hundred sixty million in Lend-Lease, which is more than we are committed to you. They have got fifty million dollars of Stabilization credit that they haven't used a dollar of," and I said, "T. V. Soong explains it that the Generalissimo wants a billion dollars in reserve to use when he sees fit." He said, "They can't use it. How can they get it in there?" I said, "I agree, and that is what is bothering me."

Morgenthau reported on January 30 that the State and Treasury Departments conferred. The record does not show whether the State Department knew of Morgenthau's incursion into the field of foreign affairs as quoted above. But Morgenthau reported that Hull "said that Russia was not to be trusted and there is no telling what would happen if with increasing Japanese victories China felt she could not look to Britain and the United States for substantial help." Hornbeck feared that the fall of Singapore, then imminent, might cause appeasers in Chungking to press for peace with Japan. He wanted to give the loan to strengthen the General-issimo *vis-à-vis* war weary elements. He favored quick action, fearing that delay would run the risk that granting the loan would coincide with fresh reverses in the Pacific war and that a loan at such time might suggest that the United States was appealing for help at "the moment when we found ourselves in difficulty." Hull "assumed there was agreement that under the circumstances financial aid to China was urgent." Hornbeck thought the amount should be US$500 million, not US$300 million as proposed by Hull on January 10. All agreed.[11]

At the cabinet meeting on January 30, the President said, "I think that it's popular to help the Chinese." Hull wrote to the President that China's "brilliant resistance to aggression . . . and their contribution to the common cause, deserve the fullest support we can give." Secretaries Stimson and Knox also wrote, saying that the loan would help China's morale and military strength.[12]

It was agreed that the President would promptly send a message to Congress. He did so, and on February 7 signed a Joint Resolution which both houses of Congress passed unanimously, providing

That the Secretary of the Treasury, with the approval of the President, is hereby authorized, on behalf of the United States, to loan or extend credit or give other financial aid to China in an amount not to exceed in the aggregate $500,000,000 at such time or times and upon such terms and conditions as the Secretary of the Treasury with the approval of the President shall deem in the interest of the United States.

A bill appropriating the funds was signed February 13. Thus it took only two weeks to complete the legislative action after the administration had made its decision.

Morgenthau told the House Appropriations Committee that to sustain the war in China "the Chinese financial and monetary system should be made as strong as possible"; that "In waging this war China has performed economic and military miracles," but that its financial system had been "severely strained in the process"; that China had made payments on schedule or even ahead of schedule on the wartime loans already granted, had shipped strategic commodities to the United States under the most difficult conditions, and had "carried out to the letter every obligation to us which it has assumed." But off the record he told a member that "we might not get a dollar back," to which a member replied, "Even so, we might consider ourselves amply repaid by Chinese participation in the war." [13]

In China the announcement of the loan was received with gratification. It was regarded as a measure of friendship and encouragement. All elements in China welcomed the credit. The Communist views as expressed in an editorial in the *Hsin Hua Jih Pao*, Chungking, March 24, 1942 (translated), contrast strangely with their later virulent anti-American attitude:

The wording of the agreement is in the spirit of true equality. The second article makes no reference to security or other serious obligations. This is unprecedented in the history of Sino-American financial and diplomatic relations . . .

Some think it unwise to neglect financial terms in making such a loan. It is our opinion that, even though China and America are engaged in a common struggle, and even though this loan is to be used in this struggle, still the Chinese people, as a matter of national pride, should after the victory repay all loans which have helped us to win our freedom.

The Sino-American loan has further improved the intimate relations between these two great nations; and has strengthened China's financial and economic strength for the struggle.

The views expressed by Chou En-lai, then chief Communist

representative at Chungking, took a different line. A representative of the Office of Strategic Services thus reported Chou's views, stated in a conference on April 22, 1942, at which Chou "offered no objection to very full notes being taken." After mentioning how anti-British sentiment was growing, Chou said:

Toward the United States, Chinese leaders and their Government present a different attitude . . . Chinese authorities think the United States is an easy prey. For example, General Chou explained, soon after the outbreak of the Pacific War President Roosevelt very properly gave a large loan to China. The Chinese got another impression. They thought, General Chou said, that since Britain and the United States were defeated by Japan, while China had resisted Japanese aggression for 5 years in the Far East, only China was able to fight against Japan, and the United States was very much afraid that the Chinese Government would make peace with Japan. Chinese authorities had therefore permitted Sun Fo to talk about a separate peace with American correspondents and at the same time had maintained contact with the Japanese in Shanghai in order to excite fears in Washington. Against this background the Chinese Government asked for a loan. First they asked for 1 billion dollars, then for 500 million dollars, specifying that no strings were to be attached . . .

General Chou said that on the American side the performance had been very good, but that Chinese authorities now think that the United States is afraid of a Chinese peace and have become very proud of their own diplomatic skill. They think that the United States is easily deceived. American generosity excites contempt and gives them reason for pride in the effectiveness of their finesse . . . A loan must be given for their five years of fighting. If the United States refused to give help the Chinese Government would threaten to make peace, but General Chou said, as a matter of fact, there is no danger at all of China's making a peace. Incidentally, he said, resistance has become a good business since help is easy to get.

General Chou said that severe limitations governed what aid the United States could give China at the present time. He said he did not think aid should be given in a way as might stimulate Chinese to demand more.[14]

Chou's interviewer, in summing up talks with Chinese leaders between April 10 and May 10, 1942, thus appraised China's attitude:

. . . not even the military catastrophes in the South Seas have set in motion the growth of a peace party. On the contrary, China is impressed with her own accomplishment in lasting six years while her Allies in Asia have been knocked out one by one within a few months. There is great national pride in China. China is confident that she stands in the vanguard of all Asiatic peoples in the fight for freedom from Japanese or Western imperialist rule. China knows that within the Japanese New Order she has no role to play except that of a slave state. With few exceptions all Chinese have always known this. Those exceptions have disappeared from the Chungking scene.[15]

STRINGS ON THE MONEY?

As soon as Congress authorized the loan, Generalissimo Chiang telegraphed instructions to Soong. There should be no specific security, no interest or fixed term of repayment, and no conditions for use of the money. The deal should be like Lend-Lease and not like the stabilization agreement of April 1941, which the Generalissimo and Kung felt was too "legalistic and stern."

The Treasury gave Soong on February 21 a draft of agreement. It provided for making available US$500 million "in such amounts and at such times as the Government of the Republic of China shall request." The final determination of the terms would wait "until the progress of events makes clearer the final terms and benefits which will be in the mutual interest of the United States and China." Article II read as follows:

China desires to keep the Secretary of the Treasury of the United States informed as to the use of the funds herein provided and to consult with him from time to time as to such uses. The Secretary of the Treasury of the United States desires to make available to the Government of the Republic of China technical and other appropriate advice as to ways and means of effectively employing these funds to achieve the purposes herein described. Technical problems that may from time to time arise in effectuating the financial aid herein provided will be subjects of discussion between the Secretary of the Treasury of the United States and the Government of the Republic of China.[16]

The Generalissimo objected to the provision for consultation, because he thought it contemplated that the United States "will in some way pass judgment on the uses to which the loan may be put." China "in any case would like to keep the Secretary informed," but the Article was unnecessary "since it makes of such voluntary acts mandatory." He wanted also some lesser changes, which at once were agreed: to wait until postwar for final settlement, to omit a statement that no interest would be charged, and to make it clearer that the determination of terms would be bilateral.[17]

The Treasury inclined not to press for Article II. They had in mind that they could freeze Chinese funds if there were any drastic change in the situation in China. Fox, who was then in

Washington, said the Chinese have had "a stiffening in attitude . . . They are a little cockier than they were. They have read about Singapore and so forth." [18] But the State Department felt it would be useful to keep Article II to reflect a cooperative spirit and also because it could help China to avoid unwise use of the funds. The upshot was proposal of a revised draft, reading as follows:

> As a manifestation of the cooperative spirit which underlies the common war effort of China and the United States, appropriate officials of the two governments will confer from time to time regarding technical problems which may arise in connection with the financial aid herein provided and will exchange information and suggestions regarding ways and means of most effectively applying these funds toward achieving the purposes which are envisaged by the two nations.

When this proposal reached Chungking, Kung asked my opinion. When I said I saw no objection to it, he indicated so strongly his impatience with any such clause that I could say nothing more. On March 19 Soong forwarded the Generalissimo's rejection, "as limiting the freedom of action in the use of the proceeds," and because it would adversely affect the public's response to the proposed sale of bonds and to other measures to be based on the loan. Also he felt that the Chinese military would think "the terms are not as clean cut as they envisaged." [19]

Despite Soong's letter of March 19, the State Department still wanted consultation. They proposed an exchange of letters to achieve the purpose of Article II. Hornbeck told Morgenthau that this would avoid a precedent of China "laying down terms to us," and that the United States owed China nothing. He felt that the Chinese were not only trying to get the money without strings, but to "score for them a first-class diplomatic victory the consequences of which in the long run will be good neither for this country nor for China." Chiang first asked for a loan but, "Now it would appear that he is asking for a *gift*." The matter, however, had gone so far that Hornbeck felt at a loss to find a way to put the United States in what he thought would be a satisfactory position.[20]

The matter went before the cabinet at Washington on March 20, and Article II was dropped. Soong agreed to write a letter saying that China would keep the American Government informed of the use of the credit. He did so and the agreement was signed March 21.[21] On April 3 Soong conveyed to Morgenthau the Generalissimo's thanks for his help and assured him: ". . . if the Secretary felt the funds were not wisely used or wished to advise or comment on their use, that the Generalissimo would be only too glad to receive his advice and comments."[22]

During the negotiations Ambassador Gauss reported that a prominent Chinese told him privately that the loan came "too easily to be appreciated or to insure provision for its effective use." Gauss detected in Chungking an assumption that the credit was "a due compensation to China for what the Chinese [regard as] our past and present shortcomings and for China's past and present resistance to Japan."[23]

50 MILLION STERLING

Late in 1941 China broached to Britain as well as to the United States the idea of a large credit. On December 24 the General-issimo asked the British ambassador to forward a request for £100 million, which with the US$500 million would bring the total to nearly a billion dollars. But the British firmly refused to think in such large terms. Their reply proposed a credit of £20 million, of which half might guarantee an internal loan in foreign currency to be sold in China, the credit to be secured upon post-war customs revenue.

The Chinese reaction was highly emotional. Did not China, as a matter of right, rate larger help after her years of fighting alone at great sacrifice? The suggestion of customs security was charac-terized as a "colonial attitude."[24] The Chinese leaders showed so much feeling and bitterness on the issue that it was hard for me to discuss it with them. This was the culmination of several things. There was smoldering resentment of long-time British prominence in China, and of the attitude of some individual Britishers who obviously looked down on the Chinese. The friction over financial issues (see chapter X) was still freshly in mind. The temporary closing of the Burma Road in the summer of 1940 under Japanese pressure continued to rankle. But everything came to a head as a result of quick British defeats in Hong Kong, Malaya, and Burma by Japan, whose forces China had stood off for four and a half years and had defeated at Changsha early in January 1942. In particular, the collapse of the British defense of Burma, cutting the land route to China, hit Sino-British relations hard. A further slant on the feeling in China—specially interesting after lapse of time—is Chou En-lai's comment to a representative of the American Office of Strategic Services on April 22, 1942, thus reported:

> They [Chinese authorities] regard the British as cunning and shrewd. Therefore, when Britain had a strong position in the Far East, the Chinese were careful to preserve friendly relations. Now that the British have been defeated by the Japanese, Chinese authorities take a contrary attitude and despise the British position, and, in fact, fail to treat the British as allies in a united war effort. In reaction to the traditional arrogance of the British, anti-British sentiment in China is developing rapidly.[25]

The British position on the proposed credit was explained to Morgenthau by Sir Frederick Phillips of the British Treasury, then in Washington. Britain was ready to grant to China all possible Lend-Lease aid and favored a combined Anglo-American credit of US$400 million, of which Britain would supply £30 million (US$120 million). But Britain was worried about her postwar balance of payments and could not grant a large "psychological" loan nor give to China an unrestricted call after the war on any unused part of a big credit. Britain felt also that each item of expenditure should be agreed in advance with China. Sir Frederick said, "The United States part of the credit would no doubt be made subject to similar conditions." [26]

The American decision to grant an unrestricted credit of US$500 million cut the ground from under the British position. When the American attitude crystallized, London at once decided to raise their figure. On February 2 they stated their willingness "to lend to China for war purposes an amount up to 50 million pounds at such times and upon such terms as may be agreed between the two Governments." [27]

In January Britain suggested to the American Government that an "Allied Economic Council" be set up at Chungking, hoping that some such mechanism might help China in her worsening plight. With a similar thought, the Generalissimo in 1941 had suggested an American-British economic mission. Growing out of that suggestion Britain sent to China late in 1941 Sir Otto Niemeyer of the Bank of England, a man with broad financial experience. Washington was never enthusiastic about the idea, although when the Treasury sent Cochran to China about November 1, he and Niemeyer were in China together for a short time and gave partial and temporary effect to the idea. Ambassador

Gauss did not favor the proposed "Allied Economic Council." He felt that if it were advisory China would disregard its views and that China would not agree to foreign participation in handling internal affairs. Nothing came of the idea.[28]

The Sino-British negotiations on arrangements for the £50 million credit went badly, as Britain felt obliged to keep to her basic position. Sino-British relations went from bad to worse. Hamilton of the State Department told the Treasury of "growing Chinese animosity to the British in the Far East," which began to be reflected in the attitude to the United States; and said he would urge the British to "hesitate long before doing anything that might further antagonize the Chinese."[29] By the middle of 1942 negotiations had practically come to a halt. The positions were too far apart. China persisted in wanting a large unrestricted credit, while Britain was not willing to give a blank check for £50 million.

From 1942 to 1944 there were intermittent negotiations. Finally on May 2, 1944, two agreements were signed. The first covered the £50 million credit. It did not differ much in substance from the basic draft proposed by the British in the spring of 1942; but annexes spelled out the uses in more detail. The British official statement said that the agreement "carries out the offer made . . . some time ago . . . for the financing of goods and services required by China in the sterling area for the purposes arising out of the war." Britain was to finance the rupee needs of the Chinese forces in India and Burma, where active fighting was then going on. Britain also would provide funds under the credit during the war to pay for transportation, for bank notes, and to help to cover the cost of orders already placed under the 1939 and 1941 purchase credits; for further purchases for war purposes; and for other purposes that might be agreed.

The agreement also provided that Britain would provide sterling backing for a loan up to £10 million to be issued in China on terms to be agreed, to withdraw redundant purchasing power. As of July 1, 1942, however, China had issued the "31st Year Allied Victory National Currency Loan" of C$1 billion. Article 5 of the loan regulations stated (translated):

Payment of interest and repayment of principal of the loan shall be made by allotment from the £50 million loan from the British Government, to be deposited in The Central Bank of China and converted into national currency.

This was based upon British willingness to support this use of the credit as indicated in the discussion with Niemeyer. But specific allocation of the British credit was only formalized in 1944. Since it was denominated in national currency, the 1942 loan was not attractive to the public, and little of it was used other than as security for advances by the Central Bank.

The second agreement of May 2, 1944, covered provision of arms, munitions, and military equipment on Lend-Lease terms. The British official statement said:

Pending signature of the agreement the cost of goods and services required from China from the Sterling area for war purposes has been met from earlier British credits, and munitions have been provided on Lend-Lease terms in anticipation of the present agreement. The limit of our assistance to China remains, as always, therefore, one of transport and not one of finance.

During the debate in the House of Commons on May 3 a Labor member asked whether any undertaking had been given that arms supplied "would not be used against the ill-armed and courageous Communist armies in China." Eden replied: "At the present moment Chinese divisions are in action alongside our own in Burma. I would not presume to postulate such question to any government which is fighting alongside our own armies."

HOW SHOULD THE MONEY BE USED?

When China asked for the credits there was no complete plan for their use. As we have seen, Kung had the idea that a large credit would greatly strengthen confidence and give important support to the currency, thus checking inflation. The American and British credits together equaled about US$700 million. That sum, he pointed out, was equal at the official rates to about C$13 billion and would provide the required 60 per cent reserve for an issue of C$20 billion. The issue at the end of 1941 was C$15 billion.

Niemeyer and I did not feel that the mere presence of these large funds would in itself help much. Sir Otto wrote in a memorandum of January 18, 1942:

I am afraid anyone who thinks that the purchasing power of the fapi in

China will in present circumstances be affected by the nature of the Chinese Note Reserve will suffer a sad deception . . .

The only thing which now affects Chinese internal prices is the volume of the Note Issue, not the form of its backing. The steady multiplication of bits of paper (which is all the Notes are) while the volume of real wealth (commodities) either remains stagnant or increases very little, inevitably results in more bits of paper being asked for before a merchant will part with a commodity. This would remain the case even if the Notes were backed by a present of all the pounds or dollars or gold in the world.

In a memorandum of February 7, I wrote:

If note circulation goes on increasing as before, the price rise cannot be checked merely because large funds are at China's disposal in New York and London, any more than the Japanese advances can be checked by the presence of large numbers of airplanes, tanks and troops in other places. Attention therefore is forced back to measures applied internally which the credits make possible.

In the first three months of 1942 prices rose faster than in any corresponding period to date, even faster than in the last half of 1941 when there was a break in confidence accompanying the new type of "stabilization" operations. Probably a main cause was China's greater isolation and Allied military reverses. In any event the new huge credits were not accompanied by a steadying of the price situation, but rather the reverse.

From the fall of 1941 there was active consideration in China of some form of internal loan secured against currency depreciation, to absorb surplus funds and be a substitute for hoarding of goods. There was general agreement that a good part of the credit should be so used.

The American Embassy at Chungking and also Fox had thought the credit might be used to some extent to encourage industrial and agricultural production in China. Also Fox and others put forward the idea of using the credit to bring in goods usable to add to production.[30] In a memorandum of February 7 I said:

China cannot now be greatly aided by imports. Projects therefore have to be carried out almost wholly with materials and labor now in China, and paid for in *fapi*. Consequently, the merits of schemes for fresh expenditure ought to be judged exactly as they were judged before the credits were granted. In other words, is a given scheme so important, as a war measure, that its benefit outweighs the detriment of spending more *fapi* and thus adding to the inflation? If existence of the new credits is used to justify schemes that should not be undertaken regardless of the credits, the situation to that extent will be worse instead of better.

The *Ta Kung Pao* of Chungking editorialized succinctly on February 4 (translated), "If these loans are used to expand our national budget or as reserve for issuing notes, then not only will there be no benefit but there will be harm."

In a memorandum of January 24 for Morgenthau, V. F. Coe analyzed the situation. He thought the chief use would be in combatting inflation by "substituting financial hoarding for commodity hoarding," as by sale of bonds, U.S. dollars, or "the shipment of gold to China and its distribution there to Chinese nationals in exchange for goods and services."[31] He also thought it might be used to help improve production and that it would have some temporary psychological benefit.

In Chungking there was some talk of direct sale of foreign exchange in China. But this did not seem very promising in the circumstances. The suggested issue of securities seemed better. There was talk also of sale of American Government obligations, but it appeared that these with low interest rates and in a foreign language would not be very attractive to buyers.

When Morgenthau and Soong concluded the agreement of March 21, 1942, which provided for the credit, the preamble said that

. . . such financial aid will enable China to strengthen greatly its war efforts against the common enemies by helping China to

(1) strengthen its currency, monetary, banking and economic system;

(2) finance and promote increased production, acquisition and distribution of necessary goods;

(3) retard the rise of prices, promote stability of economic relationships, and otherwise check inflation;

(4) prevent hoarding of foods and other materials;

(5) improve means of transportation and communication;

(6) effect further social and economic measures which promote the welfare of the Chinese people; and

(7) meet military needs other than those supplied under the Lend-Lease Act and take other appropriate measures in its war effort.[32]

The eventual use of the credit was as follows (figures in millions):

To secure dollar obligations issued in China	US$200
To acquire gold for sale in China	220
To pay for bank notes	55
To pay for textiles shipped to China	25
Total	US$500

None of the gold was shipped until the fall of 1943, when China began to sell gold to check inflation (chapter XVII). But soon after the US$500 million credit became available, China began the sale of dollar-backed securities, as described in the next section.

Of the British credit of £50 million, China used £8.1 million to purchase goods and services in the sterling area for war purposes, of which £3 million was charged by the end of 1945 and the remaining £5.1 million by July 1948. The Chancellor of the Exchequer has reiterated that the extent of this aid was limited by availability of transport, not of finance.[33]

THE FIASCO OF THE DOLLAR SECURITIES

Direct borrowing from the public, if feasible, might have absorbed surplus money and so checked inflation. In the early weeks of fighting, the Liberty Loan of 1937 was a success; but the idea was dropped when pressures to subscribe alienated influential people (see chapter III). The government thereafter made some efforts to sell bonds. But these were half-hearted and had little success, because inflation was steadily eroding the value of the money in which the bonds were denominated. In the fall of 1941, when the Generalissimo was specially worried about inflation, I proposed seeking fresh means to borrow internally, and he asked me to prepare a concrete plan. I talked with Cochran of the American Treasury in Hong Kong about possible backing by the United States of bonds to be issued in China with some form of protection against depreciation of Chinese money. Niemeyer was in Chungking when I returned there, and I found he was thinking on similar lines. We pooled our ideas, and prepared a preliminary plan which the British Government was ready to support.[34]

The granting of the large American and British credits in February cleared the way for trying such a scheme. There were the usual questions about what interest rates and maturities would be desirable. But a major question arose from the large overvaluation of Chinese money in foreign exchange. At the price level of early 1942, money had less than 5 per cent of its buying power five years earlier. But the official rate of exchange for the dollar gave Chinese money a value about 18 per cent of prewar. And, if the official rate remained unchanged, the disparity was bound to get worse. Clearly the sale of dollar-backed securities could be a costly use of dollars, and would have to be justified by results in checking inflation.

But, despite the bargain, it would not be easy to get the public to buy the bonds, as Minister Kung pointed out from the start. In a memorandum of February 2, I said, "Of course, the issue must be supported and promoted by patriotic appeals and by various forms of pressure upon persons and business organizations able to subscribe, and particularly upon hoarders and speculators." With such a program, I felt that the issue would "be a real success and help materially to check inflation." Niemeyer urged that the sales campaign be accompanied by sale of rice collected from the newly adopted land tax in kind, in order to help to break the existing high prices. That, he argued, would frighten rice hoarders into selling and let them find a place for their money in buying the bonds. He believed that steps to lower the price of the people's main food, together with drawing in currency through sale of the bonds, could have a very worthwhile effect in checking the inflation. We both urged that the issue be accompanied by tightening of bank credit, and pointed out that the government banks should not make advances to finance purchases of the bonds or buy them themselves, since such action would defeat the issue's purpose.

Kung's illness and the Generalissimo's absence delayed action. Finally on March 24 the government announced issuance of two kinds of securities. First were the U.S. Dollar Savings Certificates of US$100 million. These were of one, two, or three year term, with interest respectively of 3, 3½, and 4 per cent. Second was the Allied Victory U.S. Dollar Loan of US$100 million, a 4 per cent 10-year issue, as of May 1. The announcement stated that the US$200 million would absorb about C$4 billion, "or roughly one out of every four dollars in circulation." That, I think, was the only time after the early part of the war when there was an official indication of the actual size of the note issue.

The rate of exchange to be used gave rise to long discussion. Finally it was set at US$0.05 for the Certificates. Some weeks later the government made that rate the official rate of exchange, instead of US$0.05 5/16. For the 10-year loan, the government set a more favorable rate: US$0.06.

The Treasury felt that they should have been advised of the final plan before it was announced on March 24. Minister Kung, however, talked with Adler about the plan on March 18 and presumed he had informed Washington. When T. V. Soong conferred with the Treasury on April 11, they said they had not learned the particulars of the final plan prior to the announcement and indicated that they would criticize some phases of the plan. Soong asked the Treasury to transfer to China US$200 million forthwith as backing for the two issues. The Treasury preferred that China call for the money only as needed, because they would have to borrow and pay interest in order to deposit the full US$200 million. Morgenthau thought of going back at China and asking for some other arrangement. But the friction about possible strings on the loan was still freshly in mind, and Soong advised him to comply with China's request. So Morgenthau turned over the funds as requested.[35] When the report of the conference of April 11 reached Kung, he advised the Treasury through Soong that he would welcome their suggestions; and that he considered that the transfer of funds was essential, "in order to convince the people that use was being made of the loan without delay to prevent inflation." [36]

From the start it was clear that the issues would not succeed unless there were pressure on the well-to-do and speculators to subscribe. When the issues were announced, *Ta Kung Pao* of Chungking said on March 27, 1942, that the ordinary people had little capacity to subscribe and that it would be necessary to press the well-to-do to buy them and to force hoarders to take them in place of goods. Otherwise they would prefer to speculate for a larger and more immediate profit. Ambassador Gauss reported on May 5 that the government could force speculators and landlords to buy. But he doubted that it would be done, because "the Government . . . is itself closely allied to banking and landholding interests." Hoarding of foodstuffs, he pointed out, could already be punished by death, but the measure was little more than a dead letter.[37] The ambassador's prediction proved right, and there was no real pressure to subscribe. Furthermore, the government ignored Niemeyer's proposal to attack speculation by sale of some of the rice collected as tax in kind. Instead the government itself became a hoarder, by holding rice over and above what the army and public employees needed for current use plus reasonable reserves.

People also wondered whether the government really would pay over the dollars at maturity. In order to strengthen confidence I urged, as part of the original plan, using as trustee the Federal Reserve Bank of New York and setting aside there funds from the US$500 million loan *pari passu* with sales of the securities in China. That would have greatly facilitated subscriptions, since with a purely national setup the public would fear later requisition of the money by the government.* But instead it was decided that the Finance Minister earmark US$100 million in the Central Bank of China to effect payment of the Certificates; and for the 10-year bonds, funds for loan payments would be appropriated from the US$500 million credit. So a valuable means of adding to the effectiveness of the issues was lost.

The most serious blunder was failure to set a relatively brief time limit for subscriptions at the very favorable rates offered. Niemeyer and I proposed the plan on the basis of a well-secured issue to be sold promptly, with the aid of pressure on hoarders and those well able to subscribe. We never would have made the proposal had we dreamed that subscriptions would stay open for 18 months at a fixed rate for dollars, while the internal buying power of the national currency fell to about 15 per cent of what it was in early 1942. As the sales were handled, even those intending to subscribe could wait. They could increase their local currency funds by speculating in goods or hoarding, or by lending to speculators at interest rates of 3 to 6 per cent per month. As the printing presses rolled, and prices soared, purchase of the Certificates at the fixed rate of C$20 per dollar became more and more of a bargain.

Among those who bought Certificates, despite the uncertain-

---

* In the fall of 1939, I pointed out, the Finance Ministry authorized the government banks to receive deposits payable in foreign currency, paying 4 to 7 per cent interest. That was designed to attract capital being repatriated in view of war in Europe and help the Chinese banks to compete with foreign banks, which generally paid no interest on foreign currency deposits. But few such deposits came to the Chinese banks, for fear of later requisition by the government—only about US$2 million to the end of 1941.

ties, were many foreigners, including American army personnel. The army men were paid in American currency notes (see chapter XIV). It was highly profitable, assuming the Certificates would be paid, as they were, to sell these notes for *fapi* in the free market, and buy Certificates. In the first seven months of 1943, dollar notes could be sold for C$44 to C$95 per dollar. Thus each American dollar of notes could be converted, via *fapi*, into from two to nearly five dollars of Certificates bought at C$20 per dollar. Eventually an American army order of September 21, 1944, forbade army personnel to buy these securities. The American ambassador had earlier forbidden the embassy staff to buy them.

For many months the sale of Certificates was slow. In the first week only US$36,390 were sold at Chungking. After eight months, less than one-tenth was sold. There was a spurt of sales in December, as a result of rumors that the issue would be closed at the year end. By June 1943, after 15 months, US$47 million had been subscribed. But in July and the first three days of August, until the issue was closed August 3, US$56 million were taken up. For some time before the closing of sale of Certificates, I urged ending the whole business, while US$150 million or more of the US$200 million remained unused, unless there could be radical readjustment of the rates of exchange at which Certificates were sold.

When the sale of Certificates was ended on August 3, 1943, I again urged immediately ending sale of the Bonds. For these, with their 10-year maturity, subscriptions were even slower than for the Certificates. By the end of 1942, after eight months, only US$130,160 had been taken up. Nevertheless subscription stayed open until October 15, 1943. By October 12 subscriptions totaled only US$18 million, on which only the equivalent of US$11 million had been paid. On that date the closing of subscriptions was rumored. Sales at once zoomed. Subscriptions were closed October 15. The government, through the Central Bank and other government banks, took up nearly half which was not otherwise sold. The eventual result was that the public held about 45 per cent of this issue.

The manner of successively closing subscriptions to the two

issues, with rumored large buying by insiders, reflected on the government's good name—regardless of the facts, which I do not know. It hurt China's standing in important circles abroad. Secretary Morgenthau, reporting to the President on December 18, 1943, said that this US$200 million of aid "made no significant contribution to the control of inflation," and that such schemes "had little effect except to give additional profits to insiders, speculators and hoarders and dissipate foreign resources." [38]

It is impossible to say what amount of these securities could have been sold under a plan with realistic rates of exchange, with the Federal Reserve Bank of New York as trustee to hold the dollar funds and with governmental pressure upon those able to subscribe. Contributing to buyers' reluctance was the uncertainty when and how they could use their money when Certificates matured after one, two, or three years (mostly one year), with China blockaded and the war's duration in doubt. On the other hand, persons justifiably anxious to preserve the buying power of their money could have bought relatively stable dollars, instead of seeking safety in buying and hoarding goods or in speculation. But, whatever the amount that could have been sold, it is certain that sale of these dollar assets could not possibly have brought a real return in China comparable with their purchasing power in the United States, because of the China market's low purchasing power. Certainly a sizable sacrifice of dollar assets was justifiable in the emergency. But much of the sacrifice of assets that took place could and should have been avoided.

Since the government banks bought about a fourth of these issues, the amount sold to the public was about US$150 million. The real financial benefit which China gained from the sales cannot be exactly measured. I know of no accurate figure of the monthly deficits in this period to compare with the proceeds of sale, but a rough calculation shows clearly that the benefit was not of much over-all significance in 1942–1943. In the period of about a month from July 1 to August 3, 1943, the proceeds may have covered something like a quarter of the deficit, and in December 1942 and October 1943, perhaps a tenth. In the rest of the period the coverage was much less. There was a later offsetting benefit, to the extent that those obtaining the funds used them after the war in China's rehabilitation. But, because of continuing inflation and other disturbances, this extent probably was not very great.

For China, the mishandling of these issues was a missed opportunity. Even at the rate of C$20 per dollar, the prompt sale of a sizable first *tranche* of Certificates, say US$25–50 million within a time limit of a few weeks, could have forced substantial de-hoarding—especially if combined with Niemeyer's idea of sale of some of the rice gotten from collections in kind. Sale of other *tranches* could have followed, at rates of exchange raised successively somewhat in line with the rise of prices. Such a program could have helped to limit hoarding and check inflation. Moreover there would have been important social and political gains from requiring well-to-do persons and hoarders to buy the issues as contemplated in the original proposal. To force them to bear a larger share of war costs would have partly offset inequities of the tax system. Throughout the war the monied classes—business men, large landowners, and some civil and military officials—bore far less than a fair share of the burdens. Measures to cause them to contribute their fair share would have strengthened the government at one of its weakest spots.

XIII. THE NEAR SIEGE OF CHINA

T HE war did not wait while China and her friends were busy with immediately available projects of financial support. Worry grew whether Japan's rapid advance in Southeast Asia would entirely cut off China from Western military and material aid. It was urgent to prevent full-scale siege by keeping open a line of communications, by land through Burma if possible and in any event by air. In this book I deal with communications and military matters to the extent that is necessary and appropriate for a rounded account of aid to China, and from the angle of China's international relations. Detailed accounts of the military events are contained in the excellent studies of the official historians.[1]

DISASTER IN BURMA

American Lend-Lease aid in 1941 recognized the priority of communications. Early shipments were mostly to improve the Burma Road and to begin the railway extension from Burma to Kunming in southwest China. When Japan attacked, the congestion of supplies in Burma was already serious. It worsened as railway materials and other bulky goods continued to arrive. In December 1941, Japanese air raids on Rangoon's crowded docks not only did damage but frightened away workers.

Problems at once arose as to disposal of the big stocks of Lend-Lease goods. These came to a head with arrival at Rangoon on December 18 of the S.S. *Tulsa*, with its valuable cargo of arms and ammunition (see chapter VIII). Obviously Burma's defense, in which Britain and the United States as well as China had a common interest, had a prior call on much of the Lend-Lease stocks. Although title to the goods had passed to China, Generalissimo Chiang was disposed throughout to let the British share the supplies. But while the matter was being discussed, certain British and American officials at Rangoon took affairs into their hands by commandeering trucks and impounding cargoes. This angered the Chinese. The controversy was settled—it got even to Roosevelt and Churchill—but it left a legacy of mistrust which lasted.[2]

When Burma fell losses of supplies were heavy. Prior to capture of Rangoon, according to the official American military history,

Much equipment had been sent north, the rate hitting 1,000 tons a day as disaster neared, but it was necessary to burn 972 trucks in various stages of assembly, 5,000 tires, 1,000 blankets and sheeting, and a ton of odds and ends. A great deal of lend-lease was transferred to the imperial forces in Burma: 300 Bren guns with 3,200,000 rounds, 1000 sub-machine guns with 180,000 rounds of ammunition, 260 jeeps, 683 trucks, and 100 field telephones.

About 19,000 tons of Lend-Lease, mostly construction materials, were lost. It had been hoped to hold Lashio, the terminus of the Burma Road. But when it fell on April 29, "the Japanese gained 44,000 tons of arsenal stores." At Lashio the situation was almost unbelievably bad:

Stilwell could not get lend-lease trucks from the Chinese authorities in Lashio with which to move troops. Asked to provide 150 trucks of the 850 then in Lashio, they sent 22.[3]

When in May the Japanese penetrated China to the Salween River, many more dumps of supplies were lost.

The collapse of the British defense, cutting the land route to China, was a particularly hard blow to Sino-British relations. On December 8 and several times thereafter the Generalissimo offered to send strong Chinese forces to Burma. What happened is controversial. The British official war history indicates that Field Marshal Sir Archibald Wavell expected to bring in sufficient reinforcements from India and later from East Africa. As to China, his main concern was to have a squadron of the Flying Tigers to defend Rangoon and to get access to Chinese Lend-Lease supplies for his forces in Burma. He was ready to accept conditionally some Chinese forces and wanted others in reserve. The Chinese felt that Wavell had refused China's offer, as did the Americans present at the conferences, who so advised Washington. Finally the British had to ask Chinese aid, but then it was too late.[4] Wavell wrote later: "Obviously it was desirable that a country of the British Empire should be defended by the Imperial troops rather than foreign." [5] Discussing the British delay in accepting Chinese aid, several of the senior China experts of the State Department told Secretary Hull in January 1942, that "we had all felt that it was due to British reluctance to accept assistance from Orientals as derogatory to British prestige in Asia." [6] The reaction in China to loss of Burma was bitter. Former Foreign Minister Wang Chung-hui thus commented on April 14, 1942:

When the Japanese threat to Burma began to develop the Chinese offered to send troops to Burma. The British were, at first, indifferent; then consented to mobilization of the Chinese on the frontier but within Yunnan; then consented to movement into the Northern Shan States; then permitted movement as far as Mandalay; and finally permitted their movement to the Taungoo front. Dr. Wang said that Chinese military leaders wished from the first, to use their troops in defense of Rangoon itself. The British assured them they had the situation in hand. [7]

Churchill, with his keen mind, queried the British Chiefs of Staff on January 21 whether it might not be wise to recognize that Singapore would fall, to destroy its installations, and to "concentrate everything on the defence of Burma and keeping open the Burma Road." He said ". . . the loss of Burma would be very grievous. It would cut us off from the Chinese, whose troops have been the most successful of those yet engaged against the Japanese. We may, by muddling things and hesitating to take an ugly decision, lose both Singapore and the Burma Road." But the matter was dropped because of the strong objection of Premier Curtin of Australia, who feared for Australia's safety and refused in February the urgings of both Churchill and Roosevelt to divert to Rangoon an Australian division then at sea near Ceylon. [8]

By May the Japanese, using veterans of the Singapore campaign, had overrun most of Burma. After capture of Rangoon in early March, they gained the great advantage of sea communications. They had an efficient homogeneous force, well equipped, trained in jungle fighting, well led, and with air superiority. The Allies, in contrast, had mostly inexperienced troops of several nationalities, often poorly equipped, and the leadership had the difficulties of coalition command, which are greatest in times of defeat. Chennault's Flying Tigers did miracles, but were too far outnumbered. A final blow was failure to hold the back-door route to Lashio, near the China frontier, because of the collapse of the Temporary-55th Chinese Division which the American liaison officer on his return from the front told me "held like wet paper." That contrasted with the good fighting of other Chinese forces in Central Burma, which, however, arrived too late for the most effective use.[9]

The official British war historian cites "the British unpreparedness in practically every respect to meet an invasion of the country," which seems to have been based partly on the belief that Malaya would be held. He states that "no adequate steps were taken to build up the forces required to repel the comparatively small force the Japanese could maintain across the Siamese frontier." He concludes that a basic blunder was the failure in 1940–1941 to put Burma's defense under India Command—this was not done until December 12, 1941. Even though the British Empire was hard pressed in many areas and could not be strong everywhere, quite large forces were in India. He points out that the "front could only be in Burma." As one cause of the disaster he cites "failure to bring Chinese troops quickly into Burma." [10] Even after outbreak of the Pacific War Chinese troops promptly arriving could have helped to hold at least upper Burma, through which passed the eventual road from Assam, and the Myitkyina airport, until the monsoon in May. That could have stalled the Japanese for months and given time to build further defenses.

The loss of Burma, as the official British historian has pointed out, "dictated the future strategy of the war in South-East Asia." [11] It was essential to recover enough of Burma at least to secure the air route over the Hump, which was even more precarious now that the enemy had nearer air bases, and to reopen a land route if possible. Such action, through jungles and against strongly entrenched Japanese forces which were experienced and well-equipped and well-led, was to prove a long and formidable task.

The disaster in Burma was a terrible blow to China. Certainly it was one of the decisive factors in eventual collapse of the National Government. In Burma, China lost more than a third of her strategic reserve of troops, largely German-trained and -equipped, together with their heavy equipment.[12] Besides, the cutting of the land route prevented sending to China the vehicles and artillery and other heavy items that she so desperately needed. It was two and one-half years until the air route carried a tonnage equal to the modest amount moved over the Burma Road at the end of 1941. And, psychologically as well as materially, it became harder for a mostly besieged China to oppose Japan's might and to deal with other pressing problems. The shock to confidence caused by events in Burma speeded the inflation, which contained the seeds of dissolution. Finally, relations with China's closest friends worsened. Relations with Britain became embittered, and friction with the United States grew over Burma issues. The worsening of China's international relations, which defeat in Burma promoted, was to interfere with the close cooperation needed for the major over-all effort that alone could have enabled the National Government to cope with the problems that lay ahead.

THE HUMP: CNAC'S PIONEERING

Flights over a part of the rugged Himalayan mountain mass became the only feasible way to keep China's communication with her allies and to bring in aid in men and materials until the Stilwell Road and the pipeline were opened in the final months of the war. One of the war's miracles was the airlift, which was developed to move 73,691 tons in the peak month of July 1945, and over 5,000 tons in a single day. The foresight, efficiency, and example of CNAC, which persevered despite delays and even some opposition and sniping from the American side, cleared the way for this achievement.

The prompt opening of the Hump route was made possible by CNAC's exploration flight only two weeks before Pearl Harbor. At that time negotiations with India to begin service were not completed. But in the emergency an agreement was quickly made, and CNAC soon began flights from Chungking and Kunming to Calcutta via Lashio in northeast Burma. CNAC's main base was shifted to Calcutta from Hong Kong.

When the Japanese attacked Hong Kong on December 8, that city was ill-prepared. I spent a good part of November there, and noted that few were worried about war. Those that were mostly felt that the fortress could hold out for weeks or months until help came. The newspapers were full of complaints about the order sending away women and children, and it is said that a meeting to protest this was called for December 8. Colonel David D. Barrett, American military attaché to China, and I walked over the hills and speculated on how and when the Japanese would attack. We both believed that war was close at hand. On my last evening in Hong Kong I crossed the bay to the mainland, at dusk, to take the CNAC plane which was to fly by night over the Japanese lines to Chungking. A practice air raid alarm was on, and the terraced buildings up to the peak 2,000 feet above the bay were strangely dark—as usually they blazed with light. It was an eerie effect that conveyed to me the thought that it was my last view of Hong Kong—a splendid and tragic city— before war came.

On December 8, after Japan attacked and began to besiege Hong Kong, CNAC in a remarkable series of night flights airlifted to safety important Chinese and foreign personnel, key operating staff of the company, and vital supplies. On each of the two nights on which CNAC could operate, planes made one or two round trips to nearby Namyung, and then took off from Hong Kong for a postdawn landing at Chungking. In the bombing at Hong Kong CNAC lost two DC-2's and three Condors. But it saved there one DC-2 and two DC-3's. After the first wave of enemy planes attacked the Kaitak Airport, CNAC personnel hauled these planes to safety on roads away from the scene. A bulldozer flattened a section of fence to permit moving the planes. After this began, Bond sought confirmatory permission. When the official in charge stupidly refused, Bond engaged him in talk until there was time to complete the job, so that these vitally needed planes were no longer a target for following waves of enemy planes. Besides the planes at Hong Kong, there was one more which on December 8 was en route from Burma to China. Hong Kong telegraphed on December 8 asking that this plane be sent. The Japanese radio had broadcast that all planes at Hong Kong had been destroyed, and we at Chungking had no contrary word. For those of us responsible at Chungking for CNAC's operations, it was a tough decision whether to send into danger what might have been the only remaining plane able to maintain China's communication with the outside world. But we sent it, with instructions to pilot McDonald not to enter Hong Kong unless establishing by nearby radio that it was feasible—relying on the good judgment of Bond and his staff at Hong Kong. It was a relief to receive in the early evening, before that plane reached the danger zone, routine flight reports that other planes had left Hong Kong for China. In this dangerous operation the CNAC staff behaved with courage and efficiency.

Whether sizable cargoes could be flown over the Hump on an all-year basis was not at first clear. In the early weeks of the war Washington doubted whether other than occasional flights were possible in the monsoon season from about May to October, since the severity of the Hump weather was unknown. Bond and the CNAC organization, with long experience in flying tasks that many had deemed impossible, felt that the route was practicable. Since all depended on American support with planes, supplies, and men, Bond promptly went to Washington. He made his case. Beginning in February 1942, CNAC began receiving planes that had been ordered in 1941 as Lend-Lease. By July it had 10, and the fleet grew in the following year to over 20. In 1943–1945 CNAC operated about 25 planes, and toward the end of the war the larger C-46's were substituted for some of the C-47's and C-53's.

Early in 1942 difficulties multiplied. About May 1 the Japanese captured the airfields at Lashio and Myitkyina, in northern Burma, from which they could attack allied planes flying the most direct routes. That meant that planes over the Hump had to fly farther north and higher, with greater strain on men and planes and greater gas consumption.

Nevertheless CNAC's freight service over the Hump began in March 1942. The earlier flights were experimental, as CNAC had so few planes and lacked spare parts and maintenance facilities. The weather was bad, though this partly offset the Japanese advantage in having nearby bases. But regular service began about June 1, and from July 1 CNAC flew at least one flight daily, with few exceptions. CNAC lost only one plane in 1942. But in March–April 1943, it lost three. On April 15, 1943, Bond wrote to CNAC's managing director at Chungking:

> In spite of our tragic losses, I think our efforts have been really worthwhile. In addition to actual freight which we have carried into China and the service which we have maintained, of far greater importance is the fact that we have so thoroughly demonstrated that a substantial quantity of

freight can be flown into China. We have set a pace which must be followed by others and I am sure that this work will go on and that large amounts of freight will be flown into China, and I believe this is almost entirely due to the efforts that CNAC has made and to the results which we accomplished at a time when it was uncertain as to whether such flying was possible.

CNAC's Lend-Lease planes were assigned to bring essential military and other supplies to China and soon were put under contract with the American army for that purpose. But CNAC also had to maintain China's external and internal air-mail and passenger service. This it did with its own four planes salvaged after the attack on Hong Kong, and, when two of these were lost, with replacements which the American authorities provided after some delay. General Stilwell, following the advice of his chief air officer Brigadier General C. L. Bissell, who was deliberately promoted to that rank with one day's seniority over Chennault, was unsympathetic to use of planes in that service, contending that it was unessential to the war effort. As one close to the CNAC's operations, I can testify that most of its movement of persons and freight in this period was closely related to the war effort. The continuing appearance of these planes, maintaining regular though meager communication among the main cities of Free China and with the outside world, was a great support to the morale of the Chinese. Apparently deriving from Bissell's views, however, there was talk of the American army taking over CNAC, conscripting its planes, its pilots, and equipment. Hornbeck of the State Department opposed this in a memorandum of February 27, 1943, saying that CNAC "has a superb record in China," having "pioneered in demonstration of the practicability of flying freight between Assam and China." He said that China needed its own airline, that CNAC would do better than the army, and that the army needed CNAC's competition. China finally asked that Bissell be removed from the area, primarily because of his friction with Chennault. Bissell also had friction with the Air Transport Command (ATC) under Brigadier General Caleb V. Haynes. It was a relief to CNAC and the ATC, as well as to Chennault and his forces, when Bissell departed in July 1943.[13]

The Chinese army also had designs on CNAC. Commenting on this the State Department telegraphed to Ambassador Gauss on April 4, 1942, that CNAC ". . . has an outstanding record of efficiency over a long period and its operations afford a shining example of successful international cooperation." The pilots of CNAC, said the Department, had "a notable record of loyalty and devotion to their present management, having performed at times almost impossible feats in maintaining communications under very difficult conditions," and that "to change the set-up . . . might have highly adverse effect upon their morale." [14]

CNAC wanted to increase somewhat its internal and external services of passengers and mail, and Washington allocated to China a few more transport planes beginning in July 1943. But because of internal pressures in China, these were turned over to the Commission on Aeronautical Affairs and not to CNAC. The Commission lacked experience with this type of plane and facilities to maintain it. In a memorandum of February 1, 1944, I noted that of seven such planes four had crashed, one was unserviceable and only two were in use. Unfortunately, some of China's leaders failed to appreciate CNAC's wartime services.

As described below, the American military authorities had much difficulty in organizing an effective Hump service and in meeting the promises made to China by President Roosevelt and other high personages. General Arnold raised the question whether CNAC should control all Hump flying. General Stilwell opposed this: he called attention to the difference in pay between CNAC's experienced men and members of the armed forces, and again charged that China was interested in "nonessential Chinese commercial air routes." So the project was dropped.[15]

CNAC, however, offered to the army the benefit of its experience. At the start it made available such facilities as codes for communicating with radio stations as to operations and weather. CNAC pioneered night flying over the Hump, after the Japanese began a persistent attack on these unarmed planes in October 1943. The army soon also took up night flying. By this time the army operation was better organized and supplied. It was possible to counter the Japanese threat fairly well by routing army and CNAC planes further north, by sending out air patrols, and by bombing enemy bases. In October the enemy shot down one CNAC plane and seven army transports. But in November no transport planes were lost to the enemy, and in December only two. Also 12 of 20 enemy bombers attacking Assam fields were shot down. And ground forces successfully defended Fort Hertz, in the extreme north of Burma, an important base for American fighter planes defending the Hump.[16]

THE AMERICAN AIR FORCE AND THE HUMP

As soon as CNAC's pioneering overcame the early grave doubts about what could be done, Washington saw the need to build up promptly an effective air-lift, as basic to aid to China.[17] President Roosevelt in a message of February 9, 1942, gave Generalissimo Chiang "definite assurances that . . . the supply route to China via India can be maintained by air," saying that, "the whole plan seems altogether practical and I am sure we can make it a reality in the near future." [18] Further assurances were repeated at different levels. At first the difficulties were not fully realized, and the capacity of the route was overestimated, it being commonly said that 75 planes could move in 5,000 tons per month. But experience soon showed otherwise.

The difficulties were enormous. Transport planes were one of the scarcest items, being urgently wanted in every theater of war. The United States at the outbreak of war had in official and private service only 27 four-motored transport planes: Pan-American Airways had eight Boeing and two Martin sea-plane Clippers; TWA had five Stratoliners; and the army had one Boeing plane and 11 modified B-24's. American commercial air lines had altogether only about 400 planes, mostly two-motored. In mid-1942, when China asked for four-motored transports, the War Department stated that only 27 C-54's would be built in 1942. The War Department was reluctant to send planes to China. With operations in Europe the first priority, "Every transport sent to the CBI area was a diversion from the main effort, and the War Department so regarded the matter all during the war." [19]

There was severe shortage of engines and parts and instruments, including those for blind flying. In Assam the only adequate field was at Dinjan. Finished only toward the end of 1941, it was practically bare of buildings and equipment. CNAC's exploration plane that landed there two weeks before Pearl Harbor was the first two-motored plane ever to visit Assam. In the early months Dinjan was under tremendous pressure, being used by CNAC, the Army Ferry Command, the American and British air forces, and transient planes. Time was needed to build more terminal fields, with maintenance facilities, supplies, and quarters. The needed labor and materials were hard to get. These fields were at the end of a tenuous 1000-mile narrow-gauge railway, built to haul tea. Supply of gasoline was a major problem, first to fuel the planes for take-off over the Hump; second to build up stocks in China to supplement what the planes could take for the return flight; and finally, to supply the needs within China. Assam's climate was hot and one of the wettest in the world. Weather on the Hump was often very bad, forcing planes to fly blind at high altitudes in freezing conditions to avoid the mountain peaks. And on clear days they had to fly farther north and high, to try to avoid enemy interception. With enemy control of most of Burma, Myitkyina in the north having been lost in May 1942, there could be no good warning net. All these conditions made for strain on men and planes. The development of the mass airlift over the Hump was a remarkable achievement.

The American Ferry Command, formed March 21, 1942, with 25 transports gotten from Pan-American Airways, had great difficulty in getting under way. As early as April 17, Hornbeck stated that such information as the State Department had on its operations was "distressing," and that "the efforts of that command had not been effective so far as getting the goods to China is concerned," whereas CNAC "in the midst of many difficulties" had "done miracles in 'delivering the goods.'" [20] With the collapse in Burma in April–May, many of the army planes had to be used to evacuate military personnel and refugees to India and to drop supplies to them and to troops. By mid-1942 the Ferry Command had 12 planes, and 75 by October. There were morale difficulties due to the bad living conditions, poor mail service, lack of many needed facilities, slow promotions, and few replacements. Also the men griped about the much higher pay of the experienced CNAC civilian personnel doing the same sorts of work as military personnel.

Nevertheless the military operation began to gain headway. From the fall of 1942 its haulage over the Hump began to exceed that of CNAC by a great and growing margin. On December 1 the Army Transport Command (ATC) took over from the Ferry Command. In the spring of 1943 Washington sent Colonel Edward V. Rickenbacker to China to get his expert opinion of the situation. He reported that operations were held back by poor airdrome facilities, lack of experienced maintenance personnel, lack of radio aids and direction finders, friction in the American organization with its complicated and divided command, and poor morale of the personnel.[21] But improvement was slow and difficulties continued.

In the spring of 1943 the President gave directions that the airlift move 7,000 tons by July and 10,000 by September. Actual movement in July totaled about 4,500 tons: 3,451 by ATC and 1,054 by CNAC. In August more than 100 ATC planes per day on the average were grounded. In four weeks in September CNAC with 23 two-motored Douglas planes moved 1,134 tons. ATC moved 5,198 tons, but had 225 planes including 43 four-motored C-87's and over 100 of the new and big C-46's. However, the C-46's were found to have many "bugs" in them, and were early known in the area as "flying coffins," though when the bugs were corrected these planes helped much to enlarge the Hump tonnage. The 10,000 figure was not reached until December, when ATC airlifted 12,590 tons.[22]

CENTRAL ASIAN ROUTES

With the Burma Road closed and the airlift slow to develop, China sought other routes of supply. Early in 1943 something like 700 tons monthly was moving each way over the long Central Asian route between China and Russia. From China Russia was getting barter goods in payment for the earlier credits—metals, hides and skins, bristles, tea, et cetera. China was getting from Russia gasoline, parts for Russian trucks in service in China, and various nonmilitary items.[23] But shipments of military items stopped, or practically stopped, from the time of Hitler's attack on Russia in June 1941.

With American and British support, China tried to work out arrangements for sending Lend-Lease goods into China through Iran or Karachi and thence via Central Asia to China's northwest. It was especially important to replenish the supply of trucks, as those in China were wearing out and more could not come by air. Altogether, it seemed technically feasible to move 10,000 tons monthly or more on these routes through Russia. Also, an air route via Alaska and Siberia was discussed, to bring in planes and some supplies. It would have been very helpful if planes could have been flown to China via Alaska and Siberia, instead of via Brazil and over the South Atlantic with the long over-water crossing which was difficult for C-47 and C-53 planes, and then across Africa and Southern Asia.

Russia, however, was reluctant. She feared provoking attack by Japan in Siberia while facing a mortal threat by Hitler. Also, she wanted to keep all facilities free for emergencies. Besides, after holding the Germans at Stalingrad in 1943, Russia felt she was on the winning side, and showed less and less willingness to do anything that would help China.

Late in 1942 Russia seemed favorable in principle to transit of 2,000 tons monthly of Lend-Lease goods, in exchange for 2,000 tons from China, on a ton-for-ton basis. In mid-1943 the American Lend-Lease authorities sent forward 500 trucks for use in the Sinkiang sector, and the British supplied a similar number from India. But nothing came of the efforts. The Chinese for the first month's shipment listed 900 tons of automotive equipment, and 1,100 tons of ammunition for General Hu Tsung-nan, whose troops were lined up in China's northwest to defend against the Chinese Communists! When the first convoys reached Meshed in the fall of 1943 the Russians refused entry, apparently fearing Japanese suspicion.[24] In any case the Russians had left themselves with an out—since they knew that China's internal transport was so scarce that it was not possible for China to deliver monthly 2,000 tons of strategic goods at Hami, the interchange point in the far northwest. Perhaps Russia's willingness to negotiate was based on knowledge that China could not meet this condition.[25] In the fall of 1944 Russia finally gave permission for a convoy of vehicles to enter China via Central Asia. But before this could leave Iran it was diverted because of disturbances in Sinkiang Province. It entered China early in 1945 via the Stilwell Road.[26]

China sought also to open a route by pack train through Tibet, which had agreed to transit of nonmilitary items. But that, it was estimated, could not handle more than about 1,000 tons yearly at best because of difficulties of terrain. A pack train could make only one trip in the six months when weather conditions permitted traffic. Shipments via Tibet did not materialize.[27]

XIV. MONEY, SUPPLIES, AND STRATEGY, 1942–1943

MILITARY AID IN A WEAK ECONOMY

AMERICAN military activities in China began modestly with the mission of Brigadier General Magruder in October 1941. They grew greatly with the advent of the 14th Air Force, Lieutenant General Stilwell and his staff, the Hump operation of the Army Transport Command, the B-29 bombers, missions to train Chinese troops, and other services.

As these activities gradually developed, the United States became more and more involved with China's internal problems. Pressures on China grew. There was urgent need for airfields and related facilities such as shops, barracks, and access roads. Growing numbers of Americans had to be housed and fed, somewhat at least in the style to which they were accustomed. That problem Lieutenant General J. L. Huang and his colleagues tackled with enthusiasm and a large measure of success, considering the huge difficulties.

West and Southwest China was one of China's most backward areas, lacking much exposure to modernizing influences. Many Chinese with enlightened ideas strove hard and loyally to deal with the infinitely difficult wartime problems. But far too many had the old idea that public responsibility was a private opportunity. Relations of the rank and file of Americans and the ordinary Chinese people were on the whole quite good. But many Americans felt that "anyone who wears a tie" was a profiteer. To illustrate: I was told that when the Americans let a contract for airfields in East China, the authorities twice arrested the contractors, saying they were undependable; and then the Army had to pay almost double, to the right parties. Often there was cornering of supplies when construction was to be done. On the other hand, the American attitude often left much to be desired. On January 20, 1944, I noted in my diary:

U.S. Army needs are very inflationary, but largely unavoidable. Often they are wasteful and do not adapt to what can be done here. Buy carelessly without regard to price. But Chinese also sometimes hold them up—supply being so short. U.S. planning to export potatoes from Kunming to Dinjan despite shortages of vegetables in Kunming. Chinese killing 30 cattle daily for U.S. hostels, and supply of work animals threatened; yet Army talking of buying 50 daily to send to Dinjan. That is because there is plenty of space on planes and Dinjan is short and hard to ship enough from Calcutta, as transport is not enough to provide for needs in Assam.

I characterized the attitude of some Americans as all too often "patronizing or colonial."

How to cover American outlay that had to be met in Chinese currency became a major problem. Only the most urgent items, and in limited quantities, could come over the Hump. The Americans had to live mostly off the country, and to find locally most of the goods needed for military activities. The problem of getting money for American needs was what I called the "inward transfer problem." It was the reverse of the usual textbook transfer problem, where a country with weak finances has difficulty in finding foreign currency for payment of debts and other current obligations. Here the question was how a financially strong country could get large amounts of a weaker country's money, without too great strain on that country's economy. This problem existed during the war in places other than China, notably in the Middle East where American and British operations called for large sums in local currency. It has been met postwar, mainly in giving American military support to countries such as South Korea, Vietnam, and Laos, where the need for local currency is great relative to the country's production and foreign trade.

In 1942 and during the rest of the war both the United States and China faced hard problems in financing military aid. The budget already was seriously in deficit, apart from needs growing out of American activities. Regardless of dollars paid to the Central Bank of China in New York, the additional currency needed in China could be provided only by running the printing presses harder. What share of the additional costs in Chinese currency should China bear alone? What share should the United States pay for in dollars? At what rate should China furnish her money for dollars? And would the gain from a particular project offset the harm to China from faster inflation? These issues greatly worried both the Chinese and American leaders. Conflicting ideas on what to do gave rise to bitter controversy.

HOW SHOULD CHINA SHARE THE COSTS?

The American Lend-Lease law of 1941 contemplated that aided countries should provide reciprocal aid or benefits to the United States. This became know as reverse Lend-Lease. On June 2, 1942, China and the United States signed a mutual aid agreement, providing that China "will provide such articles, services, facilities or information as it may be in a position to supply." [1]

In the latter part of 1942 China began paying for food and lodging for American forces in China, and also for building and improving various airports.[2] The United States was paying for barracks, administration buildings, and transportation. But there was no detailed agreement. In May 1943, the United States proposed such an agreement, providing that the United States would pay in dollars for certain items of outlay in Chinese currency and China would pay for the rest, to be credited as reverse Lend-Lease. But soon the argument about the rate of exchange began to get hot. I recommended in a memorandum of November 27, 1943, that China make an agreement, within her capacity, on the ground that such action would lessen financial friction between the two governments and "strengthen the possibility of China getting in future the financial help that will be needed from the United States."

The upshot was that no agreement was made about reverse Lend-Lease. Likewise there was no agreement on how to value China's deliveries of goods and services, and only a partial agreement about money. When China was ready to sign the draft, Washington felt that first there should be an understanding about the rate of exchange. So nothing was then done. Later the American authorities in China wanted to sign up. But Washington decided against it, feeling that China would insist on valuing deliveries at exchange rates too far out of line with the buying power of national currency.[3] So China's deliveries were never definitely valued. The only specific item, but an important one, which the American records show was US$3,672,000, being the value of P-40 fighter planes which China bought in 1941 for the Flying Tigers and which were made available in 1942 when that valorous group was merged into the American Air Force.[4] Eventually the American obligation to China was canceled as a postwar setoff against American surplus property which China acquired in China and the Western Pacific area.[5]

The 21st Lend-Lease Report to Congress of September 30, 1945, just after the war ended, said that China's great contribution was its stand against Japan, which "made insignificant any material contribution measured in dollars" (page 31).

WHAT PRICE NATIONAL CURRENCY?

At first the American finance officers sold dollar drafts to the Central Bank at the official rate to get the national currency they needed. From August 18, 1941, that rate at parity was C$18.82 per US$1. As of July 10, 1942, the rate was changed to 20–1, where it stayed all through the war. But, as the printing presses rolled, prices in China soared. The overvaluation of national currency became extreme. At 20–1 the exchange value of China's money was a sixth of the prewar figure of about C$3.36 per US$1. But, approximately, at average prices in Free China, national currency at the end of 1941 had only about a 20th of its prewar value; at the end of 1942, about a 66th; at the end of 1943, about a 228th; at the end of 1944, about a 755th; and at the war's end in August 1945, about a 2,500th.[6] At Kunming, the main American base, inflation was worse than the average, and the comparison was more extreme.

Repeatedly I drew the attention of the Chinese Government to the evils of overvaluation; for example, in a memorandum of February 23, 1942, I pointed out that "overvalued rates build up a false and artificial situation, which later will have to be corrected at great cost." I urged that the granting of the large American and British loans created a favorable opportunity to adjust the rate. But the government was understandably concerned with the inflation and the fall of the value of the currency in the free market and feared the effects of a change. As it became clear that there was little chance to change the rate, I recommended meeting the situation by using special rates and subsidies and acquiescing in use of the free market for exchange.

So long as American military activities in China were small, the rising cost of national currency did not raise an acute issue. But before the end of 1942 it became clear that the ordinary GI, if he sold his dollar pay at the official rate, would not realize enough for what he would like to spend in China. So, for morale reasons, paymasters began late in 1942 to pay the American personnel in American currency notes. They did this with the full knowledge of the State and Treasury Departments and of the Chinese Government. Explaining this, Lieutenant General Brehon B. Somervell wrote to Morgenthau: "The War Department has been reluctant to have its soldiers dealing in black market operations, but for morale purposes it could not do other than authorize such a procedure in view of its failure to find other means of giving its men in China sufficient local currency to offset the unrealistic exchange rate." [7] The Army also from October 31, 1943, supplied American notes for American diplomatic and consular outlay in China, amounting to US$140,000 monthly including US$40,000 for salaries. The State Department told Ambassador Gauss that those receiving notes could "acquire Chinese currency therewith by the most advantageous means available to them." Kung told the Ambassador he had no objection.[8]

The Chinese Government did not like to see its money traded at a growing discount from the official rate. But it acquiesced in the process and made no real effort to stop it—which in any case woud have been futile. The market was commonly called a black market; but, more accurately, it was a gray market.

Payment in American currency notes took care of American military and official personnel in China. But it did not solve the problem of covering the growing American military outlay for supplies, transport, and construction. During 1943 discussions went on between the Chinese and American authorities about how to meet these needs. There were several proposals: to raise the official rate, for example, from 20–1 to 100–1; to give the American Government a special rate; to sell gold or American currency to raise funds; to arrange advances of Chinese currency as reverse Lend-Lease or as a loan for later settlement; or some combination of these. But negotiations got nowhere, and meanwhile the problem got worse. On November 2, 1943, I wrote in my diary: "If not fixed up, there will be feeling in the U.S. that the U.S. is being exploited . . . Many army personnel are sore and go home and talk." And again on November 27: "I pressed for a reverse lend-lease arrangement . . . Failure to adjust this matter will have bad consequences for China in future. Americans do not like to feel that they have been imposed upon." On December 27 I wrote that it was a common view among the GI's that China "made a profit" of the difference between 20–1 and the much higher free market rate.

On December 10, 1943, Adler recommended to the Treasury a strong formal approach to China on behalf of all interested departments of the American Government, for "reasonably equitable foreign exchange arrangements, preferably within the general framework of reverse lend-lease but assuring China of some reasonable accumulations of U.S. dollar resources." He pointed out that costs were 8–10 times those for comparable services and facilities in the United States. He favored "carefully controlled publicity regarding existing arbitrary exchange situation in China," and said: ". . . a possible suggestion of interest in the matter on the part of Congress would be beneficial here in lighting a fire under those persons inclined to be evasive and non-cooperative and desirous of continuing to exploit the situation for the purpose of accumulating large reserves of U.S. dollars out of our expenditures for the war effort." [9] The Treasury's reply of December 11 instructed him to tell Minister Kung that the Treasury could not justify continuing to buy *fapi* at 20–1 and thought it should get 100–1. Otherwise the Treasury saw no alternative but to ship and sell American currency in China pending some other arrangement.[10] On December 23 Ambassador Gauss talked with Generalissimo Chiang, pointing out that the artificial rate of exchange "might cause severe criticism that the American Government and Army are being exploited." The Generalissimo said that the official rate could not be altered, and that "both the economic and military collapse of China would result from a failure to support the currency of China." But he was willing to have Minister Kung discuss some arrangement by other means, such as reverse Lend-Lease, which the ambassador had suggested.[11]

These acute financial issues between the United States and China did not stand alone. In the latter part of 1943 they were merging with broader issues concerning Chiang's request for a billion dollar loan, supplies for China, the nature of military aid and strategy, and the status of China as an ally. These issues will occupy us in subsequent sections of this chapter and in following chapters. Also while the high and rising cost of Chinese currency was bringing friction in the military field, the situation was severely affecting private civilian agencies aiding China, foreign diplomatic missions, and foreigners not connected with their governments.

For decades foreign missionary and philanthropic activities had brought benefit to China. During the war much of this work moved to Free China, especially educational institutions and relief agencies. In the latter part of 1942 D. W. Edwards, Director for China of United China Relief, estimated 1943 remittances as follows (millions of US$):

Relief funds	7.7
Missions and education:	
Protestant	4.5
Catholic	2.0
	14.2

British and Canadian contributions for relief and education were estimated to be about US$2.7 million. Thus the total of all for the year was about US$17 million.

As chairman or acting chairman of the two American committees handling relief in China, I had direct touch with the problem.* In a broadcast to the United States from Chungking, April 14, 1942, before the financial issue became acute, I said,

The common people of China have stood up to this invasion in a way that has aroused the admiration of the civilized world. What are the reasons for this? First, there is the fortitude and resourcefulness, the strength and tenacity of these people. They have taken punishment that probably no other people could have taken and still survive. Partly also it is due to the Chinese family system. Those in need can rely upon relatives who themselves may be only a little above the margin of subsistence. Besides it is due to China's decentralized rural life based upon thousands of local areas producing most of their own food and other necessities and not greatly depending upon trade with other areas. Such an economy cannot easily be disrupted by invasion of the main routes of travel.

But to no small extent Chinese ability to take this punishment and still defy the invader is due to the care for war victims by public and private relief agencies . . .

Private relief agencies supported by the generous gifts of American funds

---

* When the foreign exchange issue began to become acute I made it clear that, because of being adviser to the Chinese Government, I would not represent the committees in taking up foreign exchange matters, or participate in committee action on them.

remain essential . . . They make possible urgently needed relief that otherwise would remain undone.

I want you to know that your money is and will be well used.

As the war dragged on, I had cause to doubt the wisdom of
making that last statement. The fixed exchange rate caught philanthropic activities in a squeeze. Sales of foreign currency were at an
unchanging rate of exchange, while costs in China were rising by
close to 10 per cent monthly on the average. Foreign gifts could
not possibly increase to offset such a rise. So some activities were
threatened with curtailment or even closing.

By the latter part of 1942 this situation began to cause acute
concern. Edwards pointed out, in a letter of October 16 to
Minister Kung, that it would be hard to raise more dollars to
offset rising costs and said that ". . . to reduce the program of work
carried on by turning away refugees, orphans, students and
teachers, the closing of colleges and schools, the reduction in the
supply of medicines, decreasing support given to the Chinese
Industrial Co-operatives, retracting the amount of medical service
rendered to the Chinese armed forces, etc., is a distressing alternative causing suffering which we do not like to contemplate." He
asked for a preferential rate of exchange for funds remitted from
abroad for relief. From the United States came reports that good
will was threatened. United China Relief cabled October 22 that
"Government and public approval our appeals may be jeopard-
ized." Clearly it would become harder and harder to raise funds
as word spread about the exchange rate situation.

Appeals to do something came from many quarters. After a visit
to Chengtu I reported to the government on March 2, 1943, that
action was urgent to alleviate the position of foreign-supported
educational and missionary activities. Some agencies, I found,
were planning wholesale reduction of staff, or closing. Most of the
institutions at Chengtu could maintain their activities for only
two to four months, even by using all their reserves. Some of
the home offices were holding back remittances, hoping that the
government would grant more favorable exchange arrangements.
My report said:

Also I was told in Chengtu that many persons are selling furniture, clothing
and other belongings to raise enough to provide a minimum living. The case

was cited . . . of a family dependent upon an annual salary of Canadian dollars 1,700—for which the exchange is about 16.66. At present prices, . . . their salary would buy only fuel for minimum heating through the winter and for the kitchen stove—leaving nothing for food and other necessities.

For some time Kung had made available government contributions in some cases to supplement gifts for various philanthropic purposes. But this was not generalized.

Meanwhile foreign embassies had been pressing for better treatment in their sales of exchange. In April 1943, the Finance Ministry directed that as a temporary war measure the Central Bank convert their exchange at the official rates, and pay 50 per cent in addition. In May this was applied also to remittances by "all cultural, missionary and philanthropic institutions." In the case of famine relief, the supplement was to be 100 per cent.

But foreigners not connected with their governments continued to be pinched by fixed exchange, as they did not at once have access to the 50 per cent supplement. Not many foreign businessmen remained in Free China. There was a sizable group of press men. All who could generally used the free market. Because of my position I did not do so, even though apparently it was not illegal. In December 1943, as the best means to cover living costs I sold for C$110,000 the better of my two radios, one which I had bought in 1939 in the United States for US$225. That was equal to US$5,500 at the official rate of 20–1. On the same day I paid C$330, similarly equal to US$16.50, for the labor of half-soling a pair of shoes with soles I had brought from India.

Remittances by overseas Chinese to dependents in China gave rise to a long controversy. Such remittances were far below the earlier high level, because Japan had overrun most of the areas in the South Seas whence remittances came. In China recipients lived mainly in occupied places, though often there were devious ways to get funds to them. Especially in the Canton area many had become dependent on remittances and were in acute need. Those who could wait were unwilling to cash the remittances when they could get only 20–1. The Bank of China was involved since most remittances came through them and they were often blamed for the adverse rate. Their pressure for a rate better than 20–1 was generally thought at the time to have been a factor in the later displacement of Soong by Kung as head of that bank.

Finally in November 1943, the 50 per cent supplement was extended to remittances of overseas Chinese and to exchange sold by foreigners not connected with their governments.

China's leaders accepted with fairly good grace the principle that defeat of Hitler was the first priority. But they resented a degree of emphasis on Europe that denied to China the minor proportion of aid that China could receive and use. In the opening days of 1942 China had defeated the Japanese drive on Changsha. While Chinese propaganda exaggerated the victory, it was real enough to cause the responsible Japanese general to commit hara-kiri.[12] For months this was the only Allied defeat of a determined Japanese thrust, and China's pride rose accordingly.

From the start of Lend-Lease, China's leaders and many Americans responsible for relations with China had been concerned about the smallness and slowness of aid. A memorandum on "American aid to China," prepared in February 1942 in the office of the Coordinator of Information at Washington, concluded that the smallness was due to "absorptions in the familiar problems of Europe rather than in the exotic far off conflicts of Eastern Asia." The delay, said the report, had been "overcome only by the most strenuous effort on the part of those in charge of expediting the Lend-Lease aid to China." [13]

Planes, equipment, and crews were started to China via Africa, to fulfill President Roosevelt's promises to Generalissimo Chiang. But many planes were grounded for repairs and parts, and many were diverted. Often items were commandeered en route, sometimes without notice or report, by officers who needed them urgently. In April 1942, the War Department took action to divert planes from China to protect northeastern India from possible invasion and to give cover to the British navy in the Bay of Bengal. The Chinese reaction appeared in a message of April 19 to Washington from Madame Chiang giving the Generalissimo's views:

If any Lend-Lease planes diverted to Tenth Group people and Army will feel themselves robbed widow's mite and will certainly resent not being treated as worthy ally who has unstintedly given all to common cause. Second, if planes necessary to defend India, etc., why not take from lot assigned to Russia or Britain who are receiving thousands from America instead of from paltry few designated for China. Third, Chinese Army and people are asking with all aid from America what has Britain contributed to Allied cause. Please inform President Generalissimo's attitude. Today British Army in Burma again retreated even from Magwe and all oil fields lost.

In reply General Arnold gave assurances that disposal of planes on the Chinese program rested with the Generalissimo and Stilwell. But the planes en route, said Arnold, seemed to be more than Chennault could immediately use, and he, Arnold, hoped some could be spared for India, where they would be under Stilwell's general command. In May the Munitions Assignment Board repossessed, with China's reluctant consent, 149,000 tons of Lend-Lease goods at Newport News, Virginia. And in July Washington, after setting aside for China in India Lend-Lease items that had a prospect of near shipment, reassigned the rest that was there.[14]

Causes of Sino-American friction were building up. Stilwell was in a tough spot *vis-à-vis* China in handling Lend-Lease matters. He bore the brunt of explaining repeated American delays and failures to meet commitments, caused mainly by priorities given to other theaters of war. His orders required him to comment on China's insistent requests, often for items which he thought impracticable or unjustifiable. And, in addition to slowness of deliveries and diversions, there were deep issues touching China's pride. China indeed had been recognized as the Fourth Power. But Generalissimo Chiang was beginning to feel that this was in name only. In a message of April 19, 1942, communicated to Roosevelt, he said, ". . . Both in the all-important matters of joint-staff conferences and war supplies, China is treated not as an equal like Britain and Russia but as a ward." He wanted China to join both the Anglo-American joint staff and the Munitions Assignment Board. Otherwise "China would be just a pawn in the game." The Board turned down both requests on June 13, in a polite message recognizing China's importance in the war. One reason was a feeling that membership in the joint staff would have involved membership in the Munitions Board, which was allocating supplies to which China could not contribute appreciably, but could only press constantly for a larger share.[15] And as to war supplies, the American military leaders felt that distribution of military Lend-Lease items in China had to be kept in American hands, because the Chinese organization was not in position to handle them properly. In a memorandum of September 23, 1944, to Hurley, Stilwell said of the Generalissimo's attitude, "What he is gagging at is L-L [Lend-Lease], and it is a serious matter of face with him that Stalin and the Br. can handle the stuff and he can't. The pros and cons are well known; the ques. remains." [16]

In contrast to the military services, the State Department was more sympathetic to China. Hornbeck pointed out in a memorandum of May 7, 1942, that Chiang "might decide to 'sulk in his tent'" unless China received supplies substantially as promised and "in reasonable proportion" to what was going to Britain and Russia. On May 20, Ambassador Gauss telegraphed that the "Chinese should have early proof that we consider China a vital theatre of the war," especially by speeding up the air transport service. On May 21 Secretary Hull sent Gauss' message to the President and Secretaries Stimson and Knox with his strong endorsement.[17]

A further serious issue arose in June. With Rommel threatening Egypt and Suez, the War Department on June 23 ordered to the Middle East from India for temporary service the heavy bombers of the 10th Air Force and some of the transports on the China run; also, some A-29 planes en route to China were diverted to the British. This diversion looked all the worse to China because, as part of the deal to build up American air power, China had agreed to furnish gasoline and bombs from its scanty stocks and had been doing so. Stilwell was instructed to break the bad news. Foreseeing trouble he wrote on June 25: "Now what can I say to the G-mo? We fail in *all* our commitments, and blithely tell him to just carry on, old top." [18] On June 26 he saw the Generalissimo, who reacted as feared and wanted "a yes or no answer to whether the Allies consider this theater necessary and will support it." On June 27 Roosevelt sent a personal message, explaining that the diversion was necessary "to preserve our lines of communication to the China Theater." The Generalissimo's reaction on June 29 was what came to be called the three demands: that three American divisions arrive in August–September to help reopen communications via Burma; that from August a 500-plane air force be maintained; and that the airlift be raised to 5,000 tons monthly by August.[19]

Generalissimo Chiang's reaction to diversions was not opposition to meeting sudden emergencies. Rather it was a deep-rooted feeling that China was being ignored, discriminated against, and not treated as an equal. The immediate issues were gradually compromised: by Stilwell's making concrete plans for an offensive in Burma, including use of Chinese troops to be trained and equipped in India; by recognizing that American land forces could not come at least for some time; by promising a 500-plane air force; and by planning to step up movement over the Hump. In July Laughlin Currie of Roosevelt's staff went to China, and his visit helped smooth matters. But the basic issues persisted.[20]

In 1941–1942 a defeatist attitude about China often obtained in American military circles, both in China and at home. Some members of the Magruder mission, after their early inspection trips, felt that months of inactive defense had "created a non-aggressive attitude in the soldiers," and reported some Chinese officers as saying that China "might be able to win this war without further fighting," because of international pressure on Japan.[21] Some American officers argued that, with the enemy in Burma, the Hump route was no longer feasible; that Japan was about to knock China out of the war; that China might make a separate peace; and that the United States could do little about it. There was even talk of evacuation of Chungking. The State Department and Ambassador Gauss in China combated these extreme views, feeling that while conditions were critical there was no imminent likelihood of a separate peace or of China's collapse. The State Department agreed with Bond of CNAC that the air route could be flown successfully with proper equipment and organization, and that Department's officers and Bond so argued with General Marshall and others. They recalled Roosevelt's promises of support of air transport to bring in supplies, and urged stepping up air support as the best antidote to the pessimism. Ambassador Gauss reported in September 1942 his view that the lessening of Chinese military resistance was not a result of any lack of will to resist but, rather, a lack of munitions and inability to replenish reserves. He felt that, understandably, they hesitated to use them unless for permanent gains, or unless they had their backs to the wall. Furthermore, the British were not enthusiastic about aid to China. In September they suggested to the American Government that China might be able to go on for another year without aid. The United States rejected the idea, stating that aid should be increased.[22]

Meanwhile, Stilwell was working hard on plans to retake Burma, and in this was getting a large degree of Chinese cooperation. But on November 24 the War Department told him that because of needs of other theaters he could not expect to receive soon the items needed for the offensive. He replied bluntly, and on Thanksgiving Day wrote to his wife: "They are too busy elsewhere for small fry like us, so we can go right ahead developing our characters and working on that shoestring I had presented to me." [23]

This general situation continued without material change into 1943, though Hump tonnage slowly increased. Also, there were issues about non-military Lend-Lease for China. The chief items related to communications. Stilwell and Bissell, his air adviser, as we have seen, were unsympathetic to CNAC as a civil air line. Also the War Department began to object to any nonmilitary program for China, the main items involved being automotive equipment and parts. The State Department and Lend Lease Administration, however, took a different view. The Lend Lease Administration told the State Department in September 1943 that it finally had to appeal to the President against the War Department, whose mistrust of China "is manifestly derogatory to China's sovereignty, . . . works to prevent the transfer to China of otherwise needed, available, and deliverable supplies," and "serves to nullify the commitments contemplated in our over-all relations with China and more specifically contained in our Master Lend-Lease Agreement with China." They favored a high-level committee under the President to review the situation, with Hopkins as chairman if possible. The State Department concurred. But this was not done.[24]

STRINGS ON AID?

When General Stilwell went to China early in 1942 he was made Chief of Staff to Generalissimo Chiang, and Commanding General of American forces in the China-Burma-India theater. His orders of February 2 were to "increase the effectiveness of United States assistance to the Chinese Government for the prosecution of the war and to assist in improving the combat efficiency of the Chinese army." In this capacity he was given control of military Lend-Lease items, which were sent to him for transfer to China at his discretion and under his supervision. Nonmilitary items, for example, arsenal supplies and transport equipment, were given directly to China without later supervision.[25]

In the spring of 1942 the War Department suggested that Stilwell and the Generalissimo agree on requests for Lend-Lease aid. In Stilwell's absence fighting in Burma, Magruder replied. He proposed a *quid pro quo* policy under which China would agree to a specified reorganization of the army, to be supplied in part by Lend-Lease.[26] Such a policy was in line with the attitude toward China formulated as far back as 1840 by Lord Napier when he advised London of "the urgent necessity of negotiating with such a government, having in your hands at the same time the means of compulsion." [27] The War Department, with approval of General Marshall and Secretary Stimson, felt that "Lend-Lease to China should not be given as philanthropy but rather on a *quid pro quo* basis, with Chinese military reforms to precede it and Chinese military accomplishments to be the sole acceptable guarantee of its continuance." [28]

When the issue arose during the summer in replying to the "three demands," Currie thought it unwise to try to put pressure on China, since the United States would not be able to meet China's wishes fully. So the President's reply, without making conditions as the War Department wished, stated that reform of the forces in Yunnan "would be of the greatest importance in obtaining our mutual objectives." [29]

For some time Stilwell's program went ahead. But as Chennault's rival program stressing air power gained momentum, Stilwell felt a lack of interest on China's part in reforming the army and attacking into Burma. On February 9, 1943, he wrote to Marshall: "Chiang Kai-shek has been very irritable and hard to handle, upping his demands no matter what is given to him, and this attitude will continue until he is talked to in sterner tones. For everything we do *for* him we should exact a commitment *from* him." The President, to whom Marshall sent Stilwell's letter, did not agree. He replied on March 8 that Stilwell had "exactly the wrong approach in dealing with Generalissimo Chiang." The Generalissimo had "come up the hard way," to reach a "position of supremacy" which he finds it necessary to maintain. "He is the Chief Executive as well as the Commander-in-Chief, and one cannot speak sternly to a man like that." [30]

Before Marshall forwarded the President's views, Stilwell had telegraphed on March 15:

Chungking cannot or will not enforce its orders in this area [Yunnan]. Our presence threatens to affect the enormous smuggling racket here, and you may expect a campaign of vilification against me personally. I have already been accused of bad faith for keeping military supplies from racketeers. The continued publication of Chungking propaganda in the United States is an increasing handicap to my work. Utterly false impression has been created in United States public opinion. Army is generally in desperate condition, underfed, unpaid, untrained, neglected, and rotten with corruption. We can pull them out of this cesspool, but continued concessions have made the Generalissimo believe he has only to insist and we will yield.

If we can train and equip the Yunnan force, we can save the situation, but I may have to call for backing in case a showdown is necessary. You may think a year of this has had its effect on me. My opinion of the Chinese soldier and the Chinese people is unchanged. It is the gang of Army "leaders" that is the cause of all our grief. With best wishes and hoping for a better picture soon.

When Stilwell got the President's views he deemed them a rebuke.[31]

ARMY REFORM VS. AIR OPERATIONS

Toward the end of 1942 plans to recover Burma began to take shape. China, with American technical and material aid, was preparing its part in the offensive, in line with Stilwell's belief that land forces were the key to military success. Preparations went forward in two places.

First was the training and equipping of Chinese troops at Ramgarh in India. This center was activated August 26, 1942, with American and British aid. To the 9,000 men who had retreated to India in good order when Burma fell were added about 23,000 flown from China. The government of India at first dragged its feet in aiding the program. But it cooperated loyally when London so directed, after American pressure through the Combined Chiefs of Staff and the British War Cabinet. It provided pay in rupees for these men and many items of local supplies whose value was about US$18 million. With good food and medical services, regular pay to the men individually and not through corrupt commanders, training, modern arms, and good leadership, this army known as the X-force soon became an effective fighting unit which could be ready to move early in 1943. These troops, who were later to fight so well in retaking North Burma in 1943–1944, vindicated Stilwell's faith in the common Chinese soldier.[32] To prepare the way for this advance, a road was started from Ledo into upper Burma.

The second part of China's preparation was the regrouping, re-training, and equipping of the so-called Y-force in Yunnan. The heavier weapons and much of the lighter would have to come from concentrating weapons already in China but were to be supplemented by increments from Lend-Lease. Training centers for infantry and artillery were set up near Kunming. American officers were assigned to the Chinese army units. By December 1942, the program was making such good progress that Stilwell could telegraph to Washington that the situation was ". . . approaching the point where it was up to the United States to make good on promises of supply and transport." Washington gave support to the whole plan by sending to India 6,000 troops, mostly engineering units, together with road-building and maintenance equipment, to arrive about April 1943, for the purpose of helping to open a land route to China.[33]

But the British in India under General Wavell were hesitant. They were unenthusiastic about retaking only northern Burma and stressed the difficulty in building the projected road to China and keeping it working during the monsoon. They felt that the road would not be ready in time to justify the effort. They were slow in developing adequate air terminals in northeast Assam and in developing communications thither from Calcutta.[34] They wavered between the project of opening northern Burma and by-passing Burma by landing in northern Sumatra and moving toward Singapore, to recover lost colonies. For Burma, the original plans contemplated an amphibious attack on Rangoon to go with the north Burma drive. But it was becoming clear that the needed air and naval superiority in the Bay of Bengal could not be had by the Spring of 1943. Wavell, supported at Washington by Field Marshall Sir John Dill, urged delay. General Marshall, however, told Dill on December 21, 1942, that he favored a limited offensive in north Burma to protect better the air route and to open as soon as possible a land route to China.[35]

Generalissimo Chiang also was hesitating. He claimed that the British had promised to provide for the Burma offensive an adequate amphibious force plus seven divisions. Churchill, however, insisted that it was not a promise but only a statement of what was then intended. The amphibious forces not being in near prospect, the Generalissimo on January 8, 1943, declined to commit the Y-force in a lesser offensive. The Casablanca conference in January of Roosevelt and Churchill and their staffs set November 15, 1943, as the tentative date for a major Burma offensive, subject to reconsideration by July.[36]

Roosevelt and Churchill, in approving the Casablanca plans for the over-all war against the Axis, emphasized "the urgency of sending air reinforcements to General Chennault's forces in China." [37] The issue was sharpening whether there should be priority in the American aid program for the Chinese army (Y-force) and the retaking of north Burma, or for developing Chennault's air forces. The remarkable success of the Flying Tigers, in defeating vastly superior enemy forces with a handful of planes, contrasted with Japanese victories in the air in other theaters of war in 1941–1942.[38] Chennault first argued in 1942 that with full authority and a force of about 150 planes, kept strictly up to strength and supplied over the Hump, he could "bring about the downfall of Japan," though later he upped the number of planes needed. His plan was to attack enemy installations and shipping in and around China, to give air support to Chinese ground forces, to bring enemy planes to combat and destroy them, and eventually to bomb Japan from China.[39] He urged these views persuasively, and they found favor with the Generalissimo. Also these views were presented forcefully to the President and Harry Hopkins. When Wendell Willkie visited China he asked Chennault to state his views in a letter to be taken to the President. Chennault did this on October 8, 1942. When Madame Chiang came to the United States in November she raised the issue with Hopkins.[40]

The President thus had to decide between backing Stilwell, supported by Marshall and the War Department, or Chennault, supported by the Generalissimo. His choice was to back Chennault, that is, the air program. The President objected to Stilwell's bargaining approach and tough line with the Generalissimo (see the preceding section). He agreed that Chennault should have a separate Air Force, the 14th, and direct access to the Generalissimo. He told Marshall on March 8, 1943, that Chennault should have "his chance to do what he believes he can do" to cause attrition to Japan by sinking ships, destroying planes, and "occasional bombing of Japanese cities." [41]

Marshall at once activated the 14th Air Force under Chennault, but warned the President that "the comparatively small air effort possible from China in 1943" would be only a beginning. The China air bases would need ground protection. *"Here is the most serious consideration* [Marshall's emphasis]: As soon as our air effort hurts the Japs, they will move in on us, not only in the air but also on the ground." Stilwell, he said, was concentrating on helping to improve China's armies. In Ramgarh, in India, he was having marked success; but was meeting "obstruction and delay" elsewhere. Unfortunately at times Stilwell incurred the Generalissimo's displeasure. But Stilwell was peculiarly well qualified by his knowledge of China and his ability as a soldier and his toughness. Marshall concluded by stating that a land route to China was necessary "to make an all-out air effort continuous and effective." [42]

The President reinforced his decision in favor of Chennault and the air program in May, after summoning both Stilwell and Chennault to Washington and hearing them and the Joint Chiefs of Staff. The latter were divided, Admiral Leahy inclining toward Chennault and General Marshall, General Arnold, and Admiral King toward Stilwell. Marshall told Stilwell on May 3 that the President favored supporting the Y-force, but that "politically he must support Chiang Kai-shek and that in the state of Chinese morale the air program was therefore of great importance." [43] The President ordered stepping up Hump tonnage with a priority for Chennault, in terms that would leave little for the ground forces for several months. The Washington Conference with Churchill and his military advisers later in May endorsed these decisions, after Stilwell and Chennault had again been heard, and decided also to open a road through northern Burma. The British favored the air side, with limited support to Chinese ground forces in China, but doubted whether enough supplies could be moved up to back both these operations and a campaign through Burma. Of the situation a few weeks after the Washington conference the official American army historians say:

As July drew to a close, the divergent trends in U.S. policy were in the open. Reform of the Chinese Army, an augmented air effort, and recapture of Burma conflicted logistically; and though Stilwell's mission was to reform the Chinese Army, to him the Chinese appeared to see U.S. air power as a substitute for a better Chinese army.[44]

The friction between Stilwell and Chennault, for which each bore responsibility, existed during most of their association in the war. Both differences of view and conflicting personalities were involved. Lack of cooperation between these strong and colorful leaders hurt the over-all war effort. Attempts to bring about better relations did not succeed.[45]

Hump tonnage did not grow much before mid-summer of 1943. There was delay because of bad weather and floods in India and failure to complete the Assam airfields on schedule. Chennault's supplies and planes were still grossly inadequate for the operations he had planned. Hence his results in the months after the May decisions fell much below expectations. There was encouragement in the claims that his forces were sinking 50,000 tons of enemy shipping monthly. But postwar reports of the Joint Army-Navy Assessment Committee indicate that the true total was not over 10,000. Particularly important, though not realized then, were the sinkings of iron ore carriers on the Yangtze River, which seriously reduced Japan's steel output. Chennault's planes were destroying many more enemy planes than they lost, a ratio of about six to one. But superior Japanese numbers and better communications began to tell. Chennault had to space his missions, waiting to accumulate fuel and ammunition and to keep planes in repair. Transport within China, from Hump terminals to East China air bases, was always a serious problem. The build-up of transport and terminals in India, however, was at last under way. Toward the end of 1943 Hump tonnage began to surge ahead.[46]

Meanwhile American-aided reform of the Chinese army was lagging. The difficulties were enormous. The better part of China's pitifully small modern forces had been decimated in six years of fighting against great odds. Military equipment and supplies and transport were scarce. In addition, there were the deep-rooted evils in the army system. The Chinese failed to concentrate in Yunnan the armies and artillery assigned there. The government feared to move some of the better units, because they were needed to restrain local warlords and in the north the Communists. A large proportion of the soldiers that were in Yunnan or that did arrive were underfed and ill. Units were far below numerical strength. While lower officer material was commonly good, the higher command was too often inefficient and/or corrupt. General Chen Cheng, whom the Generalissimo finally put in command, was a splendid choice. But in May 1943 he had to be withdrawn to take charge of repulsing a Japanese thrust toward Chungking along the Yangtze. Stilwell's infantry and artillery training schools, well staffed by American experts, were under way after overcoming local obstruction. But the Chinese Army in 1943 never sent enough men to enable Stilwell's Infantry Center to operate at over five-eighths of capacity, or for his Artillery Center at over about a fourth. Preparation by the Chinese army of supply services and operations plans met with delays. And the priority for Chennault meant that few weapons and army supplies were coming over the Hump.[47]

Nevertheless Stilwell doggedly persisted with his original directive to "assist in improving the combat efficiency of the Chinese Army."[48] In the fall of 1943 his relations with the Generalissimo became better and progress was made, though he could not put over his basic reform of amalgamating the 300 scattered, understrength and commonly ill-equipped divisions into half that number. The plan for 30 well-trained and -equipped divisions to attack into Burma from Yunnan was going better, and little by little basic arms and equipment began to arrive over the Hump.[49] But the delays were to prove costly.

The immediate result of Roosevelt's decision was to give Chennault a large degree of independence and priority of supply, but without at once contributing significantly to defeat of Japan. Stilwell, on the other hand, lost face; his army reform program languished; and his eventual recall was foreshadowed. The official American army historians felt that his position as Chief of Staff, China Theater, became "largely formal." As to Marshall's postwar judgment, they say, "After the war, as he looked back on the great argument over air power versus reform of the Chinese Army, the Army's Chief of Staff, General Marshall, commented that subsequent events had proved Stilwell to be right, but unfortunately much too outspoken and tactless." [50]

The President's decision in favor of the air program was far-reaching. It confirmed on the American side the general principle of not bargaining or bringing pressure on China for reform—though a tougher American line and some bargaining developed in 1944 (see chapter XVI). The principle of not bargaining had been forecast a year earlier by giving China a wholly free hand with the use of the US$500 million credit. On the Chinese side the air program was the line of least resistance. It accepted in effect the reluctance to deal with the gross abuses of the army system. The top leaders of both sides failed to recognize how great might have been the advantages for the future of army reform. Stilwell went so far as to say that, with army reform, "China will be able to do her part and refute her critics, and will emerge at the end of the war with the means of assuring her stability." [51] Finally, as Stilwell and Marshall had feared, the air operations prodded the Japanese into their 1944 offensive against the East China air bases. The collapse of Chinese resistance on the ground showed up the weakness of the government after seven years of stress and strain and was a disastrous and almost overwhelming blow to its prestige.

CHANGING VIEWS OF MAJOR STRATEGY

The Allied conferences at Washington and Quebec in May and August 1943, planned major moves to break the Japanese blockade in Burma. That was to lead to a great build-up in China. There was to be an offensive by the Chinese Army on the Canton-Hong Kong area supported by Allied air power and synchronized with an amphibious assault from the Pacific. "Following capture of the great ports, the combined forces would make their way into north China, from which Japan would be bombed into submission, or at least so weakened as to make successful invasion a certainty." [52] In line with this idea, Roosevelt promised that the United States would equip Chinese forces. As Chiang eventually understood it, the United States would equip at once 30 Chinese divisions (X-force), then 30 more (Y-force), and finally a further 30 (Z-force) —90 in all.[53]

The plans for breaking the blockade in Burma contemplated that land operations would begin in the latter part of 1943, with an amphibious attack on Rangoon set for January 1944. From the start of discussions in the Summer of 1942, the Generalissimo had insisted that an amphibious attack must accompany the land operations. He did not otherwise wish to risk his armies, with their meager equipment, and also his past difficulties with the British about Burma led him to feel he must get their commitment for full support. The Generalissimo had agreed to use the Chinese troops in India in the attack and also to attack from China into Burma. He "was given to understand that adequate naval forces would be available to cover the proposed operations in the Bay of Bengal at the end of 1943." [54]

But in the Fall of 1943 another view of major strategy emerged. Reform of the armies in China was lagging. American amphibious operations in the Central Pacific were meeting with success, making possible the "island-hopping" policy. And the long-range B-29 bomber was being developed. In October 1943, before the Generalissimo met at Cairo with Roosevelt and Churchill, Washington planners already felt that plans to defeat Japan should place "principal emphasis on approach from the Pacific rather than from the Asiatic mainland." [55] For China, the implications of that strategy were far-reaching.

THE CAIRO CONFERENCE

In November 1943, Chiang Kai-shek met at Cairo with Roosevelt and Churchill.[56] The famous Cairo Declaration pledged the return to China of Manchuria, Formosa, and the Pescadores. But the announcement that "The several military missions have agreed upon future military operations against Japan" [57] proved far from true.

The talks of the three leaders centered on Burma. There was hot debate whether to go ahead with plans to mount an amphibious attack to accompany the land operations. The immediate upshot, in the words of Sir Winston Churchill, was that "The President, in spite of my arguments, gave the Chinese the promise of a considerable amphibious operation across the Bay of Bengal within the next few months." [58] Chiang thereupon returned to China, while the other two leaders flew to Tehran to meet Stalin.

When Roosevelt and Churchill and their staffs returned to Cairo, the argument continued. At Tehran the emphasis was on opening a second front by invading France. Also, Roosevelt and Churchill were impressed by Stalin's declaration that Russia would later join the war against Japan. That, they thought, would provide nearby bases for bombing Japan. So, after the return to Cairo, Churchill could argue that the amphibious craft should be brought back to Europe for use in the invasion of France. General A. C. Wedemeyer, Deputy Chief of Staff of the South East Asia Command, countered the argument. He felt that a victory in Burma was important and said that all the resources needed for the amphibious operation were in sight, excepting a few escort carriers which Admiral E. J. King said he could find.[59] Chiang was not present to state his views. He had arranged to see Roosevelt and Churchill before they saw Stalin[60] and had no way to foresee that he lost an advantage by not being able to have the last word.

Finally, as Churchill put it, "I at length prevailed upon the President to retract his promise." Churchill in October contemplated an amphibious operation, but at Cairo had reserved his position.[61] Roosevelt reluctantly agreed on December 5, in the words of Admiral Leahy, to "propose some substitute to Chiang." The British Chiefs of Staff promptly moved their amphibious craft back to Europe. Leahy stated, "The Chinese leader had every right to feel that we had failed to keep a promise," and . . . "we were taking a grave risk" that China would drop out of the war. He said, "If the Chinese quit, the tasks of MacArthur and Nimitz in the Pacific, already difficult, would be much harder. Japanese man power in great numbers would be released to oppose our advance toward the mainland of Japan. Fortunately for us, the courageous Chinese stayed in the fight." King was "distressed" at the breach of the long-standing promise to China, and said that this was the only time in the war when Roosevelt had overruled his Chiefs of Staff.[62]

The Cairo meeting was planned with high hopes of giving effect to the repeated pledges that China's friends would move promptly to her relief. On the eve of the conference, Chiang and Stilwell were working together in harmony to prepare the Chinese armies for their part in the Burma offensive. Keeping of the promise Roosevelt made to Chiang at Cairo could have brought a real joint effort, significant for the future. But instead, the withdrawal of the promise ushered in a period of serious friction. The declaration at Cairo that "Manchuria, Formosa, and the Pescadores, shall be restored to the Republic of China" was fine. But would China's war-weary and disunited government be able to struggle through to claim the reward?

XV. A YEAR OF DISCORD, 1944:
MONEY MATTERS

A CHANGE OF TREND

THE seriousness of the wartime friction that developed between China and her Allies, especially the United States, has not been generally realized. The governments tried to keep it under cover, for obvious reasons of war morale. A peak in American esteem for China was reached in the first half of 1943, when Madame Chiang visited the United States and made a triumphal appearance before Congress. At that time China was "oversold" in the United States.* Thereafter a change set in. Many Americans who went to China in the war effort felt disillusioned. When they wrote home or returned and talked, their story was quite different from the common rosy exaggerations of the early period of the Pacific War. Volatile American feeling went to the other extreme, failing to give due weight to China's remarkable resistance and to make allowance for the strain on the people and their leaders after six years of war and inflation. The change in feeling, combined with the friction at the military and diplomatic level, set the scene for the postwar American attitude of strong criticism of the National Government, and even for the notion of a political compromise with the Chinese Communists. After the Cairo Conference, the change in the trend began to be apparent.

The American military historians, Romanus and Sunderland, in their excellent account of American military operations in the China-Burma-India theater, conclude that before the Cairo Conference effort centered upon the relief of China and her strengthening to become a main base from which to attack Japan. Afterward, the chief effort against Japan was made in the Pacific, and the chief object of the China theater was viewed as providing support for this effort, especially air support. These historians call

---

* On March 14, 1943, I wrote to Mrs. Young: "Many people here, both Chinese and foreigners, feel that the propaganda of China is being so badly overdone that it is bound to have a reaction adverse to China's interests."

the Conference "the watershed," and rightly state that after it "the currents flowed in a very different direction." [1]

From December 1943, several matters became closely intertwined: China's request for a billion dollar loan; the terms on which the United States obtained money to pay for operations in China; the provision of material aid to China; and the nature and conduct of military operations in China and Burma. This chapter will treat of money matters. The next chapter will deal with material and military aid.

THE AFTERMATH OF A PROMISE WITHDRAWN

From Cairo, Roosevelt at once sent word to Chiang, on December 6, 1943, that the planned amphibious operation in the Bay of Bengal was off. [2] The President asked Chiang whether he would go ahead with his attack in Burma without it or wait until it could be done, perhaps in November 1944. Meanwhile, said the President, transport over the Hump would be pushed and, after defeat of Germany, great resources would be released to finish off Japan. [3]

The Generalissimo's reaction was prompt. He feared that the radical change would cancel the lift just given to China's morale. He told Roosevelt, "the repercussions would be so disheartening that I fear of the consequences of China's inability to hold out much longer." While inclining to accept the President's view, he said, "my task in rallying the nation to continue resistance is being made infinitely more difficult." He referred to "our critical economic condition which may seriously affect the morale of the army and people, and cause at any moment a sudden collapse of the entire front." He doubted whether China could hold out for six months, let alone until November. He feared that Japan would conclude that "practically the entire weight of the United Nations' forces will be applied to the European front," and that Japan would launch an all-out attack to liquidate the China situation and thus bolster her position in the Pacific. "This," he said, "is the problem which I have to face." To help him cope with it, he asked that the Chinese and American air strength in China be at least doubled by the spring, and that Hump tonnage be brought up to 20,000 tons monthly by February (ATC moved 12,590 tons in December). For the economic emergency, which he called "more critical than the military," he asked "a billion gold dollar loan." [4]

At Cairo, the Generalissimo and the President discussed financial support for China. The records of the Conference are fragmentary, and shed little light on financial matters. But it is clear that Chiang sought two kinds of support: first, a billion dollar loan; and, second, that the United States pay the cost of its military effort in China. As to the loan, Stilwell's diary of December 6 reported the President as having said:

> Madame Chiang and the G-mo wanted to get a loan now of a billion dollars, but I told them it would be difficult to get Congress to agree to it. Now, I'm not a financial expert (!!) but I have a plan to take fifty or a hundred million dollars and buy up Chinese paper dollars on the black market. It wouldn't take much. (!!) When the Chinese found that these notes were being bought up, they would tend to hold them and the rate would come down. We might beat the inflation that way. And I'd share the profit with the Chinese Government—I'd put the notes in escrow and when they were needed I'd sell them to the Chinese Government for what I paid for them.[5]

As to the discussion of payment by the United States for the cost of American operations in China, Secretary Stimson stated: "It is understood that he [Chiang] was advised that the United States was prepared to bear the cost of its military effort in China. It is not understood that the question of exchange rates was considered." [6]

Clearly, the Generalissimo thought he had received at Cairo a broad commitment of financial support. This affected his later tough attitude in the negotiations about the rate at which the United States would buy national currency. He felt he merely was insisting on carrying out the spirit of the President's promise. Concerning the understanding on the Chinese side, I have the following in my notes of December 22: "The highest quarter [Chiang] has indicated that China is not to be asked to pay and the U.S. will pay for everything. (At what rate?) Also Stilwell had called and indicated the same principle. So it is all in the air again. There seems a misunderstanding."

SEEKING ANOTHER INJECTION: THE BILLION DOLLAR LOAN SCHEME

Ambassador Gauss had gotten wind of the loan scheme and on December 9 he telegraphed to Washington. He saw no sound basis for it on either economic or political grounds. China did not lack dollar resources. These could not easily be mobilized to combat inflation, and the use made of the US$500 million loan "does not lead to confidence that there would be a more effective handling of a further loan." Gauss saw no reason to fear that China would make a separate peace, especially now that the Allies were winning. He felt that a further loan would not check the gradual deterioration. He believed that in circles close to the Generalissimo the disposition was that "in resisting the Japs for more than six years China had done her full share and that the full burden of the conflict should now be undertaken by the United States"; also that "a strong disposition exists in the Chinese Government to exploit to its fullest American goodwill and open-handedness." He would not expect any large military effort by China, but felt China could and should do more to facilitate American military operations and especially to make "equitable and reasonable arrangements for the American financing of the war in this area." He suggested that "China should not exploit the United States in this matter. Realization by China that it is blessed to give as well as to receive and that she will be helping herself by helping us should be encouraged . . . It is my conviction that our attitude toward China should be quietly and persistently firmed." [7]

The President sought Morgenthau's views. Morgenthau said in a memorandum of December 18 that China still had US$460 million remaining from the US$500 million loan of 1942 and was getting US$20 million monthly to cover army outlay in China. He said that a loan is "unnecessary at this time and would be undesirable from the point of view of China and the United States." [8]

On December 20 the President made an interim reply. The best that could be done, he told the Generalissimo, was to plan the largest possible operation to open a route to China through Burma, with China's cooperation. Hump tonnage would be raised to 12,000 tons monthly (it in fact exceeded that figure in December, rising from 7,300 in November). The Treasury would consider the loan request. [9]

Meanwhile the State Department, in a document of December 27, analyzed the larger aspects of the loan proposal. "The United States and China," it said, "are natural and actual friends and allies." It was important that China retain its confidence in and reliance on this country, and neither move into reliance on Russia nor accept the thesis that Oriental peoples should oppose Western influence. Hence China's request should be handled most carefully. It should not be turned down flatly, but be made the occasion for a broad discussion of China's problems with special reference to financing postwar reconstruction. Such discussion might best take place by sending to China a special commission or by setting up a joint American-Chinese commission.[10]

The Treasury, however, was taking the ball. Early in January 1944, Roosevelt sent to the State Department Morgenthau's memorandum of December 18, directing that it be forwarded to Chiang. Hull questioned the wisdom of sending it "as is." He wanted a less blunt approach, as set out in the State Department document summarized above. Nevertheless, the message went foward the next day. The close relations between the President and Morgenthau outweighed the other factors. But the State Department managed to get into the message a proposal to send to Chungking a "very high class Commission," to "try to work out a complete meeting of the minds on this difficult matter." Unfortunately, however, the precise nature of the "matter" was not made clear.[11]

The Generalissimo received the President's message "affably" when Gauss presented it. But the reply of January 15 was stiff. I helped prepare the draft though I noted in my diary, "I don't agree at all," and tried to moderate the wording, as did Dr. Kung. The Generalissimo again pressed for the billion dollar loan to "enable us partly to meet the deficit of the coming war budget and also through reciprocal aid to meet a part of American military expenses in China." As an alternative he called on the United States to meet American army costs in China by buying currency at the rate of 20–1. He dwelt on China's "perilous economic situation," and her incalculable military and civilian losses since July 1937.

The proposed Commission, said the Generalissimo, would be of no use if the purpose were to discuss Treasury proposals to meet army costs. But it would be welcome if it were to deal with the Generalissimo's proposals. Unhappily the idea of a "high class" joint Sino-American commission to dicuss broad problems, including postwar reconstruction and its financing, was not presented to the Generalissimo. That proposal dropped out of sight, as a result of the President's sending Morgenthau's memorandum instead of accepting the State Department's approach.

In handing the message to Gauss, the Generalissimo said that "if the Treasury Department cannot help China financially, the American army in China will have to depend on itself after March 1," that is, finance itself and make necessary arrangements for construction, labor, and supplies.[12]

Washington gave the message a mixed reception. In a Treasury conference on January 18, Morgenthau was "mad as hell." White called the message "a very tough cable," which called on the United States, as he interpreted it, to let China know by March 1 whether the United States would buy whatever currency it needs or "that they get a billion dollar loan now."

H.M.Jr.: Supposing we call their bluff?
White: I think the cards are mostly in his hands, Mr. Secretary, unfortunately.
H.M.Jr.: Well, the billion dollar loan is out.
White: Well, unfortunately, the alternative may cost us more.

The next day Somervell told Morgenthau that Stimson and Marshall ". . . had decided that they were going to be tough with the Chinese Government. They were very dissatisfied with the cooperation they were getting in China and with the small amount of actual combat fighting which the Chinese armies were carrying on." They were ready to stop building airports if necessary and use other means to get at Japan. Morgenthau consulted the President. "The President said we should tell the Generalissimo in the cable that we would send them about $25 million of gold a month, and also that we would spend about $25 million a month"; but that ". . . he would not make a loan to the Chinese of a billion dollars." [13]

The State Department, however, continued to think beyond the immediate issues. Said Hornbeck in an extraordinarily prescient memorandum of January 18, 1944:

We are convinced that the issues in the matter under reference are of tremendous importance and that from decisions made and action taken in regard to this matter there will flow consequences of extraordinary import to the United States, to China, to the war effort, to the peace effort and to the postwar world. We believe that the issue presented in this situation calls for exercise of statesmanship of the highest order on the part both of the American and of the Chinese Governments—especially the former.

He felt that the question whether the Generalissimo was making threats or gesturing was "merely incidental," and that his words were based upon his conviction as regards the situation in China and China's capabilities after years of suffering:

If by chance Chiang is threatening and gesturing, he is doing so in the mood and after the manner of a man who, confronted with tremendous difficulties, is convinced that certain types of consideration and assistance are due him from fellow-men with whom he is associated in a common cause and who feels that such consideration and assistance are being given to others of the associates and are being withheld from him. The American Government should approach the problem and meet the issue on the merits of the case and regardless of possible errors by the Chinese in the method or the manner of their presentation of the case.

China's remarkable resistance to Japan, he said, was due partly to grit and partly to hope. But China was very tired and it would be dangerous to assume China could not collapse. China felt the United States was not doing what it could and should do to help her. At least, he said, the United States should fully meet its commitments, and go half-way or more to avoid a breach or appearance of breach with China. Such a breach, he feared, might make the difference not only between gradual increase or decrease in China's usefulness as a war partner, but between China's alignment with or against the United States and other peace-loving nations. Hornbeck pointed out that the American aid given to China during the war was like "injections." China needed another injection, and the United States should try to find some way to give it, to show confidence in China, and "to collaborate and to cooperate with them in the same spirit and in the same manner and liberality in which we do with the British and the Russians." [14]

Meanwhile the State Department was again being bypassed when it should have had the primary say. On January 19 Acting Secretary Bell of the Treasury called in State Department representatives to discuss a proposed reply first drafted in the War Department, then read to the President by Morgenthau who had since left town, and finally redrafted in the Treasury incorporating some of the President's comments. The President apparently expected the message to go forward as revised. At this meeting, General Lucius D. Clay said that the War Department realized that its draft message "might result in the American Army's pulling out of China completely," but that "the War Department has serious questions as to whether its efforts in China are worthwhile." The State Department's representatives, however, succeeded in getting time for a revision, which they worked out with the other two Departments. Finally the President approved a conciliatory message which the State Department telegraphed January 20. The President said he could not "escape the feeling that because of the distance between us there may be danger that we may fail adequately to work out our common problems and to rush into decisions which would not be in the interests of either of our peoples." He did not refer to the loan scheme but did hint at postwar aid. He said the United States would pay in dollars the equivalent of Chinese currency made available to cover the cost of all American military expenditures in China. The State Department instructed the Ambassador to make it quite clear that this latter commitment did not mean paying at the official rate of 20–1.[15] This message led to further negotiations resulting in eventual settlement of the army cost issue.

The Generalissimo's reply of February 2 was also conciliatory. He hoped for a solution of the financial issues that would be satisfactory to both countries. He did not mention the billion dollar loan.[16] As it became clear that this was out of the question, the scheme gradually dropped from sight. In a letter of April 19, Kung told Morgenthau that China was no longer asking for a new loan.[17] When Vice-President Wallace visited China in June, the Generalissimo asked him to assure the President that he "understands the necessity under which the President acted when he changed plans at Tehran," but that he (Chiang) foresaw the difficulties for China that would follow. These, however, had not proved "as bad as he feared." [18]

FRICTION OVER MILITARY COSTS

American outlay in China was growing. From US$1 million in all 1942, it mounted to US$50 million in the last quarter of 1943. The major outlay was for airfields, and there were also costs for roads and transport. Actual operations, however, did not grow in anything like the proportion that those figures suggest. Much of the higher cost was a result of getting national currency at the fixed rate of 20–1. Prices more than tripled in 1942, and again in

1943. By the end of 1943 national currency would buy less than a tenth of what it would have bought two years earlier.*

Two factors were making it increasingly urgent to work out a reasonable way to meet the American needs for national currency. First, Washington had practically decided to base in China the new B-29 bombers, to attack Japan. They would need new and expensive bases. General Clay estimated that the American program in China in 1944 might cost, at 20–1, as much as a billion dollars.[19] Second, at Cairo Roosevelt promised, in undefined terms, to meet the costs of American military operations in China.

Beginning late in 1943 there were active negotiations at Chungking. The Treasury wanted a rate of 100–1. Kung insisted on 20–1, but was ready as reverse Lend-Lease to match one for one and in some cases two for one sums bought with dollars at the official rate. That meant 40–1 or 60–1. The Generalissimo told the President on January 15, 1944, in the above-cited message, that the rate of 20–1 "is unalterable inasmuch as we cannot afford to shake the confidence of the people in *fapi*." Otherwise, he said, there would be "economic collapse" which would "seriously affect the whole military position of the Allies because of China's inability to continue resistance for any considerable length of time." [20] The Chinese view was based partly on the dubious argument that the mere holding of large dollar reserves would be a major means to check inflation.†

President Roosevelt sent a conciliatory message, despatched

* American payments for national currency at the official rate during the war were:

	Quarter	Amount (thousands)		Quarter	Amount (thousands)
1941	4th	US$1	1943	1st	US$3,994
1942	1st	27		2d	12,370
	2d	55		3d	35,681
	3d	48		4th	57,731
	4th	852	1944	January	26,431
				Total	US$137,190

† As to my discussion on the Chinese side I noted in my Diary on January 14: "Underlying views are that rate can be justified by having strong reserves, regardless of price parities, and that rate may come back to better than present after the war. Also that having more reserves will somehow stop price rise. Particular resentment at idea of 100–1 rate . . . I explained that hardly anyone knew whether there are or are not reserves or whether *fapi* spent by U.S. army are backed by US$ put up for their purchase, and urged moderation also not to close the door to further discussion."

January 24. He realized "the extent to which China's resolute war stand has rendered her economic situation acute," and suggested that Gauss and Stilwell work out a plan whereby American outlay would be around US$25 million per month. He continued:

Furthermore, since you say that your Government is not in a position to continue any direct maintenance of American troops in China, this Government, in order to cover all of its military expenditures in China, including such maintenance as well as construction, is prepared to place to your account the U.S. dollar equivalent of any Chinese funds made available under general arrangements that will be suggested by General Stilwell and the Ambassador.[21]

This message led to a *de facto* plan that let the American army get the currency it needed. They agreed in February to pay China US$25 million, and China advanced C$1 billion of local currency, followed by more advances. The US$25 million, transferred to China in March, was planned as the first of a series of monthly payments. Since China continued its advances, the work on the air bases could proceed, along with the argument.

On February 14, Gauss telegraphed that the Embassy, Army, and Adler felt China had no intention of reaching a realistic solution. They saw no advantage in further proposals "unless the U.S. Government is in position and is prepared to back up such proposals by a slowing down or curtailment of our cooperation with China financially, diplomatically and militarily." The key question was whether the military operations planned for the China area were vital. If so "and the Chinese are aware of that we are at the mercy of the Chinese Government financially." But, he felt that "a realistic attitude" would help to put relations "on a sound and reasonably reciprocal basis."[22] On February 18 I wrote in my diary that, on the Chinese side in the negotiations, the "emphasis is more on negotiation and justification of position taken as to rate than on real matter of the currency and the war. It is hard to argue or explain in conflict with views expressed. The point that a cost of US$80 for a simple chair is unreasonable, and greatly hurts China in the U.S., is missed." But on February 22 I found the attitude "more reasonable," and found hope for some form of settlement "without a rate protruding."

As to the background situation, I noted the following comment on February 1 after being rebuffed in an effort to come to grips with the fundamentals:

China's financial policy, inflation, has been inevitable. It could have been better and slowed down inflation by say a year or more. But considering how all governments operate, it is nothing to be ashamed of, and has many creditable aspects. Still the leaders do not want to admit that their policy, even tho inevitable, is responsible for all the grief. They are much worried, especially by large budget—doubling every year. They also are very worn, without vacation or much rest and very heavy responsibility, difficult decisions, seeing too many people, not delegating authority, etc. Other background: China's sacrifices and losses, smallness of U.S. and G.B. help both before and since Pearl Harbor, previous help to Japan while China fought alone. Also sensitiveness to criticism. Hence a sort of defense mechanism, and hesitation to face results of policy and to try to place responsibility elsewhere for past and future.

China should cultivate best possible relations with U.S., G.B., and Russia. But actually relations are bad. China needs help for period of internal and external peace and reconstruction, and to grow into position in Big Four. And other countries need a strong China. It will need very wise handling in all quarters.

When no progress was being made toward settling the argument, other means of financing American needs were considered. In the first quarter of 1944 prices soared, as did free market rates for American currency, because of the faster outpouring of notes resulting largely from the building of air bases. One idea was to sell American notes to control the rate. There was some danger in putting out more of these notes because of the ever-present risk that prices would come to be quoted widely in dollars. Their circulation might displace part of the national currency, hurt confidence further, and even touch off catastrophic inflation. Yet Washington thought it wise to try selling some on an experimental scale. So a parcel of US$5 million was sent in charge of an army officer going from Washington to Chungking. The parcel remained on the unloaded and unguarded plane overnight both at Kunming and Chungking, and the next day a coolie brought it intact to army headquarters. But the money was never used as contemplated. The free market leveled off and did not go above the February–March level until October. Also the Treasury held back the money in view of the unsettled negotiation.

Another suggestion, put forward by Kung early in 1944 and which the Embassy, some of the army personnel, and I supported, was to send experimentally limited quantities of selected consumer goods of relatively high value to be sold in China. In a memorandum of February 26, 1944, I gave illustrative lists of quantities and weights of goods that could be imported and sold. I pointed out that the amounts that could be realized in China thereby would be comparable with the value obtainable from an equal weight of bank notes imported. The possible revenue from such shipments would of course be relatively small. But arrival of goods would help confidence and tend to force some hoarders to sell. The possible use of some of the scarce transport capacity for such goods was based on the idea that success of the military program was bound up with checking inflation. Gauss sent this memorandum to Washington with his endorsement, as did the supply section of American Army headquarters. At a conference in Washington in March, White said he thought such shipments might be helpful. But General Somervell said transport was "definitely not available for such purposes." The Morgenthau Diaries report the following about the Vice-President's proposed trip:

> H.M.Jr.: "Wallace is to go to China."
> Mr. Pehle: "In place of the goods?"
> H.M.Jr.: "He is the goods." [23]

By June 1944, the new air bases were finished. But the financial argument continued. The American negotiators let the matter drag along, since China was providing funds in local currency for the bases and they wished to avoid risk of an impasse that would hold back the work. Kung continued to maintain that to raise the official rate of exchange was out of the question since it would cause a disastrous price rise, and that China needed much larger reserves to keep confidence in the currency and for eventual rehabilitation. The Americans argued that the inflation was caused mainly by internal factors and not by lack of reserves and pointed out that American outlay in China caused less than a third of the note increase. They did not press for change in the official rate and were ready to pay substantial dollar sums against receipt of national currency, on some reasonable basis without specifying a rate.

There the matter rested when Kung came to the United States

in June 1944, to attend the conference on postwar monetary plans.
That gave the opportunity for settlement by direct talks in the
United States. Conferences began at Bretton Woods, New Hamp-
shire, in July. The American figures showed C$20.7 billion ad-
vanced by China through July for airfields, roads, barracks, radio
stations, and maintenance. Of that sum China had agreed to pay
about C$2 billion for food and lodging of troops. About C$4
billion was for airfields built before the American army came.
There was a dispute as to which party should pay for those, and
also whether the United States had agreed to pay, over and above
the US$25 million monthly, for later-built airfields, costing about
C$12 billion. The arrangements on this point had been ambiguous.

A full-dress conference took place July 16.[24] Clay began by
proposing a lump-sum settlement of US$75 million plus the US$25
million paid already early in 1944; and also US$20 million monthly
for the three months July–September. Kung said he was ashamed
to ask for anything and wished China could afford to give without
payment. But he told of China's difficulties with inflation saying,
"Last year . . . it cost us something about ninety dollars to feed
an American soldier a day." He said:

> We in China are vegetable eaters. The poor people don't have much meat
> to eat, but of course, your boys must have roast beef and must have eggs
> for breakfast, and so forth. In England, I understand, you have to make
> application beforehand. You may be allowed an egg or two a month. But
> in China your boys need six eggs a day, and now it is cut down to four eggs.
> But you eat a pound of beef a day. In Kunming alone we are keeping cows
> and oxen to supply you . . . 12,000 catties of beef alone every day. Now
> China is not like America, because in this country you raise animals for
> the purpose of meat; in China we don't do that. In order to supply the meat
> we are feeding our oxen, used for farming purposes. I had a protest from
> the Governor of Yunnan . . . saying that cows and oxen were killed at such
> a rate that very soon there won't be any animals left to help the farmers
> farm their land.

He argued, and the Americans objected, that the cost of airfields
was over and above the US$25 million monthly that was to be
paid.

Then followed bargaining in which Clay raised his bid succes-
sively to US$90 million, US$100 million, and US$125 million.
Finally the parties were close to agreement on the latter sum, plus
US$60 million for the third quarter. The total came to US$185

million, besides US$25 million paid early in 1944. But the airfield problem was left pending, and both sides were to consult further.

For months the matter dragged. The army found that their figures had been too high and had wrongly included Chinese taxes and other items. They finally turned up with a total of C$13.9 billion, compared with Chinese figures of C$15.5 billion. Both included the Chengtu airfields. Finally at a conference on November 25, 1944, China agreed to take US$185 million in full settlement to September 30, besides US$25 million already paid.[25] That worked out as a rate of about 74–1 for the C$15.5 billion for which US$210 million was paid. The average free market rate for January–September was about 200–1. Morgenthau confirmed the arrangement in a letter of January 17, 1945, and turned over the funds.[26]

In contrast to this long argument, the settlement in 1945 for the fourth quarter of 1944 was easy. The physical amount of China's services to the army was less than in the previous quarter for which US$60 million had been paid. For costs of about C$8 billion the army paid US$45 million.[27] That worked out at a rate of 178–1. The average free market rate was about 400–1. There were no further cash settlements. Instead China's outlay in 1945 for account of the American army, the amount of which was agreed in April 1946, to have been C$103.8 billion, was covered in a set-off in the summer of 1946 against surplus American property. Altogether the United States paid China US$392 million in 1941–1945 to acquire Chinese currency. That comprised US$137 million to buy currency at the official rate from the latter part of 1941 to January 1944; and US$210 million and US$45 million, respectively, for currency advanced to September 30, 1944, and in the last quarter of 1944.[28]

THE CURRENCY SQUEEZE: NONMILITARY PROBLEMS

The 50 per cent supplement to philanthropic agencies on sales of foreign currency granted in May 1943 was far from adequate. They continued to press for a better arrangement. With costs tripling yearly, their choice was drastic curtailment or withdrawal.* Nearly two-thirds of the missionaries in Free China had

* United China Relief, according to a letter of November 15, 1943, from Director Edwards to Kung, expected to spend in 1944 in China US$8.6 million, or about

withdrawn by the spring of 1944, and an important cause was the pressure of the fixed exchange rates. The supplement was increased to 100 per cent on January 20, 1944. But that was still far from adequate. In April an American correspondent, at the request of the Chinese censor, showed me a story he proposed to send, saying that the relief dollar at 40–1 was worth only 10 cents, and that contributors were "victims of an enormous sucker game." I got him to moderate the language and make it clear that there was no discrimination against relief; but I could not conscientiously ask him to suppress the facts, and suggested he resubmit to the censor after changes.

In April the National War Fund in the United States declined to vote a grant to United China Relief, because of the exchange situation. The philanthropic organizations proposed, therefore, to use the open market. Kung agreed and, after a procedure was devised consistent with American freezing regulations, open market sales began in June. To avoid competitive selling, all groups centralized their sales in the United Clearing Board at Chungking. Demand for dollar funds was limited, but gradually it proved feasible to sell readily. Rates, however, averaged during the war only around half the black market rates for currency notes. That was because of the greater salability of notes, whereas blocked balances were in less demand.*

As the fixed exchange rates got more and more out of line, the representatives in China of foreign governments similarly found it a problem to meet their official and personal expenses. From the fall of 1943 the American Embassy covered its outlay by sale of American currency notes. The 100 per cent supplement of January 1944, applied to the personal sales of members of embassies and consulates, but not to their official outlay. Soon the British Embassy arranged to sell sterling in the free market for its needs. Others followed suit.

Obviously the fixed overvalued exchange rates bore heavily on exports. Chief of these were strategic exports such as wood oil, tin, and tungsten which the United States needed in the war. The

---

the same as in 1943. But failure to obtain a better exchange arrangement would mean "turning deaf ears to starving refugees, closing schools and colleges, shutting down orphanages, while at the same time the actual needs require an increase."

* After the war and until the Board was wound up in March 1946, rates for its drafts moved nearer to rates for notes.

Foreign Economic Administration paid a very high cost for them on a 20–1 basis, putting out US$48 million from 1941 through June 1944.[29] Also they paid for some purchases with gold. In April, 1944, tin sold in the United States at US$1,100 per ton, but the cost of producing it in Yunnan was C$600,000. That worked out at about 550–1. The black market in April averaged 220–1 or about 67 times the prewar rate of about 3.3–1. But the retail price level at Kunming in April was 688 times the prewar level. That shows the dislocation, and how out of line were such rates as even 40–1.*

The selling of exchange at 20–1 also caused for the government difficulties of a different sort *vis-à-vis* Chinese wishing to buy foreign currencies. Dollars became unbelievably cheap at 20–1. From the start of the Pacific War the blockade made import trade to Free China almost impossible, and the Stabilization Board's work in financing trade shrank greatly after Pearl Harbor. But there was a strong demand for dollars for personal reasons. Chinese businessmen or students, and indeed any who wanted a less arduous life abroad, had the chance of a lifetime to go abroad at small real cost if they could get permission. It is not surprising that many abused the privilege. I noted in my diary November 2, 1943, that "quite a number of Chinese are buying exchange at 20–1 to go to the U.S. where they can live much better and cheaper than here." And again on December 11 I noted: "My secretary wants to go to the U.S. to study—despite shortage of English language stenographers here. She didn't see what such an attitude, generalized, would do. I told her clearly but doubt the result." She and several other such secretaries left. In December, 820 students took examinations to study abroad and 660 passed. The Generalissimo finally learned of the situation and in April 1944, put a stop to students leaving China, though the ban was lifted in the fall. Also many doctors went abroad to "study," despite the almost complete lack of medical facilities in the Chinese army. I wrote in my diary, January 15, 1944: "No other country so tender with doctors in war-time. Some can properly go if not ready for work here, but most should not. Those abroad qualified for war work should be required to return."

---

* By the end of 1944, recognizing that it had become quite unrealistic to expect exporters to hand over exchange at official rates, the government by regulations of December 16 allowed them to retain the proceeds abroad to buy goods that China needed.

It was not pleasing to foreigners who were in military or civilian work in China and helping China in the war, and whose sons or relatives (including students) were in the armed forces, to see an exodus from China of students and others who should have been in China's war effort. Of course a large number of educated and patriotic men including some students and doctors served loyally in the Chinese army.[30] And a case could be made for sending abroad a limited number of students in special cases. But the attitude described, which the artificial exchange rate promoted, was all too common.*

THE ISSUES AND THEIR CONSEQUENCES

The fear of China's leaders that to change the official rate would worsen inflation is understandable. Such a fear exists in severe inflations anywhere, if official rates exist. For a government to say that its own money has fallen in value is hard. Finance ministers, in situations such as that in which Dr. Kung found himself during the war, bear a heavy and unenviable responsibility. Whatever they do is a choice of evils and may seem wrong however carefully they weigh the consequences.†

In the economic field the results of China's stubborn defense of the 20–1 rate in 1942–1945 were not of major seriousness. China was isolated and international trade and transactions were relatively small. Also a generally free exchange market was available.

But China's stubborn stand had consequences on American and

---

* During most of the war China exempted students from military duty, influenced by the traditional high regard for the scholar and low regard for the soldier in the social scale. When American forces in China began to grow there was some use of students as English language interpreters, and also in the latter part of 1943 there had been some student volunteering. On December 11, 1943, I noted in my diary the following comment of a qualified person from the educational center at Chengtu:

"Student volunteering is said to be largely for publicity. They are said to be assured that they will not be sent into any danger, and are promised scholarships later on. Their work is to be special and not fighting. Mostly they are the younger ones, 16–20, as the older ones are to be reserved for something 'more important' later. They think the war should be fought by the coolies."

† When an inflation cannot be stopped, some degree of currency overvaluation probably tends to check the price rise. But it is my considered opinion, after having been close to such situations in a number of countries, that in principle it is the lesser evil, so long as inflation has to continue, to adjust the rate periodically so that the internal and external values do not get too far out of line. Such adjustments must be carefully timed, and if possible coincide with good news and not with bad.

other foreign opinion and goodwill that were serious indeed. China could well argue that, since the American military effort was aggravating inflation in China, the United States should help to build up reserves for eventual monetary reform. The United States did that through January 1944, by paying US$137 million to buy national currency, at the 20–1 rate which was highly favorable to China. But by then the exchange rate of 20–1 had become utterly unrealistic. China should not have thought of trying to cover the huge output of the printing presses at any fixed rate. As time went on the American army was paying fantastic prices for goods and services, for example, US$1,100 for a bicycle and US$75 for a spark plug. In my diary for February 10, 1944, I noted that Stilwell said to me, "If this keeps up, they will pay us all they owe with a basket of oranges!"

After China rejected the American proposal of a rate of 100–1, and insisted on not changing the 20–1 rate, the Americans were ready to provide dollars against local currency on terms very favorable to China, but without a rate protruding. China's leaders justified their stubborn position on rates of exchange by Roosevelt's undefined promise to pay the cost of the American military effort in China. They also were influenced strongly by the withdrawal of the promise of an amphibious operation to aid in recovering Burma and above all by the serious worsening of China's internal situation.

Whatever view be taken of China's justification, the long and sometimes bitter haggling left its mark, and a feeling that China was seeking to exploit the United States. China's cause suffered badly with high American officials, with the rank and file of military and civilian personnel in or connected with her war effort in 1943–1945, and with those who had dealings with China in philanthropic and business affairs. China indeed was able to build up large dollar reserves. But in parallel she built up much ill will.

The billion dollar loan scheme had several aspects. It was not merely the Generalissimo's reaction when Roosevelt, under Churchill's prodding, withdrew his promise—though that stiffened the request into a sort of ultimatum. It was a bid for another "injection," though it exaggerated the possible help of massive credits in checking inflation. In part, the scheme reflected frustration. In two years after Pearl Harbor major American help had failed to come, while China was going from bad to worse financially and militarily. Most American aid was going to Britain and Russia. The Generalissimo feared that this indirectly invited the Japanese to wipe out China's resistance while China was left almost alone. Worn and worried, he was at a loss to understand why China, the first to resist aggression and with enormous sacrifices, received so low a priority. In part, the scheme was put forward with an eye to China's postwar needs. In part it was for bargaining purposes in the army cost argument.

The American attitude was determined mainly by immediate considerations, and little by longer-range policy. The State Department, with its background of what had been happening in the Far East and its responsibility to think about what lay ahead, had a better grasp of the delicate nature of the issues and their bearing than did the War and Treasury Departments. But the "State Department . . . was crowded out, and it vaguely knew it." [31] The President relied mainly on the War and Treasury Departments, he being commander-in-chief and Morgenthau being a close friend. The War Department and Stilwell were disturbed by China's reluctance to reform her too numerous and largely ineffective army as an effective combat force. White and other Treasury men had in 1944 a strong pro-Russian and anti-Chinese bias (see chapter XVII). Both departments were understandably sore at China's intransigence about the 20–1 rate of exchange. The State Department, though too often pushed around or ignored during the war, did manage in this instance to prevent blunt action that could have led to a costly wartime break with China.

The pressure of the War and Treasury Departments, however, along with their seizing the initiative in dealing with a sensitive foreign affairs problem, prevented an approach through the suggested commission that might have led to sympathetic attention to China's immediate and postwar problems and how best to deal with them. Certainly China's situation, after six and one-half years of war and strain, would have benefited from planning with skill and imagination as to what burdens China could carry during the rest of the war, and the kinds and amounts of aid needed. Also such a commission would have had to face the issue of dealing with China's inflation both during and after the war; whereas both China and the United States neglected that grave issue. The way could have been opened for wiser planning of economic, financial, and political rehabilitation. But success would have depended upon, first, having as both Chinese and American members of such a commission trustworthy men capable of understanding the major economic, financial, military, and international issues, and influencing their governments about them; and, second, a reasonably effective handling of the problems and a cooperative attitude on both sides.

Unhappily the split between the United States and China on these issues foreshadowed a breach which continued during the rest of the war and carried over into the postwar period.

XVI. A YEAR OF DISCORD, 1944: MATERIAL AND MILITARY AID

GENERAL James H. Doolittle's famous carrier raid in April 1942 was but a pin prick as regards Japan's war potential. But the bombing of Tokyo shocked Japanese feelings of invincibility. It led to some pulling back of planes to Japan. It caused hesitation that Nelson T. Johnson, then ambassador in Australia, described to me later as having saved from invasion Australia and perhaps likewise Calcutta. It may have influenced the Japanese to make their next big effort against American sea power, leading to the great Japanese defeat at Midway. The Doolittle raid seems to have been first proposed by personnel of the State Department and supported in the War Department. President Roosevelt warmly favored it. In 1943–1944 he promoted the idea of raiding Japan from bases in China, a project which the official army historians have said was "a project close to the President's heart." The project came to be called "Matterhorn." [1]

The idea of bombing Japanese communications and later the mainland from bases in China was favored at the inter-Allied conferences at Washington and at Quebec, in May and in August 1943. The President felt that bombing of Japan would be a "spur to China's war effort." Use of the new B-29's from China, it was argued, would "tremendously stimulate Chinese morale and unify the Chinese people under the leadership of Chiang Kai-shek." The first plans called for an eventual operation that, after a trans-Pacific invasion of Southeast China, would build up to 596,000 tons of supplies per month. Meanwhile, operations would begin ex-Kweilin, with a rear base at Calcutta. Three out of five of the big planes were to provide transport for the rest. [2]

It soon became clear that the big new planes would be far from self-sustaining, and that the operation would take a large share of the precious Hump tonnage, which in the first half of 1944 was about 13,500 tons monthly. Stilwell and Chennault each had ideas about use of Hump tonnage. Stilwell's first priority was to rebuild the Chinese army to attack westward into Burma. He consistently feared stepping up air attacks, saying, "If we go and sting them into retaliation before ready, the whole thing will fold up." He wanted first to prepare and equip a strong Chinese force to hold the East China air bases, and then to make a drive against the enemy in China—a plan which later events showed should have had high priority for China's rescue. Marshall agreed.[3] Chennault also objected to Matterhorn. He wanted to step up attacks on enemy bases and communications in China, attacks which high Japanese officers interrogated after the war said were the chief obstacle to their operations there. Wedemeyer, then a staff officer in India, agreed with Chennault.[4] I well recall that most influential Americans in China, both military and civilian, thought Matterhorn unwise.

Finally in the fall of 1943 the Washington planners favored basing the big new planes at Chengtu, about 200 miles northwest of Chungking, to get around the immediate need for stronger land forces. The President approved in principle. He broached the idea to Chiang just before the Cairo Conference, asking his support of the construction of the necessary airfields in the Chengtu area. Roosevelt offered to "make available the necessary funds through Lend-Lease appropriations."[5] In November 1943, at Cairo he got the approval of Chiang and Churchill to provide the needed air fields in China and India. This was subject, however, to further study by the staff at Washington. The staff reported that the scheme was feasible but uneconomic. They felt that bombing Japanese targets that could be reached from Chengtu, such as certain steel mills, did not promise decisive results. They favored basing the planes elsewhere.[6]

It was abandonment of the amphibious invasion of Burma, despite promises to Chiang, that helped to clinch the B-29 project. The operation was regarded as a means to salve his feelings, and it was argued that the boost to China's morale would justify the effort needed to overcome logistic difficulties. In December the Joint Chiefs of Staff approved the B-29 plan. The Joint War Plans Committee, however, argued for basing the planes in Australia. The relentless advance of American amphibious forces in the Pacific was beginning to cast doubt on the project of a major effort in and from China. The definitive base for the B-29's, it was decided on March 12, 1944, would be Saipan Island, to be invaded June 15. It was not until April 10 that the final decision was made to confirm Chengtu as an interim base. Meanwhile there were long arguments about who would command Matterhorn. Washington finally put the operation, which became the 20th Bomber Command, under direct command of General Arnold, from Washington. Romanus and Sunderland say, in their official history: "Stilwell and Chennault, therefore, had their authority circumscribed in that this great new engine of war would draw upon their reserves, would affect events in their theater, for which they would later be held responsible, but would not be at their disposal." [7]

The economic and financial arguments urged against the scheme were weighty. Conscription of labor would hurt the spring sowing in one of the richest farm areas of China. Sudden spending of huge sums for labor, materials, and landowners' compensation was bound to hurt China's vulnerable finances. These sums could only be paid by adding to note issue. And how to divide the financial burdens between China and the United States magnified the already bitter feud about financing American army needs. On January 26 Kung sent word to Morgenthau that the cost of the fields involved bringing in 60 to 150 plane loads of notes, depending upon whether of C$50 or of C$20 denomination.

In February 1944, American army sources indicated to Ambassador Gauss that for the next four months their total needs in China would come to about C$24 billion, by far the largest item being for the new air bases. Gauss, after full discussion with the American army headquarters, telegraphed to Washington on February 24, 1944, his concern about the serious impact of the plans on China. He asked: "What will be the effect upon China's already tottering economy (and upon internal political situation) of the huge expenditures planned, the doubling of the rate of note issue, the inevitable spiraling of prices, the dislocation of farm labor?" He queried whether the program was necessary and advisable militarily and wondered whether the United States was ready to take the risks and responsibility. He doubted that the Chinese leaders themselves realized the extent of the over-all picture of what the American army contemplated in China. He thought the issues called for decision by the President and the Departments concerned in Washington.[8]

There were further conferences in Washington among the State, War, and Treasury Departments leading to more exchanges of telegrams with Chungking. The State Department took the view that the bases were "not economically feasible." [9] White laid the situation before Morgenthau in a memorandum of March 27. Adler had telegraphed from Chungking that the economic situation was very serious, because of "growing disintegration of the military and political power of the Central Government, the isolation of China from the outside world and the failure of the Government to make the necessary internal reforms." China's economy "might be able to stand this extra strain," but Adler felt it "highly questionable whether we should incur the risk of imposing this strain on her unless the Army has over-riding strategic reasons for doing so." He urged cutting back plans for further large projects. White concurred in these views. The War Department reduced some of its plans. It suggested that China use some of its troops as labor battalions.[10] This was a sound idea which I and others had repeatedly urged, but which the government never used to much effect. Many of China's huge armies were poorly equipped and trained and not really usable in combat, but China was paying them anyway.

Despite the doubts, building the bases began in January 1944. It was a fantastic affair. Over 300,000 conscripted laborers, plus about 75,000 contract workers, were engaged in the work. "The Chinese hauled by hand 160,000 tons of rock and sand to build the runways needed for the planes, crushed the rock by hand and laid it stone by stone, then smoothed the surface by hand-hauled stone rollers." [11] The main work was done in about three months. The first B-29 landed April 24. The first mission was by 68 planes on June 15 against Japan's Yawata steel works, timed to coincide with the landing on Saipan.

Unhappily the fears on economic and financial grounds were justified. On February 15 I wrote in my diary: "Army spending wastefully—offering double for quicker completion, and sometimes acting as if money was of no importance. Have 300,000 men working and want 150,000 more. Hard to get enough banknotes." Dispossessed landowners were compensated by the government only imperfectly, while displaced tenants were not paid at all. The grievances carred over into the Communist phase. The Chengtu area proved very susceptible to later Communist penetration.

The note issue expansion had a sharp effect on prices and exchange. At Chengtu the three price indices showed a rise in February of 33, 34, and 39 per cent over January. The Chengtu cost-of-living index of the University of Nanking almost tripled in the six months to June 1944, and rice prices increased about fourfold.* At the same time the market for dollar notes had one of its sharpest rises. From a low around 90 about February 1 it rose to 195 February 8 and as high as 245 later in the month. The chief cause was adjustment to the outpouring of notes. But also the speculators acted on rumors that the United States was asking for a rate of 100–1. Kung maintained throughout that talk of a 100–1 rate was dangerous to confidence. I wrote in my diary February 6: "Looks as if the strain of caring for additional air operations and financing them may offset the military good and hurt Sino-U.S. relations." And on February 19: "The recent rise may or may not be the start of a more serious upward movement." In the Spring of 1944 there were ominous signs. The rate of turnover of money quickened. On one April day in Chungking money became so short that the Central Bank had to suspend

---

* The following table shows some of the chief indices for this period:

Monthly increase of:

	Average retail prices in Free China (per cent)	Cost of living in Chengtu (per cent)	Range of rice price per double shih tou at Chengtu (about 15 kg)	Free market average rate for US$ notes at Chungking
1943				
November	9	7	C$300 to 320	82
December	7	15	310 to 430	85
1944				
January	9	23	430 to 700	90–120[a]
February	16	33	730 to 820	215
March	13	11	720 to 780	247
April	11	15	820 to 1,080	220
May	11	27	1,050 to 1,430[b]	196
June	12	10		192

[a] Range at Kunming; Chungking data not available
[b] May 1 to 16 only

payments for three hours, until money could be rushed to it from a Chungking printing plant with the ink still fresh. At about the same time in Kweilin the Bank almost ran out of money and had to send a plane urgently to Kunming for more.

How did the military and psychological benefits weigh against the clear financial and other detriments to China? The operation had to draw heavily on Hump tonnage. From April 1944, when ATC began moving tonnage for the B-29's, through September, the big bombers and the fighters needed for their defense got about 55 per cent of the total. An emissary of the 20th Bomber Command wrote back to the U.S.: "Remember . . . that every single goddam thing that we send into China has to be flown in." That meant diversion of tonnage from building up China's ground forces, and from Chennault's 14th Air Force. About June 1, 1944, the Japanese started their drive which proved so disastrous to China, against the railways north and south of Hankow and against the East China air bases. Stilwell diverted Hump tonnage to Chennault to help him give air support to the Chinese armies. But, shockingly, Washington refused the Generalissimo's plea to let Chennault draw on the Chengtu stockpile for bombs, ammunition, and gasoline. Chennault pled for heavy B-29 bombing of the main base of Hankow from which the Japanese were launching their drive, and Stilwell also apparently favored this. But Washington turned down this also. The B-29's did not bomb Hankow until late in 1944, after General Wedemeyer had supplanted Stilwell and urged that action. But by then the drive had been checked.[12]

The 20th Bomber Command flew 20 missions from Chengtu. Nine were against the Japanese home islands, ten against Manchuria and Formosa, and one against Hankow. The Strategic Bombing Survey showed that the raids did little damage in Japan proper. Raids on Japanese bases in Manchuria were more effective, and those on aircraft plants and repair facilities in Formosa were "moderately successful." The official Air Force historians conclude that the missions against Japan "did little to hasten the Japanese surrender or to justify the lavish expenditures poured out in their behalf." There were no important tangible results, and the intangible ones were won at a "dear price." The supply system was "fantastically uneconomic and barely workable." They "find no difficulty in agreeing with USSBS [Strategic Bombing Survey] that logistical support afforded to XX Bomber Command in China would have produced more immediate results if allocated to the Fourteenth Air Force." The shakedown was indeed valuable, but could better have been done elsewhere.[13] The most remote and difficult supply area, halfway around the world, surely was no place to try out the still experimental B-29's.

The official army historians are equally critical. The build-up of air power without developing *pari passu* the ground forces to defend its bases was an invitation to the enemy to strike back. This he did by the drive beginning in mid-1944 to seize the whole length of the Canton-Hankow Railway and the air bases in that area. The drive even became a threat to Chungking and Kunming. Romanus and Sunderland state:

> The XX Bomber Command's B-29's, with their demands on Hump tonnage and theater facilities, conflicted directly with Stilwell's still unrepealed though practically abandoned mission of reforming the Chinese Army. That the B-29's were flying from China would be to the Japanese one more reason for a major effort there, yet B-29 demands on Hump tonnage made it even more unlikely that anything effective would be done to stop the Japanese once they moved.[14]

As to the decision that maintaining Matterhorn would help China more than giving Chennault the B-29 stockpile, they state, "If this helped China, theater headquarters was not aware of it." [15]

It was not long until pressure began to build up for withdrawal of the B-29's. In October General Patrick J. Hurley* told Roosevelt that the operation could not be justified in view of the emergency caused by the enemy drive in East China. Wedemeyer, who replaced Stilwell about November 1, 1944, promptly urged cutting back the B-29's, having in mind the need to airlift Chinese troops to defend Chungking and Kunming. He soon urged complete withdrawal, due to the need for more Hump tonnage for the Chinese troops and Chennault's 14th Air Force and to release the 312th Fighter Wing from defense duties near Chengtu. Washington agreed to some cutback and after a few weeks to full withdrawal. Early in 1945 the big planes left China.

---

* Hurley went to China in the fall of 1943 as special representative of the president, and was appointed ambassador in November 1944, succeeding Gauss.

Evacuation plans had already been made, and the orders "didn't catch the men of XX Bomber Command with their plans down." It would have been "difficult to round up a decent showing of mourners for the interment" of Matterhorn.[16]

Did Matterhorn help Chinese morale? The Chinese naturally were glad to see Japan bombed. Chiang made a speech praising the operation. But I can recall no real Chinese enthusiasm for the project in my quarter. Rather there was, on the one hand, a fear of the financial consequences, and on the other hand, the feeling of going along with American wishes, as far as feasible, because of present and prospective dependence on American good will. The financial and political effects overshadowed the military. Certainly I would conclude that the speeding up of inflation, the stimulation of the Japanese drive in East China which so exposed the war-weariness and weakness and internal division of the National Government, the economic dislocation in Szechwan Province which facilitated Communist penetration, and the added friction in American-Chinese relations far more than offset any military gains or help to Chinese morale from the B-29 operation.

In the current cold war, this episode may be a lesson against overstraining weak economies by military burdens that may damage the over-all situation because of inflation, impairment of economic conditions, social and political disturbance, and creation of added friction with the United States.

STRINGS PUT ON AID

Whereas Roosevelt early in 1943 had rejected putting strings on aid and calling for a *quid pro quo*, as advocated by his military advisers, he found himself reversing the policy a year later. The disagreement with Chiang after Cairo about military and financial matters brought a tougher line on both sides. On January 14, 1944, Roosevelt urged that the Generalissimo invade Burma from Yunnan. He said: "If the Yunnan forces cannot be employed it would appear that we should avoid for the present the movement of critical materials to them over the limited lines of communication and curtail the continuing build-up of stockpiles in India beyond that which will be brought to bear against the enemy." [17] That message crossed the Generalissimo's near ultimatum about the billion dollar loan scheme (see chapter XV).

The Generalissimo did not at once reply. But on March 27, when the Chinese attack into North Burma from India was going well and the Japanese were trying to break into Assam, he replied to renewed pressure. He felt China was not strong enough to commit the Y-force pending the desired amphibious operation.[18] The President on April 3 pointed out that the British were fighting a large enemy force on the India-Burma border that was threatening China's vital communications; that the immobilization of the Yunnan force was allowing the enemy to reinforce the troops opposing the Chinese drive from India into Burma; and that the Yunnan force far outnumbered the enemy. He said:

> To take advantage of just such an opportunity, we have, during the past year, been equipping and training your YOKE Forces. If they are not to be used in the common cause our most strenuous and extensive efforts to fly in equipment and to furnish instructual [sic] personnel have not been justified. They should not be held back on the grounds that an amphibious operation against the South Burma coast is necessary prior to their advance. Present developments negate such a requirement. The Jap has deployed the bulk of seven divisions in his operations on the Arakan, the Chindwin, and in the Mogaung Valley.
>
> I do hope you can act.

A few days later Marshall told Stilwell that unless the Y-force moved, the Lend-Lease shipments for it should end. This word was passed to War Minister Ho Ying-chin and his colleagues, who consulted the Generalissimo. The decision was to attack. On April 14 Ho telegraphed to Marshall:

> China has always realized her position with regard to offensives by United Nations, and it has only been because of time and lack of essential equipment that such action has not taken place before this time. You can rely on China doing her share, but it is hoped that you understand her difficulties. Decision to move part of YOKE Force across Salween was made on initiative of Chinese without influence of outside pressure, and was based on realization that China must contribute its share to common war effort.[19]

On May 11 the Chinese armies crossed the Salween towards Burma.

THE FIGHTING ON TWO SIDES OF BURMA AND ITS EFFECTS

Military events were now to have a major influence on aid to China, and on Chinese-American relations. Stilwell had long pressed for a pincers movement to cut off at least north and central Burma. After the Spring of 1942, when he took what he described as "a hell of a licking" in Burma, he first wanted the attack in March 1943. But the Generalissimo would not agree, and Stilwell admitted later that it was a "damn good thing March 1 is off. We'd have been hung." [20]

Even though controversies had delayed the start of half of the pincers movement from China, Stilwell had begun late in 1943 a drive from India into Burma with the Chinese X-force, strengthened by "Merrill's Marauders." On May 17 they captured the Myitkyina airport in a brilliant surprise attack. The enemy clung stubbornly to the town of Myitkyina, but by August Stilwell's men had taken it and other important positions deeper in Burma.

The Chinese armies (Y-force) that crossed the Salween on May 11, 1944, thus beginning the other half of the pincers movement, had received considerable American training and equipment, though they were not as ready as Stilwell had hoped. They attacked with great bravery against stubborn enemy resistance in tremendously difficult mountain country. They gained much ground the next month but were slowed, against American advice, by reducing strong points one by one instead of moving past them into Burma, supplied partly by air, and cutting enemy lines of support. By a narrow margin the attack failed to break through into Burma before the monsoon rains began, and the chance of a quick victory was gone. But despite setbacks the Y-force persisted. In August and September a strong enemy counterattack ground to a halt. At last the opening of land communications began to come into sight.[21]

Meanwhile the Japanese had not been content with frontally opposing the X-force. On March 7, 1944, they bid for a major victory by a drive with 155,000 men from Burma into Assam to seize the great Indian air terminals. The drive threatened both to cut the Hump route and to isolate Stilwell's forces. But after early successes the Japanese failed disastrously. By July they were in full retreat, with eventual casualties of 85 to 90 per cent in combat units and 65,000 dead in a force of 155,000.[22] General William J. Slim's British and Indian troops, with overwhelming American and British air support, had won a victory that turned the tide in Burma. Months of hard fighting lay ahead, but in

January 1945 the land route to China—which the Generalissimo generously called the Stilwell Road—was open.[23]

In the pincers drives the Chinese troops, aided heroically by the Americans of Merrill's Maurauders and later of the Mars Task Force, fought well and defeated some of Japan's best divisions, veterans of Singapore. Stilwell's faith in the common Chinese soldiers was vindicated. American liaison teams, including engineers and other specialists, helped. And the Chinese fought better because for almost the first time they had field hospital units, which the Americans organized.

Stilwell, after postponement of the pincers movement first planned for March 1943, wanted to begin the Burma campaign from both sides in October 1943. Though the drive from Assam began in December, the delay until May 11, 1944, of the drive from Yunnan meant that little good weather remained before the monsoon. So the stubborn Japanese defense on both fronts prevented opening the road into China in 1944.

The American Chiefs of Staff felt that, had Stilwell's advice been followed, "we would have cleared the Japanese from northeast Burma before the monsoon and opened the way to effective action in China proper." [24] On the other hand it can be argued that, had such a pincers movement been begun in October 1943, the Japanese would not have committed 155,000 men to the ill-fated drive into Assam started on March 7, 1944. Whether to make that drive had been quite controversial within the Japanese staff. Rather the Japanese might have put enough forces into north Burma to delay further, if not block, a junction of the two Chinese forces. The gains by these forces in the Summer of 1944 certainly would have been harder to make had not the Japanese met disaster in June–July amidst the mountains and jungles of the India-Burma border.

With benefit of hindsight, the thesis may be advanced that the right time for the Chinese attack westward into Burma was the latter part of March or early April, rather than May 11. Had that attack come some weeks earlier, when the enemy had become fully committed to the drive against the air bases and communications in Assam, the road to China might have been opened by the Fall of 1944. In that case the crack Chinese divisions from India, and part of the Y-force, might have returned to China, and a flow to China of trucks and artillery could have begun. That might have decisively strengthened the National Government and prevented the worst of the defeats described in the next section. But such reasoning is speculative. The extent to which the Generalissimo was right in insisting so long on an amphibious attack on Rangoon, and meanwhile not committing the Y-force, must be left to military experts.

DISASTER IN THE EAST

While Chinese troops with American aid were making slow progress in North Burma and West China, the situation to the east in Central and South China began to fall apart. On April 17, 1944, at the moment when China was yielding to American pressure to attack over the Salween toward Burma, the Japanese began operation ICHIGO. Their main aim was "to forestall the bombing of the Japanese homeland by American B-29's from bases at Kweilin and Liuchow." Other aims were to secure that part of China against an expected attack from India via Yunnan; to control a rail corridor from Tientsin to the Canton area in view of the "increasingly insecure sea communications"; and to "destroy the backbone of the Chinese army and force increased deterioration of the political regime." [25]

China's armies were ill-prepared to meet these great thrusts. In the north, abuse of the people by local troops in time of severe famine had been such that the troops got little aid and the Japanese were sometimes welcomed as deliverers. In the south, many troops were controlled by warlords of doubtful allegiance, some of whom were in collusion with the enemy.[26] American instructors had begun to work with the South China units known as Z-force, but so far these units had received little training and few Lend-Lease items. American officers complained that much Lend-Lease artillery and ammunition were hoarded at Kunming and Chungking. The Chinese forces suffered from having various incompetent or unreliable commanders and no proper over-all command and staff in the field. General M. F. Lindsey, head of the American East China liaison group, reported September 7, "No one here in power can tell us whether a stand will be made, who controls communications, when demolitions are planned on routes, or where 14th Air Force should best be used. With no real authority here we are just floundering." [27] At least three squadrons of the 14th Air Force were tied up in Burma, giving support to the Y-force, and not available to Chennault for use in the east. Many of the best Chinese army units were fighting in Burma and West China. Finally, China had no adequate strategic reserve, over a third of the reserve and much heavy equipment having been lost in Burma in 1942.[28]

The Japanese drive moved ahead relentlessly. Stubborn and effective Chinese defense at some points, such as Hengyang, was nullified by costly failures elsewhere. When Vice-President Wallace visited Chungking in June, Chiang told him that the defeats were caused by weakened morale. That he attributed to China's having fought for seven years under conditions of utmost hardship, to lack of help from abroad, to inflation, and to effects of the failure to open up Burma early in 1944. He asked Wallace to remind Roosevelt that he, Chiang, had told him at Cairo that "unless very early action were taken to open up Burma he could not count upon a continuance of effective Chinese resistance to the Japanese." The Generalissimo felt that if the Burma campaign had been carried through early in 1944, with amphibious support, "the effect on morale in China would have been very great." [29]

Both Stilwell and Marshall had feared that priority for Chennault's air forces over building up the Z-force would "sting" the Japanese into retaliation. Chennault, on the other hand, with the Generalissimo's support held that his 14th Air Force properly supplied could check enemy advances. Chennault believed that air support had been largely instrumental in halting three enemy drives: (1) into west China from Burma in April–May 1942; (2) in the Yangtze River area toward Chungking a year later; and (3) in the Chang-te area in the "rice bowl" of Central China at the end of 1943. It was his misfortune that Chinese and 14th Air Force intelligence misinterpreted these actions. Postwar interrogations of Japanese officers show that in each of these cases the Japanese went as far as planned, and that the withdrawals in the latter two cases were as planned. On April 29, 1943, the Generalissimo communicated to the President through Soong "his personal assurance that in the event the enemy attempts to interrupt the air offensive by a ground advance on the air bases, the advance can be halted by the existing Chinese forces." The President decided for the Generalissimo and Chennault rather than for Marshall and Stilwell.[30] But by the spring of 1944 the situation had changed. Morale was lower, the training program had lagged, and many of the best units were fighting their way into Burma, and not available to oppose the new enemy thrust.

Now events were telling the story. By September the main eastern air base at Kweilin was threatened. It seemed that nothing could hold the enemy drive. When I left Chungking for Washington in the Summer of 1944 top American officials in China told me that I might return to a government in exile.

THE STILWELL CRISIS

American-Chinese relations in matters of aid came to a head in the Summer and Fall of 1944, as the Japanese military pressure on China intensified. Vice-President Wallace, in connection with his visit to China in the early summer of 1944, recommended that Roosevelt recall Stilwell and replace him with a high officer who could gain the Generalissimo's confidence. Also at Chiang's request he recommended that the President send to China a personal representative—which led to sending General Patrick J. Hurley in August (and to subsequent resignation of Ambassador Gauss.) [31]

The War Department's answer to Wallace was to recommend to the President via the Joint Chiefs of Staff that Stilwell be made a full general, and that Chiang be urged to put him "in command of all Chinese armed forces." The memorandum of the Joint Chiefs said:

> . . . he has proved his case or contentions on the field of battle in opposition to the highly negative attitudes of both the British and the Chinese authorities. Had his advice been followed, it is now apparent that we would have cleared the Japanese from northeast Burma before the monsoon and opened the way to effective action in China proper. Had his advice been followed the Chinese ground forces east of the Hump would have been far better equipped and prepared to resist or at least delay the Japanese advances.*

Roosevelt agreed to the proposal, and on July 6 telegraphed accordingly to Chiang. At the same time Marshall telegraphed

* See the comment on this earlier in this chapter.

Stilwell, and also warned him that he must avoid offending the Generalissimo. Admiral Leahy mentions Stilwell as "publicly referring to Chiang as 'peanut' and to Lord Louis Mountbatten . . . as the 'glamour boy.'" As of August 1 Stilwell was made a full general.[32]

Through the Summer negotiations dragged on, while the Southeast China situation worsened. Chiang was ready to give Stilwell command, but under conditions which Stilwell felt would give him responsibility without adequate authority. On September 15 Stilwell telegraphed to Marshall a pessimistic report, saying that South China was lost, "largely due to lack of proper command and the usual back-seat driving from Chungking." The Generalissimo was very much worried by the unchecked Japanese advances in South and Central China and had told Stilwell he wanted to pull back the Y-force from the Burma frontier, though Chinese successes not yet reported to Chungking meant that the opening of the land route to China was almost in sight. Stilwell thought the Generalissimo did not regard the South China front as important and that he wanted to "get behind the Salween and there wait in safety for the U.S. to finish the war." [33]

Stilwell's message reached Roosevelt and Marshall at Quebec, where they were conferring with Churchill and the British military leaders. It arrived at the moment when Roosevelt and Churchill were sending a joint message to Chiang through the American and British Ambassadors at Chungking, promising to open a China port. On September 16 Roosevelt sent to Chiang through the War Department a strong message drafted by the Department. He said that to pull back the Y-force would lose all chance to open a land route and would jeopardize the Hump air route. He criticized the delay in giving Stilwell "unrestricted command of all your forces." [34]

The Generalissimo was angry. On September 24 he told Hurley that Stilwell could not be appointed and that he was convinced that "General Stilwell is unfitted for the vast, complex and delicate duties which the new command will entail." And, said the Generalissimo, "Almost from the moment of his arrival in China, he showed his disregard for that mutual confidence and respect which are essential to the successful collaboration of allied forces." The Generalissimo, however, was ready to support another American officer as commander. His attitude to Stilwell apparently was influenced by a suspicion that Stilwell had drafted and arranged the President's message. Also Chiang felt offended that Stilwell, who was his Chief of Staff and subordinate, had delivered such a strong message as Roosevelt's representative. Apart from the question whether a message should have been sent in such terms, it was a blunder not to send it directly to Hurley for delivery, and when it came through the army channel to Stilwell, he should have arranged that Hurley present it.[35]

Roosevelt's reply of October 5 said that the military situation had so deteriorated since he proposed Stilwell's command early in the summer that he no longer wanted an American to assume the responsibility. He accepted relieving Stilwell as the Generalissimo's Chief of Staff and also as in charge of Hump allocations. He further intended to relieve him of responsibility for Lend-Lease, which had been a source of friction because China did not have free disposal of the items as did Britain and Russia, disposal being subject to Stilwell's supervision. The President wished, however, that Stilwell continue to command the X- and Y-forces, because "should we remove Stilwell from the Burma campaign the results would be far more serious than you apparently realize." But the Generalissimo would not agree that Stilwell remain in any capacity. He further sent an *aide memoire* strongly critical of Stilwell's over-all strategy.[36]

Roosevelt in his final reply of October 18 said that he would at once call Stilwell back to the United States. The decisions about attacking in Burma, he said, were not those of Stilwell but of the combined American and British staffs, approved by himself and Churchill. While he would not name an American commander, he was ready to name a Chief of Staff, who would also command American forces in the China theater. For this he proposed General A. C. Wedemeyer, whom the Generalissimo already had indicated would be *persona grata*. General Dan Sultan would command in the Burma theater.[37]

Hurley's report of October 13, analyzing the issues, said that "Stilwell's fundamental mistake was the idea that he could subjugate a man who had led a nation in revolution and who for seven years had led an ill-fed, poorly equipped, practically unorganized army against an overwhelming foe." Hurley felt that the issue for the President had become a choice between Chiang and Stilwell; and that the President had to choose Chiang, since only through him could the Chinese armies be reorganized and China kept in the war. He saw clearly that the two strong personalities were incompatible.[38]

Stilwell departed at a moment when his big project of opening a road to China was nearing completion. He and his colleagues had helped China to create a strong army in India and to improve the Yunnan forces, which were driving the enemy back. His training schools and liaison teams were helping to prepare a stronger military effort by China in the rest of the war. General Wedemeyer as his successor would be able to build upon what Stilwell had begun.

Stilwell, in his final report to the War Department, discussed once again the basic question whether the United States should have put strings on its military aid and exercised control. He pointed out that he and his American colleagues had no command functions except over the Chinese army in Burma.

Holding in general to a purely advisory role, the Americans were often regarded with a jaundiced look of suspicion. In some instances our honest efforts, and our impartial action demonstrated an altruistic motive which won the respect and trust of certain field commanders. This favorable reaction to our conduct did not always hold true in the Chungking Government. In high places we were generally regarded as interlopers of cunning demeanor distributing largesse, most of which failed to materialize.

"Aid to China," once undertaken, should have been vigorously prosecuted. Fortified with a full knowledge of China's governmental venality, her economic chaos, her military weakness, a written agreement to a plan committing her to a vigorous prosecution of the war under American supervision and material assistance should have been signed before we tendered any aid.

It became increasingly obvious that a more frank and vigorous foreign policy would have helped to gain China's whole-hearted cooperation, and her acknowledgment that our cooperation depended upon determined action on her part.

He also felt that the United States should have brought pressure on Chiang for settlement of China's internal political issues, foreshadowing Marshall's postwar mission. He said:

In handling such an uncertain situation as existed in that theater of war, the Americans would have done well to avoid committing themselves unalterably to Chiang, and adopted a more realistic attitude toward China itself. We could gain little by supporting the attitude of the Chiang regime. We could have gained much by exerting pressure on Chiang to co-operate and achieve national unity, and if he proved unable to do this, then in supporting those elements in China which gave promise of such development.[39]

A basic issue was whether placing strings on aid could have extended to gaining for Stilwell the full powers he would have needed to assume the responsibility of command. Chiang during the long negotiations was never ready to grant such powers to anyone—let alone to one with whom he had had such friction as with Stilwell. To have allowed Stilwell (or another) to reorganize army leadership and the location of armies would have affected the balance of internal military and political forces.[40]

Stilwell's recall was a major event affecting Chinese-American relations. The affair has been, and it is likely to remain for a long time, a subject of controversy. Whatever the judgment, the incident had repercussions which became increasingly serious. The official American military historians state that at the Washington conference in May 1943, the President "had been solicitous in his concern not only for China but for the personal position and prestige of the Generalissimo." [41] But after Stilwell's recall leaders became less disposed to take interest in a major effort to sustain China. Washington became more ready to consider playing with the Chinese Communists, and to press for a coalition. The events of 1944 helped to set the stage for an agreement at Yalta, in terms unprecedented in American history, whereby Roosevelt was party to a deal that purported to sign away to Russia rights in Manchuria without telling China and getting her consent.*

* Concerning the Yalta agreement, Romanus and Sunderland say, "The attitude the President there adopted toward the territory and interests of China suggests that the Generalissimo's triumph of October 1944 was one of the steps that led to the Manchurian partition of February 1945" (*Stilwell's Command Problems*, p. 469).

XVII. GOLD, GIVEN AND WITHHELD

TO add to the war chest, the government collected gold and silver from the people until 1941. China's urgent need for more resources abroad outweighed the fact that payment for the metals added to inflation. There were patriotic drives, and about US$21.5 million of gold and US$9.5 million of silver were collected and exported in the first four years of fighting. Much came in the form of jewelry and ornaments, some of it donated. But in 1941 the need for foreign currencies eased, because of large credits and Lend-Lease. So the collection of precious metals was relaxed.

ORIGIN OF THE GOLD SALES PROGRAM

Gold sales were first seriously proposed in May 1942 by Hsi Te-mou, of the Central Bank. He sought ways to reduce the dependence on printing-press money. Already it seemed that sale of the dollar-backed securities, under the plan adopted, would not bring in much revenue. Sales of gold, he thought, would attract broader buying than sales of securities, given the traditional fondness of China's people for gold. He proposed selling first about 44,000 ounces (US$1.5 million) held by the Bank, and importing more gold against the US$500 million credit.

In the previous year the rise of prices had quickened, and it was vital to make every effort to check inflation. I supported the proposal to sell gold. The government was favorably inclined, but did not act at once. On December 4, 1942, I pressed the matter, pointing out that people would regard import of gold as adding strength to the currency. Distribution of gold to the public was unorthodox. It would be better to sell goods, but their import was not then feasible. Hoarding of gold was less bad than hoarding of goods. Gold sales would promote speculation in gold —which in former days had been notorious at Shanghai. Some of the gold might get to the enemy and the puppets, but this I did not consider too serious since Free China would get value from it, for example, goods. The government of course would need to have enough gold on hand or available to control the price. On balance I recommended proceeding with the scheme as a wartime expedient.

Late in 1942 Kung instructed the Ambassador at Washington to begin negotiations to acquire gold for China. This led to an extensive program of domestic gold sales. The following account of the gold situation is similar to and partly in the language of the memorandum which I submitted to the Internal Security Subcommittee of the Senate Committee on the Judiciary in connection with my testimony July 13, 1956.[1] Annexed to my testimony in the Hearings is the full text of many documents cited in this chapter.

THE TREASURY AGREES TO SUPPLY GOLD

In response to the Chinese Ambassador's approach, the Treasury agreed in December 1942 to provide US$20 million of gold, to be charged against the US$500 million credit. This gold was earmarked in the Federal Reserve Bank of New York. Shipment to China, however, was delayed. There were difficult questions about transport and insurance. Kung had been doubtful about how much gold could be sold, and did not actively press the matter. The Treasury for its part doubted whether sale of the gold would help much.[2]

Early in July 1943, Kung advised Morgenthau that inflation was growing in China, and that American needs for airfields and other facilities added greatly to China's expenditures. Kung thought it desirable to sell gold actively, and asked that US$200 million of the credit be used for shipment of gold to China. He stated that Madame Chiang, at the time of her visit to Washington in June 1943, obtained the approval in principle of Roosevelt and Morgenthau for the use of US$200 million of the credit to supply gold.

Morgenthau replied that the Treasury agreed in principle, but had previously made it clear to China that it acquiesced because the Chinese Government felt that the sale of gold to the public would help China to fight inflation and hoarding; and that such use of gold involved great costs and difficulties and the decision was primarily China's responsibility. Also, Morgenthau stated, China would be sacrificing assets which could be used for postwar reconstruction.

In response to a formal request by the Ambassador, Morgenthau on July 27 agreed to provide US$200 million immediately for purchase of gold. The reply stated:

> In order to avoid unnecessary raising of funds by the United States Treasury, it is suggested that transfers from the credit of the Chinese Government for the purchase of gold be made at such time and in such amounts as are allowed by existing facilities for the transportation to China of the equivalent amount of gold. Since it is intended that this gold will be sent to China for sale to the public, this procedure shoud not interfere with the program outlined in your message of July 23, 1943.
>
> On receipt of requests from the Government of China that a specific amount should be transferred from the credit of the Government of China on the books of the Treasury and be used for the purchase of gold, the necessary action will be taken to consummate these requests.[3]

In reply Kung expressed appreciation and said he would "request transfers in specific amounts having regard to need for the gold." [4]

Adler telegraphed from Chungking July 17, that an effective scheme to sell gold in China with adequate controls "would undoubtedly have beneficial effects in checking inflation." He hoped it could be done through the Stabilization Board.[5] But unfortunately nothing came of this idea.

The Treasury clearly recognized the desirability in principle of using gold to raise funds for war purposes as a noninflationary expedient. A memorandum of September 22, from White to Morgenthau, stated that the Treasury expected to sell about US$20 million of gold in the next three months in the Middle East and India to cover local war costs of the United States and that the amount of such sales was likely to grow. In the same memorandum White informed the Secretary, "China has asked us for $50 million worth of gold in accordance with your promise to make the gold available. I have taken the position that the gold is available as rapidly as they can ship it." [6]

A memorandum prepared by White recorded his conversation with Morgenthau on September 29, as follows:

> I said that I thought that we ought to be tough with the Chinese on the question of earmarking $200 million of gold for gold sales which they could not make before the gold could be shipped to them. The Secretary agreed. He said he thinks that we should be tough in this matter and he told me to go ahead and let them have the gold only as rapidly as it could be shipped and sold in China.[7]

In the Fall of 1943 there was discussion of possible sale of gold in China by the United States to meet American expenditures and thus overcome the disadvantages of the artificial official rate of exchange of C$20-1. Kung had no objection in principle, but thought the plan inadvisable because other governments would be likely to claim the same privilege.

Negotiations with China's representatives in Washington, T. M. Hsi, and T. L. Soong, went forward. There was no urgency about shipping gold against the US$200 million commitment. The afore-mentioned US$20 million of gold earmarked in New York was available, and the Central Bank had a stock in Chungking from which sales could begin. On November 10 these representatives telegraphed to Kung:

> Dr. Harry White assured that Treasury feel duty bound by promise to supply China with gold according to original understanding but explained difficulty in making big transfer of gold because it might cause questioning in Congress and require borrowing from market. Dr. White also stated there is no difference whether our gold is on the book of the Treasury or earmark with Federal Reserve Bank and *assured whenever we need Treasury can make transfer at any time.** We expressed our appreciation of their position and asked whether transfer in four equal lots of 50 million will be feasible as 20 million being our reserve. However Dr. White suggested maintaining all the time a revolving amount of 10 million gold in account with Federal Reserve Bank available for shipment. This means if our gold in Federal Reserve Bank falls below 10 million Treasury would make up that amount.

I urged agreeing to the revolving fund of US$10 million of gold and accommodating the Treasury by not asking them to provide gold "any more rapidly than it is actually needed for use in China" (memorandum of November 26). Otherwise they would have had to borrow the money and pay interest. But the proposal lapsed. Minister Kung hoped for larger transfers, because of his belief in the psychological value of holding larger reserves. In the light of later events it is unfortunate that China did not agree to the revolving fund and take advantage of the fact that White was then ready to facilitate shipments *pari passu* with actual needs. Such a revolving fund would have provided the gold as fast as it could have been sold, and could have obviated later troubles if the gold had been transported to China as needed.

---

* Emphasis added.

CHINA BEGINS SELLING GOLD

Gold sales began in the fall of 1943, by the Farmers Bank on behalf of the Central Bank. These sales were from the Chungking stock of about US$1.5 million. In reserve was the US$20 million earmarked in New York nine months earlier, which was beginning to be forwarded to China, and the US$200 million which the Treasury promised to supply. The first US$1 million—a million dollars of gold weighs about a ton—left New York September 28. It went by rail to Miami and thence by air through South America, Africa, the Middle East, and India to Chungking. It arrived there November 19. By the end of 1943 arrivals totaled US$10.5 million. These shipments were from the US$20 million of earmarked gold.

The Farmers Bank managed its sales so as to avoid disrupting gold prices. Sometimes the bank bought to steady the market. Total sales through February 1944, after which the Central Bank took over the selling, were only a little over US$1 million. Some had the idea that mere presence of gold in China as reserve would be a major factor in checking inflation. On November 11, 1943, I wrote in my diary: "Fear China may not make enough use of the gold, but will sit with it instead—in which case effect will be small in checking inflation." But on February 24, 1944, I noted that instructions had been given "to sell gold more actively after having held back."

Public knowledge in China of the arrangements to get gold had a helpful effect. A telegram of Adler to the Treasury November 30 said the rate of price rise had slackened for various reasons including an adequate harvest, good war news from other theaters, and the psychological effect of announcing China's gold purchase.[8] Kung telegraphed to Morgenthau the following message of December 14:

You will be pleased to hear that the recent gold shipment is one of the outstanding factors contributing to the strengthening of *fapi*, because people believe that the arrival of gold has increased the much needed reserve of our currency, thereby influencing the stability of prices. The action of the United States Government re-affirms to the Chinese people that, despite difficulties arising from the blockade and the cumulative effects of over six years of war against the invasion, China has a powerful friend desirous of strengthening China's economy as conditions permit.[9]

The Treasury in this period was giving effect to Secretary Morgenthau's decision, to "let them have the gold only as rapidly as it could be shipped and sold in China." Their reluctance about gold for China was shown by a statement by Morgenthau in a conference with his staff on December 17, 1943, at which he said: ". . . it was our fault or blame or responsibility that the gold left here so slowly. We thought that was the only way to make it last." [10] In a memorandum of December 18 Morgenthau reviewed the situation for Roosevelt. This was in relation to China's request for the billion dollar loan. Morgenthau quoted Kung's message of December 14 about the good effects of gold shipments, and said it was too early to say definitely what effect they might have. In seeking alternatives to the loan, Morgenthau recommended:

Accelerate the shipment of gold purchased by China to twice the amount we have previously planned to send. It should be possible to raise gold shipments from $6 million a month to about $12 million. At the present price for gold in the open market this would be equal to the present 3.5 billion of yuan currency that is being issued.

The impact of this two-fold program should contribute to retarding inflation, always bearing in mind that the basic reason for inflation in China is shortage of goods.[11]

These proposals clearly show Morgenthau's desire to help China to check inflation and his readiness to send to China such gold as she could really use. The "shortage of goods" argument, mentioned in the last-quoted sentence, cropped up frequently during the war on both the Chinese and the American side. In Appendix I there is a comment on the fallacy of treating the shortage as "the basic reason."

On January 19, the President in a telephone conversation with Morgenthau said he understood China was getting US$12.5 million of gold per month. Morgenthau checked with White, who was with him, and who said it was "less than that." (November and December shipments had been US$8 and 2 million, respectively.) The President wanted to send US$25 million per month.[12] The Treasury went so far as to draft a message dated January 19 for the Generalissimo which included a statement that ". . . the Air Transport Command has agreed to make additional facilities available to the Treasury for shipment of gold to China so that we hope to be able to ship about 25 million dollars a month." [13] That statement was dropped from the message sent. Nevertheless it points up the insincerity of later Treasury arguments stressing lack of transport as an excuse for not sending gold.

At this stage China's gold-selling program was only beginning to get under way. Sales by the Farmers Bank were unaggressive, and totaled but US$329,300 to the end of 1943. But demand grew after the Central Bank took over gold selling in March 1944. Sales were over US$2 million per month in May and June, and US$4.4 million in July. The proceeds began to cover a material part of the deficit of the budget. In July sales yielded about C$2.3 billion, compared with note issue growth of C$6.3 billion.

In the first half of 1944 the Treasury's operating officials, far from meeting Roosevelt's January wish to send monthly US$25 million or even the US$12.5 million that Morgenthau thought China was getting, sent a total of only about US$2 million. Of that only half had arrived by June 30. Nevertheless, until then China's gold position was not so bad. At mid-year about US$6 million of gold was on hand in Chungking. The Treasury's operators could claim that they were carrying out Morgenthau's decision to let China have the gold "only as rapidly as it could be shipped and sold."

THE TREASURY WITHHOLDS GOLD

In July 1944 the Treasury's foot-dragging began to be acutely felt. As gold sales mounted in the summer of 1944, the shortage in China became serious. On July 12 the Central Bank urgently telegraphed, asking immediate air shipments. That was the crucial moment, when the operating officials of the Treasury began to go back on Morgenthau's promises and to depart from the intent of his instructions. The Treasury sent no gold until August 3, when US$3 million went forward. And that went *by sea*. It did not reach Chungking until September 23. Three further lots totaling US$4.3 million, however, went by air in August–September. By September 30 the Central Bank had only US$215,000 of gold on hand. The last of the three air shipments arrived October 3 and was quickly sold. Then China was out of gold.

China's representatives in Washington pressed for urgent shipments. On October 2 they conferred at the Treasury with White and others. They presented a telegram from the Central Bank at Chungking, stating that recent arrivals of gold were "far from being adequate to meet outstanding contracts." The original US$20 million was exhausted, and they asked for immediate transfer of US$20 million more, to be shipped "by plane." They pointed out that "the cessation of the sale of gold would have very serious effects at this time." But White questioned the merits of selling gold.[14] Despite China's urging there was no further shipment for a month. And that lot, about US$3 million sent on November 2, went by sea; whereas all previous shipments, except that sent on August 3 in response to China's urgent appeal of July 12, had gone by air. Apparently the chief effect of China's urgent appeals was to delay shipments, and then to have them go by sea. Another lot of about US$3 million went forward on December 1, again by sea. *No more gold was sent until April 14, 1945, when about US$1.2 million went by sea.*

The Fall of 1944, when the effects of the Treasury's action began to be felt, was a most difficult period for China. The Japanese drive to take the East China air bases was unchecked and even threatened Chungking and Kunming. The fear that Japan would force evacuation of those cities greatly increased the demands for gold. In times of stress gold, being of high value in small compass, is a wonderful asset to people who fear they may have to flee for their lives. Coupled with this, the rapid growth of inflation spurred flight from the currency into whatever purchases would be likely to hold their value, notably gold. For these reasons, in the autumn of 1944 the demand for gold was unprecedented.

Demand was increased also as doubt developed about arrival of Treasury shipments, because of the meager response to the Central Bank's appeal of July 12, and the fact that no shipments went forward until August 3. When the stock in China was exhausted early in October, the doubts mounted. The situation could not be kept from the public, since the bank was out of gold for immediate delivery.

The Central Bank did not dare to stop sales and depend only on actual arrivals to sell gold. The gold price in China had long been a major field of speculation; and a soaring free market for gold, with no demand met, would have added fuel to the fires of inflation. So the bank, trusting in the Treasury's commitment and expecting deliveries even though delayed, turned to sales for future delivery. This was done partly by selling gold forward, but mainly by accepting deposits to be repaid later in gold. These sales of futures had to be made at unfavorable rates. Because of the rapid inflation, interest rates in China were then 8 per cent or more per month. Hence what the buyers would pay for the right to receive gold in six months was related to what they could make by putting out their money at interest for that period, in which the original sum would grow by about 50 per cent or more.

A memorandum by White to Morgenthau, dated December 9, said that the Chinese have been pressing to ship gold by commercial vessels, whereas the Treasury had insisted on military transport. "We have stalled as much as we have dared," said White, "and have succeeded in limiting gold shipments to $26 million during the past year. We think it would be a serious mistake to permit further large shipments at this time." White went on to say, however, that the Treasury was going ahead with its program to obtain in India "all our rupee needs through the sale of gold." [15] Some gold was available in India, and the Central Bank swapped 40,000 ounces (US$1.4 million) in New York for a like amount in Calcutta, under a deal which I negotiated with the Bank of England in the latter part of 1944.

China continued to press for shipments. O. K. Yui, who succeeded H. H. Kung as Finance Minister in December, telegraphed on December 30 that China urgently needed gold, and asked Kung, who was in the United States, to press Morgenthau to expedite shipments. On January 3 Kung wrote to the Secretary appealing to his friendship and asking his cooperation. The Secretary replied January 5 that he hoped to give a decision in the near future and was giving "fullest consideration to the best interests of China." [16] On January 18 Kung once more wrote to Morgenthau, expressing the "urgency of facilitating the shipment of gold to China and the minting of gold tokens for shipment to China." [17] The production of such tokens in one, one-half, and one-quarter ounce sizes had been discussed for many months but nothing definite had been done. The Treasury took no action on this urging. Again in a letter of February 26, Kung reviewed the situation comprehensively. He pled for immediate shipments both by air and by sea. He again urged the early delivery of gold tokens. Finally, he said that the Chinese government fully realized that gold sales were justified only by the emergency, and that it was anxious to import and sell consumer goods instead.

In a memorandum of March 2 to Morgenthau, V. F. Coe said that the situation in China was unchanged. "Ambassador Hurley agreed with you on the desirability of holding down gold shipments to approximately the same magnitude as in the past"; that is, to ship about US$7 million over the next three months. Half of this should be earmarked for promoting the production of tin in West China under an arrangement made with the National Resources Commission of China. The Treasury's reply of March 3 was a gem of dissimulation. It said:

> I am sure that you appreciate the many difficulties involved in making arrangements for the export of gold to China. As in every other phase of our activities these days, military necessity takes precedence over everything else.
>
> I have, however, instructed my men to raise again with the military authorities the possibilities of shipping gold to China during the next few months. They will inform your representatives of their findings on this matter.[18]

On April 23 Minister Yui telegraphed that the delay in shipments reflected on China's credit, saying, "I feel much concerned and distressed." The Central Bank telegraphed April 28, "We cannot overemphasize the serious effect in consequence Doctor White's default in meeting its [sic] obligations."

Meanwhile, the deficiency of gold in China steadily grew. China's uncovered commitments to deliver gold were US$12 million at the end of 1944; US$50 million on March 31, 1945; and US$84 million three months later. By June 25, 1945, speculation in gold had become so panicky that the Central Bank suspended sales, and sold practically no gold during the remaining weeks of the war.

Appendix III contains further particulars of the gold situation in China during this period.

THE CONTROVERSY: PROS AND CONS

When China was pressing for urgent shipments of gold, White gave various arguments to justify his obstruction. At the conference on October 2, 1944, he pointed out that the gold would be a valuable asset postwar, and expressed the view that if sold in China, it "could not substantially retard rising prices or the basic economic situation which was due to the acute scarcity of goods," and also that much of the gold would disappear into hoards. He made the surprising statement that "it was cheaper for the Central Government to print *fapi* than to absorb *fapi* in exchange for gold at a time when the dent that was being made by the sale of gold was not significantly large." [19] China's representatives were quick to challenge him on the size of the "dent," pointing out that in July gold sales had brought in C$2 billion against a note increase which Adler stated was C$9 (actually C$6.3) billion. In a situation where inflation was so grave, it is hard to see how anyone knowledgeable in economic matters could seriously argue that it was "cheaper" for China to print more notes than to sell gold! Also costs of printing paper money of low value are high.

In a memorandum of December 23, 1944, which he submitted to the Secretary for presentation to President Roosevelt, he amplified his arguments. The gold, he said, was being sold "in such a way as to be of benefit principally to hoarders and speculators" and much of it was finding its way to the occupied areas; it was having "practically no helpful effect on the inflationary situation"; and while it gave the Chungking government an additional source of revenue, this was "by the sacrifice of valuable national assets at inexcusably low prices." He went on to say that the Treasury had held back shipments despite pressure from China. The gold exports, he explained, clearly showed American support of Chungking. The memorandum suggested use of the shipments as a "bargaining weapon," to get Chungking to accept "your China program." The record indicates that the Secretary did not present this memorandum to the President.[20]

Let us look at the objections. There was no more reason to hold back gold for postwar use than to hold back troops because the men would be needed later. In war all kinds of assets must be sacrificed, even lives. White's objection on the ground of sacrifice of assets is without merit, if use of the assets yielded reasonable value in China and helped to check inflation. There is also the issue of what results China could have gotten with proper Treasury cooperation.

Gold was yielding good value in China. It is a striking fact that throughout the whole period of gold-selling, the value of gold in China at the official selling prices was well above the official American price of US$35 per fine ounce. It was as high as US$150 in the last part of 1943, but naturally fell as more and more gold was put on the market. Such premia on gold were usual in many parts of the world in this period. Gold prices in China ruled above those in India. That tempted smuggling, for which a number of American and Chinese military and civilian personnel had to be punished. There were cases of hijacking gold smugglers at Chinese airfields. Compared with the American price of US$35, an ounce of gold brought in China in the first nine months of 1944 the equivalent of US$89–100 at official prices and a little more in the free market. Thereafter the equivalents were lower, because gold was sold almost wholly for future delivery. But even so the equivalents in the nine months to June 30, 1945, ranged between US$37 and US$51 per ounce at official gold prices, and US$66 to US$87 at free market prices. These equivalents are calculated at average quarterly rates for *fapi* in the free market for dollar notes.*

After mid-1944 receipts from gold sales reduced materially the deficit met by the printing press. The swelling flood of paper money was the main cause of the price rise, and not scarcity of goods, as White suggested (see appendix I). Gold sales in the third and fourth quarters of 1944 were 27 and 29 per cent respectively, of the increase of note issue. In the first two quarters of 1945, the figures were 52 and 28 per cent. Figures of quarterly deficits are not available. But the proportion of deficit covered by gold sales was somewhat less than those percentages, since increase of note issue was then covering about 80 per cent of the cash deficit. A telegram from Adler at Chungking, March 11, 1945, reported that receipts from gold had become the chief source of revenue in January and February and were covering about one-fourth of the deficit.[21]

As to hoarding, the sale of gold was intended to attract the funds of those who otherwise would engage in hoarding rice or

---

* For example, in the third quarter of 1944 the average official and free market prices of gold were C$18,500 and C$20,070, respectively. The average value of dollar notes in the free market was C$209. At that rate the official and free market prices of gold in China were equivalent to US$89 and US$96, respectively. For further particulars see appendix III.

other important goods and speculate in them—in other words to divert them from that harmful activity, and thus add to the supply of goods available in the market. It was far better that people hoard gold, paid for by turning in money that could be reissued, than to have that money remain in circulation and be used in part to buy and hoard scarce goods. It was true that some of the gold found its way to occupied areas. But the buyers there were largely Chinese and in any event the government got value in local currency withdrawn from circulation for the gold that it sold, and probably Free China got goods from the occupied areas in exchange for the gold.

The Treasury made much of the argument that transport was scarce, though later Coe said, ". . . we all think that transportation is a thin excuse." [22] In January 1944, the Treasury was ready to arrange to transport about US$25 million of gold per month. The entire US$200 million weighed only about 200 tons. In 1944 CNAC flew nearly 2,000 tons of bank notes and bank note paper over the Hump. Sale of a million dollars of gold, at say C$20,000 per ounce, would have realized about C$560 million; whereas a ton of C$20 bank notes contained only about C$20 million.

The discrepancy between official and free gold prices became a bone of contention between the Treasury and China. Until the summer of 1944, when enough gold was on hand in China, official prices were kept closely in line with free prices. In the second quarter of 1944, the official price was C$18,500 and the free market price averaged C$18,803. But in the third quarter the free price began to fluctuate at levels considerably above the official price.* At the conference of American and Chinese representatives at the Treasury on October 2, 1944, Adler stated that the spread had temporarily gone as high as 60 per cent early in September, but had dropped to C$1,500 (about 8 per cent) with the arrival of gold. This appears to refer to the shipment of about US$1.5 million which arrived September 12, being the first arrival since July 12. The Chinese representatives went on to point out

* On July 16 the Central Bank, in a surprise move, dropped the price from C$18,500 to C$17,500, to trap speculators and strengthen confidence. In September it raised the effective official price to C$19,250 and in October to C$21,000, by including a supplement first of 10 per cent and then 20 per cent for compulsory purchase of Chinese Government Treasury notes. In November the official price was raised to C$24,000.

that if there were sufficient supplies of gold, the discrepancy could be obliterated. They stated correctly that "the market's lack of confidence in the Central Bank's ability to procure adequate supplies was apparently the main reason" for the discrepancy.[23] In a telegram of October 6 the Central Bank told its representatives in the United States:

> Difference between official and black market prices entirely due to stock having been exhausted. As soon as we are selling cash again difference immediately disappears . . . Public got scared because we had no more gold. All rushed for what they could grab. This unfortunately happened not due to our fault here as we requested Federal Reserve Bank for shipment by air July 12. After waiting 25 days no sight of new shipment while our stock giving out hence the black market.

Beginning in November 1944, the spread between official and free gold prices grew further. The Treasury continued to criticize China for not keeping the two sets of prices in line. But China argued quite correctly that it could not do that safely without spot gold to sell and thus control the spot price. The responsible officials in China feared that such raises would damage confidence and aggravate the inflation. At this stage, viewing the situation from Washington, I felt that the official price should have been raised more frequently and by smaller amounts, instead of waiting until March 30, 1945, to make a big increase. But the lack of spot gold, because of the Treasury's action, made any good handling of the situation impossible. A background condition promoting a rise in the free gold market was the spiraling of inflation. The average monthly rise of general prices in the cities of Free China was 18 per cent in the nine months from November 1944, through July 1945. The deficit was worse because of the costs of reorganizing the Chinese armies with American aid, growing American operations in China, and the outlay for the newly organized War Production Board which Donald M. Nelson helped to organize. Meanwhile revenue suffered from enemy occupation of larger areas.

When no American gold arrived from January 26 to June 14, 1945, the free gold market became more and more panicky. Sales at the official price for future delivery grew by leaps and bounds. Adler, in a memorandum of March 19, 1945, objected to China pegging the official price of gold so far below the free market price. He favored, however, "continuance of the sale of gold with a drastic revision of gold sales policy." He also favored issuing token gold coins of a quarter, half, and one ounce, also direct use of gold to meet expenditures. He said, "The effects of such a gold sales policy as an integral part of a broad anti-inflationary program might well be considerable and serve to keep the net monthly deficit within manageable proportions." [24] All along the Chinese Government had wanted to do substantially what Adler now advocated. But withholding of gold had made it impossible to control the free gold market and to keep free and official prices in line. Also the Treasury had delayed a decision about gold tokens.

With the gold market getting out of hand, the Chinese Government was in a dilemma. On the one hand, gold was too cheap at the official price in the face of mounting inflation. On the other hand, raising the price was always a shock to confidence and was likely to be followed by a sharp jump in the free market so long as the government did not have a stock to sell in order to control the price. And such jumps in the free market price hurt confidence and tended to cause sharper increase of commodity prices in general. Because of this difficulty, the Chinese Government delayed too long in raising the official price. Effective March 30, the Central Bank raised to C$35,000 the price of C$24,000 set November 13, 1944. The new price was just under the current free market price. But because of the lack of spot gold to control the market, the free price at once became as much out of line as ever. As to the effects of raising the gold price, the Chungking edition of the *Shanghai Evening Post* on April 1 said:

The move promptly produced skyrocketing black market prices in gold, American currency and various commodities . . .

Within a few hours after sale of gold began at the new official price, the black market price of gold jumped to CN$60,000 per ounce, and American currency in large denominations increased on the black market from 525 to 660 to one.

Numerous commodities followed suit.

It was charged in some of the press in Chungking, and also reported in the American press, that insiders had advance knowledge of the rise and profited accordingly. But the Central Bank steadfastly denied this. They stated that the only large buyer immediately before the rise was a commercial company which had just received a down payment on a substantial order to be produced for the government and was buying gold to hedge against the expected increase in its costs. However, some weeks later two minor officials of the Central Trust of China were arrested for alleged misuse of information on the gold price rise. I was in the United States during this period and have no first-hand knowledge of what happened at that time in Chungking.

SETTLEMENT OF THE ISSUE

The question of gold deliveries to China came to a head in May 1945. Foreign Minister Soong came to Washington from the San Francisco Conference on organization of the United Nations. He presented to President Truman China's request for gold and also asked for consumer goods to check the inflation. Truman asked the Treasury to consult the Departments of State and War. In a conference on the gold situation with these departments on May 1, Morgenthau said, "We've made it just as difficult for the Chinese to get it as possible, that being a sort of joint policy." [25] Representatives of those departments tended to agree with the Treasury view on gold, but undertook to give serious consideration to shipping consumer goods, especially textiles.

On May 8 Soong conferred with Treasury, State, and War Department officials. They presented to him a memorandum which recommended that China adopt an anti-inflation program comprising monetary, banking, fiscal, and administrative reforms and stabilization of foreign exchange. The memorandum proposed that China set up a "Currency Stabilization Fund" of US$500 million, to be used for purposes to be jointly agreed with the Treasury. The memorandum further suggested that China stop forward sales of gold, a program about which the Treasury had not been consulted, but said that the Treasury would try to make available limited quantities of gold. This gold, however, ought to be financed from assets other than the proposed US$500 million stabilization fund. This fund should be constituted in part from what remained of the US$500 million loan, that is, US$240 million. The memorandum went on to say, "China should investigate and cancel sales to speculators and illicit purchasers," and, "It is most unfortunate that the impression has arisen in the United States that the $200 million of U.S. dollar certificates and bonds and the gold sold in China have gone into relatively few hands with resultant large individual profits and have failed to be of real assistance to the Chinese economy." [26]

When the memorandum was read to Soong, he asked how he could combat the inflation with the US$500 million fund. He then said that he had come from the San Francisco Conference to settle matters in Washington. He read the communication of July 27, 1943, stating that the Treasury "agrees to the request . . . that $200 million be made available . . . for the purchase of gold," and that "the necessary action will be taken to consummate" China's requests for transfers of funds to buy gold. Morgenthau expressed surprise, thinking that this arrangement referred to only US$20 million, but was informed that it was US$200 million. He said that the Treasury had not envisaged sale of futures, but Soong pointed out that China made no commitment to consult when they sold gold. Soong said that he would raise the gold price and tax those who had bought for future delivery—a commitment which later was strictly carried out and a 40 per cent tax imposed in the Fall of 1945. In response to the Secretary's statement that he (Morgenthau) had tried to keep quiet the abuses in China, Soong said that he had nothing to hide—if there had been anything wrong it should be investigated, and he had so told Chiang Kai-shek. Soong also discussed the proposed delivery of textiles and goods to China, remarking that, "The country that first got beaten up by the aggressor will be the last to be rescued." [27]

The next day Morgenthau called in his staff. He was much upset by the position in which he found himself. He said that he did so many things he could not be expected to remember the terms of his letter of July 27, 1943, and that it was their responsibility to bring it to his attention.

I have given, in writing, the Chinese Government a firm commitment that they can have two hundred million dollars worth of gold . . . and you put me in an absolutely dishonorable position, and I think it's inexcusable . . .

. . . here I am acting like a huckster over something which has been settled . . .[28]

On May 10 at a further conference White told the Secretary:

. . . we had absolutely no legal grounds for withholding the gold; that what we were doing was skating on thin ice and offering excuses and we were getting away with it as long as we could . . . We have been successful over two years in keeping them down to twenty-seven million.

Morgenthau said:

I think that the Army and State Department have advised me very badly on this thing last week and suddenly Will Clayton woke up to that fact himself, entirely on his own.[29]

Despite the Secretary's attitude, White and some of his associates prepared a draft memorandum for Morgenthau addressed to the President of which they had sent a copy to the State Department for clearance, suggesting an effort be made to get China to "withdraw for the time being her request for immediate heavy shipments of gold." The report of the discussion reads:

H.M. Jr.: The first thing I want, please call up whoever has a copy at the State Department. I want them immediately withdrawn, immediately. I'm not going to follow this position. It's ridiculous. Will you please, where ever they are, get them right back . . .

I mean, you just keep going over the same ground, the same ground, the whole time. This doesn't make it plain to the President of the United States that these people own this gold, that I, over my signature, told them they could have two hundred million dollars worth of gold.

Mr. White: That's where I disagree.

H.M. Jr.: I know you do.[30]

Morgenthau decided that in reversing the policy and sending to China large amounts of gold, he should have the backing of the State Department and the approval of the President. He obtained a memorandum of May 16, 1945, from Assistant Secretary Clayton, which was confirmed in a letter of the same date from Acting Secretary Grew. That letter, while expressing doubts as to the effectiveness of the sale of gold, recommended that "the Treasury, if transportation is available, deliver the gold to China in accordance with the time schedules put forward by Dr. Soong." [31]

After obtaining the approval of President Truman, Morgenthau on May 16 wrote to Soong that the Treasury would authorize shipment of the remaining gold in accordance with the schedule requested by Soong. The letter, however, went on to question the effectiveness of gold sales:

As you know, it is my opinion that the sale of gold by China has not proved effective in combating inflation, and I am doubtful that it will prove effective. Also as I have told you, the manner in which the gold sales have been conducted and the consequent public criticism of them in China are not conducive to achieving the purposes for which our financial aid was granted.

The secretary further urged constituting the US$500 million fund, stating that: ". . . the Chinese Government's response to our proposal to institute a $500 million fund and her conduct of the gold sales program will be important considerations in our financial relations with China." [32] In these discussions with Soong, no agreement was reached about the suggested new fund of US$500 million. But on February 26, 1946, the Chinese Supreme Defence Council ordered the setting aside of a fund of that size for eventual monetary stabilization, this being done as a part of the measures taken when China reopened the foreign exchange market at Shanghai.

RESUMPTION OF SHIPMENTS

Despite the promise to accelerate shipments, the Treasury continued to send them by sea. Five shipments were made in May and ten shipments in June, by sea, the first of which arrived July 17, 1945. Beginning June 16, however, some shipments were made by plane, the first two of which arrived June 26 and 28. During the rest of the year, further large lots arrived—over US$100 million in July–October 1945.

But these massive shipments were too late to have the effect sought. Beginning in early June the gold market got completely out of hand. On June 8 the Central Bank raised the official price from C$35,000 to C$50,000. But even by that date none of the gold which Morgenthau promised on May 16 had arrived. None had even started on its way by air, though one lot sent by sea in April reached Chungking only on June 14, after the crisis. Indeed no American gold had arrived in China since January, until June 14. So in early June there was no spot gold in China to control the market, and no one could be sure when it would arrive. The free market price which on June 7 had been C$90,000 at once jumped to a range of C$105,000—128,000 in the next two days, and to C$185,000 later in June. On June 25 sales were suspended because of uncertainty how to deal with these extreme gyrations. During July the price range in the free market was C$167,000—225,000.

At the end of July the government announced a 40 per cent

tax on settlement of forward commitments and raised the official price to C$170,000. These measures practically put an end to the wartime sale of gold. With Japan's defeat approaching, a temporary deflation set in. During August the gold price slumped to C$75,000 and in September as low as $50,000.

By September an ample supply of gold was on hand and the government began the liquidation of forward commitments, collecting the 40 per cent tax. On September 28 it set the official price at C$89,000. For the rest of the year the free market price range was C$82,500–100,000.

CONCLUSIONS

Secretary Morgenthau wanted to help China and was ready to send such gold as China could really use. His reluctance to earmark or ship gold beyond what China needed for her sales program was justifiable. The deliberate foot-dragging and obstruction of needed shipments, despite China's urgent pleas, was primarily the work of White and other subordinates. It was a clear and unjustifiable violation of Morgenthau's promise. He was quick to make amends as soon as the explicit nature of his commitment was brought to his personal attention.

The Treasury withheld gold when China's need to check inflation was greater than ever before. Besides, a major factor aggravating inflation was of American origin, the spending of C$6 billion in a short time in the first half of 1944 for new air bases desired by the United States. Late in 1944 began the sharpest inflation of the war, endangering the entire war effort in China and also China's future. Surely aid in holding back this inflation should have been a major American policy. And it was clear that gold sales helped, since they covered a material part of the deficit. In 1944, despite slow-down of gold shipments, the sales proceeds of about C$21 billion nearly offset American outlay in China of about C$23 billion. Most of the Treasury's arguments are answered by the mere fact that throughout the period they sent gold without hesitation to be sold in the Middle East and India to raise money by noninflationary means.

The withholding of gold, despite the Treasury's clear commitment upon which China had relied, suggested within China doubt of American support. It hurt confidence in the government.

Thus the Treasury's action made it harder for China to hold out during the difficult last months, after seven years of suffering, and made postwar reconstruction harder.

Why this unfriendly attitude toward China? Several factors played their part:

(1) China's overly hard bargaining and reluctance to make realistic arrangements to meet American army costs in China, as to which no settlement was reached until November 1944, was unjustifiable. The argument was acute in July 1944, when the Treasury began to embarrass China by delaying shipment. Certainly soreness about China's position on army costs influenced the American attitude on gold. It helped the Treasury to gain the general acquiescence of the State and War Departments in the gold policy, though the record available does not show that they knew how definite had been the Treasury's commitment to send the gold.

(2) China's mishandling of the issue of US$200 million of dollar-backed securities did not encourage American officials to have confidence that the gold would be wisely used. But, as regards gold, it was American much more than Chinese action that prevented the sales operation from accomplishing what it could and should have accomplished. The Treasury people closed their eyes to the fact that China was getting good value from gold sales and making a good record in keeping the official sales prices in line with the market prices of gold, until handicapped by the Treasury's foot-dragging. If the Treasury had loyally supplied enough gold, the Central Bank could have avoided sales for future delivery and gotten much better prices for spot gold. Thus, the excesses that developed in the futures market, reflecting a shock to confidence, would not have occurred. And the inflation could have been somewhat slowed.

(3) Many American officials both in China and Washington felt that China had not fought as effectively as she should have after the spring of 1942. Many of them expected far too much from China. They did not sufficiently appreciate China's exhaustion; the suffering inflicted by the Japanese armies; the disorganization caused by fighting the enemy alone for seven years to mid-1944; the inability to do much against a modern mechanized army without adequate equipment and training; possible sub-

conscious reaction in China that American oil and scrap iron had previously helped Japan to fight China; the need to gird against a later Communist threat; and the subtle but fundamental damage from inflation.

(4) Finally there is the question of Communist influence. A report of the Internal Security Subcommittee to the Senate Committee on the Judiciary refers to "the Communist underground apparatus of Harry Dexter White," citing the testimony under oath of Whittaker Chambers and Elizabeth Bentley. The report states that FBI Director J. Edgar Hoover told the Subcommittee that White's involvement was "substantiated from more than 30 sources." On the other hand, members of White's family issued after his death a book fervently asserting his loyalty.[33]

The records available to me do not show specifically the motives of those concerned with gold shipments to China. Here and in other chapters I have indicated specifically the attitude and acts of White and his associates in the various dealings with China matters, so far as shown by available data. His is a mixed record. Part of the time, especially in the earlier war years, it was friendly to China; and part of the time unfriendly. I have no evidence whether there was a connection between changes in his attitude and changes in the Communist attitude to China during the war. But in any event it is clear that White's efforts in 1944–1945, while blocking gold shipments to China, to promote a US$10 billion postwar loan to Russia[34] show a strong anti-Chinese and pro-Russian bias. We felt this at the time on the Chinese side. Hsi Te-mou of the Central Bank wrote on March 2, 1945, from Washington to a colleague in Chungking that ". . . there is reason to believe that some elements in the Government here would like to 'wait and see' until such questions as the Kuomintang and the Communist Party are settled."

Certainly the withholding of gold from China aggravated the inflation, with all the grave consequences that followed during and after the war. To say how much that action aggravated inflation would be speculation. But those who held back gold, despite China's pleas and in violation of a clear American commitment, must bear part of the responsibility for later tragic events.

XVIII. THE LAST MONTHS OF WAR

IN the latter half of 1944 the war was entering its final phase. That, of course, could not then be known, and many feared it would be 1946 before Japan could be defeated. The pace of events in China became more frantic. Her armies were more widely and actively engaged than at any time since 1938. On the two Burma fronts they were increasingly successful. But in southeast China and in the north they were being routed. The United States stepped up activities in China, both in the air and in strengthening China's armies, and gave increased Lend-Lease aid. Sino-American controversies came to a head in the second-half of 1944. The army cost issue was adjusted, although a bad taste remained. The military issue was met by the removal of Stilwell and the naming of Wedemeyer. In the diplomatic field, too, there was a change as Ambassador Gauss gave place to General Hurley. The problem of the Chinese Communists became ever more acute. And in the latter part of 1944 inflation began to gain speed, with ominous portents for the future.

BREAKING THE SIEGE

The Hump Produces

Hump tonnage took a great leap forward after Stilwell's Chinese and American forces captured the Myitkyina airfield in May 1944. That made possible a shorter and lower route, while growing Allied air power greatly reduced the danger of enemy interception. From 13,686 tons in May, tonnage rose to 18,235 in June and 25,454 in July.

Meanwhile the bottleneck of communications from Calcutta to the Assam airfields was eased when American railway men under Colonel John A. Appleton, formerly of the Pennsylvania Railroad, took over the Bengal and Assam Railway on March 1, 1944. They raised tonnage 45 per cent in the first month, and more than doubled it in the next few months.[1] That proved to be a crucial move. In the first week of March, the Japanese started their great drive to take the Hump terminals in Assam, seriously threatening the air route to China. The Allies won a touch-and-go victory over the invaders in April–July, and the better working of the railway may have provided the decisive margin.

As experience grew, and more and bigger planes were sent, the Hump tonnage mounted to a peak of 73,691 short tons in July 1945 (71,042 by the military services and 2,649 by CNAC). The table below shows the eastbound tonnage, in approximate monthly averages (short tons):[2]

	CNAC	U.S. *military services*
1942, July (total)	150	85
December (total)	409	1,227
1943, 1st half	722	2,170
2d half	1,058	6,500
1944, 1st half	1,210	13,000
2d half	2,050	26,100
1945, 1st half	2,015	46,226
3d quarter	2,287	54,711

In 1945 about 60 per cent of the eastbound cargo was gasoline and oil.

The movement of goods from China to India was also important. China supplied for the Allied war effort large amounts of tin, tungsten, mercury, antimony, wood oil, bristles, silk, and tea. CNAC moved westward an average of 342 short tons monthly in the second half of 1942, and 600 to 1000 tons monthly thereafter. I can find no figures of what the army moved, except that in the second half of 1942 they moved somewhat more than did CNAC. The army's total movement of goods westward must have been much greater than that by CNAC. Besides both carriers moved large numbers of Chinese troops to India for training, in preparation for the recovery of Burma. Stories about jettisoning human cargo over the Hump to lighten planes are, I believe, apocryphal.

The total tonnage airlifted to China was about 650,000 tons. This, however, was only about equal to the cargo capacity of 70 Liberty ships, and was small relative to China's need. Shortages greatly limited the fighting that could be done in and from China. It was not until about mid-1944 that Hump tonnage equaled the Burma Road's peak in 1941. The airlift, however, was developed up to the capacity of internal distribution in China, which was limited by shortage of vehicles. The largest part of the tonnage went to Chennault and the air forces, but major amounts went to the Chinese arsenals and ground forces.

The build-up of Hump tonnage was a marvelous accomplishment under enormously difficult conditions, even though it lagged far behind schedule and fell far short of meeting China's needs. The cost was great, in men and materials. In the second half of 1943 alone there were 135 major accidents and 168 fatalities. The line of communications ran half-way around the world, about 15,000 miles from the United States. Maintaining and expanding this line was a major effort. Commanders in Europe complained that this operation deprived them of men and transport planes needed for the invasions of Italy and France. The operation, however, showed that a large-scale airlift is feasible at a cost, and its lessons were useful for later airlifts to Berlin and Korea. The official Air Force historians call the operation "the proving ground, if not the birthplace, of mass strategic airlift." [3]

The Road and Pipeline

The road, starting from Ledo in Assam, was to link with the old Burma Road near the China border in northeast Burma. To build it was a huge engineering task, because most of the route lay in difficult mountain and jungle country. Also it was a huge military task, since much of the country had yet to be reconquered. The road's chief advocate was General Stilwell, without whom it would never have been built, and after whom it was later named at Generalissimo Chiang's suggestion. From the start the project was controversial. Opponents felt that the effort needed could be used better in other ways, for example, in strengthening the airlift. The project was approved at the Quebec Conference in August 1943. The plan was to finish the road by about the end of 1944, with an initial capacity of 30,000 tons monthly, and eventually of 65,000. An oil pipeline to parallel the road was also approved at Quebec. It was expected to carry 17,000 tons monthly. Running eastward 1,800 miles from Calcutta, it was said that it would be the longest pipeline in the world.[4]

The road became important even before its completion, in the

North Burma campaign that led to capture of Myitkyina in mid-1944. In 1944 the road carried about 75 per cent of the 500,000 tons of supplies used in that campaign.[5]

By January 1945, the enemy had been driven out of North Burma and the road had been pushed ahead to link with the old Burma Road. The estimated final cost of the road was US$148 million. The first tonnage delivered to China via the new road was in February, and via the pipeline in April. Total deliveries were (thousands of short tons):

1945	Road		Pipeline
	Weight of cargo	Weight of truck plus cargo	Weight moved
February	1.1	5.2	
March	1.5	6.8	
April	4.2	15.4	0.4
May	8.4	28.1	5.5
June	7.0	28.0	5.2
July	5.9	23.4	11.6
August	4.3	15.9	10.9
September	4.3	18.6	12.4

Besides the supplies carried over the road, the replenishment of China's badly run-down road transport and the inward movement of artillery were of major importance. At the end of 1944 there were estimated to be only about 6,000 trucks in Free China, of which about half were near collapse. The road carried to China in this period 25,783 vehicles and 6,539 trailers.[6]

Three of the five Chinese divisions in Burma returned to China by road, after the Japanese defeat there early in 1945, as did the many Chinese at their Ramgarh base, in vehicles under Chinese military control. There was much illicit trade, and a joint American-British study in the spring of 1945 called the road a "Chinese army trade route." It said that shops all along the line from Myitkyina to Kunming were well stocked with goods. American troops were ordered not to inspect, in order to avoid incidents, after seizures of unauthorized goods in Lend-Lease trucks had been recovered by Chinese troops at gun point.[7]

AMERICAN AID AND THE COMMUNISTS

The "United Front" of 1937 of the National Government and the Communists broke down, as it became clear that the Communists were taking advantage of the war to promote their single purpose of taking over China. Marshal Shunroku Hata, Japanese commander in China, in his postwar comments to American interviewers, "disparaged Communist operations against the Japanese, dismissing them by saying the 'Chinese Communists merely resorted to guerrilla warfare and planned the expansion of the area under their influence and the weakening and disintegration of the Nationalist Forces through the war against Japan.'" [8]

Because the Communists, with growing guerrilla forces, were expanding their areas of *de facto* control, their possible greater participation in the fighting gradually became an issue. Bound up with this was the immobilization of sizable government forces in blockading the Communists in the northwest. In January 1943, John S. Service of the American embassy, assigned to Stilwell's staff as a political adviser, analyzed the matter while temporarily in the United States and urged careful American attention to the growing rift in China. He called attention to the possible military value of the Communist forces, especially because of their control of rural areas in North China behind enemy lines. He reported the Communists' hope that they might get "a proportionate share of American supplies sent to China." Commenting on this, Hornbeck opposed "a course of playing both sides in a foreign country, which we have never followed, and which, if followed, would be both vicious and stupid." [9] But during 1943 the issue remained alive, though nebulous in form and academic in view of the relative smallness of American aid to China, the priority of air operations, and the remoteness of Communist-controlled areas from where American land forces were fighting.

In 1944 the matter of the American policy concerning the Communists began to come to a head. There were plans for a possible American invasion of China, which might bring American troops into contact with Communist forces. Questions about the Communists loomed large in Vice-President Henry Wallace's talks with Chiang, when Wallace went to China in June, accompanied by John Carter Vincent of the State Department, and by Owen Lattimore who previously had been a political adviser to the Generalissimo on Roosevelt's recommendation. Chiang told Wallace that Americans were being taken in by talk that these Communists were only "agrarian democrats." Rather, said Chiang, they were "more communistic than the Russian Communists." They indeed wanted Japan's defeat, but they felt it could be accomplished without Chinese resistance. Hence they hoped for collapse of the Chinese Government before the end of the war, so they could take over. They "could and did use the U.S.A. (opinion) to force the Kuomintang to accede to their demands," and these tactics "make a settlement difficult." He wanted the United States "to display 'aloofness.'" He said that "no matter what the Communists say they will do, it will not be carried out." The American Government, he said, had brought much pressure upon China's Government to reach a settlement with the Communists. The "United States Army attitude," he said, "supported the Communists," and he requested Wallace on his return to America "to make it clear that the Communists should come to terms with the Chinese Government." The views of Wallace were shown in his final report of July 10, 1944, which said: "Chiang, at best is a short-time investment. It is not believed that he has the intelligence or political strength to run postwar China. The leaders of postwar China will be brought forward by evolution or revolution, and it now seems more like the latter." [10]

The American Army wanted to send a military group to the Communist base at Yenan, and Wallace raised this issue with Chiang. They wanted all possible information about enemy forces and activities in North China and Manchuria, with a view to future operations. Chiang said he realized the American Army "was anxious that all military power in China be utilized against the Japanese but . . . did not realize the threat which the Communists constituted to the Chinese Government and overestimated the utility of the Communists against the Japanese." He gave permission, nevertheless, for the American Army to send a small group to the Communists at Yenan as observers. This group shortly proceeded, headed by Colonel David D. Barrett, who had been military attaché in China, and it included John S. Service.[11]

With China facing the dangerous enemy drives of mid-1944, the American military leaders longed for use against Japan of the large government forces blockading the Communists in the northwest. Likewise they cast eyes toward the well-organized though poorly equipped Communist troops facing those forces. Roosevelt in his message presented to Chiang August 23, urging that Stilwell command all Chinese forces, said, "When the enemy is pressing us toward possible disaster, it appears unsound to refuse the aid of anyone who will kill Japanese." Realizing that Sino-Russian issues were involved, Roosevelt sent Hurley to China via Moscow. There on August 31 Molotov made his famous declaration of disinterest in the Chinese Communists and said that "his government would be glad to see the United States taking the lead economically, politically, and militarily in Chinese affairs." [12]

On September 4 the War Department indicated to Stilwell that it might provide Lend-Lease arms to a Chinese army that might include Communists. Stilwell on September 23 wanted to arm the Communists, but made it clear that they must first "acknowledge the supreme authority of the GMO [Chiang], and . . . accept command through me." He proposed arming 60 government and five Communist divisions, with priority for the former, but realized that the proposal about the Communists might well be deferred. [13]

After Stilwell's departure, the issue remained alive. In the latter part of 1944 Wedemeyer and his staff explored possibilities of arming and using Communist forces, but only if on a basis to which Chiang would agree. But Wedemeyer put strong restrictions on his staff after an OSS officer went so far in hypothetical discussions at Yenan that Ambassador Hurley felt embarrassed in his efforts to work out a reconciliation of the contending Nationalists and Communists. In January 1945, the Communist General Chu Teh asked for a loan of US$20 million to aid in procuring defection of puppet troops with their arms and equipment, and for sabotage and demolitions behind enemy lines. Hurley rejected the idea. On July 31, when the landing of American forces on China's east coast seemed a near possibility, Wedemeyer recommended to Washington that such forces should "avoid collaboration with any forces opposing the Central Government. [14]

Meanwhile the War Department felt it should have guidance, and asked the State Department for a policy statement for Wedemeyer. A statement of January 29, 1945, was given to Assistant Secretary J. J. McCloy by Acting Secretary of State Joseph C. Grew and later was sent to Wedemeyer. The long-term American objective was "a united, democratic, progressive, and cooperative

China, which will be capable of contributing to the security and the prosperity of the Far East." As a short-term objective of winning the war, the State Department "would like to see the rearmament to such extent as may be practicable to [of?] all Chinese forces willing to fight the Japanese." The statement did not suggest immediately arming the Communists, but in case of operations on the China coast, "it is suggested that our military authorities should be prepared to arm any Chinese forces which they believe can be effectively employed against the Japanese, and that they should at an opportune time so advise the Chinese military authorities." While "it does not necessarily follow," said the statement, "that China should be unified under Chiang Kai-shek," he "appears to be the only leader who now offers a hope of unification," and "the alternative to the support of Chiang . . . might be chaos," though there should be "flexibility" for the long-term objective. Hurley believed that the Communists were told of this statement, and that it stiffened their attitude in resisting his mediation.[15]

On February 26, when Hurley and Wedemeyer were in Washington, Chargé George Atcheson telegraphed from Chungking a message urging that the United States inform Chiang that "we are required by military necessity to cooperate with and supply the Communists and other suitable groups who can aid in this war against the Japanese," beginning on a small scale and without reducing aid to the National Government. The message also raised basic questions as to future American policy, including the attitude toward the National Government and how to avoid involvement with Russia over China. The message had the support of the embassy's political officers and of Wedemeyer's deputy. Hurley was angered, regarding the message as an act of disloyalty. Wedemeyer was uncertain how much value there might be in Communist military action, and was against aiding the Communists. The President agreed with Hurley and Wedemeyer about not aiding the Communists.[16]

In April Hurley again went to China via Moscow. On April 15 he told Stalin of the American desire to unify China and to train and equip its armies with "unification of the armed forces" (including some Communist divisions) under Chiang Kai-shek, and reported that Stalin agreed. Commenting on this message Chargé d'Affaires George Kennan said that Stalin "knows that unification is feasible in a practical sense only on conditions which are acceptable to the Chinese Communist Party," and that the United States should not be misled into "an undue reliance on Soviet aid or even Soviet acquiescence in the achievement of our long term objectives in China." Ambassador Harriman, who had returned from Moscow to Washington, shared those fears, and the State Department instructed Hurley accordingly.[17]

A peaceful settlement of China's fateful internal division and unification of the armies remained goals of American policy. The issue whether to arm the Communists remained in the realm of talk, there was no American invasion, and the actual action conformed to a formula agreed upon in the President's talks with Hurley on August 18, 1944, just before Hurley left for China as the President's personal representative:

> The purpose of the armed Communists being the overthrow of the Government of the Republic of China, it would be futile for the United States to attempt to uphold the Republic while arming a force bent upon its destruction. The President therefore decided that lend-lease material could not be used to arm the Communists unless and until they acknowledged the National Government of the Republic of China and the leadership of Generalissimo Chiang Kai-shek.[18]

I have here treated only the issue of American aid to the Chinese Communists, and not American or Chinese wartime handling of the broader matter of Communism in China, discussion of which would go far beyond the bounds I have set for this book.

RUSSIA'S ATTITUDE AND ACTION

After outbreak of the Pacific War Russia, so far as the evidence shows, continued to follow a technically correct policy of giving only to the constituted government of China such small aid as Russia provided. I have found no basis for believing that Russia gave arms to the Chinese Communists before Russian intervention in the last days of the war. If there were any such aid, as some Chinese believed, it could not have been large. All along, however, Russia must have known that its aid to China made face for pro-Soviet elements and helped them for the long pull.

Some Russian military advisers and technicians stayed in China until mid-1944, but apparently without much influence. Their withdrawal was then explained as due to the need in Russia. But more probably it was connected with Sino-Russian friction in Sinkiang Province and with a shift of Russian policy. When the Russians held at Stalingrad and American forces began to roll back Japan's forces in the Pacific, Russia concluded that survival of her Communist regime was assured. The danger of Japanese attack they felt had passed, China had engrossed a large part of Japan's strength for seven years, and there seemed little more that Nationalist China could contribute to Russian interests.

All through the war, and even for some time afterward, despite Russia's shift to an anti-Chinese attitude, China loyally delivered to Russia agricultural and mineral products to pay principal and interest on the Russian credits of 1938-1939. China sent part of the goods via Central Asia, and part by air to Burma and India and thence by sea. Total deliveries from 1938 to October 31, 1945, were valued at US$131 million. Considering the difficulties of getting and moving the goods under war conditions, China did well. As of October 31, 1945, arrears of deliveries, according to data of the Ministry of Finance, were US$16 million. As of June 1946, China's debt to Russia was about US$55 million, compared with estimated advances of about US$173 million. Thereafter payments by China gradually ceased. It would be interesting to know whether Russia insisted that the Chinese Communists, as a successor regime, assume the unpaid balance.

In 1943-1944 the Russian propaganda line changed from praise of China's resistance to criticism of the Nationalists and praise of China's Communists. Yet criticism of Chungking from Russia was less sharp than that by the Chinese Communists, and even than leftist criticism abroad, which seems to have been partly inspired and promoted by the party line. Russia was still heavily engaged in the war and recognized that the National Government was doing the major fighting against Japan on the mainland. Russia wanted no civil war to interfere. Also Russia could risk no interference with her receipt of war-time aid from the United States.[19] Generalissimo Chiang has charged, however, that Russia spread rumors that China thought of making peace with Japan, thus hoping to cause the United States to reduce its aid to China.[20]

Only one day before the war ended, Russia signed with China the Moscow treaty of August 14, 1945. This treaty confirmed the

Yalta agreement, designed to restore to Russia the Czarist special rights in Manchuria which Japan had seized 40 years before. An exchange of notes accompanying the treaty provided that Russia "agrees to render to China moral support and aid in military supplies and other material resources, such support and aid to be entirely given to the National Government as the central government of China." [21]

Had Russia loyally kept these promises the future in Asia would have been very different. The war, however, ended more quickly and with far less Russian effort in Asia than Russia had expected. The ink was hardly dry on the agreements when Russia started to violate them by giving active aid to the Chinese Communists. To them Russia turned over the huge quantities of Japanese arms captured in Manchuria, in Russia's few days in the war against Japan. Russia blocked the entry of Nationalist troops into Manchuria until the Communists could establish themselves there. And Russia stripped Manchuria by seizing and shipping to Siberia vast amounts of factory equipment and supplies.

Why did Russia suddenly change her policy from that embodied in the exchange of notes of August 14? Was that agreement only smoke screen to cover Russia's already existing intention to follow a different policy? Or did Russia so decide afterward? One interesting opinion is that of former Secretary of State Cordell Hull, as thus described in letter to me of December 28, 1959, from his former close adviser, Stanley K. Hornbeck:

> Cordell Hull insisted in the course of conversations I had with him during his last year that the Russians (i.e. Stalin) had intended in February and in August 1945 to live up to the provisions of the treaties to which in those months they made themselves party, until their noting, after VE Day and VJ Day, the American scrapping of our military establishment, caused them to feel that the opportunity thus afforded them to abandon that intention and embark upon the courses which they have since pursued was too good to be disregarded.

Hornbeck informs me that he himself did not and does not concur in that opinion of Russian intentions. Another view is that Stalin underestimated the strength of the Chinese Communists and their chance of winning. Supporting that view is the comment of the Yugoslav Djilas, who has quoted Stalin as saying on February 10, 1948:

. . . when the war with Japan ended, we invited the Chinese comrades to reach an agreement as to how a modus vivendi with Chiang Kai-shek might be found. They agreed with us in word, but in deed they did it their own way when they got home: they mustered their forces and struck. It has been shown that they were right, and not we.[22]

Only full access to Russian sources of information could show the whole truth; and such access does not seem near. But the record of Russia's international dealings, part of which is contained herein, shows that Russia abides by agreements only to the extent that her interest at the time and the power situation make such action seem to her advisable. Whether Russia would keep her pre-VJ Day agreements with China depended upon the National Government being strong after the war and upon the United States staying strong and being determined to support that government. These latter conditions were not present in the Fall of 1945. So Russia scrapped the 1945 agreements.

LEND-LEASE: AT LAST A SPURT

In 1945 the United States greatly increased Lend-Lease to China. The table below shows total Lend-Lease aid to all countries and to China by years (millions): *

Year	All countries	China	
		Amount	Percentage of total (per cent)
1941	US$ 1,540	US$ 26	1.7
1942	6,893	100	1.5
1943	12,011	49	0.4
1944	14,940	53	0.4
1945	13,713	1,107	8.0
1946	1,751	210	12.0
Totals	US$50,847	US$1,546	3.0

Note: Yearly figures do not add up to totals because of rounding.

The big increase of aid to China to US$1.1 billion in 1945 reflected several things. Access to China vastly improved, with the stepping-up of Hump flights and reopening a land route. The war in Europe ended in early May, easing pressure to furnish Lend-Lease to fight Germany. Moreover, China got about half its 1945 total after the Japanese surrender of September 2, 1945. About

* Letters from State Department, January 10 and March 26, 1958. Adjusted totals for Lend-Lease aid, involving reallocation of appropriations, corrections, etc., are $50,208 million and $1,602 million, respectively. These adjustments have not been allocated by years.

US$300 million represented the cost of flying Chinese troops to such centers as Shanghai, Tientsin, and Peiping to take control and receive the Japanese surrender—the only Chinese forces near to those centers being Communists. Lend-Lease to China continued into 1946, because of the large number of enemy troops in China and because of the need to equip the Chinese troops. From V-J Day through February 1946, Lend-Lease aid of US$600 million went to China.[23]

Lend-Lease goods had piled up in India in 1942–1944 because of the relatively small Hump capacity. For some time these were not properly inventoried or stored, though that condition was remedied by the Spring of 1944. The American authorities in India were then authorized to divert any War Department-procured items needed for American troops or for the American-trained Chinese divisions. China could request replacements.[24] At the end of the war many Lend-Lease goods intended for China remained in India, and others that had been ordered were "in the pipeline." China agreed after the war to buy the "pipeline" goods on long-term payment, the value eventually set being US$50.3 million. The terms were subject to alteration by mutual agreement at the time of an over-all settlement of Lend-Lease accounts. China suspended payments after the National Government withdrew from the mainland, and no over-all settlement has been made.[25]

Britain also provided Lend-Lease aid to China, but in a much smaller amount, since the United States assumed the primary burden of aiding China. British Lend-Lease to China totaled £11 million, mainly supplies and services for Chinese forces in India and Burma and sterling freights on military supplies. Romanus and Sunderland indicate that British Lend-Lease supplies provided in India for Chinese troops training there were equivalent to about US$18 million (say £4.5 million).[26]

LEND-LEASE GOODS TO CHECK INFLATION

Early in 1944 the military authorities at Washington had flatly turned down the idea of experimental air shipment to China of high-value goods, even though these might realize as much *fapi* as an equal weight of bank notes. But Kung and other Chinese leaders were deeply interested in the idea, and continued urging the project. Chiang asked the support of Wallace for this in June

1944, but nothing apparently resulted. A first step seemed to be to seek larger planes (C-46's) for CNAC, and this effort succeeded. Also I explored the availability of goods in India.

Early in 1945 China's persistent urging began to be heard. The inflation was steadily getting worse. And transport was getting better, because of the stepped-up movement by air and the opening of the Stilwell Road from India into China. On February 6, Hurley forwarded China's request for 23,000 tons of textiles as Lend-Lease, to be sold for civilian use as a "counter-inflationary measure to support currency." He said Foreign Minister Soong thought this of "paramount importance," and the Ambassador urged high priority. The American headquarters in China telegraphed on February 27 that if this operation succeeded, 1,000 to 2,000 tons monthly might be brought over the Hump. In a telegram of the same day Adler reported that the American army and the Foreign Economic Administration were thinking of the import from India of textiles to barter for food for the Chinese army. On March 14 the embassy at Chungking reported that General Wedemeyer was greatly worried by the inflation. Adler, in a memorandum of March 19 on "A program for retarding the inflation in China," urged that "everything possible must be done" to assure the inflow of textiles, which "will increase both the supply of goods and government revenues, and thereby reduce the need for expanding note issue." [27] When Leon Henderson was going to China as an American representative to study the inflation, I gave him in Washington a memorandum of March 20 which said that no quick help could be expected from taxation, and that "Obviously the best measure to check inflation is the import and sale of essential goods from abroad." I urged that "use of a small but definite part of available transport over the Hump and/or on the new road to carry goods will certainly help the total military situation by sustaining China." In April Minister Soong approached the British Government about getting goods from India, following up earlier informal discussions. The American Embassy at London reported that the British were worried and wanted to help; also they hoped that "nothing would be done to discourage Soong" and that there could be at least temporary relief. [28]

There were, however, opposing voices of rather striking accord. On November 10, 1944, White gave Morgenthau a memorandum reporting word he had received of a talk of Mao Tse-tung with John S. Service. Mao referred to the plea for cloth: "Cloth! Are we or are we not fighting the Japanese! Is cloth more important than bullets?" The Communists made their own cloth (they grew cotton in areas they controlled), said Mao, so let the Kuomintang make its cloth too! In a letter of February 12, 1945, to White, Adler wrote from Chungking: "We should turn down Chinese requests for goods on civilian Lend-Lease for the ostensible purpose of combatting inflation. There is no escaping the conclusion that the inflation cannot be really combatted in the present set up." Coe of the Treasury, in a memorandum of April 20, 1945, to Morgenthau, marshaled arguments against the project: the American textile situation was tight; transport to China must be conserved; "as in the case of gold sales the anti-inflationary effects . . . would be very small"; the Chinese had not done enough to produce textiles; and the Chinese Government tolerated hoarding of textiles.[29]

The advocates of aid to China at last won out. On April 20, 1945, Soong asked Stettinius for a priority of 3,000 tons of textiles monthly, to be sold in China to check inflation, and also he asked for trucks. Chiang had appealed to Roosevelt; American army headquarters in China supported the request. Morgenthau agreed, despite the view of his subordinates. Assistant Secretary Clayton of the State Department, with whom I had discussed it, supported the idea. Finally the army chiefs in Washington came into line, influenced by Wedemeyer's views and the knowledge that the Chinese army had improved its organization, training, and equipment and was ready to fight. In May, Washington approved procurement under Lend-Lease of 45 million yards of cloth, of which part was to be sought from Mexico and Brazil. Also 4,000 trucks were to be provided for civilian use. The War Department told the Treasury that they wanted 15 million yards monthly for six months, to use to procure food and supplies for the Chinese army. Said Undersecretary Patterson: "If they don't lick them we've got to." [30]

The war ended before import of goods could have any significant counterinflationary effect. Had the program been begun when proposed early in 1944, however, it could have been well worth while, though it is idle to speculate about how far it might have checked financial deterioration.

WARTIME PRODUCTION: THE NELSON MISSION

Under enormous difficulties Nationalist China made a "great leap forward" with wartime output in the little developed west. The growth is thus shown by official data:

	Prewar	1941	1944 Year to June 30
Spindles	17,000	100,000	275,000
Paper (tons)	200	5,200	3,611
Crude oil (gal.)	842	853,000	3,050,000
Gasoline (gal.)	5,406	263,000	3,836,000
Alcohol (gal.)	872,000	5,412,000	9,286,000
Coal (tons)	175,000	1,803,000	6,276,000

The number of industrial plants in Free China grew strikingly:

	1937	1941		1937	1941
Foundries	4	87	Cement	1	7
Machine works	37	376	Alcohol	3	133
Electrical	1	44	Paper	3	14
Chemical	78	380	Flour	6	17
Cotton mills	102	273	Iron	33	112
			Oil refineries	4	42

Many establishments of course were small, and the output often crude, but the over-all result was to help substantially to meet China's need for essential goods.

Aided by nonferrous metals flown over the Hump under Lend-Lease, the arms output in 1941–1945 was "a considerable national achievement in view of difficulties that confronted the Chinese arsenals." The Chinese workers under the efficient direction of General Yu Ta-wei showed astonishing ingenuity. Arsenals were built in caves dug into cliffs to assure protection from bombing. Production included 263,735 rifles with over 600 million rounds of ammunition; 44,718 machine guns; 10,392 mortars with nearly four million rounds of ammunition; and over 16 million hand grenades.[31]

The index of industrial production compiled by the Ministry of Economic Affairs for the area of Free China, based upon prewar as 100, was as follows:

Year	Including export goods	Excluding export goods
1939	133	133
1940	186	214
1941	243	276
1942	302	373
1943	376	520

Despite the relatively good showing there were great difficulties, and production of many essential items was far below what China needed in the war. During the latter part of 1944, the growing inflation began to be felt as a factor working against efficient production. In order to aid China in production, Roosevelt sent to China in August 1944, Donald M. Nelson, then head of the War Production Board, accompanying General Hurley. There were indications, however, that the reason for Nelson's trip was not wholly to be found in the troubles of China. In a memorandum of August 9, Undersecretary of State Stettinius said: "Things are not going well in the WPB, and the President has about decided to send Donald Nelson to Chungking along with Hurley to make a general survey of industry." [32]

Nelson spent about two weeks in China in the autumn of 1944. He found production in a sad state. Arsenals were working at only 55 per cent of capacity. Financial procedures made it hard for essential industries to carry on. Prices of raw materials often exceeded those of finished products, because of price controls of the latter. Production was uncoordinated and there was no real system of priorities.

Nelson urged unification of agencies concerned with production under a War Production Board, which China duly set up under a law granting it broad powers. Chiang asked Nelson to take real charge of the Board, even though a Chinese were at its head. Nelson agreed to work "behind the scene," and undertook to bring out some experts to help to improve output and quality and reduce costs. He hoped to double the output of war industries by the Spring of 1945. Also, to increase Hump tonnage, he helped CNAC get C-46 planes, which had larger capacity than C-47's and C-53's.

In November, Nelson made a second visit to China, bringing five experts in steel production and one in alcohol, which was vitally important as motor fuel. Other experts came later. He arranged for the Central Bank to lend C$10 billion to the War Production Board at cheap rates, and by cutting red tape, he also reduced from several months to a few days the time needed to arrange loans. The experts were competent and worked hard, but were largely frustrated by difficulties caused by mounting inflation. They helped, however, to bring about material increases in output, especially of iron and steel, machine tools, alcohol, and cement. From November 1944 to May 1945 production of some main items increased as follows (in per cent): pig iron, 46; steel, 52; coal, 35; alcohol, 30; and electric power, 8.[33]

Nelson expressed to me in October 1944 the view that production in itself was the best remedy for China's inflation, and he was ready to spend *fapi* heavily to that end. He professed not to be troubled by the risk of financial breakdown. Since the rate of price rise was already at the danger point, I cautioned him and also the Chinese Government of the risk of adding to spending unless the gains would clearly outweigh the financial deterioration that would result. In the conditions existing in 1944–1945, it seemed clear that allocation of fresh credit for almost any purpose would add to the inflation, and was justifiable only to finance the most essential activities. But he was not impressed.*

Hurley reported in June 1945[34] that the Chinese War Production Board had received from the government less funds than expected, and while it had done good work it had not done what it hoped to increase production. C. F. Remer of the State Department, who was then visiting China, did not regard the Board's expenditures as a major factor in the inflation.†

WEDEMEYER AND ARMY REFORM

For years foreign advisers, military and financial, along with

* The economic issue was the nature and extent of unused productive capacity, at a time of grave inflationary pressures. The economy as a whole was quite fully occupied with support of the war and the people's day-to-day activities of subsistence. There was no significant unemployment, but rather there were signs of shortage of man power. There were some unused facilities, as Nelson found, in arsenals and other essential industries. There were other less essential unused facilities, for example, to make iron that was substandard and of little wartime use to the economy.

† Remer reported that the expenditures of the Board had been C$2.5 billion in March and C$4.5 billion in May and that industrial loans by the government banks had been C$5 billion in March and C$8.8 billion in April. Total government spending under the budget and supplementary authorizations (according to later official data) was C$36, C$40, and C$61 billion in March, April, and May, respectively—not including advances to the American army of C$6 and C$20 billion in April and May, respectively. Thus the Board's outlay was of the order of 7 per cent of the total spending of the government; and a smaller percentage if we include advances to the American army.

many patriotic Chinese, urged basic army reform.* The German military advisers in their years of loyal service to mid-1938 made a beginning. They helped China to develop a central force, strong and relatively well-equipped, of unquestioned loyalty to the government. That force remained a bulwark of strength, though badly mauled in the first year of fighting. Yet even during the war, parts of China's huge armies were still controlled by political generals, whose loyalty was precariously gotten by subsidies and persuasion. John P. Davies of the American Embassy in Chungking described the situation in 1943:

> The Chinese Army is not an army in the sense that we use the word army. Rather it is an agglomerate of feudalistic military forces held more or less together by personal loyalties, endowments, grants of aid, threats of superior weight and indifferent toleration. The Generalissimo's relation to this armed mass is variable. A few divisions he can count upon to obey his orders fairly faithfully, within the limits of their ability. Others, no. He wisely does not attempt to issue to some of the more independent commanders orders which he has reason to believe they would not be willing to obey. Many orders are issued only after negotiation with the commander or his Chungking representative.[35]

During the stress of war and successive defeats, such a situation of heterogeneity could not be easily or quickly changed.[36]

A major cause of the army's deterioration in 1937–1945 was the inflation. Pay steadily lost its buying power, and increases were too little and too late. High officers receiving pay for their units in a lump sum all too often took money for their own uses, and engaged in trade and speculation. This had a grave effect on army morale.

Central to the army problem, and of utmost influence for evil politically and socially, was the system of conscription. Toward the end of the war the government made a start of raising the level of the army by drafting some students. These under the old attitude were above such tasks as that of the soldier, who ranked

---

* I had repeatedly urged on financial and economic grounds, during my stay in China, cutting the armies to manageable and effective size, giving adequate pay to the men that were retained; I had also urged that soldiers in the many units not busy with worthwhile military duties, who of necessity were being retained while idle yet paid and fed, be used as labor battalions for needed work that otherwise had to be paid for from the budget. The withdrawal of such men from useful labor, mainly on the farms, tended to raise prices by reducing production; while their pay with printing-press money during the war aggravated inflation. But nothing effective was done.

traditionally at the bottom in the social scale. But basically the system of conscription remained little changed during the war. Its evils were graphically put in a memorandum of August 5, 1945, with which Wedemeyer sent to the Generalissimo a report he had received. It told a tragic story, which may in part have been concealed from the Generalissimo by his subordinates. For the Chinese rural population, it said that conscription is like famine or flood, but came more often. It was a "ravaging disease" that compared to these "like chicken pox with plague."

In practice it seems that [notwithstanding the regulations] the violent forms of onset are the more frequent ones and that only office, influence, and money keep conscription out of your house.

There is first the press gang.

For example, you are working in the field looking after your rice . . . [there come] a number of uniformed men who tie your hands behind your back and take you with them . . . Hoe and plow rust in the field, the wife runs to the magistrate to cry and beg for her husband, the children starve . . .

This very rapid onset has many variations. Another way of being taken is arrest. If one man is wanted for conscription, the Hsienchang [county magistrate] arrests ten. Nine will be given a chance to buy their way out. The poorest stays in jail until the conscription officer takes him over.

. . . The conscription officers make their money in collaboration with the officials and through their press gangs. They extort big sums of money from conscripts which have been turned over to them by the officials and replace them with captives.

Private dealers in conscripts have organized a trade. They are buying able-bodied men from starved families who need rice more urgently than sons, or, they buy them from the Hsienchangs who have a surplus or they pay a man who wants to sell himself because he finds life too difficult and doesn't know any better than to go into the Army . . .

Having been segregated and herded together the conscripts are driven to the training camps . . . Over endless roads they walk, billeting in small hamlets, carrying their rice and rations and nothing else. Many of those who run away run off in the first few days. Later they are too weak to run away. Those who are caught are cruelly beaten . . .

. . . the conscripts' bodies have a great value . . . A conscript's pay can be pocketed and his rations can be sold. That makes him a valuable member of the Chinese Army and that is the basis of the demand for him . . .

If somebody dies his body is left behind. His name on the list is carried along. As long as his death is not reported he continues to be a source of income, increased by the fact that he has ceased to consume. His rice and his pay become a long-lasting token of memory in the pocket of his commanding officer.

. . . Everybody in China, including the Government, knows that the

Chinese army is too big. To cut the Chinese Army in half and to distribute equipment, rations and training facilities to the stronger half and to discharge the weaker half is a measure which had recommended itself for a long time to every military observer who came to this country. But as soldiers are primarily a source of income to officials and a source of political power and influence for generals, which general will allow himself to be robbed of his army?[37]

Thoughtful Chinese were well aware of the situation and anxious for reform.[38] A Chinese correspondent of the influential daily *Ta Kung Pao* of Chungking visited the Hupeh front in May 1943 and prepared a report for private circulation which said:

Under present conditions, which are believed to exist generally throughout the National Government's armies, a division of soldiers may be entirely wiped out by disease, starvation and desertions within two years' time without ever having participated in military operations . . .

The harsh treatment of the common people by the Chinese troops and the Japanese policy of apparent friendliness to them has resulted in making the common people hostile toward their own soldiers.

Stilwell had striven to his utmost for reform. To quote one of his many statements, this in September 1944:

We have the manpower, and we can get the weapons. I know the Chinese soldier. I have seen him fight, and he is as good as any in the world. China's army can make her strong and keep her free. We must make every effort to rebuild the Army.[39]

In 1942–1944 his efforts, for which he deserves full credit, made limited headway, despite his incompatibility with Chiang. But the results fell far short of what was needed. Regardless of personalities, the job certainly should have been actively started as soon as expert American advice was available, and pushed relentlessly as a major national policy of China. Instead, when Stilwell left, except for the armies on the two fronts in Burma, China's armies were still overlarge, underfed, underpaid, poorly equipped, badly organized, and too often badly led.

When Wedemeyer reached China about November 1, 1944, the Japanese drive from East China was threatening Chungking and Kunming. The defending forces were demoralized. He arranged to fly in two Chinese divisions plus their equipment from the Burma front and others from the northwest. They stemmed the enemy tide, aided by the fact that the Japanese halted from lack of supplies and because of their growing fear of the American advance across the Pacific.

Wedemeyer's approach to Chiang and his Chinese associates was sympathetic and friendly. He relied on advice and persuasion, instead of Stilwell's rougher ways. He quickly established good relations, which enabled him to press for reforms. Like Stilwell, he had high regard for the common Chinese soldier when properly fed, equipped, and led. He took up the task of reform where Stilwell had left it. One of his first conclusions was that "simple failure to feed the Chinese soldier underlay most of China's military problems and that the Chinese armies needed food even more than they needed guns." [40] Handing of soldiers' pay and food in lump sums to generals led to grave abuses of understrength units and nonreplacement of men. Stilwell shortly before his departure had ordered a study by his staff of the food situation. This study showed that there was enough indigenous food for a good diet in the southwest part of China, but a sampling of men from five divisions showed 57 per cent or more having at least one nutritional deficiency. One army could not even march without hunger casualties. Early in 1945 the "Logan ration," named after the director of the study, was begun. Within a few months 185,000 men were being properly fed, and became "a physically magnificent army." Army officers who had gained from the old system, however, caused some obstruction; and the Americans, when they pulled out at the end of the war, doubted whether the plan would be continued effectively.[41]

Wedemeyer could not put over the much needed drastic reduction of the number of China's more than 300 divisions. The Generalissimo ordered inactivation of about 200 divisions, but the political state of China and the advantages to individuals of having control of armies was such that most of these divisions would not quit. Wedemeyer arranged therefore to concentrate on training and equipping 39 divisions as a modern striking force. He devised a plan for having American liaison officers attached as advisers to the commanders of units, beginning at lower echelons, and several hundred Americans so served. Disagreements, which proved to be few, were to be referred to the Chinese and American officers at the next higher echelon within 24 hours for settlement, and if necessary similarly on upward to Chiang and

Wedemeyer. An experienced American, General Gilbert X. Cheves, was put in charge of the Chinese Army's supply service, with a staff which eventually included 600 Americans. That brought under control the use of Lend-Lease goods, which all too often had been hoarded or abused. A medical service was developed. Wedemeyer got the Generalissimo to create a joint Chinese-American staff, with frequent meetings. Stilwell had tried for this but had been blocked by War Minister Ho Ying-chin.[42]

When the first Chinese convoy on the new road arrived from India February 4, 1945, Consul W. R. Langdon reported from Kunming about the appearance of the Chinese troops with the convoy, veterans of the North Burma campaign:

Sturdy, cleancut, confident, and jaunty . . . they looked as unlike their local brothers in Chinese uniform as men of a different race. It did not seem possible that food, good care and training could work such a physical and psychological transformation on ordinary Chinese peasant soldier material . . . It is of interest in this connection that the Chinese spectators seemed proud of these soldiers (although they regarded them as aliens), and that General Lung insisted on inviting all of the Chinese enlisted men of the convoy to his reception, where it may be added they did not seem incongruous rubbing elbows with American and Chinese military and civilian dignitaries.[43]

The feared Japanese attack on Kunming and Chungking did not materialize. But in April the enemy tried to take the American air base at Chihchiang in Hunan Province. The newly trained Chinese troops, though not fully ready, repulsed the attack and inflicted heavy losses. The enemy had failed to take account of the improvement of their opponents. Soon the Japanese were pulling back, fearing American landings on the China coast. The Chinese forces advanced, retaking place after place. By V-J Day they had about reached the coast in the south.

As of August 1, 1945, on the eve of the war's end, China had five divisions that had been trained and equipped in India; 11 that had finished training in China; and 22 that were 50 to 75 per cent through training. Each of these 38 divisions had about enough ordnance to be operable in combat. There was, however, no proper replacement system. Much had been done, but not enough to ready the army for its postwar task of filling the power vacuum left by Japan's surrender. Romanus and Sunderland well say: "Many years had passed before rebuilding the Chinese forces within China received first priority from the Chinese and American governments; the lost years were now exacting their price in the unreadiness of the Central Government to re-establish its authority in its own country." [44]

Wedemeyer realized well that China's armies were not yet ready to maintain order, and he wanted to act vigorously. He telegraphed to Marshall August 11 that the United States might be failing to realize "the explosive and portentous possibilities in China when Japan surrenders." He feared the Communists would begin civil war and that the Japanese might refuse to give up. The War Department in reply directed him to continue to support the Central Government and to aid reoccupation by moving Chinese troops, but maintained the contradictory position notified to him on August 10 that the United States "will not support the Central Government of China in fratricidal war." On August 22, a week after V-J Day, the War Department suspended all American-supervised training, apparently because the units concerned had to move to reoccupy Japanese-held areas. Two American divisions were shortly sent to China for temporary duty to help disarm and demobilize the Japanese. But the Chinese army was soon on its own. [45]

THE PROJECTED AMERICAN LANDINGS IN CHINA

In 1943–1944 an American invasion of China had been planned as one of the major moves to defeat Japan. Stilwell's proposals to the Generalissimo to be offered at Cairo included:

In the event that communications are reopened through Burma and necessary equipment is supplied, an operation will be conducted to seize the Canton-Hongkong area and open communication by sea.

The United States would then put strong forces into South China. [46]

The American military authorities were worried about how to meet local costs if they had to land in an area plagued by inflation and almost bare of supplies. At the invitation of Major General R. L. Maxwell of the General Staff, I conferred at the Pentagon and spoke to a group of officers on October 6, 1944. I explained that China was in the danger zone of inflation, from which runaway inflation could easily develop. A major military success could greatly help to prevent this. As to the American interest in stability in China and methods of financing I said:

American military operations in China will proceed much more smoothly and efficiently if the Chinese Government throughout these areas as far as possible is a going concern. The American Army in China will require many things which it will be very difficult to get unless it is through the Chinese Government—such as labor and local supplies and local transport. Therefore, everything possible should be done both to check inflation and to sustain the Chinese Government . . .

I would urge that consideration be given to the method of financing in kind as far as the logistics will permit it. That method has been tried and has worked well in China, notably at the time of the great flood of 1931 when 15,000,000 bushels of wheat and flour were gotten from the U.S. on credit and used to employ over a million men who rebuilt 4,000 miles of dikes.

When there is a landing in China, the forces will land in an area pretty barren of supplies. The Japs have taken away all that they can lay their hands on, completely disregarding the welfare of the local area. If the military forces are to obtain the services that they will require in the way of labor from the local population it will be difficult to get them from a population that is completely undernourished. The most effective way is to bring in certain supplies, such as wheat, flour, and cotton cloth, that can be used in some method of payment in kind. The men could draw these, and they would gain in strength and be better able to render services desired by the Army.[47]

Assistant Secretary of War John J. McCloy asked me to develop the subject further. I did so in a memorandum transmitted to him October 21, which I explained I wrote in a personal capacity and not necessarily as stating the the views of the Chinese Government which I presumed would be officially consulted at the appropriate time. I also gave a copy similarly to the State Department. This memorandum urged using goods for payment in kind for supplies and labor so far as logistics allowed; selling goods for American account to get money by noninflationary means; and opening up communications with the interior, especially using small water craft, to get supplies. There were specific recommendations as to kinds of goods to be brought in and how to handle them to protect against profiteering and ensure that they would go into use and not to hoards. Such a program would have administered minimum relief to the area, as well as helped to meet military needs. Something also might be done, I stated, by selling gold, preferably tokens, coordinated with China's gold sales program; but sale of silver was inadvisable both because of its bulk and for monetary reasons. I stressed that "the methods of American military finance should take particular account of effects upon China as well as of peculiarly American problems." The memorandum concluded by calling attention to "the vital need for the future of having China as strong and stable as possible to help hold Japan in check and to steady the situation in Asia."

Especially because of the dangers of financial collapse during or after the war, I several times urged informally at this stage to contacts in the State and War Departments the earliest possible invasion of the China coast. The State Department agreed with this viewpoint, and Hamilton later told me that he advocated a timely landing and felt that failure to make it was a major blunder of the war.

Both the National Government and the Communists wanted an American landing. The government wanted the help it would bring with arms, better communications than the tenuous Hump route, the shortening of the war, and also the uplift to morale which would tend to check economic and financial deterioration. On October 6, 1944, the *Ta Kung Pao* of Chungking called for opening of a "second front" in China by the United States and Great Britain.[48] As to the Communist view, Service reported from Yenan in the Fall of 1944, that Mao Tse-tung said in an interview:

> The Kuomintang . . . fears an American landing in China only second to Russian participation in the Far Eastern war.
>
> . . . If there is a landing, the Americans will have to cooperate with both the Kuomintang and the Communists, as the Communists are the inner ring and Kuomintang is further back.[49]

I can recall no indication that the National Government feared an American landing.

Detailed plans and preparations for a landing and for the necessary related offensive by the Chinese army had been delayed by Chinese-American friction in the Stilwell period. Early in 1945, however, after the Japanese drive in Southeast China had been stemmed, Wedemeyer and his staff planned the operation for July–August. They received the approval of Chiang and the American General Staff. The prospect of carrying out the operation improved after the American landing on Okinawa on April 1, because the Japanese decided to shorten their lines in China and to try to hold the part of the coast farther north opposite the main islands. As the Japanese withdrew, strong Chinese forces began driving toward the southeast coast. These forces retook Liuchow late in June, and Kweilin about August 1. They were approaching the coast at Fort Bayard, 200 miles southwest of Canton, in the first days of August, and the American command in the Pacific made hurried plans to land at Fort Bayard. But all this was called off on August 12 after the atom bomb fell, Russia joined in the Pacific War, and Japan offered to surrender.[50]

The failure to make a timely landing on the China coast was bound up with the interrelated events hereinbefore described: the American failure to supply earlier and larger aid to China; China's failure to do more about army reform; the 1943 decision to build air power, which shifted emphasis from army reform and led to the Japanese drive against the East China air bases and the resulting defeat of the Chinese armies; Sino-American friction over army costs; the issues between the Generalissimo and Stilwell; and finally the abrupt ending of the war. Basically the American policy was a strictly military approach, and neglect of political and postwar angles. The island-hopping strategy in the Pacific was bringing good results, and the planners thought of the China theater mainly as ancillary to that operation. There was little regard for the idea that China deserved to be rescued after her years of suffering in the struggle for the common cause against huge odds, or for what would happen later. Wedemeyer has since described the basic attitude of the over-all strategy as disregarding "the vital interests of our Chinese allies, who were expected simply to go along with us, Britain, and Russia, at any cost to themselves." Quoting the official army historians, Romanus and Sunderland, he writes:

"The Joint Chiefs of Staff were aware," it is written, "that whatever might happen in China, sixty Russian divisions were promised against Japan, and these operations would sweep south and east below the Great Wall." Thus, "Chinese bases were no longer considered essential in the war against Japan." There remained only "the problems which would be created if the Generalissimo signed a separate peace . . ." There was no thought at all of the fatal consequences to China and ourselves of bringing the Soviet Union into the

Far Eastern War. Instead of trying to keep the Red Army out of China, we were happy to have her come in, and practically discarded a traditional friend, China.[51]

What might have been the gains of the government and Communists, respectively, had a landing been made in Southeast China well before the war's end? I feel now, as I did then, that such a landing of liberation would have been most helpful to the government. There was relatively little Communist strength in that area, and the landing forces would have joined up with non-Communist units. There would have been no occasion for Americans who took a purely military view, or for Communist sympathizers and/or supporters, to argue for arming Communist forces. Such a landing would have enheartened China after long years of war-weariness, and strengthened the government's prestige. It could have helped to stave off the worst stage of wartime inflation. The government would have gained experience in rehabilitating recovered territory, and at the war's end its civil organization and troops would have been located nearer to China's main economic centers. In such a postwar situation, the government would have had a better chance to put China again on the path to stability and progress.

XIX. PLANNING REHABILITATION
AND DEVELOPMENT

BY 1943 it seemed clear that China was on the winning side, even though the war's end was not in sight. Wartime problems had to have priority, but it was time to begin to plan for the future. The first need was to restore the nation as a going concern. When fighting ended, China was sure to face a huge problem of repairing war damage. Just as sure, though less clear to most, would be the need to restore a working economic system and effective government throughout the country. Businesses had been disrupted and organizations scattered. Working capital had largely gone. The government's administrative organization in occupied areas was broken, as loyal staff fled from the enemy or had to abandon their posts and were replaced by Japanese and puppets.

Also there was a vital urge to develop China's great potential and to attain in fact the place already assigned as a leading power. In past ages China at times had been second to none in civilization and culture. Nationalism and pride aimed for China again to take a place commensurate with her history, numbers, and resources.

Underlying all were two major problems. The ever-growing inflation was insidiously affecting every phase of national life. Nothing could be stable until the finances were stable. And the Communists were taking advantage of confusion to build armed forces and extend their hold over millions of people.

RELIEF AND ECONOMIC REHABILITATION

Over half of China's people were in areas that came under enemy occupation during the war. Property loss was enormous. Physical rehabilitation was basic for economic and financial recovery and for future progress.

The United Nations Relief and Rehabilitation Administration (UNRRA) was created in October 1943, at a conference at Atlantic City, New Jersey. To plan the program for China, the government set up a commission, to which I was appointed adviser. UNRRA sent to China in the Spring of 1944 two Americans, Owen L. Dawson and Eugene Staley, as consultants. Dr. J. B. Grant, a Canadian physician with the Rockefeller Foundation and then in Calcutta, was named as medical consultant. This commission worked actively with the various branches of the Chinese Government, and made a detailed estimate of future needs. T. F. Tsiang was China's chief representative in handling these problems.

In September 1944, Tsiang presented to UNRRA China's program, under the headings of food, clothing, shelter, health and medical care, transport and communications, agriculture, industries, flooded areas, welfare services, and displaced persons.[1] China asked UNRRA to provide imported requirements of US$945 million and over 2,000 foreign experts to aid in operating the program. The request, however, covered only 37 per cent of China's estimated need of US$2.5 billion of imports for the full program of relief and rehabilitation. In addition there were the costs in local currency, figured as equivalent to C$2.7 billion at prewar value of about US$0.30. These internal costs were equivalent to about US$810 million, or roughly a third of the external costs. In figuring internal costs, we used the prewar unit, because inflation made it impossible to have useful estimates in depreciating money.

China's request was reasonably realistic except in the fields of clothing, industrial rehabilitation, and public health. In the latter two fields, the proposals went far beyond restoration, into new development. This was understandable since in restoring it is easy to plan to rebuild better. But China's internal resources of men and money were limited. First things, namely basic economic and financial rehabilitation, needed to come first. The public health proposal illustrated what was involved as to internal financing. It called for total outlay in the first year of C$247 million prewar value (US$74 million), comprising C$135 million for capital purposes and C$112 million for running expenses. The total was about equivalent to the entire prewar civil expenditure of the government. I objected, urging in a letter of August 18, 1944, that China's interests would best be served "by concentrating in the first couple of years upon the restoration of monetary stability" and doing "only the most essential things." Tsiang agreed, but Chungking insisted on keeping most of the proposal.

UNRRA raised the question of how far China could pay the external costs of rehabilitation.* For advice on capacity of foreign governments to pay, UNRRA set up a committee headed by White of the Treasury, with British, Canadian, Mexican, and Norwegian members. At the request of the Chinese Government I represented China in this negotiation and presented to UNRRA a full analysis of the problem under date of July 9, 1945.[2] This analysis argued that China's prospective external assets at the war's end would be fully needed as currency reserve and to bring about financial stabilization. Prospective receipts from UNRRA and other sources, even if UNRRA provided the full amount asked, would fall short by a figure of the order of US$1.5 billion of meeting the estimated needs for rehabilitation. Therefore China considered that it was not in position to pay in foreign currency for the items requested.

China asked UNRRA's help also in meeting internal costs. China's estimate of C$2.7 billion (prewar currency), however, was far more than there was a chance of raising and spending. With a budget deficit estimated at C$1.3 billion (prewar currency) for the first two postwar years, it was vital to spend only for the most essential needs. The checking of inflation was a high priority. My close touch with European finances after World War I led me to advise all concerned that inflation in China after the war would be fully as grave a problem as during the war. Imports of UNRRA goods would help to counter inflation by adding to the supply of goods. But, beyond that, China would need help in meeting the local costs of the program. Such help should come "primarily from sale and use in kind of goods, and from sale of foreign exchange." Import of goods to be sold to produce local currency for internal costs of rehabilitation, I

---

* This was done under the terms of the Atlantic City resolution 14 which provided: "Although payment for relief and rehabilitation supplies and services shall be considered to have a strong claim on the foreign exchange assets of the applicant country, due consideration shall be given also to its needs of foreign exchange for other purposes."

urged, should be handled as far as possible through the ordinary commercial banking system, rather than through bureaucratic import and sale of goods. My proposal as to procedure was:

> . . . any system of official handling of internal sale of imports is inevitably cumbersome and bureaucratic, and will tend to interfere with restoring the normal flow of goods. Hence controlled trade and official handling should give place to private trade as rapidly as conditions permit. Therefore, as soon as imports through ordinary channels can be resumed, some simple procedure should be set up whereby to an agreed extent the original cost of the goods would be provided out of foreign funds, but the Chinese currency proceeds realized from sale would be applied to cover internal expenditures. Such a procedure might be, for example, that banks in China would open credits abroad in ordinary course for purchase of imports, the foreign exchange to be provided out of the foreign funds. The money paid by importers in Chinese credits would be turned over to the authorities concerned, less a commission to the bank.[3]

But this proposal was not adopted.*

UNRRA agreed that China should not be asked to pay the foreign currency costs. It is of interest that White supported China's proposal in this matter when it came before the UNRRA committee. I noted in my diary of July 27 that the British and Norwegians wanted to cut China's program, but that "White, supported by Canadians, said China had suffered beyond imagination, and should not be pressed to cut." † At a meeting on July 25 of a subcommittee headed by Irving Friedman, of the Treasury, Friedman remarked, according to a memorandum of the meeting, that "the more he studied the Chinese memorandum, the less he found in it with which to quarrel." The meeting developed some difference of opinion, however, about whether a large use of external resources to finance internal costs was con-

---

* I have made similar proposals since as a consultant on American aid programs. (See my letter to the *New York Times*, February 5, 1961.) But so far without success. Officials seem to feel that the cumbersome and expensive methods of governmental controls are needed to satisfy Congress.

† White's support of China in this matter contrasts with his anti-Chinese attitude in other matters in 1943–1945. In view of charges that he was part of the Communist apparatus, it could be argued that this incident shows he was independent. On the other hand, it could be argued that China's case was so clear that it would have been hard to oppose it; and also that at this time legislation to authorize American participation in the International Monetary Fund was pending, and White was being conciliatory because he hoped for an important post after the Fund came into being.

sistent with the UNRRA policy that recipient countries should primarily bear the internal costs.* The subcommittee finally included the Chinese proposals on this head, but with an indication of some difference of opinion within the subcommittee on the subject. This discussion foreshadowed difficulties met later in actual operation, in the effort to meet the heavy internal costs with the minimum of inflationary effect.

With the ending of the war in August, UNRRA's program began to go into operation. UNRRA eventually provided to China about 2.5 million tons of supplies costing about US$518 million, or more than half of the sum China first requested. UNRRA also sent over 1,000 foreign personnel. The internal costs incurred were roughly estimated as equivalent to about US$191 million, of which China paid about three-fifths and the balance came from sale of UNRRA goods and special UNRRA contributions.[4]

CAN CHINA HAVE INTERNATIONAL HELP TO STABILIZE HER FINANCES?

Stabilizing China's finances after the war was bound to be a highly difficult undertaking. In the last months of the war, inflation was beginning to spiral. The costs of taking back the occupied area were sure to be immense, revenue recovery slow, and a serious deficit certain. Large-scale external help was essential, both with money and to influence policy. Money would be in danger of being wasted unless there were "strings," in the form of understandings about the use of the aid and the internal policies needed for success. Without some form of outside stiffening, by firm, competent, and disinterested external participation in making and executing policy, stabilization of the finances was most unlikely.

After World War I, Austria and Hungary were pulled out of the tailspin of inflation only when the League of Nations helped with reforms. I was close to these events because, as the Economic Adviser to the Department of State, I had charge of matters relating to the American interest in European financial problems. In 1943–1945 I hoped for some form of external participation to

---

* Resolution 14 of the Atlantic City Conference stated: "The Council recommends that so far as possible all expenses of the Administration within a liberated area shall be borne by the government of such area, and shall be paid in local currency made available by the government of the area or *derived from the proceeds of the sale of supplies*" (emphasis added).

aid reforms in China, because conditions were so serious that nothing else would suffice.

There were several opportunities during the war to begin creation of machinery for international cooperation in helping to solve China's postwar financial problems. As early as the Spring of 1941, the British suggested a joint Anglo-American economic mission to China. Its aim would be to advise on developing the economic potential for war, the best use of external aid, and general policies for postwar reconstruction. But Washington was cool to the idea. I have already recounted the troubles then met in working out Sino-American-British cooperation in the one field of currency stabilization (chapter X). Such an economic mission, had it been properly created and staffed and had it worked with real cooperation, might have done invaluable work to help save the situation.

The next possibility of machinery to aid in financial reform was through the Chinese-American-British Stabilization Board, created in 1941. After the Board was evacuated from Hong Kong to Chungking, at the time of Japan's attack, the Board's duties were light. Foreign trade had fallen to a trickle. The British member inclined toward suspension of the Board's operations. But the other members opposed this, and Solomon Adler, acting alternate American member, telegraphed to Morgenthau on March 5, 1942, that suspension would "emphasize China's isolation" and "further weaken American and British prestige and influence here." [5] In mid-1943 the question arose of extending the American agreement, due to expire June 30. The British agreement had no specific limit, but of course ending the American agreement would end the whole arrangement. Kung was not happy with some of the terms. He was inclined at first to wind up the Board. Some elements of Chinese nationalism, stimulated by the war, were in opposition to the agreements. They argued that the Central Bank could handle future problems of exchange control, as do central banks generally; that organs like the Stabilization Board did not exist elsewhere and were unnecessary in China; and that after the war China would need credit of so much more than US$50 million that it would not much matter if the agreement lapsed.

The American Treasury too was inclined to terminate, because of growing trouble about the 20–1 exchange rate and a feeling that American sharing in the Board's work associated the United States with the rate policy. Britain, however, took a longer view. London thought the Board ought to remain, because it gave continuing contact with the British and American Treasuries which could prove invaluable in postwar monetary reform and which it would be hard to recreate.

K. P. Chen, Chairman of the Board, favored keeping it and said in a letter of June 29 to Minister Kung:

> To see China able to meet all currency problems on her strength is the fervent hope and aspiration of all. But under the present unusually difficult circumstances and disturbed world conditions, I am convinced that the closest collaboration and co-operation between our country and the United States and Great Britain is a desirable and important factor, particularly for the period of postwar reconstruction. Co-operation, not only between governments in general, but also between Treasuries and Central Banks in particular, was never more desired than it is today. The problems to be faced are so great and so interconnected that a common sharing of experience and knowledge, a common pool of resources and a closer association in matters of policy cannot but be of the greatest value. It is also my belief that a Board such as we have today, on which the American and British members sit in a spirit of sincere co-operation, could be developed into an instrument most effectively to further these ends and might be expected, if desired, to help towards reorganizing our currency system when the occasion arises.

I shared Chen's view and urged keeping the Board but amending the agreements to meet China's minimum objections. Also I urged that China should keep access to the US$50 million credit and the unused part of the British credit of £5 million.

There were numerous conferences on the problem, before and after the June 30 deadline. The upshot was that Kung became convinced that it would be wise to retain the agreements in revised form, because they would help to keep close financial relations with the United States and Britain. He telegraphed to Washington directing his representatives to see the Treasury about a revision. It was unfortunate that China did not ask a temporary extension from June 30 which I urged, to allow time for discussion, rather than let the agreement technically lapse.

On June 29 and July 6 P. W. Kuo and T. M. Hsi called at the Treasury and said that China wanted a revision "in accordance with the spirit and principles of Lend-Lease." The Treasury explained that the stabilization credit involved quite different principles. At Chungking we were preparing detailed instructions about revision when on July 26 the Treasury instructed Adler to resign unless he had strong reasons to the contrary. He replied on July 29:

> If Treasury envisages future establishment of counterpart of Board to facilitate post-war monetary cooperation, it would be preferable to preserve continuity. If not, there is no strong reason for my not resigning.[6]

The Treasury, unimpressed, told Adler to submit his resignation. When he saw Kung August 3 he reported:

> Saw Dr. Kung yesterday and notified him according to instructions. He was first taken aback but then said it was a pity that action was being taken at very time when Ministry of Finance was about to renew 1941 Agreement subject to specific revisions it had been preparing for your consideration.

On August 4 the Board stopped taking applications, understanding from Kung that it would be wound up. That caused confusion and after a few days Kung asked them to resume operations. He did not accept Adler's resignation, and the Treasury authorized Adler to withdraw it temporarily.[7]

On September 6, 1943, Kung telegraphed to his Washington representatives detailed instructions about seeking a revised agreement. They presented China's views to the Treasury and also to the British financial representative in Washington. The British view, communicated both to China and the Treasury, was that if the Board now disappeared it would discredit an organization of this type and make it hard to set up similar machinery for postwar needs. But the American Treasury held other views. On September 22 White told Morgenthau that the changes China wished could probably be arranged, but that he doubted whether the agreements should be renewed because China's official exchange rate was so out of line. Here we meet some of the results of the growing tension on army costs. Morgenthau agreed with White but wanted him first to talk to the State Department.[8]

On October 6 members of the State and Treasury Departments conferred. But the record indicates that White did not present the subject fairly. According to the State Department memorandum he said, "The most important proposal made by the Chinese was that the 1941 rate of exchange . . . should continue to govern the revised agreement," and renewal on that basis was "economically and financially unsound." He felt that absence of a stabilization agreement would clear the way for American use of the "black market," if desired. White proposed stalling and the State Department concurred. On October 13, however, Friedman of the Treasury told a member of the State Department that the changes sought by China were on "minor points":

> Contrary to Mr. Stanton's report on Mr. White's statement during the conversation of October 6, to the effect that "the most important proposal made by the Chinese was that the 1941 rate of exchange . . . should continue to govern the revised agreement," Mr. Friedman said that it was his impression that the Chinese did not discuss exchange rates specifically, though probably their silence on this point implied that they did not contemplate any change in the 1941 rate.[9]

Friedman's statement thus conforms to what White told Morgenthau, that is, that the changes China wished could probably be arranged.

On November 10 the Chinese representatives reported their talk with White. He told them that the Treasury preferred to end the agreements because they wished no responsibility for the official rate, wanted to respect China's sovereignty, and felt the Board was no longer useful. The Chinese representatives pointed out that Britain, as well as China, wanted the Board to remain. White said the United States knew that but that the agreement had expired, and he indicated that the British view would not affect the American decision.[10] That view had meanwhile been put to the Treasury by Sir David Waley, their representative in Washington. But Sir David had not convinced White. Belatedly and inadequately a member of the British Embassy presented the matter to the State Department on November 25. But the decision had then been taken.[11]

Upon receiving the report of November 10 on the Treasury's view, Kung decided to drop the matter. He never had been whole-heartedly in favor of keeping the agreements, though he had really tried for a revision. In my diary on November 19 I noted that I agreed with the British view on keeping the Board, but that ". . . fundamentally China doesn't want it. China's action partly reflects fact that T. V. [Soong] negotiated it, that U.S. Treasury did a poor job of drafting without regard for China's susceptibility, that T.V. did not try seriously to cure the defects, and ambition of the Central Bank, also feeling of nationalism." Further I noted that the British view in favor of keeping the Board as a means of Sino-American-British cooperation was disliked in Chungking, and that ". . . fundamental feeling of highest officials distrusts G.B. They wish to play with U.S. rather than G.B. internationally." When Britain proposed reconstituting the Hong Kong Committee, which operated the 1939 fund, solely to prepare its eventual liquidation, China objected; and I noted that the Generalissimo "hates the whole business."*

"Rather ironic," I noted in my diary of February 29, 1944, "that China is ending [the stabilization agreements] . . . in the midst of the greatest instability yet." In February the free market for dollars ranged between 90 and 245. China, however, was ready in the latter part of 1943 to keep the Board if Washington had been willing. The biggest factor in ending the agreements was American irritation over China's reluctance to consider some expedient to temper the effects of the unrealistic 20 to 1 rate. This irritation was part of the price China paid for her intransigence. Yet it was a pity that the advantage of keeping a framework of international financial cooperation was not presented fully and in time to the State Department either by the Chinese or the British; and by the State Department to the Treasury. And the available record does not indicate that this angle was

---

* In the latter part of November, Kung told the Board it was to cease operations from the end of the month and sent instructions to Washington and London about winding up agreements. The Board's operations were turned over to the Central Bank and the Commission for the Control of Foreign Exchange Assets. On December 8, the Board's termination became known at Chungking and was telegraphed abroad, though not officially announced.

Formal winding up entailed complex legal and technical problems, involving mainly the British side. No money was owed to the American Government, but early in 1944 the Board held about £2.25 million of funds advanced by Britain under the 1939 agreement, and about £2 million under that of 1941. Finally, in February 1944, the British Treasury gave formal notice of termination. They proposed formal reconstitution of the Hong Kong Committee that operated the 1939 fund solely to prepare its eventual liquidation, which had to await the ending of the war and learning the exact situation about presenting claims for the Chinese currency belonging to the Board, which the Japanese had seized at Shanghai and Hong Kong in December 1941. But China objected even to this formal action and the Board appointed the Central Bank as trustee to handle its affairs. The Board drew up its final accounts as of March 31, 1944. China repaid with interest the amount due to Britain under the 1941 agreement, mostly by using the aforementioned balances, and Britain repaid the British banks' subscription to the 1939 Fund (see Ministry of Finance announcement, Chungking, April 13, 1945).

ever stressed to Morgenthau. Unfortunately it could not be learned by actual experience how much the maintenance of the Board could have helped toward China's postwar recovery.

Soon after the lapse of the Stabilization Board, there was another missed opportunity to set up machinery to deal with China's postwar financial rehabilitation. At the end of 1943, the State Department wanted to arrange a special American commission, or a joint Chinese-American commission, for a broad discussion of China's problems, including the financing of postwar needs. But unhappily that idea dropped out of sight, when the Treasury and War Departments took the lead in handling the controversy on American army costs, and the State Department was crowded out.

Another good opportunity arose toward the end of the war when China sought large aid, both by credits and technical advice. To some extent the American Treasury faced up to the postwar problem when it urged China in the Spring of 1945, during the negotiations on gold, to adopt a broad program to stabilize the currency and check inflation and to set up a currency reserve fund of US$500 million.[12] But much more was needed: (1) strong emphasis by the United States on the priority in China of economic and financial restoration, and de-emphasis meanwhile of new development; and (2) seeking some procedure or machinery to develop and stiffen in China forces making for stability.

The problem of China's postwar financial stability indeed was primarily China's internal affair. But the outcome of its handling was fraught with vital consequences for the United States and the free world.

CHINA AND THE INTERNATIONAL MONETARY FUND AND BANK

A further possibility of external help in the stabilization of China's postwar finances appeared, in connection with the White and Keynes proposals for postwar monetary arrangements. The proposals were welcomed when they reached Chungking early in 1943. An international monetary agency could be invaluable in helping to restore China's finances. The American proposal, however, which became the basis of discussions, was that all countries fix in gold the value of their currencies before the Fund operated. Some countries might be able to do that soon after the war ended. But certainly China could not. Neither plan came to grips with the urgent problem of restoring the finances of war-damaged countries having acute inflation. Their stability and even their fate was likely to depend on solving this problem. For much of the world financial rehabilitation would be more urgent and for some time more important than to devise a scheme to work after recovery had taken place.

After full discussion of the plans in Chungking, there was agreement that after the war China would need a transitional period to rehabilitate the economy, national finances, and currency. The Chinese experts who met with the Treasury in Washington in June 1943 pointed this out. But they did not press very hard. On May 4, I wrote in my diary:

> Meeting to discuss with T. L. Soong about monetary plans as he is about to leave. I raised question about China's probable inability to agree on gold parity till after the war. But I was shouted down, as they do not wish to face up to this and do not want it to interfere with full membership. They also want to play with U.S. Treasury, as there will be so much need for help. But it is not wise to disregard the future—and U.S. plan is all wrong in suggesting that fixed exchange is the starting point, rather than the reform of individual situations largely by internal action but with external aid.

In support of the Chinese position, I sent informally to the State Department on July 20, 1943, a memorandum on the subject. While sympathizing with the desire for earliest possible stabilization of currency values, I felt that "Neither plan adequately recognizes the need for monetary rehabilitation as preliminary to longer-term stabilization." "Repair of . . . injured monetary systems," I said, is "quite analogous to relief and repair of war devastation—though infinitely more difficult," and "will require an all-out effort by the respective countries in a period of exhaustion," plus external help. I urged that the plans take this into account, and provide for "a transitional period of monetary rehabilitation." [13]

The views of the Chinese Government were formally transmitted in Washington on September 3. China welcomed the idea of a monetary agency for postwar international cooperation, but felt its chance of success would be greater if it could include in its scope the problem of monetary rehabilitation. The comment stressed the need for transitional arrangements and the view that stability of international exchange rates had to rest upon a sound structure of stable individual monetary systems. These in turn should be related to each other by exchange rates on the basis of which international balances of payments can be maintained in equilibrium. Therefore the first step should be to restore the individual monetary systems. China's detailed proposals were embodied in a suggested redraft of the plan, an extract of which is given in appendix IV.

Unfortunately the Treasury never gave serious thought to China's proposal. White was pursuing his set ideas about the working of a "normal" postwar system of international exchange. Surely plans for postwar monetary recovery should have had at least equal place. American interest in postwar stability through-out the world warranted a more serious effort to work out some cooperative procedure when China raised the problem in 1943.

For months representatives of the chief countries negotiated actively with the American Treasury. The Chinese experts made no headway about introducing flexibility for the fixing of initial rates. The joint statement of the experts of all the countries, which formed the basis for the Bretton Woods conference and was made public in April 1944, provided that each country should fix a gold parity for its currency "when it is admitted to member-ship" in the Fund. The Treasury was anxious to issue the state-ment at once without change, for reasons of American politics. Kung acquiesced but stated that China would have to bring up later questions affecting her ability to meet her obligations under the proposed agreement. In this matter China sought to co-operate in every way with the United States, which had granted large aid and on whom China expected to rely heavily in the future.

Clearly China and other invaded countries were entitled to have a recognized status of membership in any general postwar monetary organization, but without the risk of being obliged to agree prematurely upon a gold parity. Yet as the American-British draft stood right up to the Bretton Woods conference, such countries could not have joined at the outset. White's origi-nal conception of immediately fixed rates of exchange was based upon preparing to fight again the currency battles of the 1930's, when competitive devaluation was a serious problem. Based on experience in China I felt sure that the main postwar trouble in this field would be just the opposite—to get countries to adopt realistic rates and avoid dangerous overvaluation. On coming to the United States in June 1944, as a member of the Chinese delegation, I urged this viewpoint strongly on members of the chief delegations and pressed for flexible transitional arrangements. Professor Dennis H. (later Sir Dennis) Robertson of the British delegation was especially understanding of this need, and at the Bretton Woods conference Tsuyee Pei and I worked closely with him in drafting Article XX, Section 4, on "Initial determination of par values." That and other special clauses for invaded countries gave the needed flexibility. But there was no provision for international aid in rehabilitating the finances of war-stricken countries.

As the time drew near for the Bretton Woods conference, there were hard negotiations about the quotas of the various countries. This issue involved not only the extent to which the Fund could meet any emergency needs for drawing funds but also national prestige and voting power in the Fund. Numerous computations were made based on various formulas, and they affected the eventual decision, though ultimately it partook of the nature of a horse trade. China was anxious to be one of the "big four," with the United States, Britain, and Russia. At that stage Russia was cooperating, and her delegates signed the Bretton Woods agreements. In the earlier stages a quota of US$350 million was mentioned for China. But in the Spring of 1944 the discussion was on the basis of US$500–600 million. In a telegram of April 5, T. M. Hsi reported from Washington that the British plan would give China fifth place, below Burma-India. China objected, and White agreed with the Chinese position. When the experts' statement was published April 21, Morgenthau said that China would be among the first four with a quota in the neighborhood of US$600 million.

In the final agreement China's quota was set at US$550 million. That compared with US$2.75 billion for the United States, US$1.3 billion for the United Kingdom, and US$1.2 billion for Russia. Earlier, the Russian quota had been proposed as US$1 billion, but during the conference Russia insisted on more. Kung in a spirit of accommodation offered to agree to reduce China's quota to US$550 million in order to free US$50 million to be added for Russia.[14] Morgenthau and others went to every reasonable length in this and other matters to gain Russia's participation, and her quota was raised to US$1.2 billion. That procured Russia's signature. When Morgenthau announced at a general meeting that word had come from Moscow that Russia would sign, the gratification was intense. Russia's signature was taken as an omen that Russia would share in an effort to bring about a better state of affairs in the postwar world. But optimism was premature. Russia changed her line after the war, and as a part of her general policy did not ratify the agreements. *

An international lending institution, which became the International Bank for Reconstruction and Development, was contemplated in the original American plan. A key question for China was whether the Fund or Bank could grant credit for future monetary rehabilitation. The instructions to China's representatives urged that one or both of these agencies should be in position to do so. The final agreement for the Fund did not provide for such credits. As to the Bank, the subject remained ambiguous to the end. The upshot was a provision in Article I of the final agreement that emphasized physical reconstruction, but could be interpreted as not excluding aid in monetary rehabilitation. The Bank, however, has not entered this field.†

SELF-HELP AND FOREIGN AID IN FINANCIAL REHABILITATION

The checking of inflation is always a hard and painful task. Without foreign aid, it was sure, China could not accomplish this. Also, without proper measures of self-help, no amount of foreign aid would be enough.

Early in 1943, when China received the American and British proposals for postwar monetary arrangements, it seemed prudent to begin serious planning of postwar financial polices and action. In a memorandum of April 23, 1943, one of a series on financial

---

* Inauguration of the Fund awaited ratification by countries with 65 per cent of the quotas. American approval under the Bretton Woods Act of July 31, 1945, practically assured that the Fund would come into being. It began operations in the Spring of 1946.

† China's quota for the Bank was US$600 million, compared with US$550 million quota for the Fund. Some countries' subscriptions, including that of the United States, were set above their Fund quotas, and some below. The Bank was inaugurated in the latter part of 1946.

planning, I said, "Stabilization of prices, determination of the level of exchange, and rehabilitation of the public finances are intimately related. Without relative price stabilization, rates of exchange and the balance of payments cannot be maintained in equilibrium. And without substantial equilibrium in the budget, price stabilization will not be possible." The problem, I stressed, would have to be tackled simultaneously from many angles. The first need would be for relief and physical rehabilitation. Plans should be made for the peace-time organization of both the civil and military branches of government "on a basis of strict economy." The tax system would have to be rebuilt and reforms instituted, especially in the land tax and salt revenue. An adequately paid civil service would be essential. Plans should be adopted to deal with puppet and enemy currencies. The Central Bank should be converted into a reserve bank, on lines of the project adopted just before the war but not put into effect. Also I urged the fundamental need for land reform, comprising land registration, taxation, tenure, and utilization. In a memorandum of July 28, 1943, I recommended constituting a group of Chinese and foreign experts "to devise a sound and workable program" of land reform.

In a further memorandum of May 4, 1943, I dealt with foreign financial aid. That would be indispensable for economic rehabilitation and also to help bridge the gap between noninflationary revenue and minimum expenditure and thus check currency depreciation. It would be necessary also to reorganize the foreign debt, and to create conditions favorable to repatriation of Chinese capital and investment of foreign capital. In further memoranda of July 22 and August 9, I stressed the need to restore financial equilibrium as a precondition for economic development.

The idea was all too common that financial problems would ease once victory had been won. This flowed from the widely held idea that inflation's chief causes were shortage of goods and poor transport. One high official told me in April 1944 that once these difficulties were removed, the currency would "revive like a dry country after a rain." He felt that the currency would then revert to 20 to 30 per cent of its prewar value. But experience in some of the European countries after the first World War showed that the worst troubles were likely to come after the war. I was convinced of the danger of this in China and several times pointed out that, while prices would probably slump when victory was near, the improvement could only be temporary; and that there was danger of a still more rapid price rise after the war unless a comprehensive and solid program of political, economic, and financial rehabilitation were promptly adopted and carried into effect.

In 1943 China set up the National Planning Board,[15] but this body took little account of prospective financial problems after the war.* The Board prepared in 1944 what it termed a demobilization plan, to deal in the first postwar year with such problems as reduction of armed forces, taking back railways and industries in occupied areas, and emergency rehabilitation of communications and power. Also it worked on the five-year plan of economic development later described. That plan was to follow the demobilization plan, but whenever feasible was to begin earlier.

Repeatedly in 1943–1945 I pressed for serious and systematic organization of postwar financial planning. There were problems of great technical difficulty, especially in taking back the occupied areas, along with complicated internal and international matters. In my diary of December 22, 1943, I wrote:

> There was a meeting (21st) to discuss recovery of Shanghai. Chinese from there say there is much optimism and feeling that they should prepare. Many who played with Japs and puppets are trying to find fixers, for a price, to clear them with the Chinese Government. The meeting did not get far—same trouble of having too many people with general interest rather than a few experts to get together with some foreign experts to make plans re laws and courts, land regulations, taxation, public services, etc. Same old idea of theoretical nationalism and generalities seems to rule.

Qualified Chinese personnel were all too scarce. Yet valuable talent was available. I pointed out to Soong in a memorandum of December 16, 1944, that the number of well-qualified Chinese experts in many fields had grown, and urged a systematic effort

---

* The Board's general secretary was General Hsiung Shih-hui, who had returned from a tour of duty in Washington as head of the Chinese Military Mission. He was reported to have an anti-American attitude, growing out of lack of consideration he felt he had received in Washington. He did not speak English and was more a political than a military man. Clearly his assignment to postwar planning did not promote close cooperation with the United States, which was so important in this field.

to list them, both those in China and abroad, so that they could be brought into the postwar program. I recommended giving further training when necessary and, in particular, preparation of financial administrators. China, however, made no systematic effort in this regard. The government repeated its mistake of the prewar period, of relying too largely upon the Kuomintang and the veterans of the 1920's. So great were the problems in the entire period before, during, and after the war, that it was a grave and fatal error not to broaden the basis of national reconstruction and to seek loyal and qualified public servants wherever they could be found, both within and outside the party.

As the planning setup with the best chance of successful working, given the strength of nationalism, I proposed an inter-departmental body immediately under China's highest policy officers, aided by competent Chinese and foreign experts. Its duty would be to plan for the immediate postwar period and coordinate the plans of all branches of government. I contemplated later urging a body constituted like the Stabilization Board, with a Chinese majority and foreign members, preferably from several countries. But nationalism was so strong that there never was a favorable chance to push such a scheme.

Foreign experts would be needed in several fields after the war. As a priority I urged engaging before the end of the war a number of foreign experts in taxation, land reform, financial administration, trade regulation, and banking. In that way plans could be readied to be put into effect at once after the war. In November 1944, Kung approved my beginning to seek such experts. In December 1944, however, Soong became Acting President of the Executive Yuan and replaced Kung. Then and on several later occasions I presented the subject to Soong on the above lines and sought his authority to proceed with engaging the experts, but without success. He preferred to have experts directly nominated by the American Government. This might enhance the possibility of getting large postwar credits for economic development. In a memorandum of May 9 to Morgenthau, he spoke of the need of "a broad series of monetary, fiscal and administrative measures," and said he was "charged during this trip to arrange for American expert advice on budgetary procedure, on taxation, banking, currency stabilization and administrative reforms." [16] Nothing came of this proposal at the time. The only concrete result was the coming to China of John B. Blandford, Jr., on Washington's recommendation as budget expert, six months after the war ended, for a year's engagement.

Because of China's need for guidance and stiffening, it was unfortunate that advice from foreign sources was uncoordinated and conflicting as to postwar financial policy and action, just as it had been as to policy and action during the war. A main line of advice, discussed later in this chapter, was from influential Americans wanting China to proceed at once after the war with large schemes of development, without first controlling the galloping inflation. That attitude, which seemed to be connected with the spending ideas of the depression of the 1930's, fitted only too well with the ideas held in high Chinese circles. These spending ideas and the lack of firm and consistent American advice in favor of priority of stopping inflation, ahead of fresh spending schemes, played a part in deterring China from giving effect to such a priority after V-J Day.

CURRENCY REFORM

The key to currency reform, I stressed throughout, would be to control spending and to cover it as soon as possible by noninflationary revenues. Since it would take time to develop adequate taxes, the gap would have to be filled by revenue from sale of imported goods, foreign exchange, gold, and capital assets. Control of trade and exchange would be necessary for a time, but should be ended as soon as practicable. Meanwhile, exchange rates should avoid any large overvaluation of the currency.

The puppet currencies, which came to be the chief money of the occupied regions, posed a problem that would become urgent when these regions were liberated. As signs of Japan's ultimate defeat grew in 1943, these currencies began to deteriorate faster than *fapi*. Instead of being at a premium, puppet money went to an increasing discount. In 1945 the slump turned into panic. In a memorandum of November 27, 1944, I urged three main objectives in dealing with these currencies: "(1) all practicable regard to the welfare of bona fide Chinese holders, as contrasted with puppets and collaborationists; (2) promotion of economic recovery in the area; and (3) elimination of these currencies as soon as conditions permit." The memorandum argued that repudiation would be unjust and contrary to the first two objectives, since the chief holders were the loyal Chinese of the areas. It analyzed the various problems and made detailed proposals with regard to exchange of currencies.* Unfortunately the government made little advance preparation. It set rates that were very adverse to the puppet currencies. This partial repudiation was a hard blow to the people in the occupied areas, who had suffered through years of enemy rule. Certainly the feelings of injustice thus caused were an important factor in creating discontent with Nationalist rule and in preparing the way for Communist penetration.†

One persistent idea, which was eventually to contribute to the government's downfall, was that China should scrap the *fapi* and adopt a new currency. The currency had hardly begun to get into difficulty early in the war when this idea arose. All through the war and postwar period it was necessary to combat this notion and to stress the extreme danger of trying such an expedient until conditions were ripe for success. That meant a reasonable measure of internal and external stability and covering most of the expenditure by noninflationary means. Just when I was renewing my recommendation on the subject toward the end of the war, I noted in my diary on April 26, 1945, that Sir Frederick Leith-Ross, who had played a useful part in helping to put over the currency reform of 1935, had told a prominent Chinese that if China tried

---

* The analysis of procedure dealt with rates of exchange, which should take account of relative prices at the time in respective currencies, but should be "somewhat unfavorable to puppet curency"; seizure of unissued currency and plates; confiscation of notes held by puppet organs; refusal of exchange as far as practicable for collaborationists, though with some leniency to minor employees who were not actively collaborating; setting of maximum amounts to be exchanged, and blocking of certain bank deposits, pending investigation; the supplying of *fapi*, and choice of denominations to be issued in exchange; destruction of exchanged puppet notes; and taking back control of seized banks. To work out detailed plans I urged setting up a "Currency and Banking Commission for Liberated Areas."

† The government set a rate of 200–1 for CRB notes on September 28, 1945, though in September prices in CRB in Shanghai were then only about 30 times as high as average prices in Free China in terms of *fapi*. For FRB the rate set toward the end of the year was 5–1, though prices in FRB in Peiping were then at about the same level as average prices in Free China in terms of *fapi*. The argument made for these rates was that rates of exchange for CRB against *fapi* had been as high as 250–1, and for FRB 4.50–1. Those rates, however, partly were the reaction to outgivings by officials indicating a policy detrimental to the puppet currencies. I strongly emphasized that such rates reflected fear of repudiation or of setting highly adverse rates and that comparative prices were a much better guide.

a premature issue of new currency she "might regret it for generations." Toward the end of the war China ordered a new series of notes, though fortunately it was possible to prevent any immediate effort to issue them. This idea of a new currency finally bore fruit in the issue of new "gold" notes in 1948, whose failure was one of the major causes of the downfall of the National Government on the mainland.

In a 50-page memorandum prepared in May 1945, I analyzed China's prewar monetary system, the nature of the postwar monetary and banking system desirable for China, and the budgetary and currency measures that should be adopted for transition to such a system. Unhappily this important reform had to remain academic.

ASSETS ABROAD AND THEIR USE

In the latter part of the war, China accumulated large assets abroad. From the prewar record of US$379 million, the government's assets sank to a low around US$25 million in 1939. Then began a rebuilding as capital was repatriated when World War II broke out in September, and as China got more and more foreign help. Early in 1942 came the US$500 million credit. Then the American army paid rates highly favorable to China to buy the local money needed—US$392 million in 1942–1945. The Foreign Economic Administration paid US$48 million at 20–1 in payment for strategic materials bought through June 1944.

By the war's end, China's official external assets were close to US$900 million.* The figures seemed large. But actually it was hardly larger in relation to currency needs than were prewar holdings of US$379 million. The buying power of money had fallen throughout the world. And China had to figure on backing the currency of Manchuria and Formosa. Besides, the effort to check inflation and restore a sound currency was sure to be costly.

Besides governmental assets, private Chinese held at the war's end about US$300 million abroad, counting the dollar Savings Certificates and Bonds. In 1944–1945 there was strong popular feeling in China against those who had sent money abroad during

---

* These assets were mostly in the United States, but included about £15 million in London and unsold gold in and en route to China. Deducting funds earmarked to redeem the U.S. Dollar Savings Certificates and Bonds, there remained over US$700 million.

the war. There was a movement to take over Chinese assets in the United States. This culminated in adoption at the Sixth Kuomintang Congress in May 1945 of a proposal to ask the American Government to give names and amounts. But the American Government could not do that, and the only way was through action by China against persons in Chinese jurisdiction. I recommended against trying to take over these assets at that time, since China had no present need for more foreign exchange; conversion into local currency would be inflationary; there were difficult technical problems; and forcible action would hurt confidence, as indicated by the fact that the discussion boosted free market rates for dollars and gold.

In July 1945, I estimated that for the rest of the war and the first two postwar years China's needs for foreign exchange would exceed the sources in sight by about US$1.5 billion. That roughly covered the excess of costs of relief and rehabilitation over what UNRRA might supply. The estimate included only US$100–200 million for beginning the program of development.

It was important that China should not count too heavily on the benefits of large assets abroad. There was need to stress this, because of undue reliance in important quarters on the psychological value of reserves; an overestimate of what foreign credits could do for development as compared with self-help; and too little recognition of the priority of restoring sound finances. In a memorandum of April 29, 1944, I said, "These reserves will give China the opportunity to repair the ravages of war and put its financial house in order once more. But no amount of reserves can be a substitute for the necessary internal reforms."

DEBTS

China had been forced to suspend payments on the privately held foreign debt in 1938–1939, as we have seen, resulting from exhaustion of reserves. But with the war coming to an end the question would arise of restoring debt service. This older debt at the time of suspending payments was equal to about US$400 million. But in 1945 the sum calling for settlement equalled about US$300 million.*

* The decrease largely reflected depreciation of sterling and other European currencies in terms of the dollar; and it was assumed that Axis Governments would be required to settle debt claims of their nationals.

Of the wartime purchase credits from the United States, Great Britain, and Russia, about US$125 million was outstanding at the war's end. There was also the US$500 million American credit, all of which was spent or committed, including funds earmarked to pay the U.S. Dollar Savings Certificates and Bonds. There was the £50 million British credit, of which only £3 million had been charged by the end of 1945. China did not expect to be called upon to repay the US$500 million and £50 million obligations.

Anticipating the need to work out the treatment of these various obligations, I made in the Spring of 1945 detailed tabulations and studies of the various kinds of debt. Also I made preliminary plans as to what China should do about them. As an example, I revived a plan I had made in 1937 to consolidate the railway debt based upon a unification of the railway system. Also I analyzed such problems as looted securities, holdings of enemy nationals, and the possible revalorization in part of the prewar internal debt, whose value had been wiped out by inflation. I discussed future policy about internal and external borrowing and investment of capital. The general idea of these studies was that China ought to work out a debt settlement as soon as practicable, especially in view of the need to restore confidence and clear the way for domestic and foreign investment and new borrowing. But it would be important not to make agreements that China could not carry out, as any breakdown of payments would be hurtful. Final negotiations should wait until China "is definitely on the path to economic and financial recovery, and until China's internal situation and the international situation affecting China show a fair prospect of stability." Unhappily those conditions failed to materialize.

ECONOMIC DEVELOPMENT

China's urge for development dates back to Sun Yat-sen's imaginative but grandiose plans for communications, industry, and agriculture. In the prewar period, China made progress through less ambitious steps. But the war sadly impaired the progress.

Despite the need for all-out effort just to fight the war, the government early in 1938 adopted "Resistance and reconstruction" as the fundamental wartime policy. "Reconstruction" meant economic development. This policy worsened inflation, to the extent that money was spent for things that could and should have been postponed. It is understandable, with China's racial pride and nationalism, that her leaders wanted to start at once to redress the economic backwardness which had left her weak in the face of attack by a nation with much smaller numbers and resources. It was hard to realize that the quickest and surest way to advance after the war was to consolidate the base, by first restoring financial stability.

The roots of Communist China's Five-Year Plans for industrialization are to be found in the plans made during the war by the National Government. It was on future economic development that wartime planning placed by far the greatest emphasis. It was then commonly said in China, and also by many in the United States, that China should be developed speedily to supplant Japan as the chief industrial factor in Asia. The experts of the various Ministries worked hard and in general intelligently on specific plans for future progress. China already had a large backlog of such plans, especially for railways, highways, and water conservancy. In the 1930's, and even in the 1920's, many competent Chinese and also foreign experts had studied China's development. Much of the credit claimed by the Communists for what they have accomplished in these fields should go to their predecessors as to planning and preparation.

The plans for development were brought together in the Summer of 1945 in a scheme calling for total external costs of about US$2 billion. The objects of expenditure were worked out in detail. Over 40 per cent was for transport and communications. Over 50 per cent was for industry and mining. Agriculture was to be helped by production of fertilizers, insecticides, tools, and equipment, and by processing industries. There was provision for engineering costs and training of Chinese experts. The plans were to be carried out by a combination of public and private enterprise.

During the Spring and Summer of 1945 Soong sought in Washington large long-term credits for these projects. In memoranda of May 9, to Morgenthau, he suggested joint preparation of a program of development, mentioning the various plans for economic development prepared in China including the Yangtze

Gorge scheme. He said it was obvious that more than US$500 million would be needed.[17] That was a reference to the Treasury suggestion that China set aside a fund of that amount for postwar reconstruction of China's finances and economy. The Generalissimo and other leaders attached prime importance to the program of development with aid of big American loans. It was generally thought that Soong's political future was bound up with his success in getting such loans. Until the war ended, there was no definite decision in Washington.

Unfortunately, in the wartime planning of postwar development there was a big gap. There was no realistic planning of how to meet internal costs, or recognition of the hard fact that for every dollar spent abroad on imports of equipment and supplies a sum of the same order of size would have to be spent in Chinese currency for labor and materials. Such money could be printed. But how long could that continue? Such officers of the National Planning Board as the two Deputy Secretaries, Peng Hsueh-pei and Franklin Ho, realized that plans had to be considered in the light of internal as well as external financial capability and of measures to rehabilitate the currency.[18] But China's leaders failed to come to grips with the problem. To their credit, however, they never had a thought of doing what their successors did—to build with slave labor without regard for the welfare or even the lives of the workers.

When Donald M. Nelson went to China as the personal representative of President Roosevelt, his instructions of August 18, 1944, asked him to get the Chinese Government's estimate of the economic situation and what could be done about it and to report his own independent judgment; and to study and recommend about China's postwar economic situation and the United States' relation to it. Nelson conferred at length with Generalissimo Chiang about postwar development. He told the Generalissimo that "postwar economic problems really represent a continued development of various kinds of wartime problems." He thought that as the Japanese fall back China should make a beginning—"we must make a start right now," mentioning "erection of buildings and other arrangements in order to lay a general foundation for China's textile industry." The Generalissimo wanted Nelson to be his "chief economic adviser," and to have "the entire responsibility for China's economic reconstruction." [19] Nelson made a second brief trip to China in November 1944, and later handed over his mission to E. A. Locke, Jr., who made visits to China as special representative of the President in 1945–1946.

Nelson had the idea that greater production, even financed by the printing press, was in itself a remedy for inflation. A responsible Chinese official who came to Washington after Nelson's first visit to China, reported that Nelson had opposed a plan for large economy in the highly wasteful Chinese army. There seemed real danger of another American spending spree like that for the B-29's. I talked with Nelson in Washington on October 16, and noted in my diary:

> His approach is from production side, and he thinks China must keep present production up to capacity or will not get on in further industrializing. I stressed relation of inflation to the entire program, and to China's stability. He says they can't have stability without production, and that situation would then go to pieces. We both agree job of sustaining China must be done. He is a smart man, very sure of himself, but seems weak on his economics. I fear he may urge too expensive schemes on China.

On October 26 I wrote fully to him about the fundamentals of the inflationary problem. After cautioning of the grave consequences if inflation got out of hand, I concluded:

> I am not arguing against expenditure that is necessary for the war effort. Rather I would urge—(1) that Government expenditures be judged by a very strict test of necessity, in view of the inflationary consequences of adding to the deficit and putting more money into circulation; and (2) that the gains to the war effort likely to be realized from any given additional outlay should outweigh the financial deterioration that may result. Stated differently, China's capacity to carry a war burden is limited, and the nature of the burden chosen should be that which will do the most good.

I followed this by renewing similar recommendations to the Chinese Government.

Talk of costly programs to start immediately after the war continued, both in American and Chinese circles. Believing that such programs were totally unrealistic, in view of the inflation, I talked about the situation on March 30, 1945, with Assistant Secretary of State Will Clayton, who readily comprehended it. I noted in my diary, "I explained how limited will be the resources, and how important to have them used well. Also lack of coordination in advice to China by Nelson's people and American experts, and how unrelated to financial situation." In a memorandum of May 26, 1945, for Soong, after enumerating some of the problems that needed attention in the rest of the war and the early postwar period, I urged "a tightly knit plan covering the over-all situation," dealing with both internal and external costs of restoring the financial system, and allocating with priorities the amounts likely to be available.

Prominent among the projects was a proposal to build in the great gorges of the Yangtze River the largest dam in the world. John L. Savage of the American Bureau of Reclamation spent six months in China in 1944 at China's request to study the project. He visualized it as the source of over 10 million kilowatts yearly, or twice the capacity then of TVA, the Grand Coulee, the Hoover Dam, and Bonneville. There would be giant locks to make the river more navigable. As to the dam, Nelson said to the Generalissimo on September 19:

If this project is carried out, it will be able to do many things for China. Ships of 3,000 tons can directly sail to Chungking, the floods of the Yangtze River can be prevented, and the farms of Central China can be irrigated. The electric power to be generated will double that of the Boulder Dam in the United States. In the beginning there will be 1,000,000 kilowatts, but finally it will reach 10,000,000 kilowatts.

The cost of construction of this project will be $800,000,000 in American currency, which can be obtained in the form of long-term loans.[20]

He said he would propose that Congress approve a 50-year loan for that purpose.

On January 15, 1945, Foreign Minister Soong asked that the American Embassy recommend that the Bureau of Reclamation be asked to design, and when China has the funds, to construct the Yangtze Gorge project outlined in Savage's preliminary report; and that the Bureau be given priority to prepare a final report, specifications, and contract drawings for which China would pay.[21]

The Yangtze scheme gave rise to an interdepartmental squabble in Washington. Secretary Ickes of the Interior Department pushed for the first steps in the form of the full engineering survey of the dam site. The State Department opposed the idea, believing it was presently quite impracticable and fearing that such a survey would imply that the United States would finance the project. It should have been obvious that the scheme was nonsense at that stage of China's development, and especially in view of the rampant inflation. It was a dream for the further future, and certainly not a near-time call on the limited financial and technical resources available to China. Total kilowatt production in the area was then perhaps 50,000 kilowatts—far removed from 10 million. To justify the cost and the huge power output would have required an investment many times as great as the dam's cost in all the paraphernalia of modern cities, industrial production, transport, and distribution. Such development could not come overnight.

In a telegram of July 11, 1945, the State Department asked Ambassador Hurley to tell the Generalissimo and Soong that it felt the Yangtze Gorge project was not economically feasible for a long time to come, would involve vast outlays which would endanger financial stability, and be unproductive; also that there was no prospect for years to come, if at all, that the United States would finance it. To spend US$500,000 for a further report would be wasteful. Soong was impatient with these views and, according to Hurley's report, "remarked that if the United States did not approve the project the necessary financial assistance could be procured by him elsewhere . . . he was not interested in whether the State Department approved or disapproved. He said he knew how to handle the situation in Washington and that he would get what he wanted. He went further to say that a 'no' from the State Department is always helpful to him with the other agencies in Washington." Hurley told him that such "squeeze plays" would not work and advised him against them. Hurley thought enthusiasm for the scheme was "largely confined to certain Americans," and that Chinese backing was largely derived from intimation that the United States would provide the funds. Finally on August 30 the State Department authorized the Bureau of Reclamation to go ahead with the preliminary study.[22]

In connection with the National Government's wartime planning for the future, there was active discussion of the kind of economic system China should have. Some elements favored extensive state participation and direction, influenced by Russia's experience. Influential among these was Wong Wen-hao, Minister of Economics, a well-trained geologist and an honest and dedicated official. He favored conducting under the Natural Resources Commission a wide variety of enterprises of mining and manufacturing. He was weak on economics and disputed with me during the war the dangers of postwar runaway inflation. He later found scope for his predilection to state enterprise by joining the Communists.

The predominant view in the government during the war, however, favored a mixed economic system. There was strong support for the idea that the government should run heavy industry, leaving light industry for private capital. The *National Herald*, Chungking, a government-sponsored paper, of December 29, 1944, quoted a statement attributed to a spokesman of the Supreme National Defense Council. This statement said the policy would be to encourage private capital. State monopolies would not be too numerous and would include the chief railroads, postal and telecommunications, mints and arsenals, and large-scale hydraulic power plants. Also the government might operate in fields where private capital was not capable of doing the work, for example, in steel plants and petroleum.

Chinese and American bankers did some useful work in New York in 1944–1945 about postwar arrangements affecting banking, insurance, and foreign investment. Certain strongly nationalistic elements wanted China to impose hampering restrictions that would impede the effective restoration of foreign banks and insurance companies, whose activities before the war were strongly competitive and had been on the whole quite beneficial to China. These elements also inclined to a restrictive attitude on foreign capital, which China so badly needed. Kung took a broad view on these matters and was able to establish the view that a liberal attitude was in China's interest.

Toward the end of the war there were many discussions of a new Chinese company law. The project was nationalistic and complicated and would have worked against operation of foreign companies and investment of fresh capital. Too many of those concerned failed to realize the important benefits China would obtain from creating a climate favorable to such investment. As it turned out, postwar conditions were too disturbed to allow China to attract much fresh investment by foreign or overseas Chinese capital.

CONCLUSIONS

It is unfortunate that neither in China nor in friendly nations was there an adequate appreciation of the need for a broad program to put China's economic system and finances in order after the war. China could not do this without external aid, both in money and materials and in planning and carrying out such a program. Furthermore, a will to take the necessary action was lacking, both in China and abroad.

In China the urgency of checking inflation was downgraded because of the emphasis upon new development, rather than recovery. A sick man must stand and walk before he can run. Much of the planning on projects of development was good, and the Communists are greatly indebted to it though they do not acknowledge it. What was lacking was judgment on practicability and timing, and especially as to means to finance the heavy internal costs without ruinous inflation.* There was too little comprehension of the future financial problems and their implications, and the kind of competent down-to-earth work that was needed to determine what internal funds could be supplied and to allocate them with priority. The plans for new development took due account of the need for foreign financial and technical aid—which was then hoped for from the United States, but which later was to come from Russia. But there was lack of appreciation of what China had to do for herself, and overemphasis on what was to be done by foreign loans.

On the eve of V-J Day, Wedemeyer wrote to Marshall on August 1, 1945:

> The Chinese have no plan for rehabilitation,† prevention of epidemics, restoration of utilities, establishment of balanced economy and redisposition of millions of refugees. On the China Theater staff we have one U.S. military government officer . . . who at present is conducting a school in Chungking, teaching selected Chinese civilian officials the functions of civil affairs. This

* The weakness in doing effective planning appeared at many levels. Thus on January 7, 1944, I wrote in my diary: "Dr. C. said a laboratory was not willing to do careful work on T.B. analysis—wanted something more important. They want all the latest things, but not ready to concentrate on the common but most important . . . They want to make penicillin and do research rather than do more important things re nutrition, T.B. etc." In Washington people in government departments asked me such questions as why China so often had "too big impracticable programs"; and "why Chinese spokesman always asked for such huge sums."

† Wedemeyer was wrong in saying there was "no plan for rehabilitation," since plans for economic rehabilitation were quite advanced.

school has been established one week. I have emphasized to the Generalissimo the necessity for advanced planning in connection with the problems and he has issued instructions to his ministries. However, I am not optimistic about the results to be attained.[23]

The war ended more suddenly than had been expected. And the aggressive moves of the Communists, aided at the war's end by surrendered Japanese arms handed over to them by Russia, forced concentration on the problem of unity and survival. That atmosphere was not conducive to attention by the Chinese Government to future governmental, economic, and financial problems, no matter how vital.

The United States had a prime responsibility because Western leadership in the Far East was passing from Britain to this country. The United States, however, was not ready to grasp the implications of leadership. Had the American Government really seen the dangers of unrestrained postwar inflation in China, and the prime importance of economic and financial stability, it could have planned a major effort to help China in this field. Instead, it missed the repeated opportunities for dealing with these problems.

A complication underlying all thought of postwar arrangements was the Communist drive for power. The problem of internal unity plagued the National Government during its entire period on the mainland. In the prewar period there were the warlords and Communists. During most of the war, civil strife with the Communists was smoldering and at times active. Now, as the war drew to a close, Mao Tse-tung's well-organized movement, like an insidious disease, was widely spread in China's body, taking advantage of China's weakened condition. The threat of major civil war was ominous. So long as this situation continued, economic and financial plans could only be tentative. Yet, to press ahead with every practicable measure to bring about recovery and check inflation was bound to contribute to confidence in the government's ability to manage affairs of state. Unhappily the problems resulting from over eight years of war and destruction were difficult almost beyond imagination and proved beyond the government's capacity to solve, especially in the absence of the needed cooperation by China's friends.

XX. A SUMMING UP, 1941–1945

O UR story shows how complex and controversial in the war period were many of the interacting events concerning China. In summing up things done and not done in the period of the Pacific War, I shall not give full references, since the table of contents and index show where the reader may find more extensive treatment that supports the summary and generalizations.

FINANCIAL AND MATERIAL AID

The United States and Britain were right in turning to financial aid when Allied defeats early in the Pacific War dashed the hope of prompt military relief for China. The credits of US$500 million and £50 million showed support and boosted China's morale. This massive aid, however, fell far short of bringing the desired results. The British credit became involved in Sino-British friction, was much delayed, and China eventually used only £8 million. Use of the American credit involved fault on both sides. China mishandled issuance of the dollar obligations, which were backed by US$200 million of the credit. And the American Treasury, thanks largely to Harry D. White, blocked the timely sending of gold to China, for which US$220 million of the credit was allocated.

Sale in China of dollar securities based upon the US$500 million credit had a real potential for checking inflation. But there was no pressure on well-to-do persons to subscribe, and thus to shift their activities from hoarding necessities. The Finance Ministry failed to use the Federal Reserve Bank of New York as an independent trustee, to make the issues more attractive. And subscriptions stayed open for 16 to 18 months, at the fixed rate of 20 to 1 for dollars, although prices were rising about 10 per cent per month on the average. Despite the bargain, prospective buyers found advantage in waiting to buy the securities, since they could increase their funds by putting them out at high interest or by speculating in commodities. The sales finally closed amid charges, the truth of which I do not know, of large buying by insiders. The operation hurt the good name of the government at home and abroad. About US$150 million was dissipated without significant benefit to China.

Sale in China of gold provided under the credit could have helped much more than it did to check inflation. Gold sales were a recognized wartime expedient in several countries for raising money by noninflationary means. The Treasury was selling gold to raise local currencies in the Middle East and India at the very time it was denying gold to China, despite China's urgent pleas. The Treasury had a clear commitment to supply China with gold. China was handling gold sales well, on a cash basis, so long as the Treasury loyally sent gold. Official selling prices were kept closely in line with prices in the free market. When the Central Bank no longer had gold, it did not dare to stop sales, lest the price sky-rocket with a serious effect on general prices. Trusting in the Treasury's commitment, the Bank began to sell gold for future delivery, which did not soon materialize. Morgenthau wanted to help China, and to provide gold as fast as it was needed for sale in China. But White and his associates held back for reasons which they admitted were largely specious. When Morgenthau's attention was drawn to his promise to send gold at China's request, he was angry with his subordinates, and ordered them to make amends. But the end of the war was approaching and the damage had been done. Even then the Treasury subordinates delayed further.

The Treasury's foot-dragging came at a time when inflation was growing dangerously in China, and when Japanese troops were seizing the East China air bases and even threatening Chungking. The foot-dragging was partly influenced by the friction over meeting American army costs in China, and China's stubbornness in sticking so long to converting dollars for the army at the 20 to 1 rate despite rapidly rising prices. Another factor was China's failure to handle well the issuance of the dollar-backed securities. Also the American Government felt that in 1944 China was not doing as much fighting as she should have done. I have no information whether White and his associates had other motives. FBI Director Hoover has stated that White's involvement with the Communist apparatus was "substantiated from more than 30 sources," [1] although White vigorously denied involvement. The record shows that White, in any case, had a strong pro-Russian and anti-Chinese bias. In 1944–1945 he was promoting a US$10 billion postwar credit to Russia while blocking gold shipments to China. White's record earlier in the war shows him a supporter of aid to China. I have no evidence whether his shift of views was related to the Russian shift in the same period from supporting to opposing the National Government. On the gold issue I felt at the time and still feel that the American position was wrong and hurtful to China. Even then those of us on the Chinese side suspected skulduggery.

Washington early in 1942 wanted to put "strings" on the US$500 million credit. But the effort failed in the face of China's opposition, at a time when the American bargaining position was weak because of Allied defeats and China's victory over the Japanese at Changsha. By rejecting an agreement to consult with the United States on use of the US$500 million, China won a diplomatic victory whose results were damaging to both countries. Strings could have made for better handling of the sale of the dollar-backed securities. Also they might have brought cooperation in the program of selling gold. Such arrangements could have been made before Sino-American relations became so clouded by wartime frictions.

Besides the US$500 million credit, the United States provided large dollar resources to China through payments made to acquire local currency. This may be considered to involve aid, since the dollars were provided at rates much in excess of the fair value of the money which China provided. Because of China's weak financial position, the United States paid cash for the currency instead of claiming it as reverse Lend-Lease. Altogether the United States paid China US$392 million for American army costs: US$1 million in 1941–1942; US$110 million in 1943; US$51 million in 1944; and US$230 million in 1945. Besides, the United States paid about US$48 million to mid-1944 to buy strategic goods from China. These payments, totaling about US$440 million, were primarily valuable to China by adding to resources for postwar needs and afforded some offset for the damage to China from the more rapid inflation caused by American military operations.

How to pay for growing military operations in China's weak economy was a major problem. Only by running the printing presses harder could China provide the additional money needed. Would the gain from particular projects exceed the detriment from faster inflation? Notably in the case of the long-range B-29 bombing operation based in West China in 1944–1945, the detriment overbalanced the gain.

The division of costs between China and the United States and the rate of payment in dollars for the American share became sore issues. China insisted stubbornly for many months on being paid at the unchanging official rate of 20 to 1, even though prices in China were rising rapidly. I felt then, and still feel, that China should have been more accommodating to the American viewpoint. But, whatever the justification, the result of China's attitude was damaging. The quarrel left a feeling that China was trying to exploit the United States. China indeed was able to build up large dollar reserves. But in parallel she built up large ill will. The issue was finally compromised, but only after bitter argument. This friction became merged with other frictions over material aid and military policy. How bad Chinese-American and Chinese-British relations became during much of this period has not been generally realized. It suited the countries, as Allies, to play down the friction. But it was there none the less, and strongly colored events in 1944–1945. Moreover, it helped to set the scene for postwar relations with China.

Foreign financial aid to China, by credits and purchase of national currency at favorable rates, was adequate in amount for China's wartime needs as they actually developed in 1941–1945. But China's handling of the sale of dollar-backed securities and American withholding of gold lessened the value of the aid. The billion dollar loan, for which China asked after Roosevelt at Churchill's urging withdrew his promise at Cairo of a joint amphibious attack on Burma, would not have helped much to check the deterioration in China had it been granted early in 1944.

Lend-Lease aid to China was far from adequate. Here China suffered from the decision of "Europe first," taken at the start of the Pacific War. That decision seemed basically right then, and so seems now. Hitler was the most formidable opponent, and his overthrow would seal Japan's defeat but not *vice versa*. Also Lend-Lease aid was strictly limited by what could be flown over the Hump. The eventual development of the Hump route to carry 73,691 short tons in July 1945, was one of the most spectacular efforts of the war. But the rate of development left much to be desired. It was two and a half years before the Hump route, by moving 18,235 tons in June 1944, surpassed the Burma Road's capacity at the end of 1941, about 15,000 tons monthly. In December 1942, only 1,636 tons were carried over the Hump; and in the second half of 1943 an average of about 7,500 monthly. China fought for seven years before receiving Western aid in military supplies in an amount substantial relative to needs.

More aid could and should have been allocated to China, both to develop the Hump route more promptly and to provide goods to be delivered over the Hump. The United States failed to meet promises of aid and for some time did not send even the relatively small volume of items that could have been used. Again and again China's representatives, and those in the American Government who agreed with them, pointed out that even granting the priority of the fronts in Europe, China was not getting a reasonable proportion of Lend-Lease items, as compared with Britain and Russia. In 1941 and 1942 China got about 1½ per cent of total Lend-Lease aid; in 1943 and 1944 only about half of one per cent; and in 1945, up to the end of the war, about 4 per cent. In the fall of 1943, the Lend-Lease Administration told the State Department—both being favorable to greater aid to China—that the War Department mistrusted China and "works to prevent the transfer to China of otherwise needed, available, and deliverable supplies." [2] China after enormous sacrifices while fighting Japan alone for over four years, felt ignored and discriminated against. Hornbeck, as early as August 17, 1942, pointed out that the President had promised aid to China, but that various operating agencies of the government were impeding performance. He said with prophetic foresight: "China and the whole Far East can be lost as effective allies and, if lost, can be turned against the Occident—in absence of and for want of a little more effort on our part to convince the Chinese that we mean what we say when we praise China for the fight she has made . . . and when we promise to send her aid." [3]

Total credits granted to China during the Pacific War were equivalent to about US$700 million, comprising the American credit of US$500 million and the British credit of £50 million.

By 1942 Russian aid had practically ended. Only about half of the US$700 million was actually utilized during the Pacific War: something over US$300 million of the American credit, and the equivalent of about US$12 million of the British credit (see appendix II). American Lend-Lease during the war (including US$26 million in 1941) was about US$800 million, and British Lend-Lease was equivalent to about US$44 million. The total of aid utilized under the above heads during the Pacific War was roughly US$1.2 billion. That compares with about US$350 million utilized while China fought alone in 1937–1941.

MILITARY AID

American military aid, for which monetary costs cannot be allocated, comprised mainly the air transport operation over the Hump; air operations against Japan in, near, and from China; building the "Stilwell Road" from Assam to China, and related and limited military operations in Burma; provision of military personnel to train Chinese troops and advise in use of weapons and in tactics; and the "back-stopping" of these far-flung activities, by an organization extending half-way around the world to the United States. There were also British land and air operations at the time of the loss of most of Burma in 1941–1942, and during its recovery in 1944–1945. Finally, Russian forces invaded Manchuria in the last few days of the war, ostensibly in part to help China.

The efforts of China's Western friends were in some cases brilliant and successful, and involved great sacrifices. One need only mention as examples the Flying Tigers, the Hump air route, and Merrill's Marauders. Yet Western aid through military operations was slow and, on balance, fell far short of what it could and should have been. Unhappily some operations involved serious blunders, for which China's Western Allies and China had varying degrees of responsibility. And Russia's eleventh-hour attack on the Japanese forces in Manchuria became an aggression against China. The blunders and the aggression were to have their part in contributing to the later downfall of the National Government.

The first major disaster for China in the Pacific War was the fall of Burma early in 1942. The British military authorities in

India, as their official historian put it, failed to see that the "front could only be in Burma." They had made no serious plans for Burma's defense; and they did not put Burma under the India Command, which had considerable forces, until December 12, 1941. Field Marshal Wavell did not take advantage, until too late, of Generalissimo Chiang's prompt offer to send troops. Timely cooperative action in Burma that was reasonably possible could have held enough area to maintain and develop a land link with China.[4]

The Burma disaster of early 1942 was one of the decisive factors in the eventual collapse of the National Government. China lost a sizable part of her strategic reserve and irreplaceable heavy equipment. The cutting of the land route prevented China from getting needed artillery, vehicles, and other heavy supplies. The psychological shock of isolation hurt confidence and morale, and thus aggravated inflation. The defeat promoted friction between China and the United States and Britain, and an atmosphere unfavorable to that close cooperation that alone could have saved China.

The loss of most of Burma, as the official British historian put it, "dictated the future strategy of the war in South-East Asia."[5] With Japan holding Rangoon and most of Burma, the Allies in 1943–1945 had to fight through terribly difficult mountain and jungle country to restore a land route to China. Judgment on the strategic ideas of Stilwell, the British leaders, and the Generalissimo, as to the timing and measures to open a land route, is for military historians. In any event, Stilwell had to operate on a shoestring, for lack of enough of the sinews of war. And the bitter Japanese resistance in Burma in the Spring of 1944 delayed opening of the land route to China until the monsoon broke, and thus prevented completion of that link until January 1945. The delay was crucial. Movement to China of the strong modernized Chinese forces in Burma, plus artillery and vehicles, might have prevented much of the serious debacle in East China in the Fall of 1944 and the resulting grave political and financial consequences.

A major turning point with regard to China's rescue came late in 1943 at the Cairo meeting of Chiang with Roosevelt and Churchill. In the Fall of 1943 Chiang and Stilwell had been working well together to reform China's armies and to plan an offensive in Burma. At Cairo Roosevelt promised to Chiang, but without Churchill's concurrence, a substantial amphibious operation in the Bay of Bengal, as part of a plan to retake Burma and reopen a land route to China. But immediately after the Cairo meeting, Churchill talked Roosevelt out of fulfillment of that promise. Churchill later wrote of the Cairo Conference: "The talks of the British and American Staffs were sadly distracted by the Chinese story, which was lengthy, complicated, and minor. Moreover, . . . the President . . . took an exaggerated view of the Indian-Chinese sphere . . ." [6]

The aftermath of withdrawal of the promise given at Cairo was momentous. An immediate result was growing Sino-American friction in financial and military affairs. The controversy about meeting American army costs in China was embittered, and it was against this background that Harry White held back American gold promised to China. On the military side, the progress of reform of China's armies received a setback, and the difficulties culminated in Stilwell's recall late in 1944. The delay in opening Burma was paralleled by the forceful drives of the Japanese armies in East and Central China, intensified pressure by the Chinese Communists, and the insidious progress of inflation.

These events were ominous for the future. China's deterioration under prolonged suffering was unchecked by morale-building evidence of a determined effort by her friends to save her. The withdrawal of the promise given at Cairo amounted to a down-grading of China's importance by Anglo-American action. The United States and Britain, intent on other matters, all but turned their backs upon China's fundamental problems. In all these events the Chinese Government had its share of responsibility, as the detailed account in preceding chapters shows. But, however responsibility is apportioned, it is clear that American and British policy failed to give real thought to the potentialities. Some persons in the State Department and other branches of the American Government saw the situation clearly and urged appropriate attention to it. But these persons were too far removed from the seats of decision in the White House, the War Department, and the Treasury. Worsening relations with China promoted a less cooperative attitude on both sides, and paved the way for the arguments and decisions about postwar aid to China and how to deal with the Chinese Communists.

The decision to stress air operations, with the effect of downgrading the reform and equipping of the Chinese ground forces, is a controversial subject. Roosevelt made the basic decision in the Spring of 1943. The responsibility rested first with Chennault, who convinced the Generalissimo, who in turn with Chennault's help convinced the President against the advice of Stilwell and his supporter, Marshall. It was not surprising that the brilliant success of the Flying Tigers, against huge odds, led to optimistic estimates of what air power could do alone. We now know from postwar data that intelligence reports greatly exaggerated the damage being done by the 14th Air Force to enemy shipping, except on China's inland waterways; and also that air power had not turned back enemy thrusts, which for the most part had stopped after accomplishing their limited objectives.[7] These statements, however, are not to be taken as a reflection on the splendid work of the 14th Air Force. The official air force historians say: "Chennault's flyers developed skillful tactics and, operating with marvellous parsimony, inflicted damages wholly disproportionate to the minute force involved." And a Japanese military historian has stated that the 14th Air Force was the principal obstacle to Japanese operations during World War II in China.[8]

Stilwell felt that an immediate result of priority for air power was to sidetrack reform of China's armies. He had the highest regard for the Chinese soldier. He wrote: "He endures untold privations without a whimper, he follows wherever he is led, without question or hesitation, and it never occurs to his simple and straight-forward mind that he is doing anything heroic." And again: "I know the Chinese soldier. I have seen him fight, and he is as good as any in the world."[9] He felt, however, that lack of proper training and of modern arms was not the only reason for China's defeats. A well-qualified Chinese military analyst, F. F. Liu, has said in his study of China's resistance in 1937–1945 that, "Such strength as could be used against the enemy was incompetently managed."[10] The official American military historians of the war in this theater say that in the first years of fighting, according to the reports of the German military advisers and of Stilwell, while military attaché in 1935–1939, "the Chinese committed basic military errors: neglect of fundamental principles of strategy and tactics; improper use of supporting weapons; indifference to military intelligence; inability to adopt sound command and staff procedures; failure to establish a communications net; and failure to keep vehicles and weapons in operating condition." [11] Nevertheless these historians reported that on the eve of the Pacific War American military observers in China of the Chinese army gave the War Department "the impression of a heterogeneous force that had considerable potentialities but that was not yet an effective, well-trained, well-disciplined army." [12]

The priority for air power curtailed movement over the Hump of equipment for the land forces. But, beyond that, Stilwell felt that this priority gave China's military leaders a partial escape from the painful need to clean up the deeply rooted abuses of the army system and interfered with carrying out his instructions to assist in improving the combat efficiency of the Chinese Army. Stilwell argued that, with army reform, China "will emerge at the end of the war with the means of assuring her stability." [13] But on the Chinese side the urgency and importance of thoroughgoing army reform was never fully recognized. Stilwell helped nevertheless to lay a foundation for partial reform, on which his successor Wedemeyer was able to build later.

The B-29 bomber operation from Chengtu, which even at the time was quite controversial, has been quite uniformly condemned by postwar military analysts. The 20 bombing missions of these planes did little significant damage to the enemy. But the operation made a heavy demand on Hump tonnage, which could have been better used for strengthening Chennault's 14th Air Force and rehabilitating China's land armies. Furthermore the heavy and sudden costs of preparing the bases seriously aggravated the inflation. The strain on China caused by these costs added to the already serious Chinese-American friction over how to divide and pay for war costs.

The priority for air power, and in particular the B-29 operation, prodded the Japanese into their great offensive in Central and East China in the second half of 1944, while the Chinese armies remained unready. Stilwell argued in April 1943 that China first needed a strong ground force, and that, "If we go and sting them into retaliation before ready, the whole thing will fold up." [14] Marshall agreed with him. The failure of China's armies, aided by the 14th Air Force, to stop this drive, which even threatened Chungking, exposed China's weakness. Both at home and abroad, this series of defeats was a severe blow to the National Government's prestige and contributed to its eventual downfall on the mainland.

Until the Fall of 1943 the over-all strategic plan had been, first, to reopen the land route to China, and then with re-trained and re-equipped Chinese armies to attack the Canton-Hong Kong area, synchronized with an Allied amphibious attack from the Pacific. Next would come a move northward in China, to establish bases for heavy bombing of Japan. But the lag in military aid to China, coupled with Sino-American friction and the lag in Chinese army reform, coincided with the success of "island-hopping" in the Pacific and the development of long-range bombers. So a new plan emerged—to defeat Japan without Chinese bases and without major operations in China. Marshall told Stilwell on May 27, 1944, that his main mission was to build air power to support the Pacific drive against Japan, rather than to rebuild the Chinese armies for major campaigns in China. In line with this policy, Chennault was directed to build up reserves of gasoline out of Hump receipts.[15]

Had the 1943 strategy prevailed, China's deterioration in the final two years of the war might have been far less serious. Her armies at the war's end would have been much stronger, and they would have recovered more territory. Successes might have given the government prestige and strengthened confidence. That would have contrasted strikingly with the shock to morale from the debacle of 1944 in East and Central China. Also, the American landing forces could have brought in significant amounts of consumer goods, to use either in direct payment for services or to sell for their needs of local currency. Thus, inflation could have been retarded.

Washington's shift to main reliance on the island-hopping plan, when adopted, was no doubt militarily sound. But it mostly ignored what should have been a major political objective—the need to restore a free China. As in operations in Europe, American policy paid little attention to Clausewitz' famous dictum, that war is "the continuation of policy by other means." The policy adopted took little account of the need to sustain China's morale, or to avoid her collapse, or to plan for after the war. It added up to the old story of winning the war and losing the peace.

A final blow to China, in the last days of the war, was the invasion and occupation of Manchuria by the Russian armies. That was the supposed benefit for which Roosevelt and Churchill, at Yalta, appeased Russia at China's expense and without her knowledge. The Russian forces later handed over captured Japanese arms and munitions to the Chinese Communists and interfered with entry of Nationalist forces to take over.

From the start Stilwell wanted strings on aid and bargaining, especially to bring about army reform. Marshall took the matter to the President early in 1943, who decided that this was "exactly the wrong approach" (chapter XIV). A precedent had been created by not bargaining about use of the US$500 million loan. But later, as friction developed about sharing war costs in China, and over strategy in opening access to China via Burma, American policy changed. In April 1944 a threat to suspend Lend-Lease induced the start of China's drive westward into Burma. Then followed American pressure for Stilwell's command of the Chinese armies. The power he needed for this heavy responsibility, to reward and punish military personnel and to move armies, would have affected the balance of internal military and political forces. Chiang was opposed to giving such power to a foreigner—above all to Stilwell with whom he had had such friction. Roosevelt had to choose between Chiang and Stilwell. By choosing Chiang and removing Stilwell, the policy of seeking such strings was abandoned. But the China theater was downgraded, and the possibility lessened of major aid in rescuing China and trying to rehabilitate her as the Fourth Power.

CHINA AT THE WAR'S END

When the war finally ended in August 1945, China faced an array of difficulties that would have taxed the capabilities of any government.[16] Well over half of China's people were in areas under enemy occupation, where a Chinese administration had to be restored. Agriculture suffered from shortages of labor, animals, and fertilizers. Industry was at a low ebb, stocks of goods were depleted, and foreign trade had practically disappeared. There had been huge destruction of property and loss of capital. Invasion had broken down much of the country's business organization. Communications except by air hardly functioned. Average prices were more than 2,000 times the level of 1937, and in foreign exchange the currency gyrated in August 1945, in the range of 1,100 to 2,750 per dollar. Inflation had decimated working capital, diverted business men from normal work into speculation and hoarding, largely wiped out the middle class, and left intellectuals unhappy and disillusioned. The extremes of inflation during and after the war later gave the Communists an inestimable advantage: the people were so fed up with inflation and its consequences that they were ready to accept drastic action to end it, including seizure of capital and heavy levies on current income.

The government had commitments made before and during the war, not only for restoration of civil government in recovered territory, but also for "convocation of the National Assembly, the drafting and adoption of a national constitution, the return by the Kuomintang of the responsibility of government to the people, the termination of one-party rule, and the lifting of censorship. . . The weight of responsibility that so suddenly fell on the Government was far greater than the Government machine then existing could adequately cope with." [17]

The military situation presented tremendous problems. Over a million Japanese troops were in China proper, and several hundred thousand in Manchuria, plus nearly a million Chinese puppet troops. The Chinese Communists had about 300,000 regular troops, plus a larger number of militia. Russia occupied Manchuria with 600,000 to 700,000 troops.[18] China's army was far from ready to cope with the military problems. Army reform had lagged dangerously. Most of the troops were far from the coast and the main centers of population and trade. Yet the sudden ending of the war called for immediate action to take over recovered territory, lest it fall into the hands of the Communists or of ambitious local or regional leaders. Even before Japan's actual surrender, the Communists were claiming the right to receive surrender of enemy troops (and their arms), and to set up a rival government in the areas of Communist strength. The Communists controlled much of the countryside in the northern half of China. Japan controlled mainly the chief cities and various "strong points," together with lines of communication which were subject to intermittent attack. Japan, at surrender, could hand over to government forces only what she actually controlled. This foreshadowed the postwar situation in the northern half of China, where the government controlled cities and larger towns, and the Communists held much of the countryside and attacked railway, road, and water communications.

Russia's attitude was uncertain, despite the promise accompanying the treaty concluded on August 14, 1945, one day before the war's end, to support only the National Government. There was fear of what later happened—that Russia would deliver surrendered Japanese arms to the Chinese Communists. And immediately after August 15 the weight of American influence in world affairs began to lessen, because of the dismantling of the powerful American war machine. The United States had begun also to cut her responsibilities in China.

China's deterioration in the last two years of the war, in 1943–1945, was not surprising, after six years of struggle against Japan with only meager help. The deterioration, unfortunately, followed the exaggerated praise of China that was current in the dark days after Pearl Harbor. This sequence made for greater disillusionment, as critical first-hand reports of conditions in China began to spread in these last two years. Most of the public in the United States and Europe, to whom China was now becoming "news," had little or no inkling of what the National Government had accomplished before the war and of its then promising prospects. That was true likewise of most of the thousands of Americans who came to China after 1941 for war duty. What they then could see, without perspective, was something very different—after Japanese force had driven the government into the almost medieval western provinces, deprived China of most of her revenues, disrupted public administration, and worn down the leaders and their armies. They did not understand and allow for the insidious poisoning which extreme inflation causes in any country. To these newcomers China was the embodiment of "inefficiency and corruption." Thus E. E. Rice of the American Embassy reported from Sian on October 2, 1944, "Of the substantial number of servicemen with whom I have come in contact, I have found almost all to be adversely and almost bitterly critical of China and the Chinese and somewhat bewildered that what they consider to be the true facts about China are not, or in the past were not, available to the American public."* Rice foresaw that these feelings "may adversely affect post-war Sino-American relations," and "will influence American public opinion in the post-war period."

The impact abroad of unqualified adverse reports about China was disturbing. Writing in the New York *Herald Tribune*, December 15, 1944, I tried to put the record in balance. I drew attention to some of the National Government's accomplishments before and during the war. I stressed China's contribution to the free world by resisting Japan, the meagerness of aid to China, and the sufferings and disorganization suffered in the struggle. "American opinion," I said, "has veered from ever-praising to ever-blaming China. A wise Chinese recently remarked that China is not as good as Americans thought two or three years ago or as bad as they have thought lately . . . China, in its time of great danger, looks to the United States for help and understanding."

The developments of 1943–1945 paralleled a shift in Russia's line, which amplified the criticism of China. In the earlier years, despite the internal conflict in China, Russia praised China's heroic resistance and Chiang Kai-shek's leadership. But after holding at Stalingrad early in 1943, Russia concluded that her national existence was secure and the line about China changed. In Russia, this change was gradual, since Russia realized that Chiang was still essential to fighting Japan. But gradually the Communists and fellow travelers began attacking the National

---

* Rice's report said: "Typical officers and men have mentioned to me such things as follow: seeing few planes on Chinese airfields but many in warehouses near Chengtu; buying from the wife of a Chinese official gasolene assumed by the servicemen to have come to China under lend-lease; and several instances of catching Chinese in circumstances such as to indicate beyond reasonable doubt that they were engaged in espionage on behalf of the Japanese and turning them over to Chinese officials only to have the latter quickly release the culprits. Such matters, coming to the attention of officers and men already shocked or disgusted with the dirt, disease and squalor of Chinese towns . . . have turned many of them against the Chinese." State Department file 893.00/10-244. Such matters, even though not fairly representative, always tend to be magnified.

Government, calling it inefficient and corrupt and unwilling to fight.

The combined result, from 1943 onward, of honest reactions without perspective and of Communist propaganda, was to create an image that failed to do justice to the past accomplishments of Nationalist China. It did not allow for the unavoidable wear and tear of years of fighting against a far superior foe, plus civil war, inflation, and disruption. That uncritical image still persists widely. Even a trained historian could in 1956 refer to the National Government as a "miserable remnant of feudalism." [19]

Nevertheless, fate is inexorable. Even though China was on the victorious side, the wartime deterioration was a fact; and whatever the causes and however reasonable the explanation, it had sad consequences.

Part Three
Conclusion

XXI. AN APPRAISAL

CHINA'S CONTRIBUTION IN THE WAR

CHINA'S contribution to the total war effort, by fighting Japan alone for four years and five months and thereafter during three years and eight months of the Pacific War, has not been adequately recognized. In these long years, China struggled to the point of exhaustion. A price which China paid, besides other heavy costs, was to lay herself open to Communist domination.

The most obvious contribution was to engage an important part of Japan's land and air forces, and some naval forces. When China fought alone in 1937–1941, Japan had from about 500,000 to 750,000 men in China proper and from about 200,000 to 700,000 in Manchuria. The forces in China proper were about half the total under arms during most of the period.[1] When the Pacific War began in December 1941, China was engaging 22 Japanese divisions plus 20 brigades, compared with 10 divisions and 3 brigades which Japan used in its offensives in the South Seas, Malaya, and Burma.[2] During most of 1942–1943 Japan took a somewhat passive view of operations in China, and the number of the forces in China proper was more or less static. Some veteran troops were withdrawn for use in the Philippines and elsewhere, and replaced by less experienced troops. But the 1944 offensive, to seize the East China air bases and the unoccupied parts of the north-south railways, was the biggest land operation by Japan during the Pacific War. In this, Japan employed 620,000 first-line troops.[3] At the war's end, according to the survey made in 1950 by the Japanese Demobilization Bureau, 1,049,700 were in Japan's army in China proper. Japan then had a total of 2,343,483 in the army overseas, not counting men surrendered to Russia.[4]

Thus China, for the war period as a whole, contained on the average something like half of Japan's troops overseas. While China fought alone, the figure was well over half; in the early part of the Pacific War it was about two-thirds; and at the war's end nearly half of Japan's troops overseas, other than in Manchuria, were in China proper.

Japan's casualties in China south of the Wall to December 8, 1941, were 175,760 killed and 419,064 wounded; and from then to the end of the Pacific War, were 220,280 killed, the number of wounded being unknown. The total killed in China was 396,-040. (Chinese official figures put the total at 483,708.) The total of Japanese killed in all theaters during the Pacific War was 1,942,289.[5] After December 8, 1941, part of the Japanese casualties in China was inflicted by the American air forces. But the large number of casualties which Chinese forces inflicted in 1937–1945 belies the later charges that China did not really fight.

The China fighting caused heavy costs to Japan. In money terms, I estimate that total Japanese war costs were equivalent to sums of the order of US$9 billion in 1937–1941, and US$25 billion in 1942–1945. The China fighting absorbed the equivalent of about US$6 billion in 1937–1941, and a substantial sum, doubtless at least as much, in 1942–1945. Thus, for the entire war period, China's contribution in the fighting against Japan was to absorb perhaps 35 per cent of the costs of Japan's war effort, that is, very roughly US$12 billion of a total of, say, US$34 billion.[6]

Besides monetary costs, the China fighting forced Japan to expend large quantities of implements of war and munitions. It made a sizable demand upon Japan's naval forces, upon transport vessels and craft for China's inland waters, and upon railway equipment and vehicles. Japan could not produce or import enough raw materials to replace or adequately maintain these items throughout the war. Thus the extensive campaigns in China, especially during the Pacific War, contributed importantly to Japan's eventual economic exhaustion, which became a major factor in causing Japan's surrender without the need for invasion.

In 1937–1941 China diverted Japan from other possible adventures. Thereafter, during the Pacific War China engaged a substantial part of Japan's strength that otherwise might have been used in operations against the United States and the British Empire. China's continued resistance gave the United States after Pearl Harbor a base from which to engage Japan's air power, attack her ground forces in China and her shipping, and thus contribute to wearing down Japan's strength. The United States also was enabled to set up weather stations behind the Japanese lines in East China and thus to obtain information that was invaluable to the navy and air forces in the Pacific area.

Furthermore China helped the Allied war effort by shipping well over US$200 million worth of strategic materials, including tin, tungsten, antimony, mercury, wood oil, bristles, and silk. The shipments were to repay purchase credits, and somewhat over half went to Russia and most of the rest to the United States. Also China's resistance kept Japan from enjoying the gains from unhampered exploitation of China's production of raw materials. Thus China's farmers were induced to make a remarkably quick shift in 1938 and thereafter from growing cotton to growing subsistence crops.

The cost to China of her war effort was high. It has been stated, as showing a limited war-making power, that in 1944 China's national budget, most of which was for war purposes, was only about 3 per cent of national income, compared with American expenditure of 47 per cent of national income for war purposes.[7] That statement was roughly true, if based upon estimates of national income of *all* China. If based only upon the income of Free China, the percentage would have been at least twice as great.* The statement overlooks provincial military expenditures, which were substantial, in addition to those financed from the National Government's budget. Also it overlooks the large payments in kind for war costs, from the proceeds of land revenue in kind in 1941–1945, the estimated value of which was of the order of 25 to 35 per cent of cash payments. Finally, it overlooks the fact that a country like China, living close to the subsistence level, cannot divert to war purposes a proportion of national income that is at all comparable to that of a country like the United States.

But in any event monetary figures are misleading as a measurement of the cost of China's war effort. The Chinese people bore very heavy war costs in ways that economic statistics cannot

---

* National income estimates for China are based upon inadequate data, but the yearly prewar total may have been of the order of C$40 billion. Allowing for wartime shrinkage, the yearly income in Free China may have been of the order of C$15 billion (prewar value). Total yearly expenditures in 1941–1945 were equivalent on the average to something under C$1 billion (prewar value).

measure. Both soldiers and civilians lived largely at a subsistence level, or even below it, especially as inflation depleted the buying power of their cash income. The government often requisitioned labor and materials, either without payment or with only a small payment. China's great contribution, said the 21st Report to Congress on Lend-Lease Operations for the Period Ended September 30, 1945 (page 31), "was of course her determined seven-year stand against the Japanese. That heroic struggle of hundreds of millions of people resisting aggression made insignificant any material contribution measured in dollars."

By resisting Japan's overwhelming power, China suffered enormous losses of life and property. Chinese battle casualties, according to final official figures, totaled 3,211,419, including 1,319,958 killed, 1,761,335 wounded and 130,126 missing. That does not include the casualties of guerrillas and local militia.[8] Losses of civilian life and property were incalculable. Enemy planes bombed every sizable city and town, in many cases repeatedly. Large areas were flooded by the Chinese to block enemy advances. Millions of refugees fled their homes, with extreme privations and a heavy death rate. The health of millions was ruined by their hardships and by malnutrition. Enemy forces seized property and requisitioned labor, sometimes without payment and sometimes with payment in paper money that eventually became almost worthless. Resistance fighters and those helping downed fliers suffered brutal reprisals which often extended to their families and to whole villages.

Finally the West gained a major advantage in the war from having on its side China, the largest oriental nation. Japan's slogan, "Asia for the Asiatics," called for a vast struggle under Japan's leadership, uniting Asia against the West. But China, under Chiang's leadership, saw clearly that Japan's plan meant rather, "Asia for the Japanese." Repeatedly, China refused to consider a deal with Japan. For China's refusal to yield in the face of Japan's attack, the West should be grateful. Had Chiang Kai-shek, his armies, and people been less determined, and yielded to Japan's blandishments and offer of a separate peace, the cost in Allied lives and money of defeating Japan would have been far greater.

WAR-ROOTED CAUSES OF NATIONALIST COLLAPSE ON THE MAINLAND

In mid-1937 the Communists were only a distant threat. The government was making a good record in many fields of activity and was in course of unifying and transforming China after the chaos of the weak Peking regimes of the 1920's (see chapter I). The Japanese assault begun July 7, 1937, rudely interrupted this progress. Clearly the causes of Nationalist collapse on the mainland were rooted in events of the war. The causes comprise Japan's aggression, Russia's operations, the acts and omissions of China and China's friends, and the aggression of the Chinese Communists.

1. Japan's aggression. This interrupted China's bright prospects of 1937. It drove the government from the more modernized parts of China back into the western provinces, which in many respects were living in the middle ages; scattered administrators, disrupted revenues, and made serious inflation inevitable; killed and wounded millions of troops and civilians; destroyed vast amounts of property; disrupted the economic system; left the people and their leaders worn and weary; led to grave social unrest; created vacuums behind the enemy lines in which the Communists were able to expand; and left China broken and exhausted. Japan's leaders in 1937–1945, who chose the path of aggression, must bear the primary responsibility for China's downfall.

2. Russia's operations. By the Yalta agreement of February 1945, without consulting China, Roosevelt and Churchill, in exchange for Russia's undertaking to enter the war against Japan, gave Russia a special position in Manchuria. China was left with little option but to confirm this; but when doing so by treaty of August 14, 1945, received in exchange Russia's promise to "render to China moral support and aid," which was "to be entirely given to the National Government." [9] Russia's prompt disregard of that part of the Yalta agreement, by aiding the Chinese Communists and giving them surrendered Japanese arms, was one of the main factors in the later Communist take-over. Although Russia, in any case, might have seized a special position in Manchuria, Yalta made this possible under the guise of regularity.

3. Failures by China. China's resistance to Japan far surpassed

expectations, and China's allies have not adequately recognized, at the time and since, that it was a major contribution to Japan's eventual defeat. Likewise they have not adequately recognized the enormity of China's difficulties during more than eight years of invasion and the strain upon the leaders and people. The leaders, facing a continuing pressure for fateful decisions, were overworked, worn, and often ill. The people suffered almost unbelievably and became war-weary. Yet, however reasonable the explanation, failures took place and deterioration worsened. A major failure was the inadequacy of reform of the vast and largely ineffective armies and their leadership. China failed to use sufficiently the American aid in this which Stilwell offered, and when there was better cooperation with Wedemeyer it was too late. Had China ended the war with a well reformed army, the chance of postwar internal stability would have been much greater. In countering inflation, which could not have been avoided even with the best conceivable financial management plus prompt and massive foreign aid, China did some things well despite enormous difficulties; but also fell short of making the determined and continuing effort needed to deal with its basic causes. As China became more and more worn and weary, the government tended to rely unduly on the hope of foreign aid, as a substitute for action on military and financial problems that had to be solved mainly by Chinese. This was true of wartime issues, and also of plans for postwar development which some Chinese and American officials promoted. Also strengthened nationalism, while it stiffened resistance and helped the people to bear great hardships, made China less ready to accept needed participation of men from friendly nations in military and financial operations, and even to accept advice. Finally, the government failed to give effect to social and governmental reforms. While inflation breeds corruption in any country, in wartime China the corruption went beyond what could be deemed excusable as due to inflation and confusion. The government failed to identify itself actively with such important issues as land reform and better local government. Although preoccupation with urgent wartime needs made reforms difficult, the result was to open the way for Communist promises of agrarian, social, and governmental reform. Although the promises were deceptive, they ingratiated the Communists with the masses and the intellectuals.

4. Inflation. Although wartime inflation supplied fiscal resources, it had a ruinous effect upon government and society. It undermined civilian morale, almost wiped out the middle class, and impaired the army's morale. It made it almost impossible to govern well and thus gravely hurt the government's standing, especially at home but also abroad. It helped to create in China conditions made to order for Communist seizure. Lenin is said to have stated that the best way to destroy capitalism is by extreme inflation.[10] The hyper-inflation and monetary collapse of the postwar period could have been avoided only if the imminent danger had been clearly recognized from the start, not only by China but also by the United States and other friendly countries, and if appropriate and energetic action had been taken to counteract the danger. It has been wisely said that a generation will tolerate only one galloping inflation. When the Communists came to power, they managed to check inflation by ruthlessly seizing food, materials, and property and by commandeering labor. They had the luck to be at hand, with force and a program, when the people of China were ready to accept almost any professed remedy, no matter how drastic.

5. The failures of China's friends. Since China alone had no chance to defeat Japan, aid and support by China's friends was vital. Russian aid was substantial, prompt, helpful, and without political conditions, but it petered out after two or three years. Western aid, until the latter part of the war, was both late and little relative to China's needs. In the military field, a major shortcoming was failure in 1941–1942 to organize better the defense of Burma, whose loss cut off China. The American view, after joining the war, was for the most part strictly military, without regard for political objectives. There was little attention to rescuing a suffering ally in need, or to postwar consequences of what was done. There was even obstruction of aid, in the Treasury and War Departments. The Western nations did not recognize the potential stature in the world of the peoples of Asia. In August 1942, Hornbeck wrote thus, in analyzing the position of Chiang Kai-shek: ". . . he knows that in military councils in Washington and in London the majority of the conferees are preoccupied

primarily with considerations of occidental security and that there still prevails the centuries-old concept of occidental superiority in practically all things relating to capacity and importance."[11] The extent to which the war speeded the emergence as a world factor of the Chinese—along with other Asian peoples—could hardly have been foreseen in 1937. In China the process was quickened by the National Government's rise to power in 1928, by China's progress to mid-1937, and by her ability to avoid being conquered by Japan in 1931–1945. For the failure to understand better China's situation and needs, and to act accordingly, the United States and the Free World have paid heavily, and will continue to pay.

6. Inadequacy of planning for postwar arrangements. Only for physical reconstruction was there serious joint planning during the war by China and her friends. Both sides failed to realize that it was equally important to plan well in advance for the less tangible needs of restoring civil government in the regions to be recovered, and for financial rehabilitation. Such planning should have detailed the nature and probable extent of foreign technical and financial aid and the internal action for China to take, including a program for covering essential costs in Chinese currency with the least possible reliance upon inflation. China opened the way for this by its proposals made in 1943 in connection with the plans for postwar monetary arrangements. But Washington ignored these proposals, and China's heart was not in such prosaic action, but rather in moving at once toward becoming a strong industrial power. So advance planning was not effective. The war ended so suddenly that plans in most major fields had to be hurriedly and inadequately improvised.

7. Length of the war. Time worked against China in the more than eight years of hostilities. Given the attitudes of China and her friends, Japan's defeat came too late to allow China to be saved from the consequences of prolonged suffering and exhaustion, rampaging inflation, the errors of omission and commission by China and her allies, Russia's occupation of Manchuria, and the continuing aggression of the Chinese Communists.

8. The challenge of the Communists. All the afore-mentioned factors worked to create conditions making possible later Communist success. And the Communists, for their part, lost no time

in getting into position to profit from events. From the start of the fighting, Mao Tse-tung's fixed policy was "70 per cent expansion, 20 per cent dealing with the Kuomintang and 10 per cent resisting Japan" (see chapter IV). The Communists showed a sense of destiny, a singleness of purpose, organizing ability, and a skill in unscrupulous political tactics, that were truly remarkable. Apart from Generalissimo Chiang and some of his associates, few persons anywhere realized how dangerous and insidious was the Communist threat. Being without Russian material support during the war, the Chinese Communists had to be self-reliant. In organizing areas overrun by Japan, but which were too large for Japan to control, they developed an organization and an army which were in position to take over and use the surrendered Japanese arms which Russia handed to them after the war. They were the one dissident group in China ready and willing to take advantage of the desire for a change resulting from the critical situation and mistakes hereinbefore described, and to bid for power. Also, they could trade on the deep-seated determination that existed to gain for China a place in the world corresponding to the potential ability, numbers, and past attainments of her people.

What of postwar charges that disloyalty of certain Americans was a major cause of the Nationalist downfall on the mainland? Such an explanation is too simple. I have stated here the evidence available to me, and pertinent to this book, for the war period (see especially chapter XVII). The chief American policy makers had little background understanding of the nature and tactics of Communism. Temporary moderate tactics misled some Americans to view the Chinese Communists as "agrarian reformers" who could sincerely cooperate with a non-Communist regime. American mistakes were mainly of judgment; and whatever American disloyalty there was in the war period did not, I feel, decisively change the weight of the eight factors hereinbefore outlined.*

To sum up: China in 1937–1945 had not developed to the point where the government could cope with Japan's aggression and the many internal and international problems which it brought in train. China and her friends did many things well, but they did

---

* This is not the place to deal at length with over-all American and Chinese handling of the Communist issue in this period.

many things badly or not at all. The net result was to leave China too stricken to meet effectively the Communist onslaught.

THE ROLES OF FOREIGN AID AND SELF-HELP

Foreign aid is two-sided. For success, aid must be furnished at the right time, for the right purposes, in adequate but not excessive amounts, under the right policies, and with the help of the right personnel. And what aid can do must not be overemphasized as compared with self-help. China's wartime experience shows how hard it is to aid quickly and successfully a country with a much lower level of economic and administrative development and a very different culture. Furthermore, this experience, and its aftermath, show the danger of overemphasizing material aid and development as compared with the less tangible but vital need for reasonably sound finance and for governmental and social reforms. In these fields China needed a firm internal policy and timely and wise foreign guidance, but both China and her friends fell short badly. Let underdeveloped countries that minimize the dangers of severe inflation and the urgency of reforms heed the lesson of China!

While China fought alone there was an underlying feeling, mostly unspoken, that China needed strong allies to win against Japan's superior might. There was also the feeling that China fought for the security of other nations as well, and that they owed full support. That view was reflected in the somewhat cynical comment of one of my foreign associates, that "*China will never lose the war.*" After Pearl Harbor, when China gained strong allies, it was only natural that people in China should feel increasingly that China, after years of terrible suffering and loss, had done her share and more; and that the time had come for others to bear the main load. The expectation of aid tended to slacken efforts for army reform. Even before Pearl Harbor members of the American Military Mission, which had come to China late in 1941, reported that Chinese officers had told them that China "might be able to win this war without further fighting," due to international pressure on Japan.[12]

In contrast to that Chinese view, many of the thousands of Americans who came to China during the Pacific War expected offensive action by China beyond her capabilities. They did not realize China's war-weariness, how limited were the munitions at hand, or how brutal were enemy reprisals for Chinese attacks. Ambassador Gauss, in telegrams of February 21 and March 7, 1942, called for "a sober estimate of what we may reasonably expect from China." He said that while "the Chinese armies probably could do more by way of local offensives . . . reserves of supplies and ammunition are limited to a point where the high command does not wish to undertake extended activity until reasonably certain of its permanent effectiveness." He felt, however, that American writers and commentators were "over-emphasizing the military potentialities of China's great man-power," and that "exaggeration of China's military strength encourages complacency and invites ill-founded and detrimental comparison with other military forces." [13]

Meanwhile the Communists were without outside help or much hope of it during the war, not even—and by design—from Russia. They then could fight the Japanese only on a small scale, and for this they had to be self-reliant. That gave them a major advantage. In the summer of 1938, when loss of Hankow was threatening, Consul General Paul R. Josselyn reported from Hankow on August 16:

> Confronted with the problem of defending Wuhan the Chinese fail to show unity of purpose. The Central Government professes that a determined stand will be made but in the opinion of foreign military observers is now conserving and later will probably withdraw its best troops and equipment to ensure its transcendency in domestic politics. Central Government hope for victory in the present hostilities still rests in the economic collapse of Japan and third power economic or military intervention.
>
> Declaring that with cooperation and determination Wuhan can be another Madrid, the Communists published 2 months ago a comprehensive plan for the defense of the Wuhan area, the salient feature of which was the mobilization, training and arming of the masses. Apprehending an increase of Communist strength if the people are mobilized, the Central Government has blocked fulfillment of the program even to the extent of preventing the Communists from organizing labor and first aid corps for work at the front.[14]

Those developments foreshadowed the shape of things to come.

With China needing aid so desperately, it was natural for many Chinese to exaggerate what aid might do, especially during the Pacific War and in the economic field. The receipt of the 1942 credits of US$500 million and £50 million led some in authority to feel that mere receipt of foreign credits eased the pressure on China's internal finance. Partly for this reason a proposed cut in the army from over five million to about three million, which would have eliminated useless but costly units and added to efficiency, did not materialize—though there was also a feeling that China should keep larger numbers of troops in view of the outbreak of the Pacific War.[15] To the extent that the credits encouraged outlays that could have been curtailed without detriment to the war effort, they did harm as well as good. In planning postwar rehabilitation and development, China's leaders were too engrossed with the idea that what they mainly needed was huge American loans for new development and too neglectful of measures of self-help and financial stabilization. Basically, China's problems had to be solved by Chinese, and all too often it was overlooked that "The Lord helps those who help themselves." Thoughtful Chinese have often said that the National Government would not be in exile had it and the Chinese people helped themselves as much on the mainland as they have since done on Taiwan.*

Because of war-stimulated nationalism, China was less ready to take foreign advice and to let foreigners share in action and administration. As financial adviser, I found my advice taken less readily than before the war, when it was followed to a gratifying extent in matters of currency and internal and external financing. My colleagues until 1942, Lockhart, Lynch, and Rogers, in various branches of finance, and the foreigners in the Customs and Salt services, had a similar experience.

The American advisers were of course operating as individuals engaged by China with no related backing of the American Government. Occasionally we even faced official American opposition, notably as to the American silver-buying policy before the currency reform of 1935, and the Treasury's backing of exchange control rather than support of China's currency in a free market in 1940–1941. At times the programs and policies in which we were interested had the blessing of the American Government,

---

* On Taiwan the National Government, profiting by experience on the mainland, has made a good record both in use of American aid and in self-help. On the mainland, the Chinese Communists have relied heavily upon Russian technical and material aid, but also have made major use of Chinese labor and capital even though so harshly applied.

though not because of our nationality. To a considerable extent the official American attitude reflected a proper feeling that in our function we were Chinese rather than American.* As American involvement in Asia grew, however, the case for standing on technical grounds weakened, as compared with choosing the policy that would get the best results. It would have helped the advisers' efforts to promote greater soundness in China's wartime finances, had the American Government given to the Chinese Government, when there was occasion for aid or advice, some indication of general confidence in and support of its citizens serving China and of their ideas on financial policy. But instead, throughout the war, Washington sent to China a procession of experts—Laughlin Currie, Owen Lattimore, A. Manuel Fox, Leon Henderson, and Donald Nelson. (Similar bypassing was accorded American diplomatic representatives.) This practice of ignoring the presence in China of an American adviser inevitably tended to impair his influence. It contrasted with the British policy of relying upon the British experts in China, of coordinating their activities with British policy, and at times adding to their prestige by knighting them. Doubtless the American attitude from 1940 onward resulted partly from the fact that while the State Department generally viewed sympathetically the financial policies advocated, the Treasury did not.

The issue of "strings" on financial aid arose several times during the war.† Financial aid, to support the currency with foreign funds and to check inflation, was possible with less extensive and less obvious foreign participation than military aid. China accepted without objection a Sino-British committee to operate the British stabilization credit of 1939, and a Sino-American-British committee, the Stabilization Board, in 1941. Although difficult and

---

* Since the war, the United States has gone a long way in making available to foreign governments American personnel in the various aid programs. This is not the place to argue whether Americans can serve better as individuals engaged by foreign governments or as loaned American official personnel. How useful a foreigner can be in a given situation abroad may depend more upon the individual concerned than upon his status, provided the American Government recognizes appropriately that he is where he is and how.

† The issue of American strings on financial aid also came up after the war in connection with the Marshall mission. But they were considered in relation to pressure for political changes and reforms, and in the futile hope of bringing about internal unity by concessions to the Communists. Strings were not considered in relation to restoration of financial and economic stability.

controversial issues arose, these issues were more financial and personal (on the Chinese side) than Sino-foreign. After China became an ally, the question of strings on financial aid arose more sharply. When the United States granted the US$500 million loan, China firmly refused to agree to consult about its use and the United States acquiesced. China's diplomatic victory was costly. First it was followed by dissipation of a substantial part of the credit. Also the episode tended to set a pattern of rejecting both the offering and acceptance of advice. Later the recognition of China as one of the Big Four made it harder for China to accept external advice or pressure.

In military affairs, Stilwell in 1943 wanted to put strings on aid. He wanted to control Lend-Lease in order to bargain for army reforms and for action by China's armies. But China's leaders deeply felt that China's sacrifices while fighting alone and her surprisingly good showing against Japan gave her a moral right to receive the aid without strings and to determine its use. When the issue came to a head, Roosevelt overruled Stilwell. A year later strings were used, when Roosevelt threatened to hold up Lend-Lease aid unless China attacked westward toward Burma, and China complied. Involved with the military issues was Stilwell's antipathy to Chiang, which reduced Stilwell's usefulness and led ultimately to his recall. Thereafter Wedemeyer, a smoother worker, proved able to help the Chinese army to adopt important reforms by suasion rather than pressure, and without such friction as was earlier engendered.

Strings on aid, I feel, are right in principle. They can help an aided country to do what it should do for its own good. But use of strings is a delicate matter, as shown by the failure of the effort to install Stilwell as commander of China's armies. It is far from easy for an aiding government to change greatly the internal policies of a country that is receiving aid. Nevertheless, both China and the United States would have gained, I believe, had the United States bargained more during the Pacific War about both financial and military aid. China's occasional intimations about quitting the war should have been seen as unrealistic. But the American position was weakened because of inadequate support of China, whose cause was highly important to the United States and the entire Free World.

All through the war I hoped that the experience of the League of Nations in the early 1920's, in setting up what amounted to a temporary international control to rescue Austria and Hungary from breakdown by hyperinflation, might have been a precedent adapted to other circumstances for some sort of postwar international salvage operation for China—to help put things in order and then withdraw. Some such operation would have been desirable, to help the National Government to do what it could not do unaided, namely end inflation and set the country on the road to solvency, thus gaining prestige at home and abroad. Looking back we now can see that wartime frictions, especially between China and the United States, the responsibility for which the reader may judge from the account herein given, made such a program virtually impossible.

China's problems at the war's end, however, were so complex and difficult that financial and economic action alone would not have sufficed. To counter the internal Communist threat, action by social, political, and military means was also necessary. Only a broad and major cooperative effort on all these fronts, begun well before the war's end by China and the friendly nations, could have brought China safely through the war and enabled her to withstand the pressures both internal and external that forced her into the Communist orbit. Unhappily such an effort was not made.

Appendixes
Bibliographic Note
Glossary
Notes
Index

APPENDIX I

THE BUDGET AND INFLATION, 1937-1945

In "China's Wartime Finance, 1937-1945," soon to be published, I have dealt at length with inflation. The statement that follows is a summary based upon that account, with some of the main figures.

No conceivable action could have avoided severe inflation in China during the eight years of war. Heavy war costs could not be met by tax income, which shrank as Japan overran many of the most productive areas. The table below shows cash war costs, revenues, and the deficit covered by bank credit (in millions of C$):

Year ending June 30	Costs	Revenues	Deficit covered by bank credit	Calendar year	Costs	Revenues	Deficit covered by bank credit
1937	1,167	870	297	1941	10,933	2,024	8,909
1938	2,184	1,314	870	1942	26,038	6,254	19,784
1938 (2d half)	1,181	341	840	1943	69,325	20,768	48,557
Calendar year							
1939	2,809	580	2,229	1944	198,155	61,046	137,109
1940	5,553	1,589	3,964	1945	1,268,031	216,519	1,051,512

Land tax in kind and compulsory purchase and borrowing of grain became important after 1940. There are no accurate figures showing the value of these receipts, but I estimate the values roughly as follows (billions of C$):

Crop year ending September 30	Value
1942	6
1943	27
1944	60
1945	280

These receipts in kind became the government's most important single source of nonborrowed revenue, being roughly equal to the total of cash revenues in the three years ending September 30, 1944, and somewhat greater in the year ending September 30, 1945.

Borrowing by public sale of bonds could not cover much of the deficit. Hence by far the chief fiscal resource was bank credit: borrowing from the four government banks to mid-1942, and thereafter from the Central Bank. Most of the borrowing gave rise to the growth of note issue. In the first year of fighting, credit inflation covered roughly 40 per cent of the government's total cash expenditures, and in succeeding years between 69 per cent and 83 per cent. If we include the value of transactions in kind, the over-all picture is somewhat more favorable in 1942-1945.

The growth of total note issue, compared with C$1.9 billion as of June 30, 1937, was as follows (billions of C$): *

End of	Note issue outstanding	End of	Note issue outstanding
1937	2.06	1942	35.1
1938	2.74	1943	75.4
1939	4.77	1944	189.5
1940	8.40	1945	1,031.9
1941	15.81		

This note inflation was by far the major cause of the price rise. The rise was often blamed primarily upon scarcity of goods and lack of transport. But, despite the war, local production of basic necessities in Free China was fairly well maintained, and many items came in from the occupied areas. Clearly the active factor in the progressive rise was the flood of notes and not the progressive growth of a general shortage of goods or of difficulties of transport.

The price rise was relatively small at the start. In the first nine months the rise of average retail market prices in the main cities of Free China was 29 per cent, which compared favorably with a rise of 37 per cent in England in the first nine months of World War II. But the rate of increase in China grew, as shown in the graph on page 43. The yearly percentage increases of average prices were (in per cent): 1938—49; 1939—83; 1940—124; 1941—173; 1942—235; 1943—245; 1944—231; and in 1945—251 to August, and 230 to the end of the year. Half-yearly indices of average retail market prices in the main cities of Free China were as follows:

1937		1942	
January-June	1.00	June	35.9
December	1.18	December	66.2
1938		**1943**	
June	1.40	June	132
December	1.76	December	228
1939		**1944**	
June	2.26	June	466
December	3.23	December	755
1940		**1945**	
June	4.87	June	2,167
December	7.24	August	2,647
1941		December	2,491
June	10.5		
December	19.8		

* Issue of the four government banks, which the Central Bank took over as of June 30, 1942, plus the issues of provincial, local, and private banks. Issues of these latter three were more than a fifth of the total in 1937, but did not increase greatly and, as the other issue grew, became a minor and then a negligible part of the circulation.

Except for some periods in the first three years, the rise of foreign exchange rates in the free market lagged behind the increase of prices. The comparison appears in the aforementioned graph. Existence of the blockade as well as various controls prevented the normal interaction of prices and exchange rates. During the Pacific War the exchange market was small, except that dealings in American currency notes grew along with American operations in China. The course of rates of exchange is shown below:

1936–1941

Range in cents and pence, respectively, per C$1, selling rates at Shanghai for telegraphic transfers.

	U. S. dollars	Sterling
1936	29.50–30.25	14.25–14.56
1937	29.44–30.25	14.13–14.75
1938		
January 1– March 12	29.63–29.91	14.20–14.25
March 14– June 30	16.75–29.38	8.10–14.13
2d half	15.65–18.50	7.97– 9.02
1939		
1st half	12.50–16.50	6.22– 8.50
2d half	6.25–12.63	3.22– 6.41
1940		
1st half	4.44– 8.25	3.06– 5.03
2d half	5.16– 6.34	3.38– 4.03
1941*		
1st half	5.22– 5.75	3.16– 3.61
2d half	3.25– 5.43	2.00– 3.27

1942–1945

Range in C$ per US$1 of American notes[†]

1942	
1st half	27–31
2d half	32–50
1943	
1st half	44–64
2d half	63–98
1944	
1st half	86–255
2d half	188–680
1945	
1st half	470–2,250
2d half	650–3,250

The government made various efforts to control prices, especially after the fall of 1942. These efforts, however, did more harm than good. The controls could not be generally enforced, and when locally enforced interfered with

---

* The rates after September 6, 1941, are approximate rates in the black market.
† The rates for 1942 to 1943 are for Kunming and for 1944 to 1945 for Chungking.

the production and supply of goods. The main useful measure was provision of necessities at cheap prices to public employees.

Inflation had a devastating effect and became a major cause of the downfall of the National Government on the mainland. Inflation made it hard for the government to provide adequately for the army and for civil offices, because appropriations shrank in value before they could be received and spent. The effect upon army morale was especially damaging. Essential civil services were badly underpaid, thus impairing morale and efficiency. As the buying power of income dropped, personnel turned often to corrupt practices rather than be in want or see their families in want. Inflation promoted hoarding and speculation and brought about an arbitrary redistribution of property and income. Particularly important was the impact upon the intellectuals, notably in the universities, and inflation softened up many for Communism. Inflation made it practically impossible to govern well and seriously hurt the government's prestige both at home and abroad.

APPENDIX II

FOREIGN CREDITS AND LEND-LEASE TO CHINA, 1937-1945

This appendix contains the main particulars of the several credits which the Western powers and Russia granted to China during the war. These credits covered payments abroad for goods and services and for currency support, as specified in the table. There is also a statement of the amounts of Lend-Lease aid which the United States and Great Britain provided. Further, there is an approximation of the amounts of the credits utilized by China.

1. Credits and Lend-Lease, 1937–1941

Country granting	Date of agreement	Amount (millions)	Interest rate (per cent)	Final maturity	Security	Purpose
Russia	3/1/38	US$50	3	1943	Agricultural and mineral exports	Military supplies, etc.
France	4/22/38	Francs 150 £0.144	7	1953	Salt and mineral taxes; French Government Credit Insurance Department, 80 per cent guarantee	Nanning Railway construction
Russia	7/1/38	US$50	3	1945	Agricultural and mineral exports	Military supplies, etc.
United States	2/8/39	US$25	4½ later 4	1944	Wood oil exports; Bank of China guarantee	Nonmilitary purchases
Great Britain	3/10/39	£5	2¾	1945[1]	Principal guaranteed by British Treasury, interest by Bank of China and Bank of Communications	Currency stabilization
Great Britain	3/15/39	£0.5	5½	1943	Guarantee of Bank of China and of British Board of Trade	Motor truck purchase
Russia	6/13/39	US$150	3	1952	Agricultural and mineral exports	Military supplies, etc.
Great Britain	8/18/39	£2.859	5	1949	Guarantee of Bank of China and of British Board of Trade	Purchase of British goods
France	12/11/39	Francs 480	7	1954	Salt revenue surplus and the railway's revenue; French Government Credit Insurance Department, 80 per cent guarantee	Kunming-Suifu railway construction
United States	4/20/40	US$20	4	1951	Tin exports; Bank of China guarantee	Nonmilitary purchases
United States	10/22/40	US$25	4	1945	Tungsten exports; Central Bank of China obligation	Nonmilitary purchases
United States	2/4/41	US$50	4	1948	Tin and other exports; Central Bank of China obligation	Nonmilitary purchases
United States	4/1/41	US$50	1½	[2]	Chinese Government and Central Bank of China obligation	Currency stabilization
Great Britain	4/1/41	£5	1½	[3]	Chinese Government and Central Bank of China obligation	Currency stabilization
Great Britain	6/5/41	£5	3½	1951	Agricultural and mineral exports	Purchases in the sterling area
United States	1941	US$26			For later determination	Lend-Lease

Summary by countries, 1937-1941

The credits are listed as of the years in which they were announced, or were concluded if not announced, and are shown in millions of American dollars. The Russian credits were in dollars, and dollar equivalents are shown for the British and French credits.

	United States		Britain		France	Total Western aid	Russia
Year	Purchase credits	Stabil-ization credits	Purchase credits	Stabil-ization credits	Credits, various		Credits for military aid (etc.)
1938	25		2.3		5	32.3	100
1939			13.2	23	10	46.2	150
1940	95	50	20.0	20		185.0	
Totals	120	50	35.5	43	15	263.5	250

Amounts utilized

The approximate amounts, partly estimated, of the credits and aid actually utilized up to the end of 1941 were (amounts and/or equivalents in millions of US$):

American purchase credits	95
American Lend-Lease	26
British purchase credits	20
British stabilization credits	27
French credits	12
Total, Western credits and aid	180
Russian credits, for military aid, etc.	170
Grand total	350

For the period of the Pacific War, data of the further amounts of these purchase credits utilized are incomplete, but I estimate the amounts roughly as follows: American credits, US$10 million; British credits, the equivalent of US$8 million; and Russian credits, US$3 million.

2. Credits and Lend-Lease, 1942–1945

American

Credit of US$500 million			Lend-Lease, millions of US$
Amount used, millions of US$		Purpose	
1942	200.0[4]	To guarantee internal loans	100
1943	10.5	Gold delivered	49
1944	12.5	Gold delivered	53
	35.0[5]	Banknotes bought	
1945	111.3[6]	Gold delivered	1,107[7]
	20.0[5]	Banknotes bought	
	25.0	Textiles bought	
Totals	414.3[8]		1,309[9]

British [10]

Credit of £50 million (US$201 million)		Lend-Lease, equivalent in millions of US$
Amount used, equivalent in millions of US$	Purpose	
Charged by the end of 1945 [11] 12	Purchase of goods and services in the sterling area for purposes arising out of the war	44

[1] The British Government, pursuant to its guarantee, repaid in 1945 the British banks' subscription of £5 million.

[2] This credit was repayable on demand on 30 days' notice. But the question of repayment did not arise, because the Stabilization Board's dollar payments were covered from the Chinese banks' contribution of US$20 million and from the Board's dollar income. The credit was terminated in 1943.

[3] This credit was repayable on demand on a month's notice. China repaid it in 1944, mostly by applying the sterling balances then on hand of the 1939 and 1941 stabilization funds.

[4] The US$200 million was placed to China's credit in 1942, but was not largely drawn upon until 1944 and thereafter.

[5] These figures show an estimated division by years of the US$55 million spent for banknotes.

[6] China received only US$7 million of gold in 1945 in time to be sold, i.e., US$3 million in January and US$4 million in June. Sale of gold in China was suspended June 25, 1945. US$37 million arrived in July. The rest of the US$111.3 million, i.e., US$67.3 million, arrived after the end of hostilities. Part of the item for banknotes, and all of the item for textiles, were spent after the war ended. Of about US$156 million of the credit made available in 1945, only about a third should be allocated to the period of the war, i.e., before August 15, 1945.

[7] About half of this aid was provided after V-J Day, including about US$300 million representing the cost of flying government troops to various places to receive the surrender of Japanese troops.

[8] China received the rest of the US$500 million credit, about US$86 million, in gold in 1946-1947.

[9] In addition Lend-Lease aid of US$26 million was provided in 1941, and US$210 million in 1946.

[10] Besides the items listed below, there were official grants of £139,500 to the British fund for the relief of distress in China, and £1,500 to the Chinese Red Cross Society.

[11] In addition to £3 million charged by the end of 1945, £5.1 million (say US$20.5 million) was charged by July 1948. The total used from the £50 million credit was £8.1 million (say US$32.5 million).

APPENDIX III

WARTIME GOLD SALES, PRICES, ARRIVALS, AND STOCKS IN CHINA

A detailed statement of monthly official and free market prices of gold in China in 1943–1945 accompanies my testimony on page 1977 of the Hearings before the Subcommittee to Investigate the Administration of the Internal Security Act and Other Internal Security Laws of the Committee on the Judiciary, United States Senate, 84th Congress, Second Session, on Scope of Soviet Activity in the United States, July 13, 1956, Part 35. The Hearings on page 1970 contain data of monthly forward sales of gold and deposits redeemable in gold arriving in China.

The following table shows gold sales, arrivals, and stock in China, 1943–1945 (thousands of U.S. dollars):

	Sales		Arrivals, monthly amount	Cumulative supply or deficiency at month-end
	Monthly amount	Cumulative amount		
	Farmers Bank sales			
1943				
September	6	6		1,544*
October	14	20		1,530
November	207	227	8,417	9,740
December	101	328	2,070	11,709
1944				
January	218	546		11,491
February	605	1,151		10,886
	Central Bank sales†			
March	1,088	2,239		9,798
April	613	2,852	1,077	10,262
May	2,062	4,914		8,200
June	2,118	7,032		6,082
July	4,393	11,425	1,093	2,782
August	1,800	13,225		982
September	5,260	18,485	4,493	215
October	7,175	25,660	2,849	− 4,111
November	7,600	33,260		−11,711
December	3,185	36,445	2,949	−11,947

* The Central Bank's stock of gold held in China prior to American shipments was US$1,550,000. Adding this stock to total arrivals, and subtracting total sales, the balance on hand at the end of the period was US$20,450,000.
† Includes forward sales and gold deposits from August 1944.

1945

January	10,325	46,770	2,927	−19,345
February	12,390	59,160		−31,733
March	17,815	76,975		−49,550
April	9,240	86,215		−58,790
May	12,775	98,990		−71,565
June	16,345	115,335	3,979	−83,931
July		*	37,056	−46,875
August			36,836	−10,039
September				−10,039
October			30,489	20,450
Total			134,235	

Arrivals of gold in China in 1946 and 1947 were US$70.6 million and US$12.9 million, respectively. The total received in China in 1943–1947 was US$217.7 million. The balance of the US$220 million allocated for gold, out of the US$500 million loan, was delivered in New York.

The table below summarizes the main data of gold prices, retail prices, exchange rates, and the dollar equivalent of gold prices in China during the war period.†

End of year	Retail market prices, average	Gold price, average per Chinese ounce**	Free market exchange rate per US$	Equivalent value of gold per ounce, average
1937	118	C$ 115	C$ 3.35	US$ 34.40
1938	176	210	6.10	34.50
1939	323	400	13.30	30.10
1940	724	750	18.	41.70
1941	1,977	2,400	28.	86.00
1942	6,620	6,150	49.	125.

End of quarter		Official price	Free price	Average	Based on	
					Official prices	Free prices
1943 (4th)	22,800	12,500	12,977	83	150	157
1944 (1st)	33,300	17,000	17,895	170	100	105
(2nd)	46,600	18,500	18,803	203	91	93
(3rd)	56,200	18,500	20,070	209	89	96
(4th)	75,500	22,500	28,932	441	51	66
1945 (1st)	142,000	24,500	38,235	558	44	69
(2nd)	216,700	39,500	92,477	1,060	37	87

* Sales of gold were suspended on June 25, 1945, and practically ceased during the rest of the war.

† Retail prices are average free market prices in leading cities of Free China, based on data of the Farmers Bank of China, January-June 1937=100. Gold prices through 1942 are free prices at Chengtu as compiled by the University of Nanking; and thereafter are for Chungking as compiled by the Central Bank, average official prices being approximated for the quarters in which they were changed. Free market rates of exchange are T/T selling rates at Shanghai to 1942 and thereafter for US$ notes.

** The Chinese ounce or *tael* equals 1.00471 Troy ounces, and hence roughly comparable with the latter.

Gold prices moved generally with average retail prices until 1943, but thereafter lagged far behind. Clearly, this was due to sale of large quantities of gold.

China's receipts from sale of gold, compared with the increase of note issue, are shown below (millions of C$):

Quarter	Receipts from gold sales	Increase of note issue	Percentage of receipts from gold to note increase* (per cent)
1943			
4th	C$ 114	C$ 14,900	0.8
1944			
1st	979	20,500	4.8
2d	2,534	26,900	9.4
3d	6,067	27,400	26.9
4th	11,360	39,300	28.9
1945			
1st	29,700	57,400	51.8
2d	42,000	150,900	28.0

* Note increase was equal to 83 per cent of the estimated cash deficit in 1944, 80 per cent in 1945. Quarterly figures of cash deficit are not available.

APPENDIX IV

CHINA'S PROPOSAL FOR INTERNATIONAL AID IN POSTWAR FINANCIAL REHABILITATION

The following is an extract from a proposal which the Chinese ambassador at Washington transmitted to the Department of State on September 3, 1943, in connection with comment on the White and Keynes plans for an international monetary organization:

8. Any member nation whose monetary system is seriously disrupted by the war and which is not in position definitively to agree with the Board the value of its currency at the time when the organization commences operations may, with the agreement of the Board, elect to take advantage of a transitional period. During such transitional period each member nation so electing shall make every effort to restore monetary equilibrium through a program comprising appropriate internal measures supported by international measures taken with the aid of the organization. Such period ordinarily shall not exceed (say) two years, but in exceptional circumstances may be extended in agreement with the Board.

9. In the case of each member nation so electing, the objectives of international measures in this period shall be to give appropriate support to internal measures designed to bring about:

a) Restoration of equilibrium in its monetary system.

b) Restoration of equilibrium in its public finances, including any necessary readjustment of its indebtedness.

c) Improvement of its international balance of payments.

d) Removal of its exchange control.

e) Tentative stabilization of its foreign exchange rates preparatory to agreement with the central organization upon definitive rates.

10. Each member nation so electing shall submit to the Board as soon as practicable a tentative program for the transitional period showing the kinds and amounts of the external resources available to it to carry out the program, and the extent and nature of its estimated needs for further external assistance in attaining the objectives set out in paragraph 9. Such program shall show by stages of (say) six or twelve months each the extent of progress intended to be made toward accomplishment of these objectives. The program of assistance by the organization shall be agreed upon between such member nation and the Board at the earliest practicable date, and shall be subject to revision from time to time as the situation develops. In formulating its program each such member nation shall restrict as much as possible the amount of assistance requested from the organization in order that the available ex-

ternal resources may be applied as far as practicable to productive work of reconstruction and development.

11. A member nation so electing may arrange with the Board to hold in a special account credits available to it for monetary rehabilitation. In addition the Board may grant credits to finance monetary rehabilitation.

APPENDIX V

STRENGTH OF JAPANESE ARMED FORCES, 1937-1945

Japanese army and navy forces in all theaters and in China, 1937-1945 (thousands)*

Year	In all theaters of war		In China south of the Wall		In Manchuria	
	Army	Navy	Army	Navy	Army	Navy
1937	950	126	500	36	200	0.15
1938	1,130	145	680	36	220	0.15
1939	1,240	166	710	36	270	0.15
1940	1,350	191	680	36	400	0.15
1941	2,100	320	680	32	700	0.15
1942	2,400	450	680	32	700	0.15
1943	2,900	684	680	33	600	0.15
1944	4,100	1,296	800	32	460	0.15
1945	6,400	1,863	1,100	34	784	0.15

*Data of the Japan Defense Agency, furnished to me through the American Embassy, Tokyo, April 1960. The figures for China south of the Wall and for Manchuria are stated to be the "presumed number." The figures of men in all theaters appear to include reservists. See Ayanori Okazaki, *Nihon Jinko no Jisshoteki Kenkyu* (An Empirical Study of the Japanese Population) (in Japanese, Tokyo, 1950), p. 575.

BIBLIOGRAPHIC NOTE

The papers which I collected in 1937–1945 while serving China as financial adviser, and to whose use the Chinese Government has consented, are the chief source of information for this book. These papers, in English and Chinese, comprise letters and telegrams, memoranda, reports, statistics, periodicals, pamphlets, and books. Also I have drawn upon a partial diary, which I kept as time permitted.

Chinese official records published for this period are not extensive, other than press releases. The *Public Finance Yearbook, 1948,* in Chinese, issued by the Finance Ministry, contains considerable data. Many financial and economic data are contained in *The Money and Finance of China,* in Chinese, by Wei-ya Chang of the Central Bank of China (Taipeh, 1951). Information on a variety of subjects is contained in the *China Handbook, 1937–1943, 1937–1944* and *1937–1945,* issued by the Ministry of Information, and in *The Chinese Year Book, 1936–37* (2d issue) to *1944–1945* (7th issue), published by the Council of International Affairs in China making use of official sources. The long series of *The China Year Book,* dating from 1912 and published at Shanghai, contains issues for 1937–1938 and 1939, edited by H. G. W. Woodhead.

American Government records for this period are a mine of information. The Department of State's publication, *Foreign Relations of the United States* (herein referred to as *FRUS*), is a primary source, as are also the unpublished records of that department, to which I had access. Also important are that department's publications: the so-called White Paper of 1949, *United States Relations with China; With Special Reference to the Period 1944–1949* (Washington, 1949) herein referred to as *U.S. Relations with China, 1949,* and *The Conferences at Malta and Yalta, 1945,* Parts I and II (Washington, 1955).

For Treasury records I was fortunate to have access to photostats of a considerable part of the Morgenthau Diaries. The Subcommittee to Investigate the Administration of the Internal Security Act and Other Internal Security Laws, of the Committee of the Judiciary, United States Senate, made available to me these without restriction when I testified before them in 1956. The Subcommittee documented my testimony by publishing with it a number of extracts from the Diaries (see Hearings, *Scope of Soviet Activity in the United States,* Part 35, July 13, 1956, Washington, 1957). These Diaries, together with the publications and records of the State and War Departments, complement invaluably the story which the Chinese records reveal. Mr. Morgenthau is to be commended for preserving a record that shows so much of the process by which policy was made and carried into effect. The Diaries are closed except to Mr. Morgenthau or his agent, until opened to qualified scholars serially after 25 years have elapsed from the end of each Roosevelt term. John M. Blum, as an independent scholar working in close touch with Mr. Morgenthau, has published *From the Morgenthau Diaries, Years of Crisis, 1928–1938* (Boston, 1959); and this book contains some material on China. The study of A. S. Everest, *Morgenthau, the New Deal, and Silver* (New York, 1950), makes use of the Diaries. Also the papers of Norman H. Davis and Nelson T. Johnson in the Library of Congress, and of Harry D. White in the Princeton University Library, contain material relating to this period. In connection with charges that White was disloyal, Nathan I. White has published *Harry Dexter White, Loyal American* (Waban, Massachusetts, 1956).

British official records are not available for the whole period of study, but *Documents on British Foreign Policy, 1919–1939,* 3d series, volumes 8 and 9, contain data relating to some of the matters herein treated.

The official histories of military events, published since the war, are admirably complete, objective, and well written. The Department of the Army, through its office of Military History, has issued three volumes relating to the China-Burma-India Theater, in the series, "United States Army in World War II." These volumes, written by Charles F. Romanus and Riley Sunderland, are: *Stilwell's Mission to China; Stilwell's Command Problems;* and *Time Runs Out in CBI* (Washington, D.C., 1953, 1956, 1959, respectively). In dealing with the military phase of this story, I have found them invaluable, and they also shed much light on China's internal and international affairs. The story of the air operations is told in the official volumes edited by W. F. Craven and J. L. Cate: *The Army Air Forces in World War II,* volumes 1, 4, 5, and 7 (Chicago, 1948, 1950, 1953 and 1958). The British side of operations against Japan in Burma and India is capably and fairly told in the official history by S. W. Kirby, *The War Against Japan,* volume 2 (London, 1959). A further study based primarily upon British official documents is John Ehrman's *Grand Strategy,* volume 5 (London, 1956). The Japanese side is treated by Takushiro Hattori, *Daitoa Senso Zenshi* (The Complete History of the Greater East Asia War), in Japanese (Tokyo, 1953). I know of no official Chinese presentation of the subject, but F. F. Liu's study, *A Military History of Modern China: 1924–1949* (Princeton, N.J., 1956), contains considerable material presented from the angle of a competent Chinese participant in the war.

The memoirs and other publications of participants in these events shed light from various angles. Such books include: C. L. Chennault, *Way of a Fighter* (New York, 1949); Chiang Kai-shek, *Soviet Russia in China* (New York, 1959); Winston Churchill, *The Hinge of Fate, Closing the Ring,* and *Triumph and Tragedy* (Boston, 1950, 1951, and 1953, respectively); Cordell Hull, *The Memoirs of Cordell Hull* (New York, 1948); William D. Leahy, *I Was There* (New York, 1950); Don Lohbeck, *Patrick J. Hurley* (Chicago, 1956); Robert L. Scott, *Flying Tiger, Chennault of China* (New York, 1959); Robert E. Sherwood, *Roosevelt and Hopkins; An Intimate History* (New York, 1948); Joseph W. Stilwell, *The Stilwell Papers,* edited by Theodore H. White (New York, 1948); Henry L. Stimson and McGeorge

Bundy, *On Active Service in Peace and War* (New York, 1948); John Leighton Stuart, *Fifty Years in China* (New York, 1954); Albert C. Wedemeyer, *Wedemeyer Reports* (New York, 1958).

On Communism in China during the war period and American relations with the Communists, there is much information in the above-mentioned American official publications, especially *United States Relations with China, 1949,* and in the volumes of military history of Romanus and Sunderland. Also there is a mass of information in the official hearings: Subcommittee to Investigate the Administration of the Internal Security Act and Other Internal Security Laws, of the Committee of the Judiciary, United States Senate, 82d Congress, *Hearings on the Institute of Pacific Relations,* 1951–1952; Committee on Armed Services and the Committee on Foreign Relations, United States Senate, 82d Congress, 1st Session, *Hearings on the Military Situation in the Far East,* 1951; Committee on Foreign Relations, United States Senate, Subcommittee, *Hearings on the State Department Loyalty Investigation,* 1950. Special works dealing with communism in China during this period include: Conrad Brandt, Benjamin Schwartz, and John K. Fairbank, *A Documentary History of Chinese Communism* (Cambridge, 1952); Boyd Compton, *Mao's China: Party Reform Documents, 1942–44* (Seattle, 1952); David J. Dallin, *Soviet Russia and the Far East,* and *The Rise of Russia in Asia* (New Haven, 1948 and 1949); C. B. McLane, *Soviet Policy and the Chinese Communists* (New York, 1958); Mao Tsetung, *Selected Works* (New York, 1954); Robert C. North, *Moscow and Chinese Communists* (Stanford University, 1953); Benjamin Schwartz, *Chinese Communism and the Rise of Mao* (Cambridge, 1951); and Aitchen K. Wu, *China and the Soviet Union* (New York, 1950).

Works which deal wholly or in part with China in the war period include: Kia-ngau Chang, *The Inflationary Spiral, The Experience in China, 1939–1950* (New York, 1958), and *China's Struggle for Railroad Development* New York, 1943); Herbert Feis, *The Road to Pearl Harbor, The China Tangle,* and *Japan Subdued* (Princeton, N.J., 1950, 1953, and 1961); W. L. Langer and S. E. Gleason, *The Challenge to Isolation, 1937–1940* (New York, 1952), and *The Undeclared War, 1940–1941* (New York, 1953); F. M. Tamagna, *Banking and Finance in China* (New York, 1942); Tang Tsou, *America's Failure in China, 1941–50* (Chicago, 1963), published after this book was in type; and Arthur N. Young, *China's Economic and Financial Reconstruction,* Committee on International Economic Policy (New York, 1947).

Periodicals relating to the financial record in this period include the *Bulletin* of the Central Bank of China, in English, 1937–1940; the Bank of China's *Financial and Commercial Monthly Bulletin,* 1937–1939, partly in English and partly in Chinese, and *Fortnightly Letter on Economic Conditions in China,* 1943–1945; *Finance and Commerce* (Shanghai, 1937–1941); and, for the Japanese angle, the *Oriental Economist* (Tokyo, 1937–1945).

GLOSSARY

ATC	Air Transport Command
AVG	American Volunteer Group ("Flying Tigers")
CAMCO	Central Aircraft Manufacturing Company
CBI	China-Burma-India theater
CNAC	China National Aviation Corporation
CRB	Central Reserve Bank (puppet regime, Central China)
Fapi	Chinese Government currency (legal tender money)
FRB	Federal Reserve Bank (puppet regime, North China)
FRUS	Foreign Relations of the United States, published by the Department of State
GMO	Generalissimo Chiang Kai-shek
ICHIGO	Japanese operation of 1944 to take East China air bases and certain railways
MATTERHORN	The B-29 bombing operation from West China
OSS	Office of Strategic Services
RAF	Royal Air Force
Tael	Chinese ounce (1.00471 troy ounces)
TVA	Tennessee Valley Authority
UNRRA	United Nations Relief and Rehabilitation Administration
USMC	United States Marine Corps
USSBS	United States Strategic Bombing Survey
WPB	War Production Board
X (X-Ray) force	Chinese army based in India
Y (Yoke) force	American-sponsored Chinese army based in Yunnan
Z (Zebra) force	Chinese army planned to be reorganized in East China with American help

NOTES

I. Introduction: China Before the War

1. On the development of the United Front see *The Chinese Communist Movement, 5 July 1945*, by the Military Intelligence Division, War Department, Washington, in Institute of Pacific Relations, Hearings before the Subcommittee to Investigate the Administration of the Internal Security Act and Other Internal Security Laws, of the Committee on the Judiciary, U.S. Senate, 82d Congress, 2d Session, part 7A, appendix II (Washington, 1952), pp. 2327–2332, hereinafter referred to as Hearings, Institute of Pacific Relations. For another view see Edgar Snow, *Red Star Over China* (New York, 1938), *passim*.

2. Despatch of May 11, *Foreign Relations of the United States*, 1937, vol. 3, p. 90. Hereinafter cited as *FRUS*.

3. For an account of the American silver policy and its effects on China to mid-1937, see D. H. Leavens, *Silver Money* (Cowles Commission Monograph no. 4) (Bloomington, Ind., 1939); A. S. Everest, *Morgenthau, the New Deal, and Silver*, Columbia University (New York, 1950); and J. M. Blum, *From the Morgenthau Diaries* (Boston, 1959), chapters 5 and 10.

4. See *FRUS, 1937*, vol. 4, pp. 583, 594.

II. China in the Crucible, 1937

1. *FRUS, 1937*, vol. 4, p. 2.

2. *Ibid.*, pp. 17–18, 22–25, 28–43, 58–61.

3. Miss Dorothy Borg, writing in the *Political Science Quarterly* of September, 1957, pp. 405–433, gives a full and interesting analysis of the background and significance of this famous speech, and the issues it raised.

4. *FRUS, 1937*, vol. 3, p. 769. See also the Norman Davis papers, memorandum of November 27, 1937, in the Library of Congress.

5. F. F. Liu, *A Military History of Modern China, 1924–1949* (Princeton, 1956). This is an admirable study.

6. *Ibid.*, p. 102.

7. *Ibid.*, pp. 91, 165.

8. *FRUS, 1937*, vol. 3, pp. 482–483.

9. Kurt Bloch, *German Interests and Policies in the Far East* (New York, 1940), pp. 26, 31–33, 37–38; Liu, *Military History*, pp. 101–102, 163–164; and *FRUS, 1937*, vol. 3, pp. 481–484.

10. Molotov's statement to General Patrick J. Hurley, August 1944. See *United States Relations with China, with Special Reference to the Period 1944–1949* (Washington, 1949), pp. 71–72. Hereinafter cited as *U.S. Relations with China, 1949*.

11. Despatch of May 23, 1938, *FRUS, 1938*, vol. 3, pp. 173–181. The conclusions in the above paragraph as to the Sian incident are supported by the above-cited study of the War Department's Military Intelligence Division. That study states that the Communists dissuaded dissident government troops from killing Chiang, and that W. H. Donald, Chiang's Australian political adviser, who took part in the Sian talks, stated that Chou En-lai

"was actually the one man who enabled Chiang to depart unharmed from the . . . kidnaping." Hearings, Institute of Pacific Relations, part 7 A, appendix II, p. 2331. See also Snow, *Red Star Over China,* part Twelve, and Snow, *Random Notes on Red China* (Cambridge, Mass., 1957), pp. 1–14. Apart from the attitudes of Russia and the Chinese Communists, Chang Hsueh-liang as commander of the dissident troops undoubtedly had a major part in the decision to release the Generalissimo.

12. Hearings, Institute of Pacific Relations, part 7 A, appendix II, pp. 2330–2332.

13. Tsiang's statement to the American chargé, December 20, 1937. *FRUS, 1937,* vol. 3, p. 827.

14. *Ibid.,* pp. 69–70. See also C. B. McLane, *Soviet Policy and the Chinese Communists, 1931–1946* (New York, 1958), pp. 98–100.

15. A. K. Wu, *China and the Soviet Union* (New York, 1950), pp. 264–265. Wu was long in the Chinese diplomatic service, connected with Russian affairs.

16. Statement to the American chargé, December 21, 1937, *FRUS, 1937,* vol. 3, pp. 827–828.

17. *FRUS, 1937,* vol. 3, pp. 288–289.

18. *Ibid.,* vol. 4, p. 2.

19. Wu, *China and the Soviet Union,* pp. 263–265, and Liu, *Military History,* pp. 166–167.

20. *FRUS, 1937,* vol. 3, p. 537.

21. *Ibid.,* pp. 538–540.

22. *Ibid.,* p. 636.

23. *Ibid.,* pp. 460, 616, 711–712, 827–828.

24. Chennault, *Way of a Fighter,* p. 40.

25. *Ibid.,* pp. 47–60.

26. *FRUS, 1937,* vol. 3, pp. 565, 578, 606, 616, 780.

27. *Ibid.,* vol. 4, pp. 520–548.

28. *FRUS, Japan, 1931–1941,* vol. 2, p. 201; *FRUS, 1937,* vol. 4, pp. 530ff., and vol. 3, pp. 520, 531–532.

29. *FRUS, 1937,* vol. 3, p. 514.

30. *Ibid.,* pp. 832–833.

III. The Financial Emergency, 1937: Self-Help and Foreign Aid

1. *FRUS, 1938,* vol. 3, p. 567.

2. Everest, *Morgenthau and Silver,* p. 118.

3. *Ibid.,* p. 120. See also Blum, *Morgenthau Diaries,* pp. 481–485.

4. Chang Kia-ngau, *The Inflationary Spiral: The Experience in China, 1939–1950* (New York, 1959), pp. 213–214.

5. For data as to the development of the customs service, see H. B. Morse, *The Trade and Administration of China* (London, 1920), pp. 385–410; S. F. Wright, *Hart and the Chinese Customs* (Belfast, 1950); and S. F. Wright and J. H. Cubbon, *China's Customs Revenue since the Revolution of 1911* (Shanghai, 1935).

6. For the agreement re the Salt Administration, see the Reorganization Loan Agreement of 1913, in J. V. A. MacMurray, *Treaties and Agreements with and concerning China, 1894–1919* (New York, 1921), vol. 2, pp. 1009–1010, 1026–1029. For President Wilson's statement criticizing the 1913 agreement see p. 1025.

7. See *The Chinese Year Book, 1936–37*, pp. 891–945.

8. See *FRUS, 1937*, vol. 3, p. 877, and for further data concerning these events, pp. 858–915.

IV. Trading Space for Time in 1938:
    Communications and Military Aid

1. *FRUS, 1939*, vol. 3, p. 754.

2. Statement of Ambassador Yang Chieh, quoted by Wu, *China and the Soviet Union*, p. 269.

3. *FRUS, 1938*, vol. 3, pp. 135–136.

4. *Ibid., 1939*, vol. 3, p. 738.

5. See Liu, *Military History*, pp. 167–168.

6. Chennault, *Way of a Fighter*, pp. 62–63.

7. *FRUS, 1938*, vol. 3, p. 352; *1939*, vol. 3, p. 641.

8. *Ibid., 1938*, vol. 3, pp. 441–488; *1939*, vol. 3, pp. 46–47, 70–71.

9. Data of the Japan Defense Agency, furnished to me through the American Embassy, Tokyo, April 1960. See appendix V.

10. *FRUS, 1938*, vol. 3, p. 165.

11. Ambassador Johnson reported November 18, 1938, that it seemed that the closest the Russians came to asking a *quid pro quo* was in telling Chiang that they had a hundred planes at Lanchow, and would send more if China would continue resistance. Chiang retorted that he intended to continue resistance regardless of whether Russia helped China. *Ibid.*, p. 384–385.

12. This statement has been attributed to various sources, and regardless of its form or origin is an authentic statement of the Communist policy. See Chiang Kai-shek, *Soviet Russia in China* (New York, 1957), p. 85; A. C. Wedemeyer, *Wedemeyer Reports!* (New York, 1958), p. 283; and Liu, *Military History*, p. 206.

13. See R. C. North, *Moscow and Chinese Communists* (Stanford, 1953), p. 180. This is not the place to discuss how far Chinese Communist policy was made on Chinese and Russian initiative, respectively, or the details of the Communist movement as it developed in China during the war. Besides North's work see *Hearings, Institute of Pacific Relations*, part 7A, appendix II; Liu, *Military History, passim*; McLane, *Soviet Policy, passim*; and Chiang Kai-shek, *Soviet Russia in China, passim*.

14. *FRUS, 1938*, vol. 3, p. 137.

15. Bloch, *German Interests and Policies*, pp. 42–43.

16. Liu, *Military History*, p. 164; *FRUS, 1938*, vol. 3, pp. 182, 191–192, 198, 202, 213–214.

17. Bloch, *German Interests and Policies*, pp. 43–45.

18. *FRUS, 1938*, vol. 3, pp. 364–366.

V. Back-Stopping Resistance in 1938: The Sinews of War

1. In the latter part of March an American statement that "the Treasury will defer continuation of the monthly silver purchase arrangements with Mexico until further notice" caused weakness in the silver markets. For the Treasury view of the Mexican episode, see Blum, *Morgenthau Diaries*, pp. 493–497.

2. *FRUS, 1938*, vol. 3, p. 533.

3. Everest, *Morgenthau and Silver*, p. 121.

4. For some of the particulars of these developments in North China

the writer is indebted to a memorandum of December 14, 1939, by F. P. Ling who participated in these events as a senior officer of the Bank of China. Also see "Federal Reserve Bank of China—an Instrument of Japanese Economic Policy," in *Foreign Commerce Weekly*, Washington, August 16, 1941, pp. 4–5, 18.

5. Quoted in *Finance and Commerce*, Shanghai, September 7, 1938, p. 185.

6. *South China Morning Post*, Hong Kong, September 9, 1938.

7. *Finance and Commerce*, Shanghai, July 20, 1938, p. 46.

8. W. H. E. Thomas, *Vanished China* (London, 1952), p. 195.

9. *FRUS, 1937*, vol. 3, p. 338; *1937*, vol. 4, pp. 585–586, 595, 612–619; *1938*, vol. 3, p. 566.

10. *Ibid., 1938*, vol. 3, pp. 520–530, 555–556, 564–565, 385–386.

11. The New York *Times*, February 9, 1940.

12. Morgenthau Diaries, October 1939, vol. 216, p. 281.

13. *FRUS, 1938*, vol. 3, p. 157.

14. *Ibid.*, pp. 535–536.

15. Britain considered credits to China under the export procedure, but negotiations for such credits at this stage led to no definite result. *Ibid.*, pp. 536–538; 540–542, 552, 559.

16. Report of November 18, 1938, *ibid.*, pp. 385–386.

17. Blum, *Morgenthau Diaries*, pp. 205–206, 479–492.

18. *Ibid.*, pp. 508–509.

19. *FRUS, 1938*, vol. 3, pp. 538–540.

20. *Ibid.*, pp. 541, 544–545.

21. Morgenthau Diaries, April 1940, vol. 255, p. 183.

22. *FRUS, 1938*, vol. 3, pp. 545–551.

23. Quoted from a partial text in Blum, *Morgenthau Diaries*, p. 527.

24. White's papers at Princeton University Library show his earlier draft of the letter.

25. *FRUS, 1938*, vol. 3, pp. 320–321, 566–568.

26. *Ibid.*, p. 384.

27. *Ibid.*, pp. 566–577.

28. Morgenthau Diaries, October 4, 1939, vol. 215, p. 283. See also Blum, *Morgenthau Diaries*, pp. 508–513, 519, 527.

29. *FRUS, 1938*, vol. 3, p. 586.

30. *Ibid.*, pp. 586–590.

31. M. Shigemitsu, *Japan and Her Destiny* (New York, 1958), p. 190.

32. *FRUS, 1938*, vol. 3, p. 435.

33. *Ibid.*, pp. 377–382.

34. *Ibid.*, pp. 581–582, 590–591.

35. Reuters News Service, December 20, 1938.

VI. THE SINO-FOREIGN REVENUE SERVICES AND CHINA'S CREDIT, 1938–1941

1. *FRUS, 1937*, vol. 3, pp. 904–905.

2. *Ibid., 1938*, vol. 3, pp. 626, 629–630.

3. *Ibid., 1937*, vol. 3, pp. 904, 911–915.

4. *Ibid., 1938*, vol. 3, p. 701.

5. For the text of most of the documents, see *ibid.*, pp. 678–681, 688–694.

6. *Ibid.*, pp. 684–695.

7. *Ibid.*, pp. 695–698.

8. *Ibid.*, pp. 704–705.

9. *Ibid.*, p. 713.

10. *Ibid.*, *1939*, vol. 3, pp. 852–866.

11. For American official views on the monopoly scheme, see *ibid.*, *1942*, *China*, pp. 495–498, 502–505.

12. *FRUS, 1939*, vol. 3, pp. 810, 816–817.

13. See *Documents on British Foreign Policy, 1919–1939*, 3d series, vol. 8, pp. 231, 442, 451, 516; and vol. 9, pp. 150, 276.

VII. STALEMATE, 1939–1941: COMMUNICATIONS

1. *Finance and Commerce*, Shanghai, June 22, 1938, p. 481.

2. *FRUS, 1938*, vol. 3, p. 457.

3. *Ibid.*, *1939*, vol. 3, pp. 698, 767.

4. *Ibid.*, pp. 762–773.

5. Concerning developments in the Indochina situation in 1937–1939, see *ibid.*, *1937*, vol. 3, pp. 623, 629, 635; *1938*, vol. 3, pp. 319–320, 351–352, 375, 607–613; *1939*, vol. 3, pp. 103–105, 110, 740–741, 746–749, 755–774.

6. *Ibid.*, *1939*, vol. 3, p. 751, n.

7. The text is in the New York *Times*, July 19, 1940, p. 10.

8. See telegram of November 25, 1941, from Owen Lattimore to Laughlin Currie, *FRUS, 1941*, vol. 4, p. 652.

9. See *U.S. Relations with China, 1949*, p. 27.

10. The official British war history, S. W. Kirby, *The War Against Japan* (London, 1958), vol. 2, pp. 6–14, indicates that there was difference of opinion whether Japanese troops could invade in force from Thailand. For further discussion of the loss of Burma and its effects, see chapter XIII.

11. For a journalistic account of the abuses, see Leland Stowe, *They Shall Not Sleep* (New York, 1944), chap. 5.

12. State Department file 033.1193, Currie, Laughlin 18b.

13. State Department file 893.154/364, 367.

VIII. STALEMATE, 1939–1941: MATERIAL AND MILITARY AID

1. *FRUS, 1939*, vol. 3, pp. 136, 160, 261, 757, 764; Liu, *Military History*, p. 168.

2. Liu, *Military History*, pp. 169–170.

3. W. L. Langer and S. E. Gleason, *The Undeclared War* (New York, 1953), pp. 290–291.

4. In the fall of 1940, when Hitler had overrun Europe, the Generalissimo told Ambassador Johnson that he thought sizable American aid to China would encourage Russia to give more aid; but that otherwise he feared Russian aid was more likely to go to the Chinese Communists. *FRUS, 1940*, vol. 4, pp. 672, 429.

5. *FRUS, 1941*, vol. 4, p. 88; State Department files 793.94/16588 and 661.9331/38.

6. For accounts of these diplomatic maneuverings among the Axis powers and Russia, see Langer and Gleason, *The Undeclared War*, pp. 341ff., and W. L. Shirer, *The Rise and Fall of the Third Reich* (New York, 1960), pp. 871ff., especially p. 876.

7. *FRUS, 1941*, vol. 4, p. 954.

8. See Langer and Gleason, *The Undeclared War,* p. 625ff., and Shirer, *Rise and Fall of the Third Reich,* p. 871ff.

9. *Hearings, Institute of Pacific Relations,* part 7A, appendix II., p. 2376.

10. *Ibid.,* pp. 2344–2354.

11. *FRUS, 1939,* vol. 3, pp. 208, 308; State Department file 033.1193/9.

12. McLane, *Soviet Policy,* chapters 3 and 4.

13. *Ibid.,* pp. 103–104, 144–152.

14. *FRUS, 1939,* vol. 3, pp. 261–262.

15. *Ibid.,* p. 199.

16. Morgenthau Diaries, vol. 215, p. 282, October 4, 1939.

17. *Ibid.,* vol. 223, pp. 212–214, November 22, 1939.

18. United Press despatch from Washington, February 8, 1940.

19. Morgenthau Diaries, vol. 257, p. 178.

20. *South China Morning Post,* Hong Kong, March 7, 1940.

21. See *FRUS, 1940,* vol. 4, pp. 664–667; also Morgenthau Diaries, vol. 305, p. 213, September 12, 1940.

22. Morgenthau Diaries, vol. 308, p. 157, September 20, 1940.

23. *Ibid.,* vol. 294, pp. 37–38; vol. 307, pp. 65–77 and 148–158; and vol. 308, p. 159. See also *FRUS, 1940,* vol. 4, p. 663. A more detailed account based on the Morgenthau Diaries is given by Arthur L. Davis, in a Washington despatch of June 9, 1956, to the Buffalo *Evening News.*

24. *FRUS, 1940,* vol. 4, pp. 668ff., also Morgenthau Diaries, vol. 307, pp. 282–294, September 23, 1940.

25. State Department file 893.51/7145.

26. *FRUS, 1940,* vol. 4, p. 430.

27. *Documents on British Foreign Policy, 1919–1939,* 3rd series, vol. 9, p. 390.

28. Of the credit of £2,859,000, Chinese records show that about £265,000 was repaid by the end of 1944. A letter from the office of the Chancellor of the Exchequer, August 15, 1962, states that this credit was "only partly repaid," and that £0.9 million of the £5 million credit has been repaid.

29. See Chang Kia-ngau, *China's Struggle for Railroad Development* (New York, 1943), pp. 260–262, 280–284.

30. Okumiya and Horikoshi, with Martin Caidin, *Zero!,* p. 59.

31. *FRUS, 1940,* vol. 4, pp. 705–708.

32. See Roosevelt Papers and Morgenthau Diaries as summarized in Langer and Gleason, *The Undeclared War,* pp. 238–239, 301–304.

33. State Department file 841.248/813.

34. Quoted in *U.S. Relations with China, 1949,* p. 26.

35. C. F. Romanus and Riley Sunderland, *Stilwell's Mission to China,* Department of the Army, Washington, 1953, pp. 13–16. Hereinafter cited as *Stilwell's Mission to China.*

36. *FRUS, 1941,* vol. 5, pp. 629–630.

37. *Ibid.,* vol. 4, pp. 165–167.

38. *Ibid.,* vol. 5, pp. 635–637, 641–642. For a list of the items approved in April see *Stilwell's Mission to China,* p. 16.

39. *Stilwell's Mission to China,* pp. 16, 26–29.

40. State Department file 893.24/1124.

41. *FRUS, 1941,* vol. 5, pp. 670–671.

42. *Stilwell's Mission to China,* pp. 27–49; and Langer and Gleason, *The Undeclared War,* pp. 711–712.

43. *Stilwell's Mission to China*, pp. 37, 47.

44. *Ibid.*, pp. 23–25.

45. Letter from Department of State, January 10, 1958; *Stilwell's Mission to China*, p. 49.

46. *FRUS, 1939*, vol. 3, pp. 773–774, memorandum of January 3, 1940.

47. Chennault, *Way of a Fighter*, pp. 101–104. See also *Stilwell's Mission to China*, p. 18, which states that Admiral H. R. Stark arranged the escort because he deemed it "essential to U.S. support of China."

48. *Stilwell's Mission to China*, p. 20.

49. Chennault, *Way of a Fighter*, p. 112.

50. E. R. Stettinius, *Lend-Lease* (New York, 1944), pp. 112–118.

IX. Stalemate, 1939–1940: Can the Finances Hold Out?

1. Morgenthau Diaries, vol. 334, p. 13, December 1, 1940.

2. *FRUS, 1939*, vol. 4, pp. 181, 191–192, 199.

3. *Ibid.*, pp. 225, 227.

4. *Documents on British Foreign Policy, 1919–1939*, 3d series, vol. 9, p. 326.

5. *Ibid.*, p. 244.

6. Quoted from Reuter's News Service, July 25, 1939.

7. Reuter's despatch from Tokyo, July 26, 1939.

8. *Documents on British Foreign Policy, 1919–1939*, 3d series, vol. 9, p. 224.

9. *Ibid.*, pp. 463–486.

10. *China Weekly Review*, February 1, 1947.

11. *Documents on British Foreign Policy, 1919–1939*, 3d series, vol. 8, pp. 295, 488.

12. The main provisions of the agreements are given in *ibid.*, pp. 486–487 and *FRUS, 1939*, vol. 3, pp. 653–654.

13. *FRUS, 1939*, vol. 3, pp. 655–657.

14. *Ibid.*, p. 695.

15. *Ibid.*, pp. 206–207, 854.

16. See *Far Eastern Financial Notes*, Department of Commerce, Washington, August 19, 1939.

17. *FRUS, 1939*, vol. 3, pp. 550–557; *1940*, vol. 4, pp. 645–647.

18. *Ibid.*, *1940*, vol. 4, p. 651.

19. *Ibid.*, p. 652.

20. See the New York *Times*, October 26, 1939.

21. Morgenthau Diaries, vol. 261, p. 199.

22. *FRUS, 1940*, vol. 4, pp. 656–657. Presentation of the message, dated May 17, was delayed by exchanges between Ambassador Hu and Chungking about wording.

23. *Ibid.*, pp. 654–656.

24. *Ibid.*, pp. 658–659.

25. *Hearings, Institute of Pacific Relations*, July 2, 1952, pp. 142–144.

26. White's endorsement of July 2 on the memorandum said: "This is a copy of the preliminary draft which went to the Secretary and which I understand the Secretary took to the President." See Morgenthau Diaries, vol. 278, pp. 81–84.

27. *FRUS, 1940*, vol. 4, p. 668, memorandum of September 13, 1940, by A. A. Berle, Jr.

28. See *Ibid.*, pp. 434–458.

29. *Ibid., 1941*, vol. 4, pp. 428–430, 439–441, 672–710.
30. Quoted from Roosevelt Papers by Langer and Gleason, *The Undeclared War*, p. 300.
31. Morgenthau Diaries, November 29, 1940, p. 31.
32. The New York *Times*, December 11, 1940.

X. The New Deal in Aid for the Currency, 1941

1. *Central News Agency*, July 24, 1939.
2. See *Documents on British Foreign Policy, 1919–1939*, series 3, vol. 9, pp. 341, 391, 490, 513.
3. *FRUS, 1941*, vol. 5, pp. 629–630, and vol. 4, pp. 81–95. The latter contains parts of Currie's report. He made useful proposals on land tax in kind, banking reform, supply of goods, and transport by road and air. He endorsed the Generalissimo's idea of an American-British economic mission, which was partly realized by the visit to China of Sir Otto Niemeyer and H. Merle Cochran late in 1941.
4. State Department file 893.51/7269.
5. Morgenthau Diaries, vol. 450, p. 365, October 14, 1941; vol. 496, p. 288, February 1, 1942.
6. *Ibid.*, vol. 334, p. 13, December 1, 1940.
7. *FRUS, 1941*, vol. 5, pp. 601–602.
8. Re the recommendation of freezing, see the extract from Currie's report in *ibid.*, vol. 4, p. 93. Currie's other recommendations cited above are not included in *FRUS*, but are from the State Department's photostatic copy of the full text, which latter is in the Franklin D. Roosevelt Library, Hyde Park, New York.
9. See *Scope of Soviet Activity in the United States:* Hearings before the Subcommittee to Investigate the Administration of the Internal Security Act . . . of the Committee on the Judiciary United States Senate, 1957, part 35, pp. 1959–1961.
10. Morgenthau Diaries, vol. 387, p. 322, April 10, 1941.
11. *FRUS, 1941*, vol. 5, p. 667.
12. Chapter V, and *FRUS, 1938*, vol. 3, pp. 157, 385–386, and *1939*, vol. 3, pp. 665–666.
13. *Finance and Commerce*, May 14, 1941, p. 482.
14. Central News Agency, Chungking, June 20, 1941.
15. *Finance and Commerce*, July 9, p. 39, and July 16, p. 61, 1941.
16. Quoted in *ibid.*, July 9, 1941, p. 39.
17. State Department file 893.51/7253.
18. Morgenthau Diaries, vol. 238, p. 150, January 29, 1940, and vol. 263, p. 161, May 16, 1940; *FRUS, 1940*, vol. 4, p. 659.
19. Feis, *Road to Pearl Harbor*, pp. 142–144; the New York *Times*, January 19, 20, 1941.
20. *FRUS, 1941*, vol. 5, p. 621.
21. The quotation is from an extract from Currie's report, a photostatic copy of which the State Department later obtained from the Franklin D. Roosevelt Library, Hyde Park, New York. See *FRUS, 1941*, vol. 4, p. 93. The Editor of Foreign Relations told me in 1959 that no record of the Generalissimo's communication is in the Department's files.
22. Morgenthau Diaries, vol. 390, pp. 4–7, April 19, 1941.
23. Feis, *Road to Pearl Harbor*, pp. 227–228, n.

24. Morgenthau Diaries, vol. 405, pp. 471ff., June 6, 1941. This was the forerunner of White's proposal which Morgenthau transmitted to the President and Secretary of State November 18, 1941, in what proved to be the final stage of negotiations before Pearl Harbor. That proposal would have sought a full settlement with Japan based on withdrawal of Japanese forces from China, a "final settlement of the Manchurian question," change of the American immigration restrictions to put China and Japan on the same basis as other countries, credits of US$2.5 billion to Japan, trade agreements, and removal of most of the American fleet from the Pacific to face Hitler's threat. *FRUS, 1941,* vol. 4, pp. 606–613, and *Japan, 1931–1941,* vol. 2, pp. 769–770.

25. For an account of these matters which makes use of contemporary and postwar data including the Tokyo War Crimes Documents, see Langer and Gleason, *The Undeclared War,* pp. 629ff.

26. *Ibid.,* pp. 641–645.

27. *FRUS, 1941,* vol. 4, pp. 832–833, and vol. 5, p. 681.

28. *Ibid.,* vol. 4, p. 851.

29. Langer and Gleason, *The Undeclared War,* pp. 654–655, 708.

30. General License no. 58, U.S. Treasury Department, July 26, 1941.

31. Wilfred Fleischer wrote in the New York *Herald Tribune,* of July 27, 1941: "Japan must move quickly to consummate her conquests in Asia or face economic ruin and defeat . . . The Japanese are now with their backs to the wall and they must carry on with the struggle they have so rashly embarked upon or renounce their dreams of empire in Asia. The die has been cast."

32. Langer and Gleason, *The Undeclared War,* pp. 651–654, 708.

33. Morgenthau Diaries, vol. 472, pp. 208–214, November 24, 1941.

34. *Ibid.,* vol. 450, p. 259, August 23, 1941.

35. *Ibid.,* vol. 485, p. 368, January 14, 1942; vol. 496, pp. 286–287, February 1, 1942.

36. *Ibid.,* vol. 472, p. 209, November 24, 1941.

37. *United Press* and *Reuters News Service* despatches from Shanghai, October 14 and 15, 1941.

38. Morgenthau Diaries, vol. 463, p. 159, November 18, 1941.

39. Letter of December 24, 1959, to the author of this book.

40. The text of this letter of December 7, 1941, is in the record of the Hearings of the Subcommittee to Investigate the Administration of the Internal Security Act and Other Security Laws, of the Senate Committee on the Judiciary, July 13, 1956, part 35, pp. 1961–1964.

XI. A SUMMING UP, 1937–1941

1. *U.S. Relations with China, 1949,* p. 32; letter of August 15, 1962, from the Office of the British Chancellor of the Exchequer; Russian data from the records of the Chinese Finance Ministry.

2. State Department file 893.51/7145.

3. *Finance and Commerce,* November 23, 1938, p. 402.

4. *FRUS, 1941,* vol. 4, p. 395.

5. *Ibid.,* pp. 503, 552–553.

6. Memorandum of October 25, 1941, by William R. Langdon of the Far Eastern Division, *ibid.,* pp. 545–546.

7. *Ibid.,* pp. 660–661.

8. *Ibid.*, p. 665.

9. *Ibid.*, *Japan, 1931–1941*, vol. 2, pp. 769–770.

XII. Massive Financial Injections

1. Morgenthau Diaries, vol. 485, p. 350, December 16, 1941.

2. *Ibid.*, vol. 485, pp. 357, 361, January 3 and 9, 1942; *FRUS, 1942, China*, pp. 432–433.

3. Morgenthau Diaries, vol. 484, p. 186, January 9, 1942.

4. *FRUS, 1942, China*, pp. 433–435.

5. Morgenthau Diaries, vol. 485, pp. 252–253, January 13, 1942. See also *FRUS, 1942, China*, p. 441.

6. Morgenthau Diaries, vol. 485, p. 211.

7. *FRUS, China, 1942*, p. 450. See also Morgenthau Diaries, vol. 485, pp. 96–97, January 12, 1942; vol. 489, pp. 369–372, January 28, 1942; and vol. 490, p. 41, January 30, 1942.

8. *FRUS, 1942, China*, p. 443 and 443n.

9. *Ibid.*, pp. 444–447.

10. Morgenthau Diaries, vol. 487, p. 280, January 17, 1942; vol. 489, p. 366, January 28, 1942; vol. 491, p. 100, February 2, 1942.

11. *Ibid.*, vol. 490, pp. 149–150, January 30, 1942.

12. *Ibid.*, p. 161, January 30, 1942; vol. 491, pp. 88–90, February 2, 1942; *FRUS, 1942, China*, p. 454.

13. Morgenthau Diaries, vol. 494, pp. 1–22, February 9, 1942.

14. *Ibid.*, vol. 580, pp. 93–94, OSS report of September 5, 1942.

15. *Ibid.*, pp. 76–77.

16. *U.S. Relations with China, 1949*, contains the text of the draft agreement, pp. 479–481, and the final text, pp. 511–512.

17. Morgenthau Diaries, vol. 503, pp. 614–615, letter of March 3, 1942.

18. *Ibid.*, vol. 507, p. 144, March 12, 1942.

19. *U.S. Relations with China, 1949*, pp. 483–484.

20. *FRUS, 1942, China*, p. 487; Morgenthau Diaries, vol. 509, p. 113, March 19, 1942.

21. The text of the agreement is given in *U.S. Relations with China, 1949*, pp. 511–512. See also *FRUS, 1942, China*, pp. 419–495.

22. Morgenthau Diaries, vol. 513, p. 58, April 3, 1942.

23. *FRUS, 1942, China*, p. 475, telegram, March 1.

24. Morgenthau Diaries, vol. 485, p. 113, February 18, 1942.

25. *Ibid.*, vol. 580, p. 92, OSS report of September 5, 1942.

26. *Ibid.*, vol. 491, p. 4, February 1, 1942. See also *FRUS, 1942, China*, p. 447.

27. Morgenthau Diaries, vol. 491, p. 94, February 2, 1942.

28. *Ibid.*, vol. 489, pp. 375–376, January 25, 1942.

29. *Ibid.*, vol. 530, p. 220, May 21, 1942. See also *FRUS, 1942, China*, pp. 517–523.

30. Morgenthau Diaries, vol. 482, p. 213, January 3, 1942; vol. 495, p. 492, Fox's memorandum of February 11, 1942; vol. 499, pp. 428–430, despatch of January 8, 1942.

31. *Ibid.*, vol. 488, pp. 62–63, January 24, 1942.

32. *U.S. Relations with China, 1949*, p. 511.

33. See the Chancellor's *Third Report on Mutual Aid*, October 1946 (Cmd. 6931), pp. 7–8, supplemented by a letter of August 15, 1962, from the Chancellor's office.

34. See the letter of January 27 from Sir Frederick Phillips of the British Treasury to Morgenthau, *FRUS, 1942, China,* p. 447.

35. Morgenthau Diaries, vol. 515, pp. 269–287, April 11, 1942.

36. *Ibid.,* vol. 521, p. 173, April 20, 1942.

37. *FRUS, China, 1942,* pp. 516–517.

38. *U.S. Relations with China, 1949,* p. 489.

XIII. The Near Siege of China

1. The relevant works of the official historians are: from the American side, Charles F. Romanus and Riley Sunderland's three volumes, *Stilwell's Mission to China, Stilwell's Command Problems,* and *Time Runs Out in CBI* (Washington, 1953, 1956, 1959); and W. F. Craven and J. L. Cate, *The Army Air Forces in World War II,* vols, 1, 4, 5, 7, *passim* (Chicago, 1948, 1950, 1953, 1958); and, from the British side, S. W. Kirby, *The War Against Japan,* vol. 2 (London, 1958), and John Ehrman, *Grand Strategy,* vol. 5, *passim* (H. M. Stationery Office, London, 1956). For the Japanese side, see Takushiro Hattori, *Daitoa Senso Zenshi* (The Complete History of the Greater East Asia War), in Japanese (Tokyo, 1953). I know of no corresponding Chinese history, but considerable information is contained in the book by F. F. Liu, *A Military History of Modern China, 1924–1949.*

2. See Kirby, *The War Against Japan,* vol. 2, pp. 19–21; *Stilwell's Mission to China,* pp. 57–62; and *FRUS, 1942, China,* pp. 573–576.

3. *Stilwell's Mission to China,* pp. 84, 134–135.

4. See Kirby, *The War Against Japan,* vol. 2, pp. 16–19; and *Stilwell's Mission to China,* pp. 50–57, 84–85.

5. Supplement to *London Gazette,* January 1948, quoted by Herbert Feis, *The China Tangle* (Princeton, 1953), p. 25; *Stilwell's Mission to China,* p. 55.

6. *FRUS, 1942, China,* p. 7.

7. Interview with representative of the American Office of Strategic Services reported in Morgenthau Diaries, vol. 580, p. 124.

8. Winston Churchill, *The Hinge of Fate* (Boston, 1950), pp. 56–58, 155–166.

9. For full accounts of the campaign see the official histories: Kirby, *The War Against Japan,* vol. 2, *passim,* especially pp. 218–220; and *Stilwell's Mission to China, passim.*

10. Kirby, *The War Against Japan,* vol. 2, pp. 101–104, 218–220. See Chapter VII re my unsuccessful effort in the spring of 1941 to arouse greater interest in the defense of Burma.

11. Kirby, *The War Against Japan,* vol. 2, p. 220.

12. Liu, *Military History,* p. 213.

13. See *Stilwell's Mission to China,* pp. 252, 272, 275, 285, 345–346; also Craven and Cate, *The Army Air Forces in World War II,* vol. 4, pp. 448–451. See *FRUS, 1942, China,* p. 663. For strong criticism of Bissell in his dealings with Chennault, see R. L. Scott, *Flying Tiger: Chennault of China* (New York, 1959). My dealings with Bissell on behalf of CNAC indicated his lack of comprehension of the part CNAC was playing and could play in the war effort.

14. *FRUS, 1942, China,* p. 674.

15. Craven and Cate, *The Army Air Forces in World War II,* vol. 4, p. 413.

16. *Ibid.,* pp. 467–468.

17. For a full account see the official history, Craven and Cate, *The Army Air Forces in World War II*, vols. 1, 4, 5, 7.

18. *FRUS, 1942, China*, p. 576.

19. Craven and Cate, *The Army Air Forces in World War II*, vol. 1, p. 352; *Stilwell's Mission to China*, pp. 164–165.

20. *FRUS, 1942, China*, p. 677.

21. Craven and Cate, *The Army Air Forces in World War II*, vol. 4, pp. 446–447.

22. *Ibid.*, vol. 4, pp. 439–446, vol. 7, pp. 123–125; Romanus and Sunderland, *Stilwell's Mission to China*, p. 284.

23. *FRUS, 1943, China*, p. 602.

24. *Ibid.*, pp. 606, 612–613.

25. For documents on these negotiations see *ibid., 1942, China*, pp. 591–623, and *ibid., 1943, China*, pp. 590–619.

26. Romanus and Sunderland, *Stilwell's Command Problems*, p. 292n.

27. See *FRUS, 1942, China*, pp. 624–631, and *ibid., 1943, China*, pp. 620–644.

XIV. Money, Supplies, and Strategy, 1942–1943

1. *FRUS, 1942, China*, pp. 566–572. For the text see *Executive Agreements Series No. 251* or *56 Stat. 1494*. This agreement was similar to one which the United States and Britain signed February 23, 1942.

2. For further information re provision by China of hostels and subsistence for American forces in China, see Romanus and Sunderland, *Stilwell's Command Problems*, pp. 290–291.

3. State Department files 893.51/5-2644 and 893.24/5-345 and 5-3045.

4. 27th Report to Congress on Lend-lease Operations, March 31, 1948, p. 54.

5. The New York *Times*, September 1, 1946.

6. See appendix I and the graph on page 43.

7. Morgenthau Diaries, vol. 689, p. 168, January 3, 1944.

8. State Department files 103.91702/3783 and 893.24/1672.

9. Morgenthau Diaries, vol. 683, p. 81, December 10, 1943.

10. *Ibid.*, p. 94, December 11, 1943.

11. *Ibid.*, vol. 687, pp. 204–209, December 23, 1943.

12. *FRUS, 1942, China*, p. 21.

13. State Department file 893.24/1298.

14. *FRUS, 1942, China*, pp. 579–583; *Stilwell's Mission to China*, pp. 114–117, 159–160.

15. *FRUS, 1942, China*, p. 33; *Stilwell's Mission to China*, pp. 157–159.

16. Romanus and Sunderland, *Stilwell's Command Problems*, p. 451. See also *Hearings, Military Situation in the Far East*, before the Committee on Armed Services and the Committee on Foreign Relations, U.S. Senate, 82d Congress, 1st Session, Part 4, June 21, 1951, pp. 2873–2874.

17. *FRUS, 1942, China*, pp. 41, 48, 55.

18. *Stilwell's Mission to China*, pp. 157–162; T. H. White, ed., *The Stilwell Papers* (New York, 1948), p. 119.

19. *FRUS, 1942, China*, p. 89; *Stilwell's Mission to China*, pp. 169–172.

20. *Stilwell's Mission to China*, pp. 177–190, 198, 224–225.

21. *Ibid.*, p. 43.

22. *FRUS, 1942, China*, pp. 43–67, 90–92, 119, 138–139, 148–152.

23. White, *The Stilwell Papers,* pp. 171–172; see also *Stilwell's Mission to China,* pp. 222–245.

24. *FRUS, 1943, China,* pp. 505–514.

25. *Stilwell's Mission to China,* pp. 74, 159; *FRUS, 1943, China,* pp. 506–511.

26. *Stilwell's Mission to China,* p. 160.

27. H. B. Morse, *The International Relations of the Chinese Empire* (London, New York, 1910), vol. 1, p. 142.

28. *Stilwell's Mission to China,* p. 223.

29. *Ibid.,* pp. 160, 185–186, 223–225.

30. *Ibid.,* pp. 278–279.

31. *Ibid.,* p. 282.

32. Romanus and Sunderland, *Stilwell's Mission to China,* pp. 212–221; *Stilwell's Command Problems,* pp. 279–280.

33. *Stilwell's Mission to China,* pp. 234–241, 247.

34. *Ibid.,* pp. 290–291, 331–334, 341–344.

35. *Ibid.,* pp. 247–250, 290–291, 331–334, 341–344; Kirby, *The War Against Japan,* vol. 2, pp. 291–297.

36. *Stilwell's Mission to China,* pp. 247–250, 254–260, 271; Kirby, *The War Against Japan,* vol. 2, pp. 291–297.

37. *Stilwell's Mission to China,* p. 271.

38. Chennault claimed for the period to October 1942, an 8–1 record of enemy planes destroyed. (See Chennault, *Way of a Fighter,* p. 212.) General R. L. Scott, Jr., states that this group was credited officially with 299 enemy planes from December 18, 1941, to July 4, 1942, confirmed by outside sources, and that perhaps as many more were lost but not discovered and confirmed. This was done, he states, with never over 49 planes operational, and with loss of eight pilots killed in action and four missing, plus nine accidentally killed. See Scott, *Chennault of China,* p. 70.

39. Chennault, *Way of a Fighter,* pp. 212–216.

40. *Ibid.,* pp. 212–216; *Stilwell's Mission to China,* pp. 250–261.

41. *Stilwell's Mission to China,* pp. 278–280.

42. *Ibid.,* pp. 280–281.

43. *Ibid.,* p. 325.

44. *Ibid.,* p. 341. For a full account of the arguments and military decisions see *ibid.,* pp. 262–333.

45. See the three previously mentioned volumes of Romanus and Sunderland, *passim;* and *FRUS, 1943, China,* p. 131.

46. *FRUS, 1943, China,* pp. 336–339, 347.

47. *Ibid.,* pp. 292–296.

48. *Ibid.,* p. 74.

49. *Ibid.,* pp. 376–379, 385.

50. *Ibid.,* p. 283.

51. Memorandum of September 29, 1943, for the Generalissimo, quoted *ibid.,* p. 373.

52. Romanus and Sunderland, *Stilwell's Mission to China,* pp. 388–389.

53. *FRUS, The Conferences at Cairo and Tehran, 1943,* pp. 889–890. See also Romanus and Sunderland, *Stilwell's Command Problems,* p. 64. At the war's end only about a third of the program had been completed, and the American Government took the position that the undertaking was for the war period only. See chapter XVIII.

54. Kirby, *The War Against Japan,* vol. 2, p. 305.

55. Romanus and Sunderland, *Stilwell's Command Problems,* p. 53.

56. See *FRUS, The Conferences at Cairo and Tehran, 1943,* Washington, 1961. Not only do the documents contain little about economic and financial matters, but information about the reaching of major political and military decisions is often sketchy. Records of some of the principal meetings were not made, and the happenings have to be pieced together from various sources, including the later writings of some participants. Re the matters discussed in this Section see especially pp. 159–160, 340–351, 364–365, 543, 545, 561–562, 672–681, 700–711, 719–726, 758, 815–817, and 855–856. *Stilwell's Command Problems,* by Romanus and Sunderland, pp. 63–71, contains an analysis and information supplementing the afore-mentioned publication.

57. Romanus and Sunderland, *ibid.,* p. 66.

58. Sir Winston Churchill, *Closing the Ring* (Boston, 1951), p. 328.

59. Romanus and Sunderland, *Stilwell's Command Problems,* p. 70. For a detailed account of the argument, see pp. 63–71.

60. *FRUS, The Conferences at Cairo and Tehran, 1943,* pp. 56, 72–73, 77.

61. Churchill, *Closing the Ring,* p. 328. The Prime Minister's directive which Lord Louis Mountbatten, who commanded the theatre in Southeast Asia, received October 23, 1943, contemplated an amphibious operation. See Ehrman, *Grand Strategy,* vol. 5, p. 148. Ehrman states that the British explained verbally to Chiang before the end of the conference that the operation "will be taken into consideration" (p. 164). Ehrman states that "almost certainly" Roosevelt promised to Chiang by November 26 a "considerable amphibious operation" (p. 165). Churchill, in a Minute of November 29 cited by Ehrman (p. 571), "wishes to put on record" that although the proposed operation was to be carried out solely by British forces "he has never been consulted upon it," and "specifically refused the Generalissimo's request" that it be done simultaneously with land operations in Burma.

62. William D. Leahy, *I Was There* (New York, 1950), pp. 213–214; Romanus and Sunderland, *Stilwell's Command Problems,* p. 71.

XV. A YEAR OF DISCORD, 1944: MONEY MATTERS

1. Romanus and Sunderland, *Stilwell's Command Problems,* pp. 49, 82, 362–364.

2. Chiang had not been told just what operation was intended, and it later developed that the South East Asia Command still had resources for a limited amphibious operation. See *ibid.,* pp. 71, 75ff.

3. *Ibid.,* p. 71.

4. For the full text of the message of December 9, 1943, see *ibid.,* pp. 74–75.

5. White, ed., *The Stilwell Papers,* pp. 251–252. See also *U.S. Relations with China, 1949,* p. 488, and *FRUS, The Conferences at Cairo and Tehran, 1943,* pp. 804–805, 845, 861.

6. *U.S. Relations with China, 1949,* p. 499.

7. Morgenthau Diaries, vol. 683, pp. 39–43, telegram of December 9, 1943.

8. For the full text of the memorandum, see *U.S. Relations with China, 1949,* pp. 488–489.

9. Romanus and Sunderland, *Stilwell's Command Problems*, pp. 79–80.

10. *FRUS, 1943, China*, pp. 487–489.

11. Telegram of January 5, 1944, to Ambassador Gauss, State Department file 893.51/7727A.

12. See *U.S. Relations with China, 1949*, pp. 492–495, for the text of the message and Gauss' report.

13. Morgenthau Diaries, vol. 695, pp. 51–56, 170–179, January 18 and 19, 1944.

14. State Department file 893.51/7732.

15. State Department file 893.51/7732, 7735a and 7741a,b.

16. For the text see Romanus and Sunderland, *Stilwell's Command Problems*, pp. 300–301.

17. Morgenthau Diaries, vol. 741, p. 91, Morgenthau's letter of June 8, 1944, to President Roosevelt.

18. *U.S. Relations with China, 1949*, p. 559.

19. Morgenthau Diaries, vol. 702, pp. 137–139, February 19, 1944.

20. *U.S. Relations with China, 1949*, pp. 492–493.

21. Morgenthau Diaries, vol. 695, pp. 272–280, and vol. 696, pp. 25–28, January 24, 1944. See also Romanus and Sunderland, *Stilwell's Command Problems*, pp. 297–301.

22. Morgenthau Diaries, vol. 701, pp. 280–281, February 14, 1944.

23. *Ibid.*, vol. 712, p. 55; vol. 733, p. 34.

24. *Ibid.*, vol. 755, pp. 13–64, July 16, 1944.

25. *Ibid.*, vol. 798, pp. 203–248, November 25, 1944; vol. 810, p. 171, January 17, 1945.

26. The Treasury made public the settlement January 23. They explained payment of cash for war-connected services as due to the fact that it related to a period before there was an arrangement with China for Lend-Lease and reverse Lend-Lease. The New York *Times*, January 24, 1945.

27. Morgenthau Diaries, vol. 859, pp. 28–29, letter of June 24, 1945.

28. The figure of US$137 million is taken from documents prepared by the Treasury for the Bretton Woods negotiations of July 1944, on reimbursing China for American army costs. The detailed monthly figures show disbursements of US$6 million for personnel, over and above the US$137 million, but most of the US$6 million was paid out in American currency notes sold in the free market. See Morgenthau Diaries, vol. 754, pp. 52, 55. A War Department resumé dated May 19, 1944, puts the figure at US$155.5 million. See *U.S. Relations with China, 1949*, pp. 497, 501. I cannot explain the discrepancy unless the US$155.5 million is a preliminary figure that includes the US$25 million paid in March 1944, in consideration of advances of local currency for which no rate was fixed.

29. *U.S. Relations with China, 1949*, p. 501.

30. In 1945 under Wedemeyer's influence China began to make some use of students in the army, but it was too late for very effective action. See Romanus and Sunderland, *Time Runs Out in CBI*, pp. 247–249.

31. Herbert Feis, *The China Tangle*, p. 61.

XVI. A YEAR OF DISCORD, 1944: MATERIAL AND MILITARY AID

1. Romanus and Sunderland, *Stilwell's Command Problems*, p. 112.

2. Craven and Cate, *Army Air Forces in World War II*, vol. 5, pp. 15ff.

3. Romanus and Sunderland, *Stilwell's Mission to China*, p. 322.

4. Romanus and Sunderland, *Stilwell's Command Problems*, p. 111; and

Time Runs Out in CBI, p. 359. For Chennault's view see his *Way of a Fighter,* pp. 276–279.

5. *FRUS, The Conferences at Cairo and Tehran, 1943,* p. 173.

6. Craven and Cate, *Army Air Forces in World War II,* vol. 5, pp. 20–30. Postwar studies showed the rightness of this view about steel, since the Japanese industry was producing at far below capacity due to shortage of raw materials, though that was not known in 1943. See Romanus and Sunderland, *Stilwell's Command Problems,* p. 16.

7. *Stilwell's Command Problems,* pp. 113–114. See also Craven and Cate, *The Army Air Forces in World War II,* vol. 5, pp. 25–46.

8. State Department file 893.51/7750.

9. *Idem;* and Morgenthau Diaries, vol. 702, pp. 137–139, February 19, 1944, and vol. 705, pp. 160–165, March 1, 1944.

10. State Department file 893.51/7550; also Morgenthau Diaries, vol. 714, pp. 215–216, March 27, 1944, and vol. 740, p. 337, April 13, 1944.

11. *16th Report to Congress on Lend-Lease Operations,* June 30, 1944, p. 48.

12. Craven and Cate, *The Army Air Forces in World War II,* vol. 5, pp. 81–87; Romanus and Sunderland, *Stilwell's Command Problems,* pp. 368–369.

13. Craven and Cate, *The Army Air Forces in World War II,* vol. 5, pp. xv–xvi, vol, 4, pp. 171–175.

14. Romanus and Sunderland, *Stilwell's Command Problems,* p. 116.

15. Romanus and Sunderland, *Time Runs Out in CBI,* p. 161.

16. Craven and Cate, *The Army Air Forces in World War II,* vol. 5, pp. 150–152.

17. Romanus and Sunderland, *Stilwell's Command Problems,* p. 298.

18. *Ibid.,* pp. 306–308.

19. *Ibid.,* pp. 310, 312, 314.

20. Quoted by Romanus and Sunderland, *Stilwell's Mission to China,* p. 262.

21. Romanus and Sunderland, *Stilwell's Command Problems,* pp. 329–360, 389–398, 423–424, 433–436, 471–472.

22. *Ibid.,* p. 195.

23. For a detailed account of these campaigns see *ibid.,* pp. 119–256, and Romanus and Sunderland, *Time Runs Out in CBI,* pp. 77–141, 206–230.

24. Memorandum of July 4, 1944, to the President, in *Stilwell's Command Problems,* p. 382.

25. T. Hattori, *Daitoa Senso Zenshi* (The Complete History of the Greater East Asia War), Tokyo, 1953, vol. 3, p. 247, quoted by F. F. Liu, *A Military History,* p. 219. See also Romanus and Sunderland, *Stilwell's Command Problems,* pp. 316–320.

26. Re the doubtful allegiance of certain generals, and Chiang's reluctance to supply them, see Romanus and Sunderland, *Stilwell's Command Problems,* pp. 320, 371–372, 401–402, 408–413; and Tang Tsou, *America's Failure in China* (Chicago, 1963), pp. 111–113.

There was much trade between the free and occupied areas, and local commanders often yielded to the temptation to engage in it or tax it. This tended to create "a vested interest in an undisturbed front." *FRUS, 1943, China,* p. 45.

27. Romanus and Sunderland, *Stilwell's Command Problems*, pp. 320–327, 367, 371–374, 423.

28. Craven and Cate, *The Army Air Forces in World War II*, vol. 4, p. 539; F. F. Liu, *A Military History*, p. 213.

29. *U.S. Relations with China, 1949*, pp. 551–552.

30. Romanus and Sunderland, *Stilwell's Command Problems*, pp. 21–22, 325–326; *Stilwell's Mission to China*, p. 320. See also chapter XIV.

31. See Wallace's report of July 10, 1944, a photostat from the Franklin D. Roosevelt Library, Hyde Park, N.Y., in State Department files, and the Hearings before the Subcommittee to Investigate the Administration of the Internal Security Act and other Internal Security Laws, of the Committee on the Judiciary, U.S. Senate, 82d Congress, 1st Session, Part 5, October 18 and 19, 1951, pp. 1363–1455. See also Romanus and Sunderland, *Stilwell's Command Problems*, pp. 374–379.

32. Romanus and Sunderland, *Stilwell's Command Problems*, pp. 381–384; Leahy, *I Was There*, p. 256.

33. Romanus and Sunderland, *Stilwell's Command Problems*, pp. 384–387, 418–430, 435–436, 438.

34. For the text see *ibid.*, pp. 445–446.

35. *Ibid.*, pp. 447, 452–453.

36. *Ibid.*, pp. 458–464.

37. *Ibid.*, pp. 468–469.

38. *Ibid.*, pp. 462–465. For a detailed statement on June 21, 1951, of Hurley's views on the Stilwell affair, see *Hearings, Military Situation in the Far East*, part 4, pp. 2863–2881.

39. *US. Relations with China, 1949*, pp. 69–70.

40. See Tsou, *America's Failure in China*, pp. 88–124, for comment on this issue and the internal political issues involved.

41. Romanus and Sunderland, *Stilwell's Command Problems*, p. 469.

XVII. Gold, Given and Withheld

1. See the Hearings, July 13, 1956, re "Scope of Soviet Activity in the United States," Part 35, Washington, 1957. Hereinafter cited as Hearings, Part 35.

2. *U.S. Relations with China, 1949*, p. 485.

3. For the texts of these communications see *ibid.*, pp. 485–488.

4. Message telegraphed July 31, 1943, through Chinese Embassy, Washington.

5. *FRUS, 1943, China*, pp. 429, 431.

6. Morgenthau Diaries, vol. 666, p. 179, September 23, 1943; Hearings, Part 35, p. 1986.

7. Morgenthau Diaries, vol. 668, p. 68, September 29, 1943; Hearings, Part 35, p. 1987.

8. Morgenthau Diaries, vol. 682, p. 83, November 30, 1943; Hearings, Part 35, p. 1987.

9. *U.S. Relations with China, 1949*, p. 488.

10. Morgenthau Diaries, vol. 685, p. 26, December 17, 1943; Hearings, Part 35, p. 1990.

11. *U.S. Relations with China, 1949*, pp. 488–489.

12. Morgenthau Diaries, vol. 695, p. 176 *et seq.*, January 19, 1944. See Report of the Subcommittee to Investigate the Administration of the Internal

Security Act and Other Internal Security Laws, to the Committee on the Judiciary, U.S. Senate, 84th Congress, 2d session, December 31, 1956, section V, p. 72.

13. State Department file 893.51/7732.

14. For the minutes of this meeting, see *U.S. Relations with China, 1949*, pp. 502–504. For analysis of the arguments, see the following section.

15. Morgenthau Diaries, vol. 802, pp. 1–3, December 9, 1944; Hearings, Part 35, pp. 1993–1994.

16. Morgenthau Diaries, vol. 807, pp. 257–259, January 3 and 5, 1945; Hearings, Part 35, p. 1994.

17. Morgenthau Diaries, vol. 814, p. 381, January 18, 1945.

18. *Ibid.*, vol. 824, pp. 230–236, March 2, 1945; vol. 825, p. 171, March 3, 1945; Hearings, Part 35, pp. 1999–2002.

19. *U.S. Relations with China, 1949*, p. 503.

20. From Harry D. White papers, lodged at the Princeton University Library, received by the Internal Security Subcommittee of the Senate Judiciary Committee, September 30, 1955. See Morgenthau Diaries, vol. 846, p. 35, where Morgenthau states on May 10, 1945, in suggesting a letter to the President, that "there was a letter originally written on that to Mr. Roosevelt which I never took over."

21. Morgenthau Diaries, vol. 827, part I, pp. 53–55, March 11, 1945; Hearings, Part 35, p. 1997. I was then in Washington and did not obtain detailed figures of the deficit by months.

22. Morgenthau Diaries, vol. 845, pp. 314–322, May 9, 1945; Hearings, Part 35, p. 2023.

23. *U.S. Relations with China, 1949*, p. 503.

24. State Department file 893.51/4–1245. Adler's memorandum outlined a policy of retarding inflation, in connection with Leon Henderson's visit to China.

25. Morgenthau Diaries, vol. 843, p. 106, May 1, 1945.

26. *Ibid.*, vol. 845, p. 170–179, May 8, 1945. For the text of the memorandum, see *U.S. Relations with China, 1949*, pp. 504–505.

27. Morgenthau Diaries, vol. 845, pp. 211ff., 340, May 8, 1945.

28. *Ibid.*, vol. 845, p. 314ff., May 9, 1945; Hearings, Part 35, pp. 2022–2023.

29. Morgenthau Diaries, vol. 846, p. 32ff., May 10, 1945; Hearings, Part 35, p. 2026.

30. Morgenthau Diaries, vol. 847, pp. 36–37, May 15, 1945; Hearings, Part 35, p. 2029.

31. Morgenthau Diaries, vol. 847, pp. 144–145, May 16, 1945; see also *U.S. Relations with China, 1949*, p. 507.

32. Morgenthau Diaries, vol. 847, pp. 149–150, May 16, 1945. For text of the letter see *U.S. Relations with China, 1949*, pp. 507–508.

33. See the Subcommittee's Report, section V, December 31, 1956, 84th Congress, 2nd session, p. 71; and Nathan I. White, *Harry Dexter White, Loyal American* (Waban, Massachusetts, 1956).

34. Morgenthau Diaries, vol. 808, pp. 196–197, January 9, 1945; Hearings, Part 35, pp. 2035–2036.

XVIII. The Last Months of War

1. Romanus and Sunderland, *Stilwell's Command Problems*, pp. 254, 268–270.

2. CNAC data are from my files, received as CNAC director, and are converted from metric tons to short tons. Military data are from Craven and Cate, *The Army Air Forces in World War II*, vol. 4, pp. 443–446, vol. 7, pp. 117–151; and Romanus and Sunderland, *Stilwell's Mission to China*, pp. 163–167, 284, *Stilwell's Command Problems*, p. 112, and *Time Runs Out in CBI*, p. 14. For some months of the year ending in mid-1944 the official military historians do not give exact figures, and I have estimated the missing data by reading figures from the charts which Romanus and Sunderland present.

3. Craven and Cate, *The Army Air Forces in World War II*, vol. 7, pp. 117–139, 151.

4. See Romanus and Sunderland, *Stilwell's Command Problems*, pp. 10–15, 139–142.

5. *Idem*, p. 389.

6. Romanus and Sunderland, *Time Runs Out in CBI*, pp. 138, 317–318.

7. *Ibid.*, pp. 364–365n.

8. Quoted by Romanus and Sunderland, *Stilwell's Command Problems*, p. 433n.

9. *FRUS, 1943, China*, pp. 193–199, 201.

10. See memorandum of the conversations in *U.S. Relations with China, 1949*, pp. 553–555, 559; also Wallace's report of July 10, 1944 (see note 31, chapter XVI).

11. Quotation from *U.S. Relations with China, 1949*, pp. 554–555. For a fuller account of the background and work of the Wallace Mission and of the political issues involved see Feis, *The China Tangle*, pp. 145–165.

12. *U.S. Relations with China, 1949*, pp. 67, 72.

13. Romanus and Sunderland, *Stilwell's Command Problems*, pp. 420, 431, 451–452, 455.

14. *U.S. Relations with China, 1949*, pp. 86–87; Romanus and Sunderland, *Time Runs Out in CBI*, pp. 72–75, 249–254, 337, 391.

15. The text of part of the statement is quoted in Hearings, Military Situation in the Far East, Part 4, June 21, 1951, pp. 2929–2930. See also Romanus and Sunderland, *Time Runs Out in CBI*, pp. 336–337; Lohbeck, *Patrick J. Hurley*, pp. 339–340; and Wedemeyer, *Wedemeyer Reports*, pp. 302–320.

16. For the paraphrased text of the message see *U.S. Relations with China, 1949*, pp. 87–92. For further light on views current in 1944–1945 about arming the Communists, see Feis, *The China Tangle*, pp. 268–272, and State Department Loyalty Investigation, Hearings, Subcommittee of the Committee on Foreign Relations, U.S. Senate, 1950, part 2, p. 2,069.

Edgar Snow has reported a conversation with Roosevelt which took place March 3, 1945, a month before Roosevelt's death, in which Roosevelt indicated that he might be willing to provide supplies to the Chinese Communists. See Snow, *Journey to the Beginning* (New York, 1958), pp. 347–349, and *Random Notes on Red China* (1936–1945) (Cambridge, 1957), pp. 125–130. That apparently was before the President decided to uphold the views of Hurley and Wedemeyer.

17. The messages are quoted in *U.S. Relations with China, 1949*, pp. 94–98, and are summarized and their implications discussed by Feis, *The China Tangle*, pp. 283–289.

18. D. Lohbeck, *Patrick J. Hurley* (Chicago, 1956), p. 280.

19. For analysis of these complicated changes in the propaganda line,

see North, *Moscow and Chinese Communists*, pp. 185–187, 202–203; and McLane, *Soviet Policy*, chapters 3 and 4.

20. Chiang Kai-shek, *Soviet Russia in China* (New York, 1957), p. 105.

21. The text of the treaty and related documents is given in *U.S. Relations with China, 1949*, pp. 585–596.

22. Milovan Djilas, *Conversations with Stalin* (Harcourt, Brace & World, Inc., New York, 1962), p. 182.

23. *21st, 22nd and 23rd Reports to Congress on Lend-Lease Operations*.

24. Romanus and Sunderland, *Stilwell's Command Problems*, pp. 283–284.

25. *23rd Report to Congress on Lend-Lease Operations*, pp. 67–72; letter of October 14, 1959, from State Department.

26. The British figures are from the Chancellor of the Exchequer's *Third Report on Mutual Aid*, October 1946 (Cmd. 6931), supplemented by a letter of August 15, 1962, from the Chancellor's office. See also Romanus and Sunderland, *Stilwell's Command Problems*, pp. 279–280.

27. Despatch 293, April 12, 1945, from the American Embassy, Chungking, file 893.51/4–1245.

28. Morgenthau Diaries, vol. 823, part I, pp. 179–180, February 27, 1945; vol. 828, part I, p. 197, March 14, 1945; and vol. 839, p. 337, April 24, 1945.

29. *Ibid.*, vol. 793, p. 143, November 10, 1944; vol. 829, part 2, p. 343, February 12, 1945; vol. 839, p. 43, April 20, 1945.

30. *Ibid.*, vol. 848, p. 116, May 21, 1945; vol. 850, p. 33, May 29, 1945; and vol. 851, pp. 29–30, June 1, 1945. See also State Department files 103.9169/2–645, /2–2645, and /6–445; 124.936/2–2745; 893.24/6–145; and 893.50/4–2145.

31. Romanus and Sunderland, *Stilwell's Command Problems*, pp. 413–414n.

32. State Department file 740.0011 P.W./8–944. See also the New York *Times*, August 21 and 22, 1944, and *Asia*, March 1945, p. 123.

33. Nelson's report to the President, December 20, 1944 (partly printed in New York *Times*, January 27, 1945) and Embassy despatch 460, June 6, 1945, State Department files 033.1193 Nelson, Donald M., /1–1245 and /6–645. Bank of China, *Fortnightly Letter on Economic Conditions in China*, July 16, 1945, p. 7.

34. See Hurley's despatch of June 6, 1945, State Department file 033.1193 Nelson, Donald M.; Remer's report of June 12, 1945, file 124.936/7–945. The total which the Board made available to various industries was C$10.5 billion up to August 15, 1945, or a little more than the C$10 billion authorized in the latter part of 1944. Bank of China, *Fortnightly Letter*, September 1, 1945, p. 5.

35. Memorandum to Ambassador Gauss, March 9, 1945. *FRUS, 1943, China*, p. 27. For a good analysis of China's military problems, see Liu, *Military History*.

36. Tsou, in *America's Failure in China*, quotes Stilwell's idea that the Generalissimo feared that the commander of a reformed army might "challenge his position as China's leader" (*Stilwell's Mission to China*, p. 353); and states the view that, with army reform, "The power and influence of military and political leaders not belonging to the Whampoa faction would have expanded" (pp. 78, 112).

37. Romanus and Sunderland, *Time Runs Out in CBI*, pp. 369–373.
38. See for example the discussion of the army system by Chang Kia-ngau, *The Inflationary Spiral*, pp. 126–128.
39. Romanus and Sunderland, *Stilwell's Command Problems*, p. 427.
40. Romanus and Sunderland, *Time Runs Out in CBI*, p. 65.
41. *Ibid.*, pp. 241–247.
42. Wedemeyer, *Wedemeyer Reports*, pp. 295–298, 322–326, 335–338; Romanus and Sunderland, *Time Runs Out in CBI*, chaps. II, V, VIII, XII, and *Stilwell's Mission to China*, pp. 156, 384.
43. State Department file 893.154/2–1245.
44. Romanus and Sunderland, *Time Runs Out in CBI*, pp. 368, 394.
45. *Ibid.*, pp. 394–396.
46. Romanus and Sunderland, *Stilwell's Command Problems*, p. 57.
47. From report prepared by the War Department and furnished to me.
48. Morgenthau Diaries, vol. 787, p. 277, October 7, 1944.
49. *Ibid.*, vol. 796, p. 244, November 18, 1944.
50. Romanus and Sunderland, *Time Runs Out in CBI*, chaps. XI and XII. Threat of a landing, though none was made, had its effects on the war. The fear of a landing held back General Okamura's forces late in 1944, when they were threatening Kunming and Chungking, and led Tokyo to overrule his plan for trying to knock China out of the war. *Ibid.*, p. 350.
51. Wedemeyer, *Wedemeyer Reports*, p. 327; see Romanus and Sunderland, *Time Runs Out in CBI*, pp. 5–6.

XIX. Planning Rehabilitation and Development

1. The program is summarized in a pamphlet, "Relief and Rehabilitation in China," published at Washington, UNRRA document R and R1.
2. UNRRA document CS-CFC/AP(45) 9, 11, revised 9 July 1945.
3. *Ibid.*, pp. 3, 9, 12.
4. An excellent comprehensive account of the working of the program is the report prepared by Harry B. Price, *UNRRA in China, 1945–1947*, published by UNRRA, Washington, 1948. The figures above are from pp. 11, 14, and 32 of that report.
5. *FRUS, 1942, China*, pp. 498–499.
6. *FRUS, 1943, China*, p. 465.
7. *Ibid.*, pp. 465–466.
8. Morgenthau Diaries, vol. 666, p. 177; vol. 668, p. 68.
9. *FRUS, 1943, China*, pp. 469–471.
10. Morgenthau Diaries, vol. 678, pp. 336–338, November 19, 1943.
11. *FRUS, 1943, China*, pp. 474–475.
12. *U.S. Relations with China, 1949*, p. 504.
13. For the text of the memorandum, see Hearings, Internal Security Subcommittee, Part 35, pp. 1981–1983.
14. Morgenthau Diaries, vol. 756, pp. 184–191, July 20, 1944.
15. *FRUS, 1943, China*, pp. 62–63, despatch of June 12, 1943, from Embassy, Chungking; and pp. 127–128, memorandum of September 21, 1943.
16. State Department file 893.51/6–745.
17. State Department file 893.51/6–745.
18. *Ibid.*, 893.50/9–1444, despatch from Ambassador Gauss, September 14, 1944.

19. See State Department file 033.1193, Nelson, Donald M. /8–2244; and report of Nelson's mission, State Department file 893.00/10–1244.

20. *Ibid.*, 893.00/10–1244. See also an article by Nelson, *Colliers*, May 12, 1945.

21. State Department file 893.64A/1–2645.

22. State Department files 893.51/8–1845; 893.64A/7–1145; and 893.-64A/8–845; and 893.64A/8–3045.

23. Romanus and Sunderland, *Time Runs Out in CBI*, p. 390.

XX. A Summing Up, 1941–1945

1. Report of the Sub-Committee to Investigate the Administration of the Internal Security Act and Other Internal Security Laws to the Committee on the Judiciary, U.S. Senate, 84th Congress, 2d Session, Section V, December 31, 1956, p. 71.

2. *FRUS, 1943, China*, p. 509.

3. *Ibid.*, *1942*, pp. 138–139.

4. See chapter XIII and Kirby, *The War Against Japan*, vol. 2, pp. 101–104, 218–220.

5. Kirby, *The War Against Japan*, vol. 2, p. 220.

6. Churchill, *Closing the Ring*, p. 328.

7. Romanus and Sunderland, *Stilwell's Mission to China*, pp. 336–339, and *Stilwell's Command Problems*, pp. 21–22.

8. Craven and Cate, *The Army Air Forces in World War II*, vol. 4, p. viii; Romanus and Sunderland, *Time Runs Out in CBI*, p. 359.

9. White, ed., *The Stilwell Papers*, p. 124, and Romanus and Sunderland, *Stilwell's Command Problems*, p. 427.

10. Liu, *A Military History*, p. 223.

11. Romanus and Sunderland, *Stilwell's Mission to China*, p. 6.

12. *Ibid.*, p. 32.

13. *Ibid.*, p. 373.

14. *Ibid.*, p. 322.

15. Romanus and Sunderland, *Stilwell's Command Problems*, pp. 363–364, 466.

16. For a more detailed account of economic conditions at the end of the war, see Arthur N. Young, *China's Economic and Financial Reconstruction*, Committee on International Economic Policy (New York, 1947), pp. 12–13.

17. Memorandum given to Wedemeyer by the Chinese Government in 1947. See *U.S. Relations with China, 1949*, pp. 817–818.

18. *Ibid.*, p. 817.

19. E. F. Goldman: *The Crucial Decade* (New York, 1956), p. 117.

XXI. An Appraisal

1. Data of the Japan Defense Agency. See appendix V.

2. Hattori, *Complete History*, vol. 1, pp. 314, 319, 330. Quoted by Liu, *Military History*, pp. 204–205, 209.

3. Liu, *Military History*, p. 219.

4. Hattori, *Complete History*, vol. 4, p. 441.

5. Data furnished to me by the Japan Defense Agency through the American Embassy at Tokyo, April 1960. Chinese figures show a total of 326,753 Japanese killed to December 8, 1941, and 156,955 thereafter, a total of

483,708; and calculate the wounded as four times the killed—compared to the Japanese-reported ratio in 1937–1941 of about 2.4 to 1. See *China Handbook, 1950* (New York, 1950), p. 182; the grand total there shown contains a large arithmetic error.

6. It is hard to make a precise estimate because published Japanese official data of wartime expenditures appear conflicting, being compiled on different bases. See Sorifu Tokei-kyoku (Statistics Bureau of the Prime Minister's Office), *Nihon Tokei Nenkan* (Japan Statistical Yearbook), 1949, pp. 800–803, 850; and Bank of Japan, *Economic Statistics of Japan, 1953*, pp. 171–172. The Bank of Japan and the Japan Defense Agency have kindly helped me to get and interpret the available data. The figures that follow seem to me best to show the situation.

In 1937–1941 while China fought alone against Japan, total Japanese military expenditure was about ¥38 billion, equivalent at average exchange to roughly US$9 billion. Japanese data do not show the amount spent in Japan for the China fighting, but only the expenditures in China. Contemporary data of the State Department, however, state that in those years the China fighting "absorbed about 25 billion yen of Japanese expenditure on war effort" (memorandum by Hornbeck, February 16, 1942, *FRUS, 1942, China,* p. 21). That figure was equivalent at average exchange to about US$6 billion. These data indicate that the "China incident" absorbed in those years something like two-thirds of Japan's military outlay. That was a heavy burden on Japan's economy, and one result was an inflation which roughly doubled prices in that period. Also Japan had to export gold heavily—US$702 million to the United States alone in 1937–1941—reflecting the heavy buying of oil, scrap iron, and other materials needed in the war. Offsetting the strain on the economy, however, was the fighting experience which Japanese forces gained in China.

For the period of the Pacific War, 1942–1945, Japan's total military outlay was of the order of ¥200 billion. Since Japanese prices more than doubled in these years, it is hard to give dollar equivalents. An approximation might be US$25 billion. There is no basis for estimating very closely what part of those costs related to the China fighting. China was engaging something like half the Japanese troops overseas, other than in Manchuria. But naval and air war is much more costly than land fighting, and many battlefields were much more distant than nearby China. Hence the costs related to China in 1942–1945 were certainly less than half the total, perhaps more nearly a fourth.

7. Romanus and Sunderland, *Time Runs Out in CBI,* p. 10.

8. *China Handbook, 1950,* p. 182.

9. *U.S. Relations with China, 1949,* p. 587.

10. I have been unable to find a reference to this in his published works. J. M. Keynes may have been one of the first to mention this oft-quoted statement. See *The Economic Consequences of the Peace* (New York, 1920), p. 235.

11. *FRUS, 1942, China,* p. 137.

12. Romanus and Sunderland, *Stilwell's Mission to China,* p. 43.

13. *FRUS, 1942, China,* pp. 24–25, 28.

14. *FRUS, 1938,* vol. 3, p. 262.

15. See Morgenthau Diaries, vol. 485, p. 112, January 12, 1942.

Index

Harvard East Asian Series

*The East Asian Research Center at Harvard University
administers research projects designed to further scholarly
understanding of China, Korea, Japan, and adjacent areas.*

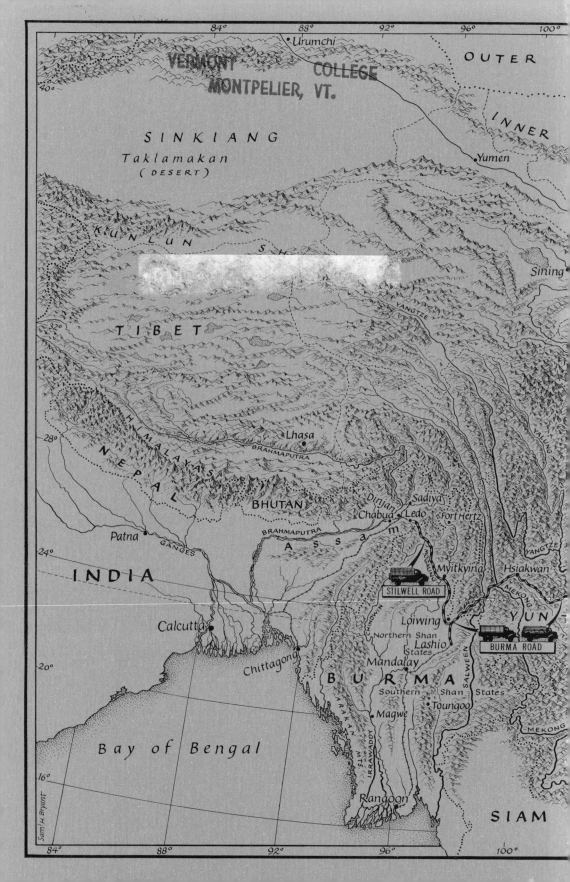

OUTER

INNER

SINKIANG

Taklamakan
(DESERT)

Urumchi

Yumen

K U N L U N

S H

Sining

T I B E T

YANGTZE

40°

32°

28°

H I M A L A Y A S

NEPAL

Lhasa

BRAHMAPUTRA

BHUTAN

Dirjan
Sadiya

Chabud Ledo

Fort Hertz

A S S A m

YANGTZE

Patna

GANGES

BRAHMAPUTRA

INDIA

24°

STILWELL ROAD

Myitkyina

Hsiakwan

MEKONG

Loiwing

Y U N

Calcutta

CHINDWIN

Northern Shan
States

Lashio

SALWEEN

YALING

BURMA ROAD

Chittagong

Mandalay

SALWEEN

20°

B U R M A

Southern Shan States

ARAKAN MTS.

Magwe

Toungoo

MEKONG

Bay of Bengal

16°

IRRAWADDY MTS.

Rangoon

SIAM

Sam H. Bryant

84°   88°   92°   96°   100°